Oma, Mu and Me

Jean Kaye

with love

Rene

Dedication

For those who are forced to seek refuge and for all
the descendants of Olga

Much of the material concerning St Denys School in
Chapter 16 comes from a book in my possession –
undated, and with no ISBN number – by Kathleen E
White, entitled St Denys School, Oxford

Originally know as
Holly Trinity Convent School

Oma, Mu and Me

Irene Gill

Fivepin.

Fivepin Limited
91 Crane Street, Salisbury, Wiltshire, SP1 2PU
www.fivepin.co.uk

British Library Cataloguing in Publication Data
A catalogue record for this book is available from the British Library

© Fivepin 2006
ISBN 1 9038774 2 3

Printed in the United Kingdom by Lightning Source Ltd, Milton Keynes

Contents

OMA, MU and ME: Family Tree

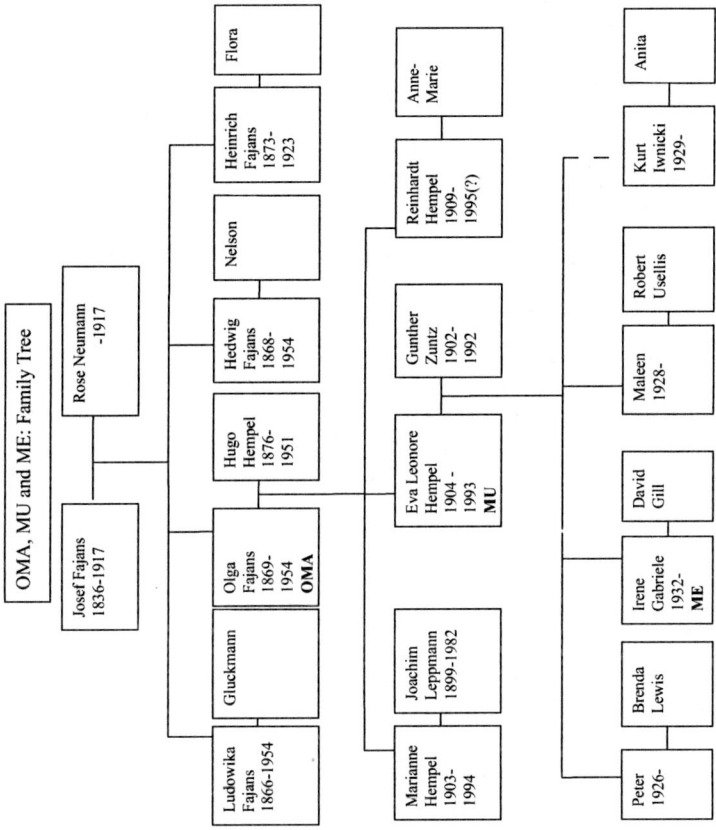

Chapter 1

In 2002, we visited Gdansk, the Polish city on the Baltic: a beautiful place, with fine houses, noble churches and public buildings with tall, pointed spires and pinnacles. We – my cousin Dudu, my husband David and I – wanted if possible to see the places where my much admired grandmother, my Oma, lived and moved and had her being as a child, more than a century before, when it was a German city, and called Danzig. In her memoirs, she calls the street where she grew up Hundegasse – Dog Street – and I found it: Ulica Organa, as it is called now. It is one of the parallel pedestrian streets of ornate, colourful, Dutch-style terraced houses, their stepped façades topped by human or animal figures, or a golden sun, or a star, and decorated porches.

So a house like that was Oma's home, when she was a child, in the late nineteenth century. Here is how she remembered Danzig, in her old age:

House in Ulica Organa

'The town, right in the North of Germany, near the sea, passes through my mind continually, almost like the sea itself, changing constantly and yet always the same. Sometimes it is the colours that memory brings to the surface: the old grey houses, the velvet green of the ramparts embracing the city like motherly arms, above all the luminous red of the Church of Mary, glowing as if it was on fire, a red I have only seen on the old churches of the Baltic towns. At other times it is shapes that memory conjures up: those needle sharp spires on the Town Hall sparkling like gold in the evening sun, and the old pointed gables in all their variety. But sometimes human figures arise from the past that fit into the framework of those old streets, bringing with them a wealth of colourful life, which I would like to pin down before it all vanishes into oblivion. I see it all like images woven into grey silk; as my memory casts its light now here, now there, astonishingly brightly coloured figures become visible, and then fade away again.'

My cousin Dudu knew Oma far better than I did, having lived with her for many years, in Persia/Iran, and in America. I envied her a little for that. I was born in her house in Freiburg, in Germany, and we lived with her there for three years until we had to flee from the Nazis; but of course, I cannot remember those days. My memory of her is based on the two occasions when I saw her later, once in Denmark, and once in England: a short, stout woman with silver hair in a bun on the top of her head and large blue-grey eyes gazing affectionately at me over the top of her glasses. But we exchanged letters, and my mother, Mu, talked about her often; so she was always very important to me. I was brought up to admire her for her achievements, being one of the first women doctors in Germany, and for her forthright ways, her wit and intelligence and self-confidence. For instance, she refused to obey the absurd diktats of fashion which in her young days expected women to wear corsets and long, uncomfortable dresses dragging on the ground: she designed straight, ankle-length dresses for herself, with a useful pocket. She refused to be fettered by convention. When her husband became insufferable to her, she took their three children (including my mother, Mu) to the other end of Germany and set up as an independent, self-supporting woman.

But Danzig/Gdansk was where she passed her formative years; and it was curiously reassuring to see places on which her eyes had rested, so long ago. The great Church of Mary, for instance; but it was not 'luminous red' any more; the brickwork was blackish, due perhaps to the fires that had engulfed the town during the last days of the war, when Hitler decreed that it should be one of the 'fortress towns' and 'fight to the finish'. The church had survived, though it had suffered; but other fine buildings we saw and admired had not. They had been recreated after the war.

Oma was born in 1869 in Thorn/Torun, the city of Copernicus; the family moved to Danzig/Gdansk when she was very small. Her name was Olga Fajans. Her father, Josef Fajans, was a prosperous businessman; he traded in grain, which was carried on rafts and later on steamers down the River Weichsel/Vistula/Wisla; from Danzig it was exported across the Baltic and the North Sea to Western Europe. Those fine pedestrian streets, including Dog Street/Hundegasse/Ulica Organa, lead down to gateways through the great wall along the River Mottlau/Motlawa, a branch of the Vistula/Wisla. Looking out over the calm water you see the Speicherinsel, Granary Island, Spichrzow in Polish, where great-grandfather Josef Fajans stored the grain prior to shipping it to Western Europe. Family tradition claims that he cultivated long finger-nails so that he could carry samples of grain in them to show to potential customers. But when we were there, most of the grain stores on the island were still in ruins, as everything else had been at the end of the war – and now we did see 'luminous red brick walls' – broken crags rearing through the bushes and saplings that had grown up among and through and on them.

According to my mother, Oma's father's father had been an innkeeper. This was one of the few professions open to Jews. Men would spend everything they had on drink, go home drunk, beat their malnourished wives and children, and beget more children. The peasants' wives considered the Jewish innkeepers villains – taking all the money and sending home a blind-drunk man. But Josef's father persuaded peasants not to spend everything on alcohol, reducing the drunkenness in his part of Poland and winning so much respect that he was even elected to represent his district in the Sejm – an almost unheard-of honour for a Jew – his integrity had prevailed against all obstacles.

His wife bore him one child after the other. His most passionate desire was that his children should be better off than he, and the only way to achieve this was education. Jews were only allowed to attend the Tora and Talmud schools. Josef was the oldest, and at the cost of enormous sacrifices he was sent to Breslau/Wroclav, then a German city with a famous university. He would have to get through the university entrance exam, the Abitur, first. He walked all the way, barefoot in wet weather to save his boots. He was aged about sixteen. He had to be sure to reach a Jewish settlement before nightfall, so that he could sleep in the synagogue and be given a little food. Josef was an enthusiastic scholar and student. Of course there was no way his father could send him anything like enough money, and he had to work as a shop assistant for his living, twelve hours a day, keeping himself awake at night with strong tea and wet towels to study. He lived in a tiny box room with only a candle for light and no heating; it got so cold in winter that the walls and ceiling were covered with ice, and he wrapped himself up in old potato sacks and anything else he could find. He had to learn German as well as the subjects required for his exams. Just before he was to take them, news reached him that his father had died.

So he had to return home. Being the oldest he had to undertake the duties of head of the family – earn money, arrange marriages for his sisters, provide dowries for them, get the boys qualifications, and care for his feeble-minded mother. He was now seventeen. He did not want to be an innkeeper. He got into the grain trade with one of his brothers, who somehow, it seems, earned the title Admiral of Warsaw. (Another brother emigrated to Australia and is said to have married an aboriginal princess – and to have brought her to Germany once to meet the family. We are very proud of this link with royalty.) There was a great deal of traffic on the River Weichsel/Vistula in those days; not only grain, but great rafts of logs, with families living on them, floated down to Danzig, taking half a year for the journey. Josef lived in Thorn/Torun at first, before moving down to Danzig on the mouth of the river. When he had solved most of his family's problems, and had in fact become quite rich, he fell in love with Rose Neumann, daughter of a cultured but penniless family. Her father was a dreamer who never earned enough, was always in debt, and enjoyed life. His wife Johanna was highly educated and far superior to him intellectually, but she did not know how to deal with practical problems either, living in higher spheres.

She wrote a book of fairy tales, which were very moral and didactic. Now when Joseph asked for Rose's hand in marriage, her father said: 'My dear young man, I advise you not to. You have just got your own affairs in order, your business is prospering, and now you want Rose! You must know that you wouldn't just marry Rose, but the whole family, we will all be a drain on your purse' – and so on. But nothing deterred him.

Oma was very fond of her grandfather Neumann, and wrote about him in her memoirs:

'I lost him when I was quite small, but he is among my favourite childhood memories. He remained as he was born: innocently addicted to the pleasures of life (not excluding alcohol, if I rightly interpret the colour of his nose). Unencumbered by any strong sense of responsibility, he fathered six children and did little else for them, apart from being good-natured and affectionate. He was a businessman, but devoid of business acumen – in fact he was almost chronically bankrupt. But how lovable! As soon as he woke up in the morning he would be whistling the themes of a string quartet or a symphony, for he was very musical. He would stand on the table on the balcony for half an hour at a time to watch the swallows that nested by the ceiling there. He would take me by the hand when I was a little girl and go to the beach at Zoppot with me. There we would "lie on our tummies" – that was the formula – to build sand hills and tunnel through them, and to talk. I cannot remember what we talked about, but it was all good and enjoyable: not deliberately instructive yet extremely interesting and stimulating for me. He was a philosopher in all but name, able to distinguish the essential and the inessential. What he considered essential was: living in Nature; appreciating the beauty of the world; peace within and around oneself; and goodness. Financial success, external honours, possessions, ambitions: those were things he considered inessential. There was always room at his table and in his house for poor relations, but he was not interested in their tales of woes. When he was old and hard of hearing so that he was unable to follow the conversation of the invariably large company at his dinner table, he might ask the person sitting next to him: "What are they talking about? Family jeremiads? All right." And he would stop trying to listen and let his thought wander in pleasanter realms. When his daughter Rose, who was my mother later, longed to have her voice trained, there was, as usual, no money available. He consoled her by saying: "Never mind. Genius always finds its way." And he was right, in a way: she went on singing all her life, her voice untrained, unspoiled, – and glorious.'

Oma liked to trace the contrast in the characters of her parents, and how they were reflected in their children:

'Yes, my darling mother! Her innocent serenity, her charm, her musicality, her adaptability, the grace she showed in her dealings with people – in fact all

the light-heartedness she inherited from her father – it was these Neumann qualities that ensured the happiness of our childhood. As for my father: he was wholly admirable, the embodiment of honour, responsibility, duty – yet each of his four children went through crises with him which led to our leaving the parental home. He was a tyrant; he was an ascetic, and expected those around him to possess those qualities which made him so admirable – and so difficult to live with. But opposites attract, and he had fallen in love with our mother, Rose, who was so utterly different from him. His youngest child, and only son, Heinchen, was a "Neumann" through and through, with nothing of the paternal Fajans in him. He was musical, he played the violin as beautifully as our mother sang; he was even-tempered, carefree, good-natured, and anything but an ascetic. All these qualities, which Papa secretly loved in women, he could not tolerate in his son. He had no warmth, no understanding for him. Nor for my sister Hedwig (Hedchen), though she took after him, even in appearance, and in her strict morality. That was not what he was drawn to in women. His favourite was his first-born, Ludovika (Lutka). She and I are a complete amalgam of our mother's and our father's characteristics, and apart from a few crises I got on very well with him.'

In Danzig, Josef was quite a patriarch. Visiting musicians would stay in his house. In addition to the three girls, Lutka, Hedchen, and Olga, and one son, Heinrich, they had three or four nephews staying with them. They also owned a house by the sea at Zoppot/Sopot, where they would stay in the summer. It was called a 'rubber house', because though it was quite small, any number of people seemed to be able to stay in it.

Their world was Germany, Prussia, middle class, though it was no more than a small island surrounded by Poland. But officially, Poland had ceased to exist, having been swallowed up by its neighbours, 'partitioned' between Russia, Austria, and Prussia; even the Polish language was forbidden; schools and universities had to use Russian or German, depending which neighbour's gobbet they were in. Previously, from about 1250, the kings of Poland, recognising that their country had a swashbuckling aristocracy and an earthy peasantry and nothing in between, invited German merchants and craftsmen to come and settle in his country and form a middle class. Along with the Germans came Jews, more and more of them, fleeing from the pogroms of Western Europe, until there were more Jews in Poland than in any other country. (It is a bitter irony that the biggest pogrom of all should have been perpetrated in the south of the country, near Cracow, at another of those places with a Polish and a German name: Auschwitz/Oswiecim.) Many Jews went on using their medieval German dialect, which absorbed Slav and Hebrew elements and came to be known as Yiddish, and kept their religious and social customs, living together in the shtetls, or little towns.

But the Fajans family distanced itself from those orthodox Jews. One theory is that the family must have come to Poland many centuries before from Faenza in Northern Italy, home of the glazed earthenware known as majolica in Italy and faience in France, as the name Fajans suggests. Oma, growing up during Germany's boom-years following victory in the Franco-Prussian War of 1870–71, though of Jewish descent, did not come from a shtetl or speak Yiddish or practise the Jewish faith. She considered herself German. She was an atheist. In fact, decades later, as a child in Oxford, I still received a distasteful image, passed down the generations, of the Ost-Juden, the 'East-Jews', the women in flouncy red skirts with bits of torn lace, the men with ringlets, all with low standards of hygiene and honesty, and, above all, a funny accent when they spoke German. It was always possible to raise a laugh by mimicking their accent. But one of them contributed to the family's store of practical wisdom. It begins with the words: 'Wenn ein Warrier...' and it means: 'If a lunatic asks you for anything, you must promise it, with a sacred promise. But – you don't keep it'.

We know all this, and a good deal more, because Oma was fond of talking about her past, and when she was over 70, she started writing her memoirs, which finally filled three black-covered exercise books. They are in my possession now, and I love reading them. I also have boxes of her letters to my mother (the earliest written in the 1920s) and to me. She always wrote from edge to edge of the paper, in the same unfaltering, very legible hand, probably with the same fountain pen, in German (but not in the traditional German handwriting called Sütterlin, and never using the ß, only ss – another instance of her refusal to be bound by convention) until her death in California in 1954. She sometimes repeats herself, and when she notices this, crosses out whole pages angrily. She does not even mention the fact that she was Jewish until she comes to describe her marriage: it played no part in her consciousness, though it was to have such a devastating effect on her life later.

Here's how she remembers life in that house in Dog Street:
'Life was never dull in our house, what with Papa's uncontrolled temper and Mama's incorrigible carelessness – and the great number of children. There was a good deal of friction between us children in our remote nurseries, where our parents did not interfere with us, as well as between our parents. My father expected my mother to keep housekeeping accounts, and this she was constitutionally unable to do. He could not understand why she did not simply write down everything she spent in the course of the week; so she would rack her brains as the end of the week approached, and produce absurd statements like this famous one:
> Parsley.........10Pfenning
> Beggar..........10 Marks.
This would lead to shouting and door-slamming and tears.

They went for a certain walk every Sunday afternoon, which always took them past a certain coffee shop where everyone who was anyone in Danzig met and drank coffee and chatted. He abhorred that. And while Grandma always tried to coax him to the door and then to open it casually, she never succeeded in tricking him into entering. It was her dearest wish, because gossip was her greatest pleasure. But he thought it would be idiotic; they could drink coffee at home, cheaper and better. He would have died for her; but he was quite incapable of giving in to her in such a small matter.

When I was grown up and living abroad, Heinchen, who was still at home, wrote to me in a letter: "Everything is the same as ever here: little tantrums from Papa, little tears from Mama." But those tears were not tragic. Our parents loved each other faithfully right to the end of their long lives.

I was not afraid of my father. At 8 o'clock every morning, after the others had gone to school, I went for a walk with him and my dog, Harras.'

'The others' went to school: she did not. She was sometimes feverish, and the doctor believed she had a 'shadow on the lung'. This meant, among other things, that she was free to go on these early morning walks:

'We generally met our Scottish friend, Mr Stoddart, with his dog, Tello, and together we walked on the green ramparts that embrace Danzig. Harras was a rather coarse, often ferocious Newfoundland; Tello, a pedigree pointer, was – like everything to do with the Stoddarts—much more refined. We regarded the Stoddarts with some awe, as typically English (not Scottish!), which at that time meant elegant, stylish, fashionable. Occasionally the Stoddarts' man-servant would be waiting for us instead of Mr Stoddart and ask us to take Tello, as his master could not come. Which of course we did. But if the situation was reversed, Harras would never dream of going with the Stoddarts. Much as he loved his walk, he refused to be separated from me. We were always together, and were known as "The little miss and the black Satan". We would walk as far as the Russian Grave before returning home.'

::*:*:*:*

When we visited Gdansk, all those years later, Dudu, David and I, we went to the Lenin Shipyards, scene of the heroic uprising by Solidarnosc in the 1980s, with clusters of drooping, inactive derricks. Then we took a footpath that seemed to lead to an attractive tree-covered slope. We came past a building covered with the Solidarnosc logo, and climbed the hill behind it. On the far side a steep descent took us to a narrow valley where brick structures tunnelled into the hillside: clearly some sort of military bunkers. As we ascended the opposite slope we could see the curve of the ridge. Was this the 'green arms of the ramparts' that embraced Oma's Danzig? Following a pleasant path through the trees, we came to a tall stone monument, blank on the first three sides we looked at, but with an inscription in Russian on the fourth, and a mosaic of St George and the Dragon. A memorial to Russians who had lost their lives here – Oma's 'Russian Grave', perhaps, the destination of Oma's pre-breakfast walks with her father and Mr Stoddart and the dogs Harras and Tello. As we walked on along the arc, with the town on our left, past more brick-built fortifications – meeting a number of latter-day dog-walkers – we were retracing their footsteps, and I indulged in a fantasy of two sober-suited gentlemen pacing along steadily – and a lively little girl running hither and thither among the trees with two dogs.

That illness, that 'shadow on her lung' in her childhood had, I think, a lot to

The grassy ramparts

The Russian Grave

do with her independence of mind and spirit. She wrote about it in her memoirs:

> 'It was a source of great joy to me. I was "delicate", often ran a temperature, so I had to be "nursed", to spend as much time as possible in the fresh air, to stay in bed late – all sorts of things which I thoroughly enjoyed. I felt well in myself – even now I enjoy really euphoric states when I am feverish – so I could hardly blame my older sisters when they, trudging past me, snug in my bed, early in the morning, on their way to breakfast and school, dropped acid comments like: "Aha, poor little Olga is feverish again, is she? Could it be a case of Sloth Fever, I wonder?"'

It may also account for the fact that she was closer to her father than her siblings, and not afraid of him. She even played pranks on him:

> 'It was my father's custom to take an after-dinner nap in the reception room, known as "die kalte Pracht" – cold splendour – because of its grand furnishing and lack of heating. He insisted that one of his daughters should massage

8

his head while he slept. Once, when it was my turn, I got bored and started plaiting his thick hair into tiny pigtails, which I tied up with coloured wool. He woke up with a start and hurried down to his office in the basement – where his chief accountant said: "Ahem, Mr Fajans, sir, I think you ought to look in the mirror." He did so – and came storming upstairs in a fury. But I was waiting for him at the top of the stairs with my arms outstretched. Before he could say anything I embraced him and said: "My darling Papa, I love you so much!" This took the wind out of his sails, and he sat patiently while I restored his head to normal.

He was at other times a most irascible man. At mealtimes there would often be rows for some reason or other, when he would seize a plate or a glass and fling it onto the floor in a fine display of fury. I decided to try to put a stop to these scenes. So one day I put an ordinary empty flower-pot behind the samovar by Mama's place at the table, and told her that when next he lost his temper and started throwing things, she should give him a taste of his own medicine and smash this flower-pot. Now in our house there existed a modest silver sugar bowl which Mama had been given as a wedding present, but was not allowed to use, because Papa thought it was too "showy". Only glass or china ones appeared on the table, and in the course of time these would occasionally get broken. On one such occasion, when Mama had forgotten to replace it, she put the silver one out, as a temporary measure. But Papa raised no objection, so she made bold to leave it in use. She loved pretty things. But on the third day, the catastrophe came: Papa noticed it, and flung it, full of lump sugar, on the floor. I stared at Mama imploringly: NOW! And, trembling with alarm at her own temerity, she seized the flower-pot and threw it down onto the silver sugar bowl and the scattered sugar lumps. It broke into a hundred pieces. The effect surpassed my wildest dreams. Papa was so overwhelmed by the violence of this act that he rose, his face as white as chalk, and left the room. And he never threw things again.

We went for a family walk every afternoon at exactly the same time, with Papa and Mama in front, arm in arm and in step – I can still see my dear little mother bouncing up and down as she strove to keep in step with her long-legged husband. Behind the parents we children had a certain amount of freedom; but if my father came to some obstacle, a "danger", say a cow pat, or a ditch or a puddle which had to be crossed, then he would stop and wait until he had got us all across at the spot he designated as the most suitable. I, being a bit of a revolutionary, probably out of opposition to him, usually brought up the rear, amusing myself in my own way; and if I noticed what was happening I would do anything, struggle across the ditch or whatever at the most inconvenient place, just so that I would not have to submit to his guidance. As I grew up I found it galling to have to ask him for every little thing, be it a ticket for a concert or a play or a train – not that he was not always most generous. Nothing concerning our health or our education was too expensive.

*****

A short train ride from Gdansk took us to Sopot, the seaside resort. It was called Zoppot in Oma's day, and the train was a double-decker. Here they spent the summer months. We wanted to see the beach where Oma went for long walks, often singing or reciting poetry to herself, with a book tucked under her arm to read at some convenient spot.

Her dog, Harras, was her only companion and her protector, for he was a strong dog, keen on fighting and prone to bite. She wrote about this dog at some length in her memoirs:

'My father had to pay a lot of money for torn trousers, bitten legs and the like. No dog in the street was safe from his attacks, and we had to muzzle him long before the law about muzzling dogs came into force. His first muzzle was made of leather and he soon disposed of that. So he was given a metal one. All this only made him dearer to me, because with his protection I was able, and allowed, to indulge my passion for long, solitary walks, which would otherwise have been impossible for a girl in our society, surrounded as we were by ruffians and stabbers and rapists.

When we walked along the beach I would take off my shoes and stockings and bury the lot in the sand. I would never have found them again after a walk lasting between one and three hours, but Harras did, infallibly. The only time he was a nuisance was when I swam, as he was determined to save me from drowning, dived in after me, seized my arm quite painfully between his teeth and towed me back to the beach. In the end I had to lock him up in a bathing hut for as long as I was in the water.

The fishermen who lived on the Hela peninsula beyond Zoppot used to earn a little extra money by plunging into the sea up to their necks and carrying people ashore from their boats. They also carried the bathing huts out into the shallow sea. These huts had no floors. Ladies, having got partially undressed inside, would dip into the sea where no one could see them. But I had no time for such nonsense – I swam openly in the sea.

I hardly ever went out without Harras. When I started having private lessons, to make up for missing school, Harras would sleep quietly in a corner until I was ready to leave. When I was in my room, doing my homework, or reading, he would stand at the window, which had to be kept open for him, summer and winter, with his front paws on the window sill, watching the passers-by. If some not particularly important acquaintance came past, he would wag his tail politely. But if certain close friends or, in particular, any "admirers" appeared, he would turn his head to me and call me, quite distinctly.

One of these admirers was a cousin, Heinrich, nick-named Pips, a violinist, a serious, decent person – but the most ridiculous eccentric. He was a nail-biter, and full of complexes, inhibitions, and the like. He would turn quite green if he saw two girls kissing: physical expressions of affection nauseated him. He worshipped my mother, and was more or less in love with each of us three sisters in turn in his gauche, undemonstrative way. He spent a lot of time in our house, and gave us flowers. When his liking for me was at its height he was very fond of joining me on my walks on the beach at Zoppot, or in the forest alongside the beach, always, even under a blazing August sun, in his thick, dark, buttoned up jacket. I urged him to take it off and he was quite shocked. "I am not in the habit of appearing before ladies in my shirt sleeves," he said. He always brought a big white silk handkerchief expressly for the purpose of spreading it under my head when I lay down. He was absurdly spinsterish and old-fashioned, and my uninhibited behaviour gave him a lot of pain, especially when I was in my early teens and derived a positively diabolical pleasure from ridiculing him. Once, when he came to a big party at our house, and was shaking hands all round in his awkward, comical way, I rushed forward, flung myself at his feet and cried in mock ecstasy: "Light of my life! Star of my nights!" The poor fellow must have wished the earth would swallow him up. I still feel guilty when I remember that episode. But at that age I was a dreadful tease: I would do anything to raise a laugh. At a wedding we attended in Warsaw my good, respectable older sister was deeply embarrassed by my cheek and impudence which had a group of cousins surrounding me roaring with laughter at my remarks, until my father's step-brother Leopold Wotkowicz drew me gently aside and pointed out that my behaviour was nothing to be proud of.'

She was probably making fun of the Ost-Juden – the 'Eastern Jews'. She did learn some Polish, and was proud of her ability to communicate with Slavonic-speaking people all her life. In the course of her lifetime Poland went through further transformations. She was 50, in 1919, and living in Berlin, when the First World War had ended and the Versailles Treaty resurrected Poland from its 'partitions'. She was 70, and living in Persia (Iran), when Hitler unleashed the Second World War on 1 September, 1939, by invading Poland; in fact Granary Island/Spichrzow in Danzig /Gdansk was the scene of some of the first bombardments of the war, resulting in those red-brick ruins that we saw. But to Oma, Gdansk was always the beautiful German city Danzig, the scene of her childhood and youth. And Zoppot/ Sopot was the setting for her great romance.

Chapter 2

Oma as a girl with her dog Harras

Oma did not go to school, but she was not growing up entirely without education: she shared private lessons with two sisters, Becky and Marie Baum, alternately at their home and at the Fajans'. It was to these classes that Harras accompanied her. Here too her cheeky sense of humour led her to behaviour which she deplores, looking back across the decades in her memoirs. Their elementary teacher was a Fräulein Hellmann. *'We did not consider this withered, pedantic old maid (she was all of 25!) superior to us. I criticised her constantly, never accepting her corrections without arguing – I must have offended her enormously on many occasions. I remember one day when she left the Baums' house in tears. When Dr Baum heard of this, he drove after her and begged her forgiveness in the name of her tormenters. Later I realised how wrong my treatment of Fräulein Hellmann was and felt deeply ashamed. And we became friends.*

We also had French with a Parisian, Mlle Fechez; literature and history with Preacher Röckner; and English.

Becky and Marie's mother, Frau Baum, was an unlovely, highly intellectual woman, and she influenced me more than anyone except my father in those days. She did not treat us like children, but talked to us as if we were adult. This stimulated independent thinking and judgment in me, and hastened my precocious mental development – and my precocious critical faculty. She was not in the least concerned with housekeeping or with the care of her six children plus one foster child, their training, their clothes, their behaviour; but on the other hand she was passionately involved in their mental development. She taught them all herself at first, and did not let her daughters go to school: they, and I with them, were taught by private teachers. Only her two sons went to the grammar school, presumably at her husband's insistence. We were not allowed any religious instruction, only bible stories from the Old Testament. She was descended from the Mendelssohn family; there were portraits of Moses and Felix on the walls.'

'Independent thinking' was always a characteristic of Oma. But these good and stimulating relationships with the Baum family turned sour later. The first discordant note was struck when Oma's lovely sister Lutka had been chosen to be Snow White in a 'tableau' for charity – and Frau Baum persuaded the organiser to use Becky instead; this roused great bitterness in the Fajans family. Both Becky and Marie left Danzig to study, and Marie later became a close friend of the famous writer Ricarda Huch, and published her memoirs. Oma was indignant to find there was no mention of her long intimacy with Marie in the book. She never forgave Marie for this slight. Many years later, after the First World War, Marie gave a political talk in Freiburg, where Oma was then living; so she decided to go along. She remembers that Marie

'...spotted me when she was already standing at the lectern and to my great surprise came down off the podium and walked through the whole auditorium to greet me. She probably expected me to come "back-stage" after the lecture; but I made myself scarce and never saw her again. The wounds she and her sister inflicted on me with their disloyalty and arrogance have never healed.'

It seems extraordinary that Oma should harbour a grievance over such a long period. I suppose it was the down-side of her solid self-esteem, which also led her to presenting herself as a good example. I have letters which she wrote to me in which she criticises me for having too many boy friends: she herself, she writes, had had many friends who were boys and men, and prided herself on the fact that there was never the slightest whiff of eroticism between her and them. She only had three emotional affairs in her life. It was on that long, curving, sandy beach lapped by the shallow Baltic sea at Zoppot that the first of them began. It was immensely important to her all her life. She writes about it at length towards the end of her memoirs:

The beach at Zoppot/Sopot

'One day I was lying on the beach at Zoppot, as I often did, a healthy, happy girl of fourteen, when a young man of about seventeen walked past. And I fell in love with him, then and there; and this love dominated my whole being thereafter.

His appearance fascinated me, as nothing else ever did, before or after. Perhaps it was because he was so very different from me: tall, slim, with a pale, serious face, large, blue-grey eyes that gazed into the distance without even noticing me. He seemed to embody everything I had ever felt or dreamed of that was beautiful, spiritual, ideal, unworldly – it all seemed to be there in his pensive, introverted, dreamy gaze. From that moment, everything I did, thought, desired was focused on him.

I soon found out that his name was Hans Schubert (no relation to the composer), and that he was the oldest of the three sons of a wealthy baker, owner of a coffeehouse, a Konditorei, in Danzig's main street, the Langgasse. He went to the same grammar school which my brother Heinchen, aged ten, had just started. Several of my friends knew him, and I got all sorts of information about him out of them. Like us, his family had a holiday home in Zoppot.

At last we were introduced by one of our mutual friends, and from then on I would see him almost every day in the street, my heart pounding. He would remove his hat with a deep bow and what I believed was a meaningful expression in his eyes.

I do not know how he came to take an interest in me, unless it was my adoring glances; but it was soon obvious that he endeavoured to meet me as often as possible – as I did him – but without ever saying a word. In Zoppot we would meet on the beach, and on the double-decker train that carried commuters into Danzig and back again. The boys used to sit on the upper deck. Some would make a point of sitting above their girl friend and lowering a flower or a bouquet down to her on a piece of string. Once, when this happened to my high-principled sister Hedwig, she flung the flowers – beautiful roses – indignantly out of the window: she was not to be bribed or bought by a bunch of flowers!

I got no roses from Schubert. My passion, that burned ever more strongly, was nourished only by his deep, earnest glances, at our ever more frequent, silent encounters, which he was just as keen to devise as I was. For instance, in Danzig I resumed going for pre-breakfast walks with my father and Mr Stoddart and the dogs on the wooded ramparts, as far as the Russian Grave. As often as not, I would hear a familiar tune being whistled: Beethoven's F-Major Romance. I would fall back so that I would be unobserved when, soon after, I received my greeting – but never more than the doffed hat and the deep look. In time my innocent father noticed this youthful early morning walker and expressed his approval for his healthy habit.

Near the Schuberts' house in Zoppot was the North Park; I would often *sit on one of the benches there and read – and he would as often come past, always with the same silent greeting. Or if I was walking along the beach with Harras, I would be aware of Schubert walking some distance behind me with his dog, or coming towards me. There was never anyone else to be seen, and I always hoped, in vain, that he would speak to me.*

These silent but intentional meetings, devised with so much care on both sides, were the oh! so pitifully inadequate nourishment for our love for three long years. Then came the unforgettable 25 September 1886. Once again, I had observed that he was following me along the beach, so I went inland to the little wood at Thalmühl, sat down on a bench, and waited. And he stopped in front of me, and spoke. I almost fainted. He escorted me home; and later I returned to that bench and scratched the words: Hans loves me – in Greek – on the back: I found them still there, many years later.

Now we spoke to each other almost every day, at least during the summer months, when both our families were staying in Zoppot. But there was never a word, not a hint of love, so that I was never sure of his love.

One major event in this the so-called love-life of my youth took place in the Thalmühl wood, where we were going for a walk. Our two dogs, my Harras and his Hector, started fighting furiously. When I tried to calm them down, Hector gave me a deep and painful bite in my arm. Schubert was terrified and took me to his parents' house nearby, where his mother, whom I had not met before, looked after me. She undressed me, cleansed the wound and bandaged it, very tenderly.

Schubert started coming to our house quite frequently – not to see me, but to play string quartets with my brother Heinchen and two friends, Richard Simson and Wenzel. They would play in Heinchen's room, which had been separated from mine by a thin partition, so I was virtually present at these quartet evenings and got to know and love the music – which was often by his namesake, the great composer Franz Schubert. We also met at little parties at the homes of mutual friends; moreover his parents invited me to musical evenings at their house, where I was sometimes the only guest apart from the players – in what capacity, I wondered, with what title?

When his class took the Abitur, the school-leaving exam, the school celebrated by putting on an opera in which he was to sing the tenor part. I thought this would be the breakthrough. He was going to sing: "He sees the virgin stand before him, glorious in the splendour of youth" and he would make it obvious that he meant me, of course, me – plain little girl that I was. At last his true feelings for me would be revealed, if only in song, I thought. But what a disappointment! He had a hangover from the previous evening's party, and the words and tunes that seemed so significant to me were rattled off without any feeling whatsoever. However, afterwards there was a ball at a friend's house, and there, at last! he showed me clearly that he preferred me to all the others; in fact, late in the evening he walked me home. What is more, because of a late frost the pavement was slippery, and he was bold enough to offer me his arm, which I was bold enough to take. Bliss! But the longed-for words were not spoken.

Soon after that he went away to study, first at Marburg and then moving from one university to another, as was the custom in Germany; he was only at home in the vacations. Then, when I went out, I would make a point of walking along Langgasse on the side opposite to his family's house and Konditorei, hoping to see him standing at the first floor window, looking out for me – in which case he would be sure to come after me. If I was with Hedchen, she would be bound to notice this stratagem, and would hiss at me indignantly: "Shameless hussy!" Little did she know that I always felt unsure of him, since he never declared himself. But surely he would one day! To myself, I called his parents Little Beaupère and Little Beaumère, privately considering them my in-laws. They were clearly fond of me; indeed the relationship between me and Beaupère became quite affectionate. We went for long walks together, when he would confide in me. As an apprentice baker, he had walked as far as France and England to learn his trade, had then started a small bakery in Danzig, which had prospered. Now he wanted to give his three sons a better start in life than he had had. All three of them went to the grammar school; Hans and the youngest, Paul, whom I called "Shrimps" because he was so shy and reticent with me and with girls generally, went to university; Shrimps studied chemistry. They were all given excellent music lessons, violin, cello and piano, and sometimes, when I came past the Schuberts' house in Zoppot, right by the beach, I would find Little Beaupère by an open window listening to them playing a trio; he would beckon to me to join him. He was worried about Hans. So he was "studying". But what? Now it was theology, then it was philosophy, then singing and violin, then he was writing – what was his goal? Where was all this taking him? He was talented in many different ways, and was drawn hither and thither.

Beaupère himself was a member of the male voice choir. I sometimes went to their practices and almost died with suppressed laughter, partly because of the absurdly unsuitable songs these solid middle-aged citizens sang, about pretty girls waiting in vain for their lovers, and the like, partly because of the extreme contrasts in tempo and volume, surging and swooping from fortissimo to pianissimo and back again, under the baton of their conductor Kisielnicki, and partly because of their long beards wafting up and down, casting grotesque shadows on the wall.

His was not the only choir in Danzig. There was another, very big, mixed one. My mother was on the committee, and she and I sang in the sopranos. We performed the most demanding works, such as the St Matthew Passion, the Paradise and the Peri, Caesar Franck, the Ninth Symphony, and many more, with great enthusiasm. In the university vacations

Schubert seldom missed coming to a practice, sometimes to sing, sometimes just out of – musical? – interest. I imagined he came because of me and always looked out for him. The woman who sat next to me must have noticed it – once, when we were singing the chorus in the St Matthew Passion that goes "Whither has your friend gone?" when Schubert just happened to have left she gave me a most significant look. But by then, my idolatrous love of Schubert, which had been going on for some years, must have been wellknown in our town. We were seen so often, together, and I daresay I was not able to disguise myself or conceal this overpowering emotion within me. But I was never sure of him.'

*****

One day, walking through the poorer part of Danzig, Oma saw a small, grubby child sitting in the street. He looked so much like Schubert – with the same grey eyes – he could have been his child. And so she decided to adopt him, then and there. It was not in her nature to hesitate.

'What's your name?'

'Hans Hildebrandt.'

Even that coincidence filled her with emotion, though Hans is a very common name

'Take me to your mother. Please.'

He led her to his mother's flat. She turned out to be a slatternly woman with too many children by different men. Oma didn't waste any time. She simply asked the woman if she could adopt Hans, or foster him.

It seems to have been settled very quickly. Presumably she led Hans across the railway line, and through the gateway into the old centre of Danzig with its handsome buildings, to the Hundegasse and home. But her father seems not to have been very pleased with this idea; indeed, he was outraged at the suggestion that there would be room for him somewhere in their house. It became necessary for her mother to intervene and suggest a compromise. As it happened, their cook, Margot, had recently left to get married. She would surely be pleased to look after little Hans if they gave her some money. So this was settled.

Oma clearly felt responsible for the boy and must have visited Margot and him regularly, talked to him, studied his school reports, and given Margot the money. On one of these occasions, she found the boy was upset because he couldn't go to the school sports day: he didn't have the correct white shorts. It was too late to buy any, so Oma decided to make him a pair, though she hated sewing and was no good at it. She asked Margot for a pair of his shorts to use as a pattern. Her motto was always: If it's something other people can do, then I can do it. She unpicked the shorts, carefully, remembering which piece was attached to which; pinned them to some white material, cut round them, and stitched them together exactly the same. It took her most of the night to do this; but early next morning, she took them to Margot's house. Hans was overjoyed. But these brand-new shorts already had a patch on the seat. There had been one on the old shorts, and Oma hadn't dared leave it out.

In 1888, when she was eighteen, Oma had to have an operation to rectify a squint. Afterwards, as a kind of reward, or consolation, her father let her go to see her close friend and former fellow pupil, Becky Baum, who was studying music in Leipzig.

Becky was not the only Danzig person studying in Leipzig. There was Becky's lover, Morchen Liepmann. And there was Hans Schubert. The four of them had a great time together. Morchen and Schubert would call for Becky and Oma at their boarding house to go on expeditions in the sparse, wintry countryside, or to museums, theatres, concerts. She and Becky insisted on paying for themselves. In the Gewandhaus, sitting next to her Schubert, she heard the great Schubert's 'Death and the Maiden' quartet for the first time. The impression it made on her was unforgettable. She loved all Schubert's music – and never called her reticent lover Hans, only ever Schubert; the glorious music was like a nimbus clinging to the name. And the love of Schubert's music persisted down the generations: I find it quite overwhelming myself.

Oma's idolising love for Hans Schubert is strange – and she realised it herself. She wrote:

'Yes, although in all those years Schubert never uttered a word of love, let alone touched or kissed me, still I was convinced in myself that he loved me too, even if not as exclusively, as boundlessly as I loved him. He had no notion of the depth of my love. He regarded me as a cheerful, natural being, approaching life from the light, cheerful side, in contrast to his phlegmatic nature. He had no idea how I suffered for him, how I longed for him, worshipped him, idolised him. Many years later, when we were both over fifty, we exchanged the poems we had written about each other in those years of our youth, and then we both understood what had been going on inside us for the first time. Here is one of his, which shows how totally he failed to understand my feeling for him:

All the others can see it
Only I cannot.
All the others believe it,
Only I do not.
Only I cannot find in those shrewd eyes
Any trace of the love that glows.
She thinks it's fun, the spirited girl,
To tease this earnest, introspective fellow

And lead him by the nose.

And the truth was that I was, figuratively, lying at his feet, lost in admiration, adoring him!

Finally I could not stand the uncertainty any longer and decided to bring things to a head at any price, even if it meant losing him. I wanted to force Schubert to reach a decision. I resolved to leave him for a whole year, hoping that he would realise at last that he could not live without me, and would utter the longed-for words. I would go abroad. I would go to England, and teach.

So I prepared myself for examinations in German, English and French, and passed them after five months. Then I informed my father of my plan. All I wanted from him was my fare. I told him that I wanted to prove to him and to myself that I could support myself. This was not easy for him: men in those days prided themselves on providing for their women-folk, and felt they were failures if a wife or daughter earned her living.

Of course, my real reason for going was Schubert. I wrote to him – he was in Berlin at the time – saying that I felt our friendship was beginning to seem like a shackle to him, that I was therefore going to disappear from his life completely, for a year in the first instance, by going abroad; there was to be no correspondence between us. I expected his reaction to give me certainty, one way or the other. I lay in bed with a fever (literally) awaiting his reply, which came by return of post – and was so delightful, so unambiguous, that I could harbour no more doubts. He wrote that he could never live without me, could not do without me, and could not agree to my suggestion: he loved me too much to do without any contact with me. And he concluded with a poem:

It's no mere candle-light that burns and dies
No mere reflection of those lovely days
When all my happiness I saw in you
If I proclaim today my inmost truth:
You faithful girl, it's true that I love you.

The poem did give me pause. All those negatives, that "you faithful girl", made me aware of his doubts. But I dismissed these thoughts: the longed-for words had been uttered at last. Before leaving for England, I was going to Berlin with my father and my friend Mieze Baum, and then to the Harz mountains for a holiday with them and two cousins. Since Schubert was in Berlin, I arranged to meet him alone in an art exhibition at the Lehrter station.

I felt like a bride now, ready to fling myself into his arms. But what happened? He greeted me with his usual formal bow, called me Miss, did not refer to our letters with a single word, and followed me to the garden where my people were waiting for me. I obliged him to agree to meet me next day in the Deer Park; that was all.

When we met there, he behaved like a madman, rushing to and fro and declaring he neither could nor would ever marry, because of a strain of insanity in his family (his parents were closely related) and finally rushed off without a word of farewell. In my despair I feared suicide – he had been harbouring such thoughts for some time – and sent him an anxious telegram – in those days it would have been unthinkable for me to go to his flat alone.

I received a reassuring reply, so next day I set off for the Harz mountains as planned with my father and friends, and not long after I went to England. I do not remember seeing him again before I left, but – still hoping – I sent him my address in London, c/o the Adelmann Teachers' Institute.'

Chapter 3

It was late autumn when Oma, aged 21, went to England. She thought she was rather good at English, after all the tuition she had had, and expected to have no trouble with the language. But when she got off the train at Victoria station, she writes:

'I found the railway officials so incomprehensible – and they me – that I thought I had accidentally come to the wrong country.

I had been seasick on the crossing from Vlissingen and was feeling very sad, because of Schubert's rejection. I made my way to Miss Adelmann's Teachers' Institute, and showed her my tutors' reports, since I didn't have a school report; and rightly or wrongly my tutors all praised my talents, intelligence, knowledge, and so on. These glowing reports enraged Adelmann. She started shouting at me, accusing me of having made them up myself. Nevertheless, I was taken into the dining room for lunch. I was appalled at the strictness of the regime. "I see someone taking a bite out of a piece of bread and butter!" Adelmann suddenly screamed across the long tables. After the meal, I was surprised to see all the aspiring teachers and governesses lined up on either side of the corridor. Adelmann paced along the ranks like a general, and slapped those that met with her approval so hard on the shoulder that just watching made me flinch.

In those days it was fashionable to wear your hair with a fringe on your forehead – but for Adelmann, that was unbearable coquetry. If anyone came to her place with a fringe, she had to remain in solitary confinement until the hair had grown long enough to be plaited in. Moreover, they all had to wear bonnets, like nurses. Of course I refused – I never wore anything on my head – and she upbraided me for my rebelliousness.

I spent two weeks in all in London, in a gloomy bed-sitter, made even gloomier by a pea-soup fog, which really frightened me. When at last it lifted, I walked around the streets. Normally Oxford Street was busy and as I walked along it, so young, so alone, so sad, it seemed to me that the English had no heart, as if, even if I fell over, dead, or ill, they would walk past me, silent and unconcerned. I misunderstood their reticence, especially towards foreigners, and felt they were being hostile if they did not give me a friendly look as they passed by. I soon discovered how wrong I was.

After a few days, Adelmann offered me a job to teach German. It was only au pair, but I accepted it at once, anxious to get away from her and her Institute. It was called Cedar House, a finishing school at Burnham Beeches, near Slough.

Slough was a little town with fewer than 8 000 inhabitants in the 1890s, when Oma went there. It has grown enormously, with a great deal of industry. Burnham Beeches, while almost engulfed in housing, remains a lovely forest of ancient beech trees, as it was in her day; and the local library was able to show me these old photographs of Burnham Beeches and of Cedar House, the property, in 1891, of a Mr G Hill; but that no longer exists.

However, it was to this house, in 1891, that Oma made her way, and rang the bell. Let her continue the story:

'The door was opened by a pretty, smart and rather snooty parlour-maid: "Oh, the new governess," she said dismissively. But then I was taken to the Principal, Miss Gosset-Hill, an excellent person. Her elderly father lived and taught at the school too, as did her younger sister, Miss Tottie. Her mother, a petty, miserly old woman, was the housekeeper. And there was a French governess too, a young, charming, superficial Parisian. At first I had to share a room with her, divided only with a curtain. Other teachers came to the school by the hour: a singing teacher, Mr Stubbs, from the famous choir of St George's Chapel, Windsor, and a riding instructor who came twice a week for the oldest girl, Louisa Cave, and twice for the little ones. They were dressed just like ladies in long riding habits with a train and hard hats, and looked very sweet, enthroned on their side-saddles. All the girls came from the best families. There were six aged sixteen to eighteen, four aged twelve to fourteen, and two little sisters aged six and seven, with a baby sister who was not even a year old. These three little children had been abandoned by their mother, and brought to Cedar House by their father. The baby was only with us for a short time.

Now a new life began for me, very different from what I was used to as the daughter of a wealthy, respected man in Danzig. The girls were divided into two classes by age. The two smallest were taught by Miss Tottie. I did as much work as I could, to deaden my gnawing grief over Schubert. I gave private lessons to "faithful Baisie", a rather untalented Irish girl of twelve, *because she burst into tears whenever she could not keep up with the others in class. I found I could teach her, in an unorthodox way, and she was enormously grateful. Louisa, the oldest girl, very talented in languages and in painting, was soon a real friend. The French woman attached herself to me, as I was her age and spoke her language. In fact all the people in Cedar House gave me nothing but friendship and love – except perhaps that parlour maid. I had a few battles with her. At mealtimes she would serve first the pupil on my right, then the pupil on my left, and only then, me. So after observing this silently for a few days, I got up, walked round the long table to Miss Hill, and asked her whether this order of serving was at her behest? Miss Hill's embarrassment, and everyone else's, was acute. But from then on I was served before the pupils.*

It was considered unladylike to fetch such things as lamps (we used paraffin lamps) from the nether regions; one had to ring for them. One evening I rang, several times, and there was no reaction. It was the parlour maid's revenge for her humiliation in the dining room. So I kept my finger on the bell till the whole household came rushing to my room in alarm. I simply said I had been ringing for a lamp without success. Nothing of the kind ever happened again.

I often went out walking in the meadows or in Burnham Beeches, a park-like forest or a forest-like park, with ancient beech trees of enormous girth, and often hollow trunks in which two or three people could easily stand. Mendelssohn is supposed to have composed his music for "A Midsummer Night's Dream" here; there is a memorial which attests to it. When I roamed about there alone I often sang to myself, quite loudly. One day a farmer spoke to me and asked me if I had sung a Swedish song the night before? He had a small boarding house at the edge of the forest where painters, chiefly, came to stay for weeks, or even longer. And the previous evening an old Swedish painter had jumped up at supper, saying he could hear a Swedish song. He ran out, followed by all the others, some with lanterns, but they had been unable to find me. I had stopped singing. This conversation was the beginning of a great friendship between me and the farmer, Titus James. He showed me his charming house and garden, where the Mendelssohn Memorial stood.

Sometimes I took one or other or all the older girls with me on my walks, which was a much appreciated favour. One November day I stood in a glade, leaning against a tree, watching the girls laughing as they ran about trying to catch the falling leaves before they reached the ground. They thought that was lucky! I was so immersed in my sorrow, I felt so old compared to them, though they were only my juniors by a few years, I was so hopeless, so lonely, that Louisa must have noticed it. For one or two years later, when I had been back at home for quite a long time, I came across the song in Schubert's "Winterreise" about the last leaves on the trees: the poet "hangs his hope" on one leaf and feels that if that leaf falls to the ground his hope will be lost. This brought the scene in Burnham Beeches so vividly to my mind that I copied the poem in a letter to my friend Louisa and asked her if it reminded her of anything. Her description of that scene came by return of post – though of course she knew nothing of my unhappy love. Louisa persuaded me to take riding lessons with her twice a week, which I greatly enjoyed. In general all the affection I received from old and young did mitigate my grief as time went by.

One or two months after my arrival in Slough, a twenty-page letter was forwarded to me from the Adelmann Institute in London; in it, Schubert gave me my final dismissal, as it were. He was writing from a water-cure clinic in Harzburg. It was a horrible letter, full of quotations, chiefly from Goethe's "Faust" Part 2; in fact it was quite impersonal, but so unambiguous that I could draw only one conclusion: it's finished, finally finished. Soon after reading it I had to give a lesson. One of the eighteen-year-old Irish girls suddenly ran out, weeping noisily, and a little later Miss Hill came to me and said I need give no more lessons, as I appeared to have received bad news from home – the girl must have deduced this from the look on my face – but was to be left entirely in peace. I told no one there about my grief, but they all treated me with touching consideration and tact. Later the same day I sent Schubert back all his letters without any further comment apart from a request for mine to him. They arrived a few days later, complete, and I wanted to regard this chapter as closed now. But the truth is that I dragged my love and my sorrow and my unquenchable hope around with me for three more long years.

Otherwise I have only pleasant memories of the rest of my stay in England. The pupils liked me and showed it in every way: the two little ones would wait for me at the bottom of the stairs, put their arms around me and call me: "Darling sweet little Fräulein!" I was often asked to chaperone girls when they wanted to go shopping in the little town of Slough, rather than the flirtatious young French teacher, because I was so virtuous. For that reason I was also chosen to be present during the girls' music lessons with Mr Stubbs, rather than Mlle Fillon, who would have enjoyed the – oh so rare – company of an attractive young man. I was impervious to his charms. I always sat in the poorly heated music room with a big shawl round me and blue glasses on my nose, reading or writing, completely ignored by Mr Stubbs. Once, when a pupil asked me to play the accompaniment to a Schubert song and I disposed of the shawl and the glasses he looked quite astonished to see me emerge as a young and not really ugly girl.

Once, when I acceded to Mlle Fillon's request to come with me on one of my walks and headed for my beloved Burnham Beeches, she implored me to go to "the town" instead.

"Mais que voulez vous y voir?" I asked.

"Un pair de pantalons, Mademoiselle," she sighed.

About a year later, when she was back in France, she sent me notice of her engagement. I sent her my congratulations and added: *"Alors vous avez un pair de pantalons tout pour vous seule!"*

Once the school held a *"penny concert"*, as it was called, for charity, and I had the nerve to sing the Elsa aria from *"Lohengrin"*: 'You breezes that my laments so often sadly filled…'.

The applause that my unskilled singing received at the school went to my head. A glowing review of my singing appeared in the local rag. I sent a cutting to my family with the heading: "A Prophet in his own country ….". Moreover, the vicar of a little town nearby, who had heard me, paid me a visit and asked me to take part in a concert in his parish, and to do him a personal favour by singing a song he particularly liked: "In einem kühlen Grunde". Often a girl would come to me when I was sitting at the piano and say: "Oh Fräulein, do sing 'Elend'", or: "Please sing 'Mein Herz'" – both from Schubert's "Winterreise".

*****

In the Easter holidays I went to Paris, where my cousin Julie Wolfthorn, later wellknown as a painter, was living with her friend Jelka Rosen, who later married the composer Delius, and another cousin, Meta Neumann, who was being trained as a singer. I got a room in the Rue de Vaugirard, where they all lived, and was plunged into the wildest Bohemianism. In my respectable English governess's garb, with corresponding behaviour, I was an inexhaustible source of amusement to the whole gang, who exploited their unsupervised freedom in every way. All the painters in the group had pictures in an exhibition which was about to open, and one of them, a Portuguese, Sancho Pinto, invited me to the vernissage, a kind of preview to which each exhibitor could bring one guest, while the general public were excluded. He was to pick me up at a certain time, but he arrived early and waited in the corridor, leaning against the door. When I, not dreaming that he was there, and still – oh horror! – in my petticoat, opened the door to get my shoes, poor Sancho Pinto fell full-length into my room. I felt besmirched for life, having been seen in my petticoat, and by a man! That's what we were like in those days. Once, when I was sixteen, and opened the door – again, to get my shoes, and in my petticoat – I slammed it shut again, because my dog Harras might see me. In my defence I must add that on that occasion I saw the folly of my action and opened the door again immediately and let him in.

I cannot really understand how I came to develop this ludicrous prudishness. Of course, there were some very strict rules in my youth. For instance, there was no communal bathing. There was a bathing place for women, and, at a considerable distance from it, a men's bathing place. Family bathing places did not come in till much later, and they were strictly for families; bachelors and single girls were not admitted. But my prudishness was excessive, and it meant I was a square peg in a round hole in that Bohemian set-up in Paris. One evening, coming out of the Opera late and alone, I was walking up and down the Boulevard des Italiens, vainly seeking one of the booths where they sold tickets for the omnibus. A gentleman who evidently misinterpreted my going to and fro in the night spoke to me and offered me his company. I was speechless with horror at this affront and leapt into the first cab that came along – which was far too expensive for my sparse resources. Arriving at the house where I was staying, my terrors were reawakened by a gentleman who entered the front door at the same moment as I, and, like me, took a candle, a room key and some post from the shelf on the wall, and followed me up the dark stairs. After the "frightful" incident on the Boulevard, my terror was absolute as I heard the stranger's footsteps behind me, climbing up and up the stairs to my room door: I felt hunted. But luckily the stranger went on up; he had no evil intentions whatever. However, on another evening, when I again climbed the stairs to my room with a candle and my room key, I found my door unlocked, to my alarm, and when I went in hesitantly the candle fell from my hand as I was embraced – pulled onto a man's lap in the dark – and kissed! My screams for help fortunately caused the perpetrator to reveal herself as "Frink", a painter from Argentina, who belonged to my cousin's circle, and had dressed up as a man to be amused by my consternation.

She was not the only one who liked to wear men's clothes, with a masculine haircut, even in the street, though this incurred severe police penalties. I was so innocent at that time that I knew nothing about sexual perversions, which played a not inconsiderable role in those Bohemian artists' circles. Lesbian affairs were not rare and were hardly kept secret. Only I was so ignorant that I sometimes played and sang for a lesbian couple whom I found very likeable. They asked me to, to help them go to sleep, while they cuddled in a four-poster bed. The "masculine" partner was a very manly looking, tall, stately girl called "Singe" (from Grisinger) who only ever dressed as a man. At the vernissage that Sancho Pinto took me to, all the women painters had robed themselves in the craziest, most striking, picturesque fashions, with enormous hats (cheap, from Bon Marché), ancient brocade dresses inherited from great-grandmothers, long trains, etc. I, in my ultra-respectable English governess's costume, must have looked quite absurd among them.

I returned to Burnham Beeches until the autumn, when my self-imposed year of exile was over. Then I spent almost all my savings on presents, and went home.

I had a travelling companion, a young man I had never seen before, but

Oma (centre, front, standing) among the artists at a fancy dress party in Berlin later

we made friends immediately. He was an English clergyman, a Baptist, called Streuli – the name was Swiss, but the Streulis had been British for generations. He was going to Dresden to visit a married sister. At first we just looked at each other, very often. But on the ferry, where I was again dreadfully seasick, he was a Good Samaritan to me, and we drew closer to each other. In Düsseldorf we parted, he to Dresden, I to Berlin. For three years thereafter we wrote to each other, and he sent me souvenirs from his many journeys. And we were to meet again.

Chapter 4

Oma's feelings for this young Englishman, Streuli, seem to have existed in a different part of her psyche from her love for Schubert. This was still dominant. Despite the long and horrible letter from Schubert, and the return of his letters to her and hers to him, Oma simply could not believe that her strong feeling that they belonged together was false. She writes:

I was by no means cured of my nine-year-old love sickness. All my thoughts, as I returned from England, were concentrated on one point: "What will our first meeting be like?"

The very first day after my return to Zoppot I hurried out to the beach, where I hoped to meet him. I went up onto the low ridge that runs parallel to the shore, climbed the narrow path we both knew so well, past the bush where he had lain so often in hiding, waiting for me to come into sight on the beach below – as he described in a poem which he wrote when he was about nineteen, but which I did not get to see till he was about fifty:

A boy lies stretched out on the ground...
A bush with gentle sympathy
Conceals him with its yellow leaves ...
Won't she come this morning either? ...
Then the bush begins to rustle ...
Someone's whistling near at hand.
There she is! And down he tumbles
Till he lands before his darling ...

That was where I was walking that day, looking down to the beach – and there he was at last, with his father, evidently heading for the Kolibka Grotto, as I was. I got there first and sat down on the low stone table in the grotto, where I could see the sea, but not the beach. I was trembling. Little BeaupPre saw me at once from the entrance and came towards me with outstretched arms, full of pleasure and surprise, and greeted me like a favourite daughter. But as for Schubert – he bowed, silently, stayed by the entrance, avoided my eyes. His father looked at us, taken aback, understanding nothing, only feeling that something was wrong, and soon put an end to the situation by going away, after an almost tender farewell. And Schubert went with him.

A year before, when I went to their house to say goodbye before going to England, his mother had said to me, softly: "Do marry our Hans!" And I had answered briefly: "It takes two." And when BeaupPre escorted me out through the garden, he had asked: "Does Hans know you're leaving?" And I just nodded silently. But he hadn't come to see me before I left. And now our

*reunion was just as negative, and so he remained, whenever and wherever
we met. He did not speak to me, stayed away from me, avoided looking at
me. Just once, at a friend's wedding, he attempted some sort of rapproche-
ment, shyly and clumsily, but was foiled repeatedly by other people's chance
interruptions. Then he went back to Heidelberg, where he was studying.'*

*****

She expected her father to be impressed by her year in England, having done
what she set out to do, and generally having proved herself to be competent.
She even repaid the money he had lent her for the journey, half expecting
him to let her keep it; but he put it away in a drawer without a word. As she
recalled, many years later:

*'I thought that when I returned I would achieve greater independence from
him and get a monthly allowance, as my brother Heinchen did as a student.
But my father did not comply, not wishing to lose his custody over me. So I
advertised English lessons in the local paper and quickly got a number of
students. But to have a daughter doing paid work was a terrible disgrace. He
implored me to cancel all the lessons, and promised to do everything I asked.
I complied, and for the next years I lived the life of a rich man's daughter,
with no real duties, no work, no substance in my life, in my parents' home. I
had plenty of freedom, went on trips and outings with them or with a
woman friend – and felt unhappy and dissatisfied.'*

Most young women in her position were really waiting to get married, as her
elder sisters already had; her still unquenched passion for Schubert ruled
that out for her. But she could and did still play her part in family life.

Her father went to Karlsbad once a year because of his gall bladder, and
naturally his wife accompanied him. Every year she had a new dress made
for that trip. At that time fashion dictated that dresses had to be so long that
ladies had to hold them gathered up in a great bundle when they were out, to
keep them clean. This exasperated her sensible, practical father. He forbade
his wife to wear such dresses. Of course Oma, his daughter, refused to wear
them, but her mother thought it was necessary to keep up with fashion.
And she did.

From Oma's memoirs:

*'One day I received a very agitated letter from Papa in Karlsbad. He had, as
usual, gone for a walk on the promenade with Mama on their first day there,
arm in arm, of course, so that she had to take huge strides to keep in step with
him, who was so much taller. And then he noticed, indignantly, that in defi-
ance of his wishes she was wearing one of the excessively long dresses and
holding the train bundled up in her hand. Irritable as he normally was,
doubly irritable because of the Karlsbad cure he was undergoing, he left her
standing there and returned to the hotel without her. "And then that woman*

left me all alone in Karlsbad and went to Berlin, when she knows perfectly well that this will ruin my stay here!"

A letter from Mama arrived by the same post. "Mindful of your wise instructions, I decided that on this occasion I would not put up with Papa's outrageous behaviour. I enquired about trains to Berlin, ordered a cab, and packed my suitcase. Papa saw me and said: 'What's the meaning of this?'

'I'm going home.'

'Have you got any money?'

'No. You'll have to give me some.'

'What about keys?'

'You must give me those too.'"

Finally he escorted me to the station, every inch the concerned husband, bought my ticket, gave me money and the key, and stood like a stone statue, watching me depart."

I wrote back to my father immediately, pointing out that Mama was old enough to choose her own dresses. To Mama I wrote: "How could you do that to him? If he can't stand your dress being so long – cut it! Whom do you want to please, after all? So cut it, and go back to him."

Well, she did go back to him, but without shortening the dress. And he received her with relief and walked the promenade with her in her long dress without a murmur.'

❉❉❉❉❉

Her brother Heinchen, too, gave her a brief sense of purpose. He was studying law in Königsberg to the east of Danzig, along the Baltic coast. It is called Kaliningrad now, and belongs to Russia, but was then the capital of German East Prussia and a venerable university town, home of the philosopher Emmanuel Kant. Heinchen was expected to write home regularly, but – as she writes –

'...his letters home became rarer and rarer and finally ceased altogether, which affected the parents in accordance with their temperaments: Father was furious, Mother anxious. So I wrote him a loving sisterly letter, asking him to confide in me, as he was obviously in some sort of pickle. His reply was brief: "You are my dear, good sister and I thank you. But I'm in a mess, and no-one can help me out."

There was only one thing for me to do: I had to go to Königsberg to see for myself. I told my mother, implored her not to let Papa know, got her to give me all the money she could lay her hands on, asked our man-servant, Friedrich, to come to my room very quietly, in his socks, at six in the morning to get my suitcase and take me to the station. "Very well, Miss Ollchen," said faithful Friedrich, and did as requested, obviously thinking to himself: " At least I'll be able to see who she's going off with." But – even more shockingly – I got on the train all by myself.

30

At Königsberg I took a cab to Heinchen's digs, and rang the bell. The landlady opened the door.

"Good afternoon. Is Mr Fajans at home? I am his sister."

From the landlady's visible disbelief at the word "sister" I drew my own conclusions about Heinchen's lifestyle.

"No, he is not at home. He's on duty on the parade ground."

Aha – so he was a part-time soldier!

"Could you get a message to him to let him know that I am here?"

"I could."

"And could I wait in his room till he comes?"

"Yes, why not. This way, miss."

When we were in his room, I casually took off my stiffly starched cuffs, inscribed with my name Olga Fajans inside in indelible ink, and let her see it, to dispel her doubts. Then I took her into my confidence, or rather I encouraged the landlady to confide in me.

"Does my brother owe you any rent?"

"Well yes, as a matter of fact, he does. For two months."

"I see. Do you know if he has any other debts?"

"Well, there are these bills from the beer shop," she said, almost apologetically.

"Let me give you the money for his rent. And would you be so kind as to take this money to the shop, to pay his bill there?"

"Certainly, miss. And shall I go to the parade ground and tell him you're here?"

"I would be most grateful."

So she hurried off, and I sat down on a lumpy green sofa with little crocheted doilies everywhere to wait. There were frightful oleographs on the walls, and a wardrobe with Heinchen's violin case on top, thick with dust. That confirmed my worst fears. He must be in a very bad way if he wasn't touching his violin any more. I found a book, Dostoyesky's Crime and Punishment, which did not make my wait in that uncomfortable room any rosier. Then there was a ring at the door, and a familiar voice asked:

"Fajans at home?"

The landlady replied quietly that his sister had arrived.

"Sister? Ha!"

The caller laughed in a good-humoured way and soon the door was flung open to reveal – my old friend Richard Simson!

"Olchen! It really is you!"

I assured him that it was, and to while away the time he took me for a stroll round the unlovely town of Königsberg and its pitiful surroundings. We returned to the digs, and at last Heinchen came, and embraced me affectionately. But then he said, "Can't talk now. Dead beat. It's been a hellish tour of duty. Must sleep." And he flung himself down on the bed and slept for two hours. When he woke up, he declared that he was famished.

"Must celebrate. Not every day a fellow's sister comes to visit him. Come on – I know a decent restaurant."

We had wine with our meal and talked and laughed together for a long time. When at last he and I returned to his digs he was exhausted again.

"Can't talk now. Must sleep first. So must you. Here – you have my bed. I'll sleep on the sofa in the landlady's sitting room. Look, she's got it ready for me. I asked her to. Look, Olchen, I'm sorry, but I have to be on duty again very early. You wait here, all right? Sleep as long as you like, make yourself at home. I'll be back in the afternoon. Then – "

"Then we can talk?"

"Then we will talk."

And so at last, after the best part of another day, he made his long confession. I got him to tell me what debts he had, promised to pay them off, and to get his monthly allowance increased. In return I got him to promise to let me know if he ever owed more than ten marks at the end of any month. I kept my promise; he, alas, did not. Then he confessed that he had contracted syphilis, as so many young men did in those days, when sex before marriage was unthinkable, and marriage before they were securely settled impossible – unless they had the fortitude to be totally abstinent until they were at least thirty years old. This had to be kept secret from the parents. Like many of my friends, he had to go in for a cure, which I arranged for him before I returned home.

It seemed to be successful. Years later, he married, and had children, and was a successful judge in a small town – when the syphilis, which, it turned out, was only dormant, became active again. He died young. People suspected that he had contracted it through being unfaithful to his wife. Only I knew that it was because of his "youthful indiscretions".

*****

'One of the trips I had planned was to meet Marie and Becky Baum in Zurich and travel with them through Switzerland, then along the Rhine, and finally to go on a walking tour in the Harz mountains. The journey to Zurich would take me through Heidelberg. And Heidelberg meant Schubert: he was studying there. I was so unhappy, so incapable of freeing myself from my love, so deeply wounded by Schubert's behaviour, that I resolved to use this opportunity to force him to speak to me. I went to his mother and asked her to write to him to tell him when I would be arriving at Heidelberg station and asking him to meet me there. I did not want to write myself.

The train entered Heidelberg punctually and there was Schubert standing on the platform. We greeted each other silently with a handshake. After we had walked several paces, I said: "Let's go to a quiet place where we can talk without interruption."

He took me to a wine garden, where it was already nearly dark, and we sat opposite each other at a table. And there I started telling him how I felt, for the first time in all those long years. I reminded him of our long friendship, how I had been his closest friend during the years of his youth; asked if I had ever failed him as a friend, touched just superficially on our shy, never outspoken love, which nonetheless each of us recognised in the other, reminded him of the walks on the Danzig ramparts, and how he used to whistle the theme of the Beethoven romance, and how we looked out for each other on the beach at Zoppot, and finally asked what I had done to deserve to be thrown aside like a worn-out garment, and whether he considered me so petty that I would be unable to continue to be his friend, even if he no longer loved me in the other way.

He said nothing, but in the dim twilight I could see that there were tears falling from his averted eyes. At first I was petrified. That was the last thing I had expected! I got up, went round to him, held his head against my breast, and wept with him.

Then the unexpected happened. A miracle. All the pain, disappointment, the aching, endless longing for his love – left my heart and made way for an almost motherly pity, while I caressed him, not as a lover or a beloved, but as a mother caresses. I was liberated at last; I felt the burden of my grief lift off me. Now I wanted nothing but his friendship, and from that moment, for the first time, I could contemplate building up my life without him, away from him, without him, without waiting to be united with him, married to him. We both felt relieved. He too was happy that we had come close to one another again. He would not let me continue my journey that same evening, as planned, though Marie and Becky Baum were waiting for me – instead, we spent the whole of the next day together, walking in Neckargmünd and Neckarsteinach, and finally we parted as the best of friends. And so we remained until he died at the age of 67.

⁕⁕⁕⁕⁕

It was after that meeting in Heidelberg that Oma, free at last from the shackles of her frustrated hope of marriage to Schubert, decided to study medicine.

This was an extraordinary decision for any woman to take in the year 1895. Europe's women were just beginning to fight for their rights. In Britain, the suffragette movement did not really start until 1897; it was 1903 before Emmeline Pankhurst and her daughters founded the famous Women's Social and Political Union. Only Switzerland allowed women to study medicine. Oma was not a feminist, in fact, she had no time or sympathy for feminism. She was simply herself: a self-assertive person – as she writes:

'...from an early age I had always followed my very own, independent paths, rebelling in almost every respect against the customs of the time. I remember one occasion when I was a child on a visit to Thorn, when the whole family, and numerous aunts, cousins, etc were getting ready for a trip in coaches, I hid in a distant room, because I wanted to stay at home alone, for no apparent reason. I knew no other girl in my young days who spent hours every day walking alone, or rather with a biting dog. Neither of my sisters did, nor any of my girl friends. And none of them washed from head to foot in cold water every morning, as I did. It was also very unusual for the daughter of a wealthy man suddenly to wish to prove to him that she could be independent of him and earn her own living as a governess in England. And I taught myself, and passed in English, French and German in a quarter of the time normally allowed. When I came home after a year I wanted to go on earning money by giving private lessons, and only gave up the plan because my father begged me to, and agreed to give me an allowance. Now, having spent between two and three years in the hateful condition of living at home with no real work or duties, I made up my mind to become a doctor. This was again was quite eccentric; women were not admitted to study or take exams in medicine in Germany, and there was no one else in our town who had hit on such an "absurd" idea. A woman might perhaps get permission from individual professors to sit in on their lectures, but she could not be matriculated, nor take any medical examinations. But I was encouraged by some professor friends, who wanted to use me as a sort of guinea-pig for the experiment of women's studies, and so I resolved to try my luck at a German university whose rector was willing to back me up: Freiburg.

Once again I went to my father with an extraordinary request; once again he asked for 24 hours to think it over, and then agreed. What a generous father I had! He also agreed to my once again completely unconventional method of preparing for the Abitur, the university entrance exam. Remember I had never been to school, had only been given some rather haphazard private lessons with Becky and Marie Baum. But I was already 26, and I was in a hurry. I gave myself a one-and-a-half year deadline; I would sit and pass the exam in the spring of 1897. Everyone who heard of my plan laughed at me: it would be impossible to cover the syllabus in such a short time. But I was determined. I found tutors for maths and for Greek and Latin, and had two hours a week for each of those three subjects. When I told the Greek and Latin teacher that I wanted to get through the syllabus from scratch in one-and-a-half years – the grammar school allowed nine years for Latin, six for Greek – he thought I was mad, until he saw how I worked. I asked my brother's maths teacher to give me lessons, but he declined. He had sworn never to teach girls again, because he had suffered the torments of hell in his first appointment at a girls' school. He was still quite young when I called on him, good-looking, and positively smart for a teacher. Why had he *suffered? He explained: as soon as he entered the classroom, the girls would all stare at some point or other in his clothes: sometimes his shoes – he looked down nervously, they seemed all right – sometimes at his tie, or his cuffs – always as if there was something wrong. It made him so nervous that he gave up the position. In the end he did take me on, and was very pleased with me, only the poor fellow had to mark an awful lot of exercises that I had done at home, which meant a lot of work for him.*

After a few months my parents moved to Berlin, and I with them. I had to find new teachers there. I found a good maths teacher whom I had known in Danzig, but I did not know any teachers of Latin and Greek. So I went to Helene Lange, who was a well-known feminist and educationalist, to ask if she could recommend a teacher. And there, as four years previously with Adelmann in London, I observed that very competent, unmarried females are simply insufferable: self-confident, domineering, like sergeant majors. In fact, Adelmann was a friend of Helene Lange, who now poured scorn over me for my cheek in thinking that I could cover the whole syllabus in one-and-a-half years; it would require three, or was it five years. When she went so far as to maintain that I would above all be unable to write a German composition in the correct form I got up and left, without getting a recommendation for a teacher. I found an excellent one without her help.

I went for a short rest cure in Switzerland, at Lenk – and there I received a letter from Streuli, the young English Baptist minister, whom I had got to know on the journey home after my year at Burnham Beeches, and with whom I had been corresponding ever since: he was going to be in Switzerland at the same time, and wondered if we might meet, for instance in Grindelwald, where he would be staying for a while with some friends. So without hesitation, when my stay in Lenk ended, I went to Lauterbrunn for the night, or rather, half the night: I got a lad to come to me at two o'clock in the morning and guide me to the path at Wengern Alp and the Kleine Scheidegg. From there I walked on alone to Grindelwald, where, according to our arrangement, I would find a message from him at the Post Office, or he one from me, depending on who got there first. Well, I found his letter to me, with his address, set out for the hotel named, and suddenly a young man in sports clothes stopped in front of me. We hadn't seen each other for years, and hardly recognised each other, which did not prevent us falling deeply in love with each other. But I was true to my old, puritanical principles: never show, certainly never say how you feel! So we parted for the second time after a few days, and I went home to Berlin and got on with my studies.

In the following September, Streuli visited me at my parents' home, and then for the first time in my life – I was already 27 – I lost my inhibitions. For the first time I felt the bliss which silent, wordless, profound, youthful love can never give, which arises from kisses and caresses and irresistible tenderness.

He left after a few days, and I plunged into my studies again, until at last I was ready, and passed the Abitur at the beginning of 1897, as planned, confounding all the pessimists. The written part was spread over several days and went without a hitch, except that I angered the French teacher who was invigilating me and one other candidate by not using the dictionary available for the pathetically easy translation from French into German.

And in the spring I went to Freiburg, full of the highest expectations.'

Chapter 5

From Oma's Memoirs, Spring 1897:

'I was met at Freiburg station by two of my Danzig friends, Georg Rodenmacher and Georg Pietrkowski, whom I called Pieter, who were about to take their final exams, and Franz Keibel, Professor of Anatomy. He walked on my left side and explained, in deadly earnest, that being the first and only female at the university I would have to be tremendously careful, virtuous, reserved, since not only the whole university, but the whole town would be watching and criticising.

"You cannot possibly live in student digs," he said. "I have taken the liberty of booking you into a boarding house where you will be, as it were, under supervision and well looked after."

Freiburg

But on my right side my two friends, Georg and Pieter, were whispering about some digs they had found for me – "right close to where we are. You'll be your own boss there, independent, unsupervised, and live the way it suits the three of us!"

My good angel on one side – two tempters on the other! In the end I accepted that it would be best for me to stay in the respectable boarding house, at least at first.

But the semester was not due to begin for another fortnight, and so I had time to commit my first sin. I set off for Colmar, to meet my English friend, and I spent two weeks travelling in the Vosges with him: surely the loveliest, happiest time of my life! Now I was not living only in dreams, in unfulfilled desire, in yearning and fearing as I had in all the long years of my youthful love for Schubert. Here was blissful fulfilment.

There was only one thing that came between me and Streuli, and that was religion. Our attitudes were diametrically opposed. For him, it was the crown of existence; it meant nothing at all to me. I was an out-and-out atheist, and had been ever since I was a child. I could only accept the ethical part of Christianity; in fact he often said that in that respect I was a better Christian than anyone in his congregation; but that was all. I knew that I would wreck his life if I married him, for it soon became apparent that I was *stronger than he, and far more likely to pull him over to me, than to be drawn into his faith. In the end, we both accepted that, and when in 1899 I had passed my examinations and was to leave Freiburg for Breslau for my practical studies, we parted. We parted in the midst of our beautiful love.*

But for the time being this relationship enriched the first two years of my medical studies; for not only did he visit me every few weeks for two or three days; he came over from England for all the holidays and we went on wonderful trips together, to Switzerland, to France, the Ardennes ... And my studies did not suffer from these interludes; on the contrary, they gave me energy, élan, they made me receptive to new ideas. I was undaunted by any difficulties.

And there were plenty of those. While I found anatomy, zoology, botany and physiology intensely interesting, the two subjects that dominated the early semesters, namely physics and chemistry, bored me. They were completely new to me, and I had no talent or understanding for them. I could just about cope with physics, thanks to Professor Himsted's brilliant teaching; but chemistry remained a book with seven seals to me. Our ancient professor, Kiliani, had no idea how to make the subject interesting. He would come in and, without so much as a glance at his listeners, go to the board, turn his back on us, and start writing up incomprehensible runes. I copied them anxiously while listening to what he was saying. The student sitting next to me did exactly the same.

"Do you understand?" I whispered to him.

"Not one word," he whispered back. I was greatly relieved. Well, I thought, I'm not the only idiot here. Yet by dint of laborious rote learning I managed to get through the exam, in the end.

My total lack of ability in this field might be explained by the fact that the afore mentioned Professor Keibel, being a friend of the family, had taken it upon himself to compile my timetable, and sent me to the organic chemistry course, which was probably a mistake, since I didn't have a clue about inorganic chemistry. But I enjoyed the other courses and look back on them with pleasure, remembering zoology with Professor Weismann, physiology – especially of the sense organs – with Professor von Kries, and anatomy with Professors Wiederheim, Keibel and Gaupp. Professor Keibel taught embryology.

Being the only female in the university, my days were brimful with amusing little events. The students, all younger than me, could not keep their eyes off me, even during lectures. They had no idea that I was already 28; they thought I was very attractive and were keen to get to know me. There was one, who was already familiar with hashish and opium; he wanted to study "the modern woman" embodied in me, and always sat next to me in the lecture theatres and the laboratories. He sometimes laid an ultra-modern book between us to start a conversation. Only when I said, naively, that the only literature I could talk about was Schiller's "Maid of Orleans" and "The Bell" did he leave me alone and declare to others that I was the world's worst bluestocking. That was fine with me. I had my two friends, Georg and Pieter, who called on me every evening after supper for long walks in the forests and hills, sometimes till the middle of the night; every Sunday they took me out for a glorious expedition into the country. This came to an end after my first semester, which was their last. Later I had two other friends, one called Berg, and Leo Zuntz (whose son in the fullness of time was to marry my younger daughter). Later still, I nominated a young man to be my friend and constant companion: a country boy, who struck me as inwardly and outwardly clean, and intelligent. His name was Hugo Hempel, and he was in love with me. This did not bother me. I had my Englishman for loving.

The professors all fussed over me and spoiled me as if I was a dainty little creature. Even the chemistry laboratory technician would sometimes wait for me before a lecture and whisper: "Please don't be frightened – there will be some bangs today". And the professors would ask me solicitously: "Are you keeping up all right?"

The students observed me closely. If I wore a new blouse they would all stamp their feet enthusiastically. Since I lived quite a way outside town, I always came in by bicycle – which was almost as unusual for a woman in those days as studying medicine. It earned me a nickname: Strampel-Olga (Pedalling-Olga).

It was customary for students to pin a visiting card to the seat where they normally sat in lectures. Mine was forever being adorned with hearts and arrows; diminutives were added to my name, sometimes Greek ones. All sorts of things gave rise to harmless little pleasantries. When I asked one aged laboratory assistant called Eschle, who was distributing microscope slides, for one with heart tissue, he burst into a popular song, bellowing: "Heart, my heart, why so sad?" If I put on a clean lab.coat, he cried out: "Just look at our Miss Fajans! Doesn't she look like a little angel?"

And so on. I was old enough not to be embarrassed by all this. It was never spiteful. And I still had my English lover. Until 1898. But then I passed my examinations; and I parted from him.

I moved to Breslau, where my oldest sister, Lutka, lived with her husband, a magistrate named Gluckmann, who worked at the County Court, and their three children.

*****

Breslau, like Danzig, now belongs to Poland, and has a Polish name: Wroclaw. And we – Dudu, David and I – visited it, too, in 2002. It is a fine city on the River Oder/Odra with a great cathedral and a splendid market square with an ornate Gothic town hall and a big university. In Oma's – and

Lutka's – time it was a proud, self-governing, German municipality, with a famous university; a flourishing industrial town, due to Bismarck's policy of Germanisation of all that area known as Schlesien/Silesia. But it too was smashed to smithereens in the Second World War, and after the war was given to Poland: the German inhabitants fled to the West and were replaced by Poles. Almost everything we saw had – like the fine buildings in Gdansk – been brilliantly reconstructed under the Communists. Oma writes in detail about her studies:

> 'It was a real joy for me to study under the excellent professors in the medical faculty there, Mikulicz, Pfannenstiel, Neisser, Czerny, Flügge, Uthoff, and Fitelm. Most of them were very helpful to me and overrated my abilities – possibly because until this experiment with me, that am of quite average intelligence, they had never come across an academic woman before, and were accustomed to regarding all women as intellectually inferior. Only the pharmacologist Fitelm, an old roué, recognised that my way of thinking was radically different from the other students', though I generally reached the right conclusion in the end. Once he set us a small problem: How much of the actual substance will a patient receive from an injection of a 3.5 solution? While most of the others quickly wrote down the answer, I had to brood long and deep and cover reams of paper to work it out. Fitelm walked around, glancing at the students' papers. When he came to me, and saw my long, involved calculations, his face lit up with a happy smile. "Miss Fajans," he said. "Now I know exactly how your brain works!" When it came to the final oral examination with him, knowing of his weakness for the feminine, I bought myself a sky-blue blouse. That helped me against his better judgement, and he gave me a Grade 1.
>
> In fact, my thought processes were often different from other students'. Another example is still vivid to me. Hugo Hempel, who was so much younger than me, and who had come to Breslau from Freiburg at the same time as me, was sitting beside me in the embryology course, studying sections of an embryo through microscopes. I could not for the life of me make sense of my section, and deplored this fact to him. He jumped up. "It's quite simple!" he cried, and he poked his head between his legs and showed me how the section had been cut and which parts it had touched.
>
> Mikulicz, the wonderful surgeon, was as hard as steel with his assistants – strict and demanding; but with his students he was wise and instructive, and as for his patients, he treated them with indescribable kindness, gentleness and understanding. When a little old woman was brought into the lecture theatre just before her operation for a strangulated hernia, so that the students could all see the hernia, Mikulicz whispered to us to file past her rapidly – she was in great pain – but to take a close and careful look. Meanwhile Mikulicz stood in front of her, so that she could not see the students, and spoke to her encouragingly: "Now my dear, it'll soon be over, and then

you'll be lying in bed comfortably. Do you like coffee? You do? Nice and strong, with cream and sugar? Doctor, please see that this patient gets a good cup of coffee straight after the operation." And so on; all the while he was stroking her hand, and signalling to us to hurry up.'

* * * * *

When we were there in 2002, we were shown round the university, much of it very modern; but the medical faculty looked as it must have looked in Oma's day. It was particularly gratifying to find not only a street named after Professor Mickulicz, whom she so warmly admired, but also a marble memorial to him: clearly her opinion of him was widely shared. It was also strangely moving to see modern students, many of them female, going in and out of the doors, up and down the steps, as she must have done – though she would have been in long skirts.

Memorial to Professor Mickulicz

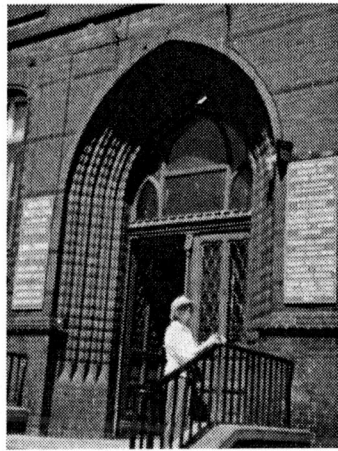

Entrance to the Department of Surgery

'Some of the clinical assistants were opposed to women studying,' she records. 'They argued that if a woman wanted to study like men then she should not expect to be treated as a lady; in fact, they treated me as coarsely as possible, taking delight in allocating patients to me whose ailments were located in parts which I would find really embarrassing. One day I was assigned a patient with a diseased penis. I was in despair, and gave Mickulicz, who had not been listening, a despairing glance as I walked past him. He quickly grasped the situation and yelled at the malicious assistant: "Dr X! Miss Fajans will have this patient!" – a case of breast cancer.

I often worked at a small hospital belonging to the Patriotic Women's

Guild. A young, very charming doctor was in charge: Dr Tietze. When his first ever course of lectures was announced, only four of us signed up for it. One day Tietze's friend Pfannenstiel, the gynaecologist, asked him how the course was going.

"Badly", was the reply. "Twenty-five per cent of my students are ill."

"Good gracious! What's up? An epidemic?"

"No. Miss Fajans has got nephritis."

This illness was followed with sympathetic concern in Breslau's medical circles. The first time I reappeared in the hygienist Flügge's class, the kindly old gentleman asked me to come to his room after the lecture. There he questioned me closely about the course of the illness, and asked if I was wearing woollen underwear.

"No, I'm not."

"But you should. You must! For at least six weeks!"

"All right, I will."

"Is that a promise?"

"I promise."

We shook hands solemnly to seal the promise, and I bought and wore woollen combinations as demanded. Many years later I passed them on to my eldest daughter.

When I presented myself to Dr Tietze as an assistant he accepted me with pleasure.

"I want to make you a good doctor," he said. "If you agree, I will keep you fully stretched. I will be very demanding. I'll chase you around, I will shout at you at times."

"Good," I answered. "That's what I want."

Now a very strenuous and many-sided apprenticeship began for me. During an operation, I might be in charge of the anaesthetics when he would suddenly tell someone else to take my place. "Sterilise!" he would shout; or "Pass the instruments!" Or he would ask me to fetch something without telling me where it was – I was to work things out for myself. One day I was told to shave the head of a patient with a head wound that was to be stitched.

"But doctor, I've never – "

"Good, so this is your first time."

I was told to stitch a wound.

"But doctor, I've never – "

"Fine. You've seen me put in stitches? Well, get on with it then. The patient's drunk and won't feel a thing."

I had to prepare dirty feet for operations. But I also had to train a young theologian who wanted to be a First Aider, to keep him busy, to find suitable tasks for him to do. Soon I had to perform minor operations myself under Tietze's supervision.

Strict as he was, he was also generous with his praise, and it was thanks to *him that later, when I was a country doctor in Ferch, I was able to perform surgery in the most unsuitable surroundings imaginable without a qualm. Another thing I learned from Tietze was the ability to observe suffering and pain without being overwhelmed with pity. He was a true friend to me.*

In fact, there was one case that moved me deeply. A Polish boy of about thirteen with severe osteomyelitis was operated on at regular intervals to remove splinters of bone and so on. He was so weak that he could not be given any more narcotics, so he suffered the most ghastly pain. I was the only one who knew any Polish, so it was my task to encourage him, to comfort him, to occupy his mind. One day when I was talking with him I suddenly fainted: I had been ill with the aforementioned nephritis for days without giving in to it. Tietze discovered that. And it was Tietze who later on removed my tonsils.

I also assisted the gynaecologist Pfannenstiel, who was fond of me as well. In his clinic I was chiefly an observer of his operations. Then he sent me to his outpatients' department, which was run by his first assistant, a certain Dr Krömer – one of the younger medical academics who were furiously opposed to women studying. Krömer's method was to ignore me. He would vanish behind a curtain with the patients without letting me watch. After several wasted days I told him that I would go to Pfannenstiel and complain about the "training" I was receiving. This scared him. He maintained he was only excluding me because the women would be embarrassed in front of me!

On the delivery ward, each student was allocated a pregnant woman. We had to spend the night on the ward. Many of the women were called "house pregnancies" – wretched women and girls, often unmarried, who did domestic work and made themselves available for examination by the students, often for months, in exchange for free confinements. I was deeply affected by the groans and screams of the women giving birth. But one very tall student was inspired to imitation. He lay on a bed, and, merrily assisted by the nurse on duty, and to the great mirth of the other students, he mimed a birth. I reported him and the midwife to the professor next day: he expressed indignation; but as he himself was rather coarse, nothing much was done about it.

The pathologist, Professor Ponfick, a comical, rosy old gentleman, always blushed when he saw me. He tried to avoid this as much as possible, turning his back on me so that I could not see the specimens he was dealing with, except by using cunning, or even force. This was not ill-will on his part – only embarrassment. Amusing stories about him circulated in Breslau. Once he ordered a cab, and when the coachman asked: "Where to, sir?" Pontick replied: "Just go; I'm sure I'll remember soon." After a long, aimless drive the coachman took him back home, received his fare, and Pontick returned contentedly to his study. Another time, at Christmas, his wife remarked that she would like a new carpet for the following Christmas. To avoid forgetting this, Pontick bought a carpet straight away and left it lying rolled up in the attic. Months later, when his wife happened to go into the attic, a cloud of moths rose from the remains of the carpet, most of which they had consumed. It was said that when his cat had kittens he ordered a second, smaller hole to be cut in the back door next to the existing one, so that the kittens too would be able to run in and out.

At the end of my final examinations, I was waiting anxiously with three other students in a side room to be told if we had passed in pathology. At last Pontick came and released us from our fears, except that one of us had failed the microscopy part. This student was an intelligent, hard-working, and very poor man for whom an extra semester would be a catastrophe. He turned as pale as a sheet, leaning against the wall for support – a picture of woe. I screwed up my courage and, making the most of my special position as the only woman, stepped in front of the deeply alarmed professor.

"This student is far superior to the rest of us in knowledge and skill. It is unthinkable that we have passed and he has failed. It must have been caused by some unfortunate accident. You will have to give him a second chance and let him repeat the microscopy test straight away."

Everyone was dumbfounded.

"But – but – " Pontick stammered, "A fail is a fail. There has never been an immediate retest!"

"Yes, I know, Professor. But there has to be a first time for everything."

And so on. I managed to fix things so that my unfortunate colleague was summoned back next morning and given another slide to study through the microscope. Anxiously, I ran there to support him, though of course he was supposed to be kept in complete isolation: I was taking a risk, acting illegally again. I wanted to open the door very quietly and secretly – when it was flung open by Pontick, who cried, quite jovially: "Come in, come in, your friend has passed!"

The written part of the final pathology examination was a complete farce. When I heard what was to happen, I was shocked at first; but I was implored from all sides not to oppose this venerable institution and bring it to light, since all the students had got through the exam by this method for years. So what happened?

The evening before the exam a cab pulled up outside the caretaker's flat at the Pathology Institute with one or two friends of the candidates and a large number of text books covering all the various topics. These were stowed away in the caretaker's flat – he was in league with the students – and next morning four selected friends sat downstairs in front of the stacked-up books. Upstairs the candidates entered and the attendant, who was also in the know, held out a bag containing numbers. Each number related to a topic – but we already knew which number went with which topic: the boys *had written them on their cuffs; I had a slip of paper with the list of numbers and topics. Each in turn took a number out of the bag. If the topic did not appeal to us, we put it back and took out another number. The attendant waited patiently. Finally we went into another room where the answers to the actual questions were to be written, in strict isolation, of course. But soon the attendant came in on the pretext of having to deal with the fire, went behind each candidate, collected the question papers, and took them to the friends downstairs. They busily cut the relevant pages out of the text books, which the attendant, armed with a carafe of water or similar camouflage, took up to the candidates in bundles. And now, well supplied with the facts, we wrote our excellent essays.*

Other institute attendants were also in alliance with the students against the perfidious danger of exams. The attendant at the Institute of Surgery, for instance, gave a veritable crash course in bandaging in the basement just before the exam. I was so far ahead of my fellow students (thanks to Tietze!) that I assisted him in instructing the others.

Two other women came to study medicine at Breslau, and we three spent one semester in Heidelberg: that part of Germany – Baden – was one of the first to allow women to matriculate and enter the university.

I took my finals in 1902. Soon after, I married that young fellowstudent, the peasants' son, Hugo Hempel.'

Chapter 6

So in 1902, after completing her Staatsexamen, which qualified her to practise medicine, though she still had to write a dissertation, Oma decided to
marry, and she picked her fellow student, Hugo Hempel, to be the lucky
man. He was the youngest of the nine children of a farmer in Saxony, in the
south of Germany, at a tiny place called Zschoppach. He and one brother,
Carl, were sent off to study medicine. The farm had belonged to the
Hempel family for decades – and it still did when we – David and I – visited
it in 1972 and again in 1995; it cannot have changed much in appearance,
though it was rather dilapidated.

The Hempel farm at Zschoppach

The buildings date back to 1773, a
handsome stone-built quadrangle,
with the family's living quarters on
one side, barns and workers' rooms on
another, stables for a horses and cows
and calves, garages for machinery, and
a huge midden in the centre.

She did not love him. But she
wanted to get married, and she wanted
to have children. Moreover, she writes:
'...now I was roused, all the more
strongly and irresistibly, because so
belatedly, and I believed I could not live
any longer without love, without being
loved, passionately loved. And Hugo
seemed likely to give me what I needed.
My sensuality, roused so belatedly and now fully satisfied for the first time,
masked the absence of true feeling. I liked him well enough. On the whole,
he appealed to me. He was clean, inwardly and outwardly, hardworking,
competent, keen on his profession – and he loved me with all the untarnished
passion of his youth – he was eight years younger than me! I considered this
to be no bad thing. I would have found it hard to accommodate myself to a
man of an age more appropriate to mine, who would expect some sort of sub-
missiveness from me and resist my boundless desire for independence. I
thought I would be able to have a good marriage with Hugo, one that would
satisfy us both and make us both happy, since he admired me, believed me to
be the fulfilment of all his dreams, and shared my interests, at least profes-
sionally. As for me, I felt that love was something I gave up when I parted
from Schubert and from Streuli. I thought that the fact that I did not love

Hugo was of no significance. I thought I had worked it all out very cleverly. And that was my big mistake. And my guilt, as I recognised later.

The time came for her to meet his family, and now, for the first time, it seems, the fact that she was Jewish became significant to her. Hugo feared that his parents would not accept her – the only Jews they knew were dealers in cattle and farm produce, and mutual cheating did not lead to mutual respect. So at his urgent request, she had herself baptised before the wedding – it made no difference to her, being an atheist – and agreed not to tell his family that she was Jewish until they had got to know her better. From an early age, she had been an atheist. She once told us that she 'belonged to the generation that preferred to say "oxygen" rather than "god".'

In fact, she need not have bothered. She records that the parents were actually very fond of her:

'After about a year, they came to visit us, and I decided to stop sailing under false colours: I told my father-in-law the truth – and also Hugo's reasons for keeping it from them for so long. At this, he got up, came to me, took my head in his two hands and said, in his broad Saxon dialect: "That Hugo is a stupid boy. Olga, if I could love you still more, I'd do so now."

Our married life began in Munich, where Hugo started specialist training in the ear, nose and throat department in the University Clinic, while I worked in the Gisela Hospital for Children. My immediate superior was Dr Hutzler, a big man, covered all over with red hair, with green eyes. He was very clever and excellently well trained medically – and I loathed him from the bottom of my heart. He was a sadist. The little patients were terrified of him – and that seemed to please him. One small boy had had a tumour removed from his chest and was now given a new dressing almost every day. As soon as his mother opened the door to the treatment room he started screaming if he saw Hutzler in the distance. Once, when Hutzler was busy, I beckoned to the child to come to me and bandaged him: he did not make a sound. From then on he always ran straight to me and let me do whatever I had to without a murmur. But one day, when Hutzler noticed the unwonted silence, he called out: "That child is my patient" – whereupon the panic, the screaming started again. He was one of a number of doctors I got to know who could and probably did later support the Nazis in the ghastly experiments.

Like other men, he obviously thought that if a woman had the effrontery to study medicine, then she was no lady, and her life should be made as difficult as possible. When he was using the stethoscope, or examining a patient by tapping and listening, he insisted on absolute silence; but if I was using either of these methods he would often sit on the table holding a noisy conversation. Finally I protested.

"Sir," I said. "If you, with your great experience, require silence when

47

you are examining a patient, how much more must I need it, having only just qualified!"

After that he did refrain from that kind of disturbance.

I had not been working for long at the Gisela when I became pregnant. Now I kept fainting. Luckily, this usually happened only in the mornings, and my duties at the hospital started at two or three o'clock and often continued into the evening. At times a doctor had to go into distant parts of the town or its suburbs, and Hutzler liked to send me on the more unpleasant calls. Once he sent me out into the country to a gipsy encampment only accessible on foot. Scarlet fever had broken out among the children. After that I went to the head doctor, Professor Trumpp, and asked him if he thought it was right that I should be chosen for such visits, when there were several young male colleagues available. This led to my being relieved of all evening visits, though at that point no one had any idea that I was almost five months pregnant – thanks to the loose clinical coats!

One morning I was asked to go to the hospital to help with the anaesthetics during an operation. I did not faint every morning, so I thought I could take the risk. However, I suddenly felt it coming on in the middle of the operation. I only just had time to press everything into the hands of the doctor standing next to me, and then I fell down. I woke up in Trumpp's room, lying on a sofa. He looked at me anxiously, and said, diffidently –

"Doctor – might … ?"

"Yes, you are right. I've been keeping it secret because I want to get in as much practical experience as possible."

"I see. Well, you must decide when you want to stop."

Now Hutzler's behaviour changed. If I had done about two hours' work, he sent me into his room to lie down for half an hour, and brought me a glass of milk and plenty of chocolate. He was much more considerate in other respects, too. I continued working well into the sixth month, and then started doing some research for Professor Trumpp.

The birth of my first child, a girl, Marianne, was exceptionally difficult, and involved the use of forceps, which damaged my peritoneum. Afterwards I was very ill with septicaemia – and who should appear at my bedside with a bunch of roses but Hutzler. He went to great lengths to ease my situation. He saw at a glance that lying on my back all the time hurt my knees. The next day he brought an adjustable knee support of his own invention. And he supported my aching back by pushing the back of a chair under my pillows, so that I could use the seat as a back rest. He also realised that the old hag who was supposed to be nursing me was repugnant to me and quite useless. He excused himself and went out with her. After about ten minutes he returned.

"She's gone," he said. "One of the Grey Sisters will be coming in quarter of an hour."

So I was cared for by a nun. Hutzler came every day, entertained me, was indefatigably helpful, so that I was bound to be grateful to him despite my persistent dislike.

Some years later he was on trial before the medical disciplinary court: he had been trying, through all sorts of intrigue, to have two professors removed from the Gisela and to get himself appointed its director. Before the case was completed, he shot himself.'

*****

'When the baby was six weeks old, and I was still very weak, Hugo got an appointment in Marburg, so we had to move. I gave up the research I had been doing for Professor Trumpp. Hugo had to carry me down the four flights of stairs and into the cab, and at the end of the journey he had to carry me again, for we were to live in a boarding house on the Schlossberg, and the coachman considered the hill too steep for his horse. We only stayed there for a short time; it was a wonderful place, and I convalesced rapidly. Then Hugo found a flat and engaged a maid, as I could not do any work yet, apart from feeding the baby and looking after the housekeeping.

After only five months I had reason to think I was pregnant again. I could not believe it, and asked Pfannenstiel, my professor in Breslau, who had transferred to Giessen, not far from Marburg, to confirm my suspicion – which he did. He gave me a severe talking-to.

"A woman with your intelligence and knowledge has no right to risk another pregnancy so soon. You are in a poor state of health – and I daresay you faint quite often, as you did before – am I right?"

"You are."

"Well now, here's what I suggest. You enter my clinic at least a fortnight before term – say, in early October."

I did so – only to find that the chief assistant in the clinic was none other than that Dr Krömer with whom I had crossed swords in Breslau! During the almost unbearable waiting time I was to accompany Krömer on all his rounds and watch his examinations. I was revolted by the insensitivity, in fact the brutality with which he treated the "house pregnancies". And when it came to my own very difficult and protracted labour – it went on for 24 hours – which he was supposed to be supervising during the night, he sat in the next room, busying himself with some writing task, completely unmoved by my irrepressible moans and groans and my fear that the forceps would be used again, with the same dire results – torn peritoneum and septicaemia – as before. Pfannenstiel wanted to avoid this at all costs and implored me to hold out as long as possible. Krömer had been told to watch the progress of my confinement very closely; but he did not come in once during the night. Towards morning I sent for the professor, and he urged me to carry on for one more hour: if no progress has been made by then, he would intervene.

But I managed; little Lorchen was born without the forceps – and then, when I was lying in bed, relieved: then Dr Krömer paid me his first visit. I turned my back on him. I refused to speak to him. When my friend and protector, Pfannenstiel, asked why, I explained in no uncertain terms. Krömer said, "Ever since Breslau I've known you dislike me, so I thought it would please you best if I showed myself as little as possible."

"Have you ever asked yourself why I disliked you so?"

"Well, you were annoyed with me when I didn't let you into the cubicles where I was examining patients."

"That's nothing compared with my disgust at the way you treated those poor young women, the 'house-pregnancies' – as if they were dirt, as if they had no rights, no feelings! And here I have seen that you are just as coarse, just as brutal as ever."

He stared at me. "Coarse? Brutal? No, no, I assure you: that is far from the truth." He went to the window and stared out for a long time. When he turned to me again, I was surprised to see that there were real tears in his eyes.

"I may be clumsy," he said. "I know I have no style, no elegance, no charm. But those things are only skin deep. I beg you, try to see me as I really am, underneath. Please don't think so ill of me!"

For the rest of my stay in the clinic he was exquisitely polite and considerate to me, so that I could not maintain my sharp rejection of him; and yet inwardly my dislike of him, as of Hutzler, was unchanged, in spite of everything.

*****

She doesn't mention one thing that was to be so important later. When Lorchen – my mother, Mu – was born, and baby Marianne saw her in her mother's arms, Marianne screamed so much that Oma asked the nurse to take the new baby away, as Marianne was so distressed. In fact she did not stop screaming until Lorchen had been taken out of the room. Oma must have described this scene more than once as the children got older, as a surprising and amusing example of – what? Sibling rivalry? Marianne's precocious insight into the situation? Whatever the reason, it was a powerful factor in my mother's lifelong feeling that her existence was unwanted – and that she was treated unfairly. But Oma's memoirs continue quite cheerfully:

'We had two good years in Marburg. I was happy with my two charming children, whom I had desired for so long, and was not particularly worried about not getting on very fast with my medical training. I had started a thesis, under Pfannenstiel's supervision, on pelvic dilation in various positions in any corpses that became available. But then, in 1905, Marianne, aged one-and-a-half, fell ill. She lost weight, was as pale as ivory, had no appetite, could not sleep. At first we had no idea what was wrong with her. I

took her to the *University Clinic and tuberculosis was diagnosed. I was advised to take her
up into the hills somewhere. At first I chose the
highest spot accessible from Giessen, where
Pfannenstiel now worked: whenever a new
corpse was delivered to his clinic, I was summoned by telegram, and my dear mother came
to look after the little girls. But Marianne's condition got worse, with alarming temperatures
rising all the time. I got in touch with some
friends who had a farm very high up in the Harz
mountains, and they offered me hospitality very
warmly. So I had to give up work on my thesis
for the second time. Hugo's brother Carl
Hempel was in practice in Magdeburg, and I
asked him to take over Marrianne's treatment.
He agreed, examined the little child, and found
she had TB in the bronchial glands. He was*

Lorchen and Marianne

very experienced, and gave me excellent advice regarding medication, diet,
life-style – always out of doors, even in the autumn. The temperature graph
started levelling out, and with devoted nursing and dieting and fresh air
Marianne started putting on weight again. And I was convinced of the
importance of fresh air.'

*****

'Now we felt able to discuss the question of where we were to settle: somewhere where Hugo, and I too, if possible, could find work. We investigated
many towns, including Dresden, but there was no opening anywhere for an
Ear-Nose-Throat doctor. Then we heard that the only ENT specialist in
Thorn in – the town of my birth – had just died, and a replacement was
urgently needed for a large practice: many Polish farmers and labourers
crossed the frontier to get medical care. An added advantage was that my
father's name, Fajans, was well thought of in those parts, as he introduced
steamer traffic on the Vistula. So we set off for Thorn. If only we had settled
in Thorn – things might have been very different! But we broke our journey
in Berlin, and here a cousin of mine, Dr Auch, who had a big practice in the
west of Berlin, took me aside and asked me if Hugo was well qualified.
    "He is."
    "And is he conscientious?"
    "He certainly is that!"
    "Can you guarantee that?"
    "Certainly – but why?"
    "Because as it happens we are looking for a reliable ENT specialist. He*

can be sure of a brilliant practice if he is up to it."

Now I made my second big mistake. The first was marrying Hugo when I did not love him. The second was persuading him to give up Thorn and settle in Berlin. Coming from a long line of peasant farmers, he would have been much better suited to that semi-rural practice.

He soon had the promised "Praxis Aurea" – the golden practice – but being a simple son of the soil he was completely out of place there. The unexpectedly high income, the great appreciation he received from his colleagues, and from his patients, the flattery of the rich, pretty high-society ladies: all this went to his head.

As soon as my friends in Berlin heard that we were going to settle there, I received numerous letters, invitations, expressions of welcome. Right at the start we were invited to a big party by the Lord Mayor, Reicke: he had been a friend in Danzig when I was still a girl. But of course Hugo did not know anyone at the party. Being devoid of social graces he did not speak to anyone. He just stood behind my chair and kept murmuring: "Let's go home, Mother" – while I was in the middle of most interesting conversations.

Soon I gave up all social intercourse for his sake. I tried to put up with his many short-comings: his continuing immaturity, his awkwardness in the presence of his superiors, his self-consciousness in any social situation. I made do with what he could give me, and tried to be a good wife. It meant giving up almost all my old friends, male or female, as he was stiff and almost paralysed in their company and consumed with a childish jealousy, even of my parents, sisters and brother.

I started working at the Dr Hugo Neumann Children's Outpatients' Clinic every afternoon, first taking my children with their very reliable nanny to Berlin Zoo for an afternoon in the fresh air and the stimulating setting. Since Hugo was employed at another outpatients' department in the same part of Berlin – a very poor part – we generally travelled together on the same train part of the way. He got out at Friedrich station; I had to go a few stops further.

In 1909, when Marianne was six and Lorchen five, I became pregnant again.'

*****

'One day, I received a letter from Streuli, the English clergyman who had been far more than a friend for three years. It was about twelve years since we had parted. I had told Hugo all about him, and about Schubert too, before we got married. Now he was coming to Berlin for a Baptist Conference and asked if he could come and see me and get to know my husband, too, and the children. I told Hugo, and asked him if he would like to meet Streuli. His only response was: "If that fellow dares to set foot in my house

I'll throw him downstairs."

"I see."

For some days, Hugo did not speak one word to me. He was consumed with jealousy. I did not consider this justified; nor did it occur to me to forgo the pleasure of seeing my former lover again. So I wrote to Streuli and asked him to meet me at the station where I normally left the train; and requested the clinic to let me have that afternoon off.

The day on which I intended to carry out this sinful plan approached – and Hugo seemed have resolved to put his jealous rage behind him. He spoke to me quite normally, and headed towards the station together with me as before: apparently he wanted a reconciliation. Once again we sat in the train together as far as Friedrich station, where he took his leave of me, confident that I would be going to the Neumann clinic.

My plan worked perfectly. Streuli was waiting for me as arranged, and in spite of wind and rain we spent the hours I normally worked at the Clinic happily strolling about what was probably the ugliest part of Berlin.

I caught the usual train to go home. But when I turned the corner and looked up at the windows of our flat, I was surprised to see the whole family, and my sister Hedwig, looking out for me. When I opened the front door, Hugo pulled me into his room.

"Have you been with him?"

"Yes."

He switched off the light, so that we could not be observed from the other side of the street. Then he came up to me threateningly.

"If you lay a finger on me," I said, "you will never see me or the children again."

Well, he did not touch me. But from then on he was always angry with me for my so-called adultery – which he probably did not really believe in himself. My lapse had come to light when, wanting to put an end to the long period of estrangement, he tried to phone me at the Clinic, only to be told that I had not even arrived. At first he was frightened. He phoned Hedwig, and she went to the police to ask if any accidents had been reported. They reassured her, saying that brief disappearances were usually caused by rendezvous. She came to report this to Hugo, and they phoned all the accident and emergency departments – and then saw me coming round the corner hale and hearty. At that moment Hugo remembered my asking if he would like to meet Streuli.

For the remainder of my pregnancy, Hugo ignored me completely. He would not even help me when I went into labour. So I phoned my old friend Leo Zuntz, who now had a maternity clinic in Berlin, and he saved me from the worst pains by giving me brief anaesthetics; finally, at my urgent request, he ended the confinement after only seven hours by using the forceps. I could not believe it was all over.

"Use the forceps – good things, forceps," I kept murmuring, still only half conscious.

"Why – are you expecting twins?" asked Leo. "One boy has been born so far!"

And so I held our son, Reinhardt, in my arms. Thanks to Leo's help, I had felt almost nothing, in contrast to my two previous confinements. I recovered so quickly that I was able to go to the market after only five days.'

*****

'One day, Schubert visited me. We had not seen each other for eighteen years. He was married, and brought his little son to meet me. When they were leaving, I escorted them to the front door. As we passed Hugo's room, he flung the door open; then he demanded: "Who was that?" I told him truthfully, whereupon Hugo threatened to fling him, too, down the stairs, like Streuli, should he ever dare to show himself again. So I had no alternative but to meet him elsewhere. Why should I deny myself that pleasure? Once we went to the park at Charlottenburg with our children; sometimes we met at the home of mutual friends when, as in the old days in Danzig, they were playing quartets. After one such occasion he escorted me home, and we stopped en route at the Roman Café.

And that was where it happened. For the first time we talked uninhibitedly about our youthful love, and the feelings we had never quite revealed to each other. Now at last, when we were both married and had children, we were able to speak freely about the past, lifting the veil from so much that had not been known or understood at the time.

I asked him if he ever loved me in an erotic sense – for I never felt he did, and indeed I always endeavoured – as was normal in those days – never to let anything of the sort arise in our association. He replied that he never felt erotic in my presence, only after we had parted. So my stupid prudishness, my false pride, had triumphed, with the result that our feelings were never expressed in a natural way, but were suffocated in all sorts of unwholesome inhibitions.

After his first and only (because of Hugo) visit to the flat in the Nürnbergerstrasse, his wife Blanche came to see me, to get to know me. We soon became friends. Before leaving, Blanche asked me to show her pictures of myself when I was younger.

"Before today I only knew about you as a very young person, from Hans' stories about you."

"Oh, it really isn't worth the trouble – I was never pretty."

"Oh yes you were! Hans says so!"

That is the first compliment I ever got from him. Blanche was a very good wife for him, far better, I realised, than I would have been. Blanche was soft and pretty and graceful, and she accepted him as he was and tried to *make life easy and pleasant for him. I would have tried to get him to fulfil his promise in some way, to be more than a talented dilettante.*

He was over 40 when he married Blanche. One day he told me how it came about.

"I woke up one morning with the alarming realisation that I had got engaged to Blanche the night before, which was against all my principles, as you well know: I was determined never to get married. I was in despair, rushed to her, threw a fearful scene, rushing around the room, tearing my hair and shouting: 'I cannot and will not get married, never, never!' Now if it had been you, Olga, you would have left the room without saying a word and it would all have been over. But do you know what Blanche said? She was kind and concerned, and said, 'Hans, dear, you're so nervous. Lie down and have a little nap.' How could I get disengaged after that?"

Chapter 7

Hugo – who seemed to be so "clean, inwardly and outwardly" – changed – for the second time. The first change came about when he married Oma, and became so shy, awkward and withdrawn that she gave up many of her social contacts. But now his success as a doctor in Berlin changed him again: he became arrogant and overbearing, intolerant, jealous, suspicious, dictatorial. Life with him became almost intolerable, both for Olga and for the children. Here's how my mother remembered him:

'*My father was an unhappy man, and he spread a great deal of unhappiness around himself. I do not think he was "normal", being both sentimental and brutal, cunning and credulous, highly sexed and highly puritanical. A first class specialist doctor and a failed farmer. He was a cloud in my life, black and threatening, and I can hardly remember a single good day with him. I still have terrifying dreams about him. He was big, with a tendency to obesity, a big bushy beard, and his very small eyes behind thick glasses always seemed to me to be either terribly tired or else cunning and malicious.*

Sometimes I felt sorry for him, but his only response was a kick. Mother once told me that he hated me "because I looked so Jewish", and had asked her never to leave him alone with me as he might harm me: this when I was just three years old.

He worked ceaselessly, never enjoyed a moment's leisure, and most of his patients adored him. There can be no doubt that he was a gifted and conscientious doctor. Some of the time he worked in a "Poliklinik", i.e. with poor people, and that was where our housemaids came from.

One, Ida Grommek, from Rosengarten in East Prussia, stayed with us for good. She was a good-looking, proud woman, intelligent, and in time she was an effective assistant to him in the surgery; moreover she was a good cook. But she did not like children – we called her the dragon. At breakfast time she would comb our hair, very roughly, so that it hurt; and if we behaved badly she would clasp her hands and groan: "Is this what middle-class children behave like?!" Fate was not kind to her. Her devotion to my father was doglike. Because of her poor hearing, the telephone was a big problem for her. This led to terrible rows. On one occasion, when she had mixed up some names, my father was so furious with her that he not only shouted at her, but beat her. Then he went out, and we said to Ida: "You must go. You cannot stay here." And she seemed to agree, and was ready to go. But when my father came in, and said, "Ida, get me some tea," she went back into the kitchen.

The flat in the Nürnbergerstrasse in West Berlin was quite large, seven rooms plus bath, kitchen and maid's room. But Hugo requisitioned nearly all of it for his growing ENT practice. The two large front rooms were his consulting rooms, but the children's room next to them was in constant use for favoured patients, enabling them to jump the queue. The telephone was in the dining room, so he, and patients, were forever coming in to use it when Oma was having coffee there, or helping the children with their homework, or reading to them. Then they had to keep absolutely silent until the calls were finished. The long corridor was used for hearing tests, during which no one could use it, though it led to the bathroom and toilet. Since it had to be available for patients all the time, she often had to whip the children out of the bath, wet and covered in soap, and take them to the unheated bedroom. This freezing cold bedroom was where she had to receive visits from her parents and friends; the children's bedroom was just as cold and even more uncomfortable. In the kitchen Ida boiled pus-covered instruments and blood-soaked bandages on the cooker side by side with their lunch. There was just one room into which the practice seldom penetrated: a pretty room, where she had her grand piano, and where she and the children were more or less undisturbed. Unless, of course, there had been an operation. Then the patient was brought in here so that Oma could, if necessary, stop any late haemorrhaging.

She tried to persuade Hugo to rent part of the flat opposite, so that the practice could be moved in there, and their flat be freed for family life. In vain. So she decided to force the issue. She ate almost nothing, she hardly slept, she thought of nothing except her intolerable situation – until she was so run down, so weak, that she fainted several times and her pulse was weak and very fast. In the end she spent all her time on the sofa, her eyes shut.

It worked. Hugo was so worried by her condition that he finally signed a contract for two rooms in the other flat. It took a fortnight for Olga to recover her deliberately damaged health.

Meanwhile the children were developing: Marianne, very close to her mother, doing very well at school; little Reinhardt strong and healthy; and between them, Lorchen, my mother, Mu. The fact that she was very pretty, with a bright, original mind, tending to "lateral thinking", counted for nothing. She knew only too well that she was not as dear to her mother as Marianne and Reinhardt, that her birth, in contrast to theirs, had been unwelcome; and she had some minor deformities – club feet, a partial curvature of the spine – which did not handicap her physically in any way, but which must have contributed to her stammer and her nail-biting, and her chronic under-achievement at school.

'I can only look back on scenes from my childhood with horror,' she wrote when she was quite an old woman. *'It seems to have been an endless chain of wrongdoing and punishment. Father tried to do gymnastics with us.*

Marianne was quite good at it, but I was incapable of even the smallest jump in his presence, and almost every "lesson" ended in tears for me, and praise for Marianne. Any kind of competition was beyond me, I never had enough self-confidence. My father hated my inhibitions, which sometimes inverted into cheekiness. No one tried to understand my nail-biting or my stammering. Both my parents were convinced that I was sinful, since I did not control either; and they believed that I actually wanted to do badly at school; the best medicine they could think of was beating, and both of them were generous with that. Of course Father was the worst, he was so huge, and as strong as a bear; it was quite impossible to defend yourself against him, or to hide. Mother beat me far more often, but afterwards I still felt human. Once, when Father had beaten me especially savagely because of my nail biting, Mother came to my bed, where pain, bitterness and despair were keeping me awake. She spoke encouragingly: my sense of honour would surely help me deal with such a petty problem as nail-biting, and so on. While she spoke, and I was feeling grateful to have someone willing to speak to me, I was busily biting my nails. When she noticed, she yelled at me, and left me with the words: "No sense of honour, no will to improve, you're not worth bothering about!"

*****

But at other times, as she looked back at her childhood, my mother saw nothing but great happiness and pleasure. She was born on 25 October 1904, and when she was very small the family used to go to a small place called Walkemühle for holidays.

'I was just three or four years old, but I could still find my way around there today with my eyes shut. The mill was by the road, with a giant chestnut tree in front of it. You could look across meadows to the "big frog pond". There were so many frogs croaking in the night that you kept being woken up by them. On the other side was the farmyard, with the red mill house opposite, where the owners lived. There was a stream that turned the mill wheel, all overgrown with nettles and other weeds, a wonderful place for ducklings and chicks, and there were masses of them there. And there was a horse called Hans, a friend of the family but also of the summer visitors. He was allowed to run around free by night, often even in the afternoon, when we children would be lined up anxiously on the veranda. Because Hans would go mad with joy. He would rush around, fling himself onto his back and kick his hooves up in the air. There must have been cows, too; I can remember the cowshed, but I'm not too sure about the cows.'

Friends and relations would join them at Walkemühle, including Leo Zuntz, Oma's fellow student at Freiburg, who was now married and father of two daughters and a son, Günther (who – very much later, was my father). Mu writes:

'Opposite the cowshed there was hill of sand which you could slide down. Günther Zuntz showed me how to glide down elegantly, but I could only do it on my backside. But then he was two years older than me. Of course no one dreamed that Günther and I would be married one day and have children. There were glorious forests all around, with masses of fungi and berries. What a lovely time we had! The house was tiny; I slept in a cot under the stairs right by the front door. Marianne, who was one year older than me, slept in our mother's bed. We two, being so small, ran around naked most of the time – and our bottoms were permanently stained blue, because of all the blueberries. I think we had pancakes with blueberry sauce every single day, and chanterelles.

There were many visitors apart from the Zuntzes: older cousins, and our beloved aunts, Luise and Julie Wolf, the artist, whom we always called the

Marianne and Lorchen

Günther

Little Wolves, often came and brought more friends with them. They would all sleep in the attic, on straw, not in individual beds – there was no room for beds. Each person had a nail in the wall for a towel. How my mother managed all that, and fed everyone, is a mystery to me. I can remember nothing but peace. We went swimming in the morning; Aunt Julie sat on a sort of post at the edge of the water used by hunters and painted. Later, Julie and Mother created a dwarves' cave for us under a fallen tree, lined with moss and with little silver beds for the seven dwarves, and a better one for Snow White, and silver chairs. They even created a water supply! There was a slight hollow on the tree trunk, in which rainwater collected. Mother took an artificial flower from a fashionable ladies' hat, (she herself never wore a hat), pushed its hollow stalk through the roof of the cave into the water, which ran into a hollowed out chestnut. The water could be turned on and off with a safety pin. In the evening we always left chopped up leaves by the cave. Next morning we would find that they had all gone – so the dwarves had eaten it all up in the night. Sometimes they left a few bits; evidently they had not felt so hungry on that occasion. It was all quite realistic and convincing.

The forest was dense and, to me, seemed to be endless. We had to walk through it for a long time to get to the station. Generally we went in the coach pulled by Hans the horse; but if my father came for the weekend, Mother would usually walk with him through the forest to see him off. Once, coming back alone, she lost her way in the dark and was terribly afraid. There was a mass-murderer at large in those days, called Sternnickel. When Mother sat under the chestnut tree alone in the evening to read, she always had a lamp beside her, and a pistol with the safety-catch off. I don't think she knew how to shoot, but the idea was that Sternnickel would run away at the sight of a determined woman and a pistol. This was never put to the test. But that evening she was alone, without her pistol, and she thought she saw Sternnickel everywhere. The junipers looked particularly frightening in the moonlight. She had no idea where she was and was sweating with fear. Then she saw a bit of white paper lying in the moonlight, which was so bright that she could read it: Günther, 3 underpants, Dora, 2 pinafores, and so on. It was a laundry list of the Zuntzes! So she could not be far from the house, and in fact she soon reached it. In general, Mother was quite fearless; but she said she had sometimes felt that someone was standing behind her, or looking at her from behind a juniper tree – and she had panicked.'

✽✽✽✽✽

Back at home in Berlin, in the flat in the Nürnbergerstrasse, they would often visit Oma's parents, Rose and Josef Fajans, who lived in the leafy suburb called Grunewald. Mu loved these grandparents as much as Oma loved her grandfather Neumann when she was small. Her description of them tallies quite well with what Oma tells us about her parents in her account of her childhood in Danzig. Here's what Lorchen wrote about them when she was a grandmother herself:

'My happiest times as a child were those I spent with my grandparents. We never asked for anything better. I remember the house so well that I could find my way round it in the dark to this day. I remember the pictures on the walls, the marvellous old Baroque cupboards. They lived in Grunewald, at number 5 Jagowstrasse; it was a comfortable and spacious house. We went there every Sunday afternoon; up a stone staircase to the front door and, in summer, both grandparents would be standing on the top step to greet us. Grandmama was short and stout, Grandpapa very tall, a bean pole, and looked majestic. Grandmama was all love and warmth. "Well, Ollchen,"

she would say to our mother – her name was Olga – as soon as she saw us, spreading out her arms, "well, children, I've been waiting for a long time." In the winter they would both be standing inside the house; that meant going up a few more steps, a heavy curtain was pulled aside, and there were the two old people on the top step. Greetings were always the same. While she, small and rotund, bent down to embrace us lovingly, Grandpapa would be standing immobile so that we had to stop on a lower step. He would not move; we had to clamber up to kiss him. On one occasion we thought this was a bore and maybe he didn't really want a kiss, so we didn't make the effort. He didn't say a word, went into his room silently, and didn't join us at the coffee table as usual. He felt so hurt that he stayed in his room all the afternoon. Grandmama and Mother took turns running to him, trying to explain away our heartlessness. In the end we were sent in to give him a very belated kiss. He sat stock still at his writing table, did not look at us, so we forced our kisses on to him, and then everything was all right again. That's what he was like: incapable of revealing himself and his great affection, but thirsting for tenderness. Grandmama understood him, and he loved her immeasurably.

On winter evenings we would all sit at the round table and look at the pictures in the big Doré bible. We were never bored. We were not allowed to speak, but it never occurred to us to do so. Grandmama had dolls for us, which we couldn't take home; but almost every time we visited she had made them some new clothes. There was an espalier with a morello cherry on the south side of their house, but we were never allowed to eat them from the tree – which is when they taste best – but only when they were served in a bowl at table.

Their maids certainly had a hard time, but they stayed for years and only left to get married. I remember one called Emma. She gave me a little silver horse that pulled a carriage made of a shell. A wonderful present. Her room was in the basement with a good window looking out into the garden. Everything was clean and neat and comfortable. I liked being there with her, and in the kitchen. Much later I realised how hard life must have been for servants: under constant supervision, with very little "time off", never a whole day, I believe! And always on call. Emma married a widower with one child, and we went to the wedding with the grandparents. Mother had warned us not to make any remarks, for instance about the flat being small and in a poor part of Berlin called Wedding. As one used to say "in our circles", Emma had been extremely well trained by the grandparents, for which she should be grateful (and she was). She really loved the grandparents, and the years she spent with them were halcyon years for her.

One day when I was five and Marianne six, our housekeeper Ida startled us by giving us each a rucksack and telling us we were going to stay with the grandparents. "But why? Ida, tell us why? What's going on?" – "You'll know soon enough."

We stayed in a guest room at the top of the house. It had a balcony for Grandfather's plants. His Puritanism extended to the plants. They were not allowed to turn towards the sun; he would always turn them back. So it was not so much a greenhouse as a home for cripples. After a few days we returned home to the Nürnbergerstrasse – and at last the secret was out: we had a baby brother, Reinhardt.

The First World War put an end to this solid and secure life. Neither of the grandparents lived to see its end, and how thankful I am that they did not have to experience the so much more dreadful horrors of the Nazis. Grandpapa wept with joy when "The Kingdom of Poland" was announced: he could not, at his age, see through that swindle. For he loved Poland: all over the house there were oil paintings with scenes from Polish history; for instance, an elegant salon, a lady dressed in lace weeping on an armchair, weeping children in velvet and silk, a young man with a pistol in his hand stands facing a horde of Russian soldiers who have just broken into the palace. Unforgettable! But my mother and her sisters did not share this love for the Poles: they called them Polacks – I'm sorry to say – and described them as unreliable and unwashed, draped in torn lace, given to high-flown utterances in comical German, and generally absurd.

When Rose died in 1916 Josef was so heart-broken that he followed her within the year. That was a dreadful year. One of his sisters was with him all the time; he also had a female housekeeper and his daughters visited him every day. But he had become an insufferable hypochondriac, lived for his digestion, refused to brush his teeth. He only spoke about Rose. One day Mother was in the room next to his, waiting for the nurse to finish caring for him, so she sat down at the piano and sang a few Schubert songs. Rose had had a bell-like voice, and when she sang people stopped in the street and called: "Da Capo!" and "Bravo!" My mother's voice, though clear and sweet, was small in comparison; but now, almost for the first time, he really listened to her singing, and when at last she went in to him she found him bathed in tears. "My child, I thought it was Rose. I never knew you could sing so well." From then onwards she always had to sing to him.

His death was a relief, and in death he was as handsome and majestic as he had been in his best years. Things were getting worse in Germany at that time, in 1917, and his daughters could not go to the crematorium with the hearse, as there were no cabs or cars.

I am reluctant to leave the grandparents. They are buried in Halensee, between Berlin and Grunewald. On their grave there is a grey stone with a rose rambling over both of their names. I remember their house in Grunewald so well. I remember the pictures on the walls, the marvellous old Baroque cupboards – five, I think – but above all I remember how safe one felt with them. I have Grandmama's armchair here in Oxford, and another upholstered chair, her writing table and her sewing table.'

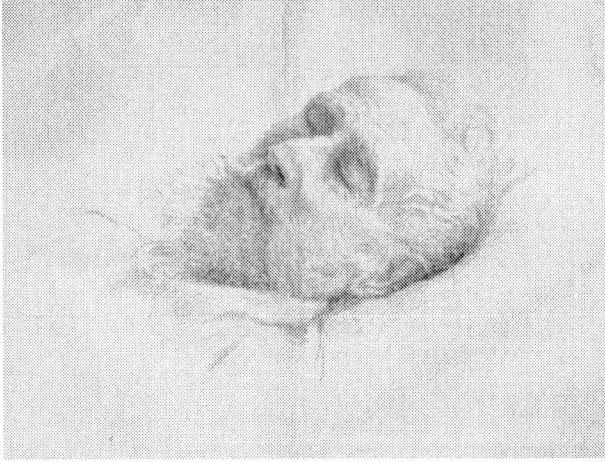

Josef Fajans on his death-bed. Drawing by his son-in-law, Ernst Nelson

I went to that cemetery at Halensee with David, but we could not find their grave and were told that after a certain length of time, if graves are not tended by relatives, they were made available for new burials. So it is as well that they have their memorial in these pages.

*****

My mother also remembered every detail of those obligatory afternoons in the Zoo, when her mother was at work, and when she was old she wrote a description of them which was published in Bongo, the Berlin Zoo's house magazine, after her death, in 2002. Here it is in English:

The Elephant Gate to Berlin Zoo (restored since World War II)

'Our mother was a fresh-air-fiend, convinced that fresh air had saved Marianne's life, so every day, after lunch, we had to go out for at least two hours, regardless of what the weather was like. Incidentally, this fresh air business was not a simple matter: There were no cars in the road in those days, but an awful lot of people, all sharing in that air, so my mother was afraid that our share, the "air pillar" above us, might be too narrow. That was why time spent on our big balcony was only an optional extra, and didn't count as "Fresh Air" no matter how cold it was: while it gave onto a whole rectangle of gardens, too many people were breathing there. Likewise on the roads. Well, obviously it was not our mother's intention that we should go for a walk in the streets, but in the Zoo, which was only a few minutes' walk away from our flat.

However, we dawdled in the street. First we stopped outside a shop called "A Gruetzmacher, Milliner". Being Puritans we had nothing but scorn for hats. During the war the two shop windows were quite Puritanical enough in all conscience, a few feathers, one pathetic little hat, that was all. Still, we imagined how the feathers could be attached to that hat. and jeered at the silliness of it. Then we came to a baker's shop, which was glorious, even in the war, because it smelled so good. Before the war mother bought little gooseberry tarts there, absolutely delicious. Also, in that same dim pre-historic, pre-war time, there had been Alexander cakes costing five pence, a sort of macaroon, which one got occasionally if one had been exceptionally good. We stood there for a long time, imagining how wonderful it was going to be when one could buy such things again.

Next we came to some blocks of flats. One of them was called London, and we asked ourselves if the police were blind. Only spies could be living there. We were all wildly patriotic. Once, in a post office, an old lady came in wanting to send money abroad. Staggering! Of course the clerk was not in the least helpful, and the rumour soon spread out onto the street: there was a spy in the post office! So when this old lady came out, quite a crowd of children were waiting for her and started throwing potatoes at her. Probably we joined in, yelling: "Spy! Spy!"

The next shop was "Hamburg-Altona in Berlin", a fishmonger's, selling mainly smoked fish. We often ate kippers or pickled herrings, very tasty. But as the naval war intensified, this source of joy dried up. Then we came to a fashion shop, where dresses could be bought for 100 Marks – incredible – and a wonderful florist. Next to it lived our friend Horst Klee. He also spent his free time in the Zoo, and we had a lot of fun there together.

Now we had to cross a busy main road. Several trams ran past here, with trailers, and cabs and so on. Opposite was the great Elephant Gate to the Zoo: two gigantic stone elephants rested here, and the roof was set up on their backs. We all had season tickets and could go in as often as we wanted.

Once we were inside the fun could begin. First there were big flower-beds with beautifully manicured lawns between them; all, of course, fenced in and not to be stepped on. What a challenge! But you had to be careful, because if a warder caught you, your ticket would be confiscated. For the next few days you had to go in through the administrative building and confess your misdemeanour to the officials there. They would record it in a big book. Finally your ticket would be handed back to you with the warning *never to step on the lawn again. We would curtsey and say thank you. I can't remember ever promising to be better in future…*

Then it was top speed to the lion house if the weather was cold. There certainly would not be any fresh air there, but how would Mother know? We stayed there for a considerable time, met our friends, and were privileged to watch them being fed. Sometimes there were lion cubs to be seen, who had a separate cage with their mothers, since the paternal feelings of the lion are not to be trusted. These little animals were most beautiful, and they played around their mother so happily. Of course, they didn't know that they would never be free. Sometimes a lioness rejected her young; then a big female dog was found, whose pups were killed; thereupon she would be locked into the cage with the lion cubs. I once witnessed this puppy-murder, it was very bad and I screamed at the keeper to stop, but it made no difference. Still, we did get a little vengeance. There was a notice on all the cages which said: "Never hurt an animal for fun, it feels pain as you do." So from now on, whenever we saw that keeper, a mixed chorus of voices bellowed that slogan, with an addition: "Even puppies feel pain when they are beaten to death with a broomstick". That keeper did not love us.

After the lions we went to the bears, brown ones, and one polar bear, who had a big pool in his cage and swam around in it in all seasons. But we were depressingly aware of the loneliness of these animals, generally just one bear to a cage. You could go up a staircase and look down at the animals from above and possibly feed them. They stood on their hind legs and waited – it was hard to resist their pleas. Of course feeding the animals was forbidden, because they might be given unsuitable food, but if we had anything, stale bread or the like, then we were confident that it was the right thing for them.

There was a tall shrubbery on one side of the bear cages, and we liked to go through it, since it was forbidden, and we discovered that there was a bear locked in right at the back there; he never saw his fellow prisoners or the many visitors. We never found out why this bear was isolated. Of course we often visited him. He was deeply depressed and just kept running along the fence, taking no notice of us or our bread; surely his solitude had made him melancholy. He became a symbol to me.

Now we would run to the Little Skunk House, a really wonderful place to stay. There were anteaters there, and very small monkeys that were so sweet and friendly. The smell was pretty strong, but it was nice and warm. Hence our saying: "a warm fug is better than cold ozone." Then through the deer park to the giraffe house. The deer were always out of doors, and between their enclosures we could find the loveliest liverwort in bloom, which we picked, of course. After all, it was very easy for us, as we made our little brother watch out and warn us if a keeper came into view. Our mother was delighted when we brought her a nice bunch of flowers.

Just in front of the giraffe house there was a marble statue, wrapped up in winter, of a centaur, half man, half horse, who had laid a fabulous snow-white marble lady across his back. There was a huge mosaic over the entrance which depicted a giraffe hunt in Africa. That was horrific. Also there were machines there in which one could see cinema films if one had some money. Of course we never had any money, and though Horst Klee tried using smooth buttons we could only ever see the first picture. But occasionally some Croesus had put in money and turned the handle and then, finding the show too silly, left it before the end. That's what we hoped for every day, and we turned the handle in the hope there would be something to see. If ever there was we all flung ourselves at the machine together, so that no one could see anything anyway.

The giraffe house was warm, and it was circular, with a real winter garden in the middle, full of shrubs and palms, a fairy-tale place. The giraffes were wonderful. In that house there were also some glass enclosures for delicate dwarf gazelles, and big gazelles too, and similar animals whose names I have forgotten. We strolled round, or sat on one of the benches, the winter garden behind us and the animals in front.

After a while we would run to the hippopotamus house. Two hippos lived there, unbelievably ugly, colossal beasts. They had a pond. The water had to be changed from time to time; then the animals had to be coaxed out of the water and driven into a locked room. I don't know how the keepers managed it. After several hours, they were allowed to go back into the water, which was now clear. We would sit and wait under a hippo skull in a glass case (donated by Baron von Bleichroeder, one of Germany's biggest bankers). The liberation of the huge animals was very exciting and well worth waiting for.

Once, one winter's day, I did something very mean. I had a snowball in my hand, and a hippo, probably in expectation of some titbit, opened its enormous mouth. I threw the snowball in, and was then very alarmed when the hippo dived down under the water. Of course I thought I had given the poor animal a dreadful stomach ache and was full of remorse. But when I went back there next day he was just the same as ever, lolling about in the water.

Next came the ostrich house, and that was quite magical. Not only because the ostriches and other long-legged birds were very astonishing, keeping quite still, but because there was a painting on the back wall opposite the entrance which looked absolutely real. It showed the Memnos statue, half submerged in water, with women round it washing clothes. But from the barrier where you had to stand you could see what looked like real sheep by the water, an avenue of reclining sheep. It was painted so wonderfully that you could not believe it was a picture. Once, shaking with fear, I climbed over the barrier and ran as fast as the wind along a strip of real sand – and crashed into the wall with the painting on it. So now I knew it was *only a painting. It must have been a masterpiece, for I can still see it with my mind's eye, and can almost hear Memnos, turned to stone, groaning in the morning, when his mother, Aurora, the Dawn, kissed him, but could not liberate him.*

The elephant house was next door, with an African elephant who was on very good terms with his keeper, who only came half way up his leg. There was an Indian elephant just opposite, but they never came together. There was an elephant skeleton in the middle, which was a bit eerie.

The rodent house was great fun. You could play with the animals through the fence. Above the cages there were pictures of rodents dressed up in human clothes, with names like "Burglar Rat", "Soldier Hedgehog", and so on: about ten of them. We knew them all by heart and could recite them in the correct order. But there you are: I can only remember two of them now. Outside there was a squirrel in a cage which kept turning in the wind so that the poor creature could never settle down or get into the rodent house, though it was only a few centimetres away. I used to dream about that.

There was a small monkey house opposite, and that's where Marianne, my sister, then aged about five, got bitten by a monkey she was giving a peanut to – not badly, just a scratch, but she screamed dreadfully, and Mother led her away from the cage and left me behind. This instantly threw me into despair. I screamed, and flung myself down on the ground, where-upon everybody said: Just look at that poor child, she's been bitten by a monkey; and I was fed chocolate and sweets till my mother came rushing back all out of breath and gave me a big smack for misleading people and getting so many goodies which I was not entitled to.

Another warm place was the house of the big apes, chimpanzees and gorillas; but I never really liked them. Next to it was the playground, where we met our friends and played marbles. It was a real craze. You came with your bag of marbles and said: "First?" to anyone there, to decide who would have the first go. In time we all collected numerous marbles, most worth just 30 or 40 (30 or 40 what? I never found out), but some as much as 500. It was very exciting. There were parallel bars and the like for the boys to do gymnastics, but we girls only had a sunless and joyless area behind the monkey house. However, that's where we used to meet our friends, espe-cially Mila and Werner Süssenguth. Mila was an excellent person, patient and kind to her brother, who was quarrelsome and always cold and tearful. But Mila had brilliant ideas, for instance to swim in one of the ponds, which was not allowed, of course, and so full of water weeds that we only just man-aged to get out again, covered in mud. Another time she lit a fire among the bushes and we cooked semolina and maggi cubes that we had brought from home in pond water. Of course we were spotted right away and had to put out the fire and take our saucepan to a bench. It was only lukewarm and tasted awful, but we could not throw it away – there was a war on.

Sometimes we climbed up into a hayloft where Horst read us funny stories. Reinhardt – aged about four – kept watch at a window, and if he saw some-one coming he would warn us and we would rush down the ladder and hide Reinhardt in a waste paper basket, because he couldn't run fast enough. Later we would go back and find him still sitting quietly as we had left him, covered in old newspapers. In the winter, when the flamingo pond had just frozen over, but was not thick enough to take our weight, we sent Reinhardt out to break us off some pieces of ice to suck. But he slipped up and there he was sitting with his little bottom in a hole in the ice, unable to get out. We had to lie full length on the ice and inch towards him, pull him out, sopping wet, and rush home with him. We were never punished for such deeds, but Reinhardt was praised for his spirit of sacrifice.'

Chapter 8

My mother talked to me about Ferch very, very often as the years went by. Ferch was the village where her family had a weekend and holiday home after the farm at Walkemühle was destroyed by fire. It played a similar role in their family life as the Zoppot house had in Oma's childhood. I was regaled with endless detailed descriptions of the place. It was an earthly paradise; there were endless supplies of ripe strawberries, the cherries were as big as tomatoes, the tomatoes as big as apples; the meadows were full of sweet-smelling flowers, and the nearby lake was of almost supernatural beauty: there was nothing and nowhere as wonderful anywhere in the world.

I think the reason why Mu remembered it with such intense love may have been that here her parents were reasonably harmonious together. Moreover, her mother, Oma, found fulfilment there, as a doctor as well as a smallholder and a mother. As she writes in her memoirs:

'I would have found life with Hugo completely intolerable if we had not bought a plot of bare, sandy land, just over an acre, on a hill at the village of Ferch, opposite Potsdam and Werder at the southern end of a lake, the Schwielohsee, in 1909, just after Reinhardt's birth, where we decided to build a house for our weekends and holidays. In such matters we always got on famously. We both loved living in the country; we saw eye to eye in financial matters; Hugo had earned, and saved enough in these three years to pay for the purchase and the building in cash, without needing a mortgage or incurring a pennyworth of debts, provided we were careful. So for a time this was my task. Hugo's practice left him no time to attend to details, and he had sufficient confidence in my common sense, intelligence and responsibility to entrust the whole undertaking to me.

I rented a small holiday flat in Ferch, very close to our plot, got hold of a competent local builder, worked out the plans and the estimates with him, cut out anything that was beyond our means, even when it meant reducing the ground plan, because the ground floor needed thicker walls and therefore more bricks, so that the house was not as wide and low in its proportions as we would have wished, but rather too tall and narrow for beauty. I intended to conceal this with climbing plants and vines, and so I did in quite a short time. Since I did not use an architect, but only my intelligent builder, I was able to design the interior precisely to suit our requirements. It turned out better than expected. Hugo dug a very deep well – the groundwater was very low – and set up a huge barrel as a reservoir with pipes running the length of the fairly steep plot. Right at the bottom we established beehives – there were fourteen in the end. These were Hugo's main hobby until the war broke out:

then I had to take charge. In the yard we had a stable, washroom and toilet, and we kept one or two goats, a lot of poultry, a duck pond, and a most beautiful pony from the zoo that I had fallen in love with, as well as numerous doves. From the house we had a wonderful view across woods and the lake to Werder and Potsdam.

The sandy soil, infested with couch grass, was dug over to a depth of one-and-a-half metres, cleaned and manured, and then the garden was laid out. Flowers, vegetables and strawberries were my department, while Hugo looked after trees and bushes, mainly selected fruit trees. Everything flourished wonderfully, and soon we had an abundance of everything and were able to give away large quantities to friends and relations and later, in the war, to soldiers. I always set out from Berlin with the children at midday on Saturdays; Hugo would follow in the evening. I suppose those days at Ferch were the best days in our married life.

Now I set up officially as a doctor for the first time and soon I was very busy, as there was no other doctor far and wide, and when the people there – mostly peasants – needed medical help they had had to send for someone from far away at great expense, and with great delays.

First I introduced major reforms in infant feeding, as the infants I was called to were in a pitiful state, and the mortality rates were far too high. The women were mostly out in the fields and hardly ever breast-fed their babies; they thought they were doing the best thing for them if they gave them condensed milk, and nothing but condensed milk, though they all had a cow or at least a goat in the stable. It was not easy to convince them that even fresh goats' milk, if no cows' milk was available, would be better than expensive tinned milk, even if it was genuine Swiss, and that fruit juice and vegetables should be introduced very early. The great success of these methods soon convinced them.

One summer there were numerous cases of pneumonia, and once again my treatment was highly successful. I lent my baby bath to those people who did not have one and taught them how to do hot and cold fomentation – and not one patient died. Of course none of the modern methods were available in those days.

But my main speciality was "minor surgery", which I practised in very awkward circumstances. When I finished studying, local anaesthetics were only just coming in, and I had no experience with them. So I hardened my heart and performed the most daring operations without any anaesthetic. It was out of the question anyway, as I never had an assistant. My patients never complained. They thought that was just how things had to be, and they had the utmost faith in me and my skill. As in the case of the infants, I was once again very lucky – or perhaps my frequent attendance at Alexander Tietze's operations in Breslau meant that I was particularly well trained.

My operations took a somewhat unusual course. I got the patient –

usually a man – to sit on a couch, in front of my small operating table; I sat behind it and after the first vigorous cut the patient fainted because of the pain and keeled over onto the couch. While he was unconscious I continued operating, bandaged him, and finally brought him round with cognac or rum; he was usually pleasantly surprised that it was all over. However, this method of anaesthetising by pain does not work with women: they just scream and scream.

Since someone might be injured on a Monday, and then wait for my return on the Saturday, I often had to deal with suppuration in an advanced state, or concealed foreign bodies – for instance a fish hook buried in a man's thumb; the skin had grown over it so I had to dig and burrow for a long time till I found it. One man had inflamed ligaments in his hand, and during the waiting period the glandular swelling had spread right up into the forearm. I had to clean out an old forester's infected glands. A boy came whose lower lip and chin had been ripped open by a guard dog. I did not dare to stitch it, for fear of infection; instead, I cleaned it thoroughly, placed a thin tampon with iodine between the surfaces of the wound, and pressed them together with sticking plaster. All that could be seen later was a thin white line.

I believe I owed my successes to Dr Tietze's great interest in me, Germany's first female medical student. But luck played a part too. One "white Easter", when we had a snowstorm, the four-year-old child of my builder fell ill early in the week; a doctor was called in at great expense who declared that she must be taken to Hermannswerder for an operation for peritonitis on the Saturday. Her father had already harnessed the horses to an open cart; but her mother would not let them go till Dr Hempel had come to Ferch and been sent for. I found the child unconscious, no reaction in the pupils, pulse almost imperceptible, abdomen distended – that had led to the incorrect diagnosis of peritonitis. But I recognised that it was acute pneumonia and realised that the child would not survive a cross-country journey of many hours in an open cart in that weather. I brought her back to consciousness by means of hot and cold fomentations throughout the night. When I went home at about five in the morning the child was sleeping peacefully. A few hours later I went back, somewhat apprehensively, and found the child sitting up in bed and playing. On another occasion a young man with acute appendicitis was taken back to Berlin by Hugo and was operated on in a hospital just before the appendix ruptured. Once a woman came across the lake in a motor boat to see "the doctor" – and found me in my gardening clothes.

"My husband has suddenly become deaf and is rushing around like a madman!"

"Quite suddenly?" I asked.

"Yes!"

"Don't worry. That can be put right in a few minutes. Wait while I

change."

Respectably clothed, with the few instruments I would need – a probe and a syringe – since I had no doubt that a plug of earwax had slipped back – I crossed the lake with the woman in her motor boat and was able to release the man from his panic and despair.

Another time it was the village mayor who came to see me with swollen, red, weeping eyes: a case of neglected conjunctivitis. I told him there were two treatments: a mild, rather slow one (boracic acid) and a very painful but much quicker one (silver nitrate). Since it was spring, and there was a lot of work on the farm, he opted for the quick one, which he endured without flinching. When he stumbled down the stairs, half blind from the drops in his eyes, he searched in vain for his wooden clogs, which he had left at the door, as was customary; little Reinhardt had put them in the duck pond as boats.

Beside my medical work, the farming was my greatest pleasure, and here my interests coincided with Hugo's more than in any other area. He was always happy in Ferch, and full of appreciation for the way I had adapted to this way of life, despite my urban background. I looked back on my years as a rich man's idle daughter in Danzig – the most "work" a young woman in that position could do was a little dusting – and was hugely relieved that now I was truly busy, planting and sowing, weeding, harvesting, bottling fruit, juice, purees and poultry, as well as extracting honey from Hugo's hives – I enjoyed it all. It made me really happy to see the full jars of honey glowing in their various colours: almost red after the fruit blossom, white and snowy from acacias, golden from lime blossom, and so on.

The farmyard at Ferch: Mu on the left with a maid, Oma, Marianne, Reinhardt and friends at the back

So at least when we were in Ferch we lived peacefully and affectionately, for several years, until one day a neighbour told me of the murder in Sarajevo. I knew at once that that meant war. I hurried back to Berlin with the children, and found Hugo already making preparations to enlist. During those last few days he did not leave my side for an instant. His love, his trust, moved me deeply. We had lived together quite well for those twelve years, despite some differences. Those derived in part from his irrational jealousy and in part from his desire to impress me, to assert himself somehow.

*****

For Lorchen, the weekly trip from Berlin to Ferch was a glorious adventure in itself; I heard about it again and again. When there was no one around to describe it to, she got out her typewriter and wrote it all down:

'I could go on about Ferch for days. The more I think about it, the more I remember.

When we were young we looked forward to the weekend all through the week. On Saturdays, when school ended at midday, Ida would be standing at the school gate with our rucksacks, and would take our school satchels home. Then we rushed to get the train to Potsdam, and ran onto the Star Steamer which took us to Ferch in two and a half hours. How we landlubbers admired the sailors and the cabin boys, who jumped ashore to tie the ropes and put down the gangplank!

My God, how lovely the lake was, with forests everywhere! At first it was just a river, the Havel. But then our lake opened out, Lake Schwielow. I can never forget what a joy it was to see the great lake before us without anything to obscure the view. It filled you with pride, you felt like royalty. First we went across to the other side, then back to the middle of the lake, and there was Petzow on the right, an old manor house, where Herr von Rochow lived. Everyone was afraid of him – there was a rumour that he shot anyone who entered his park. Yet we always went to Petzow every autumn – the walk from Ferch took about one-and-a-half hours – to collect horse chestnuts. Of course horse chestnuts are completely useless, but so irresistably brown and glossy. We lugged great rucksacks full of chestnuts home. On the opposite side of the lake was Flottstelle, a very poor place as I remember it, very sandy, but with a little café where you could get raspberry juice, if Mother was feeling very extravagant, which did not happen often. And I can still see the rather pathetic blackcurrant bushes there, all covered in sand. The next stopping place was called Ferch Neue Scheune (New Barn), where there was a very popular bathing place – it even had changing cabins and a pole in the water with a sign saying: "This far for non-swimmers, only strong swimmers beyond." We learned to swim very early and loved it. We mostly bathed at a spot nearer home, with no luxuries, where we would hide in the rushes to change and often got into the water from a rowing boat.'

'It took about quarter of an hour to get from the landing stage at Neue Scheune to our house, but the steamers did not run in the winter and then we had to go by train to Lienewitz. The walk through the woods from Lienewitz took about three-quarters of an hour. The grandparents often came to Ferch, preferably when my father was not there, and we would meet them at Lienewitz. Grandma had a weak heart, and wherever the path went

Schwielohsee – with swimmers

uphill we would hear Grandpapa's voice: "Slowly, Ro." And her reply: "Yes, Jo." Which however never changed their – never rapid – tempo in the least. There were three paths from Lienewitz: the Long Way, which we used if we were being fetched by a horse and cart, the Other Long Way, which took us to the other side of the village and closer to our house, and the Forbidden Way, which we generally used. It was the shortest, but the most strenuous. We also called it the Uphill, Downhill path because that was what it was like. You could only manage it if you did not have too much luggage. I can still see the view across the lake when you had got almost to the end of the Uphill, Downhill path, and the cushions of wild thyme with the most wonderful butterflies on them, and immortelles too. I often walk along those paths in my dreams, through a pine forest, which has a wonderful smell. Mother thought the coniferous trees were deplorable, mere matchsticks. She was used to the beech trees by the Baltic. Every time we came to a little stand of deciduous trees Mother went into ecstasies and long stories of Danzig and Zoppot were bound to follow. We never grew tired of them. There is no denying that pine forests are not the best sort of forest. The ground is covered with pine needles and cones, so that it is not pleasant to walk barefoot. But the sound of the wind in the pines is very special, like the sea, Mother said. It is quite an experience to lie under the soughing trees. The stems are a reddish gold and bare quite high up. We saw deer and hares in the forest, and foxes, and lots of birds, and plenty of wild mushrooms. We always used to pick great baskets full of fungi, raspberries and strawberries too. Wherever the ground was not carpeted with pine needles or sparse grass it was pure sand. The carts left deep ruts, which made it hard going for the horses, creeping across the sandy heath with heavy loads; and when it was frosty a little dog like my Marjellchen could only get along with great difficulty. The Uphill Downhill path had three ups and downs. Then you came to an area of young trees, with birches, beeches and oaks among them. There were vast quantities of mushrooms here. A little to one side of the path there was an abandoned tree nursery. The trees were tall and black, because they were too close together; it was an uncanny place. However, you would fight your way through if you saw golden chanterelles glowing in there. Picking wild mushrooms is just as exciting as hunting, and it would be blasphemy to leave a good one. Then it was downhill, with a stand of birches on the right, and after another bend you came to a giant oak, a truly magnificent tree, many hundreds of years old, for sure. Then the narrow path, with beech trees on the right, turned and we came to the place where we went tobogganing in the winter, and then into the village. Here was the big meadow with oak trees; you could not see the lake yet. Around 1916, when we were going bathing, we met a group of wounded, convalescent soldiers there, with their nurses. It was their last day before they had to go back into the hellfire. Mother had tears in her eyes. But being a practical person, she took a couple of sturdy lads home and loaded them with honey, jam, fruit and juice. She was never one to sit and weep. She was outraged by the war, but she could not see a way out. She was incapable of hating the Russians, or the French, and wherever there was an opportunity to say or do something kind, she did it, without any fuss. Once she discovered a sadistic non-commissioned officer was making life even harder than it had to be for some prisoners of war. Straight away she went to him and told him to stop. When that did no good she went to the Ministry in Berlin and succeeded in having that sadist removed from his "soft number" and sent to the front. I use the word "sadist". Of course, it was nothing in comparison with what was normal some years later in our country.

There was a big old-fashioned oven close by that meadow, under a huge chestnut tree; a brick-built tunnel that would be crammed full of brushwood which, when it had been burnt, left the bricks burning hot. The charred remains would be pulled out using long poles and the whole oven would be swept clean with juniper twigs that had been dipped in water. Then the loaves would be pushed in on long poles and the door shut. Afterwards you could have your own cake baked for a few pence. What a glorious smell! Once in late autumn I came upon a gipsy family there, who had

no horse, only a dog cart. They were just getting ready to leave. The clouds were racing across the sky, the wind was blowing the dead leaves. A boy about my age was loading the dog cart and I wondered where they would go. That was the first time I had seen homelessness, and felt it.

Next we came to the little alder wood, where the alders all stood with their feet in the water of the swamp. Their roots formed little islands. You had to jump from one island to the next, if you didn't want to get into the water. It was treacherous and might be dangerous; besides, you were covered with leeches if you had just played there for a little while. In front of the swamp was the most beautiful sycamore in the world. Not just because it was so big; its growth was perfect, since no other trees hemmed it in. No matter how tired we were, coming from Lienewitz, we always turned aside from our path to look up into the filigree of its crown: it was a joyful reunion every time. On the other side of the path there was a good place for dog violets behind a big oak. Moreover, there were rowans there. My father often pulled up saplings with his monstrously powerful hands to plant in our garden. But they never prospered, since he had not used a spade, and had damaged the roots.

Then we were out of the woods. Cornfields in front of us, the raspberry hill, and a ring of houses. On the left was Ulrich's garden, a row of plum trees permanently (so it seems to me now) laden with luscious fruit. Ulrich was also known as the Old Goat of Ferch. Then you saw the house, built like a medieval castle, of the evil magician – Attorney Naruhn, from Berlin. He was our deadly enemy. Because, before he started building on "our" hill, he had visited Mother, and had admired our incomparable view across the lake. Then, as she used to say, "the monster goes and plonks his box precisely where it cuts our view of the lake in half." He was a wretched little shrimp of man, and married Bertha the Cow, a huge woman, but they never had any children. His mother and sister also lived in Ferch, in a caretaker's flat, in dire poverty, wrapped up in shawls and coats, summer and winter. Naruhn was a megalomaniac, as his building demonstrated. But he ran out of money, and went all over the place trying to buy second-hand doors and furniture, which then didn't fit into the castle properly. And he had cypresses planted all along the fence, several hundred of them, which all withered and died in the sandy earth. By some trickery he had gained possession of

Naruhn's Castle

the path between our properties. One day we received the following written message: "Herding cattle on my private road is forbidden." He must have meant our hens, that ranged freely everywhere.

Our hill was uninhabited when we settled there, apart from a brown wooden house called Kieköver, but in the end there were four houses. A pastor lived in one with his family. One of his sons had tuberculosis – most poetical – the other one was called Martin and was wonderful. Enge, my sister, loved Phillip, the tubercular one, but Martin, the blond hero, was my ideal. Not that we ever spoke with them. But we would stand on our balcony for ages, peering down at the grey house, and reporting exciting news items to each other: Phillip has gone out at the back into the wood, Martin has come home with two friends, and so on.

You could smell our hedge roses from afar: wild English roses they were called. And then at last you were at our gate. What joy, when we got there at last! Straight out into the garden, up into the trees if the cherries were ripe, and there were quantities of berries, and asparagus beds, and so on. Very often we had one or two friends with us, who would marvel at the garden, and the lake, and our almost absolute freedom. But on the Sunday we had to be in Lienewitz by 4.20 if we were to get back to Berlin at a reasonable time. Usually we were heavily laden, but as it was all wonderful fruit and vegetables we never complained, especially not during the war and the blockade, when there were such terrible shortages.

There were two birch trees right by the house. A concrete path led from the gate, with dahlias on either side. My grandfather had given us most of the roots, but when he saw how prolifically they bloomed here, he said reproachfully to Mother: "My child, surely this is against nature." Mother dearly wanted to have an English lawn with standard roses in the middle. But lawns are not possible in the Mark Brandenburg, unless you can water them non-stop. There were pinks all round, in tussocks. In front of the house there were some trees, and nothing was to be pruned; Mother wanted things to grow naturally. The shade was delicious: one often gasped for shade in Ferch. This whole area was a terrace – another long-cherished dream of my mother's. Earth was brought in wheelbarrows, and with endless patience she would pull the yard-long roots of couch grass and convolvulus out of it. She would show us the "eyes" where new plants would grow, "and just think," she would say, "if just one tiny bit stays in the soil the whole garden will soon be overgrown with it." We shuddered.

The house in Ferch

And she would struggle for hours to anchor the earth wall with stones, plant-ing house-leeks in the gaps.

My father designed the garden "scientifically", so all the paths were dead straight, three parallel paths and two across, though Mother would have pre-ferred winding paths. The middle one was widest, with strawberries on either side. In Ferch we had strawberries from May till October, by the bowlful. By a crossing there was a boulder; Marianne sat here, reading, while Reinhardt, my friend Lisa and I galloped about on our hobby-horses. Whenever we passed her, Marianne would stretch out a hand and say, in a pathetic tone of voice: "This poor old woman begs for a kind donation." And we three fools were kept busy supplying her with handfuls of strawberries or other fruit, or it might be peas or fresh carrots and so on. Then she would squawk: "May God reward you, kind lady." By another crossing there were sweet smelling violets. Then there were asparagus beds, and sixteen beehives. When she was dealing with the bees Mother had to wear an old pair of Father's trousers, tied up with string at the ankles, with a jacket secured in the same way, so that the bees could not crawl in, and a wire mask over her head with a little door for a pipe. A charming sight.

When we went swimming we would go across a big, moist meadow. It had drainage ditches which joined together in a small, very fast flowing stream, which ended in the lake. The peasants drove their carts through the stream – that was good for the wooden wheels. There were beautiful flowers on this meadow, and the night before Mother's birthday (25 July) we all went there to pick Grass of Par-nassus, a flower I have never seen anywhere else. There were also various types of dianthus, scabious, harebells, saxifrage, stonecrop, cats foot, dogroses and thyme. I think every flower in Ferch had a sweet scent.

Path across the meadow

After Mother had left Berlin and gone to live in Freiburg, and I was staying with my father, I sometimes went to Ferch with him. Ferch was to be my inheritance. Marianne got to study, Reinhardt got a farm, and I was to get the house and garden in Ferch. But it was not to be. Ferch had to be sold to pay for Reinhardt's agricultural studies and his farm.

Before we emigrated in 1938, I went to Ferch with Leo Zuntz and my children. We walked through the completely overgrown garden, but not into the house. That was the last time I saw it.

Irene Gill

Now, not a day passes but I am in Ferch, going for a walk, or to the little shop, or simply going through the garden, and an infinite happiness fills me. Sometimes I feel that if I could only see our garden fence once more, could just sit under our little birch trees again, that I could then die at once. The earth opens, and I am at home.'

Chapter 9

If we as children ever got separated from Mu – going for a walk in the country, or on a crowded shopping street – we would hear her whistle a certain tune: do – so – do-do – ti – la – so, and would immediately reply by whistling: re – so-la-so-do – as we hurried to rejoin her. This was the opening of the theme song of the Wandervogel, an organisation she and Marianne belonged to when they were girls in Berlin and which Mu often told us about. It must have been something like the Ramblers, as it involved long walking tours; but it was run entirely by young people, adolescents; and the emotions and ideals behind it were at a pitch never approached by the British group. Mu loved it, though when she came to write about it in her old age she had had to recognise that those emotions and ideals were so close to nationalism that the Nazis had been able to absorb the whole movement into the Hitler Youth without much trouble. But when she was a girl, she had no idea that there was anything political about it.

'We had a wonderful time in the Wandervogel,' she writes. 'What a lot of friends one had in those days! I remember them so well. One was accepted for what one was, one belonged, one was important to the others. I think that was the happiest time in my life. And yet there was the war going on, the killing and the destruction – and hunger, because of the blockade and a series of cold, wet summers resulting in bad harvests in Germany. For us, the Wandervogel was thoroughly apolitical. I suppose we were living in Cloud Cuckoo Land, not recognising the strands of racism and nationalism in it; but we were young, you see; we took ourselves very seriously, and what we talked about endlessly was our inner lives. And we did have inner lives.

There were separate groups for boys and girls. Luz was our leader, and a very suitable subject for hero-worship. I had a crush on her, and even today, when I think of her, my old love is rekindled. Vera Lachmann came on at least one of our hikes. She and her sister Nina remained dear friends all my life. I remember Vera heroically volunteered to clean the great cooking pot – a dreadful job, as there was no hot water and it was black from the wood smoke and encrusted with dirt. All she had to clean it with in the nearest stream was sand and bundles of grass or straw.

Cooking was always fun, but when I consider that everything was carried on our backs – the big pot, whole cabbages, etc. – then it all seems more like a penance to me. We cooked out of doors, which was not always easy, since the wood was often so wet it produced nothing but smoke. The food consisted of potatoes and carrots, or potatoes and turnips, or cabbage – we each brought whatever we could and tossed it into the pot. Underdone and lukewarm when the fire didn't burn well, it was not too different from

Mila's dreadful concoctions in Berlin Zoo. Sandwiches made with artificial honey or dripping were all shared. Mother used to give us really excellent sandwiches to take along – because of the food we produced on our land in Ferch. Moreover my father's family, our Saxon relatives, were farmers, and sent us good things, like a parcel of potatoes I remember, each potato wrapped in tissue paper, as if it was as precious as an Easter egg – which at that time it was. So we were probably better fed than most people during the blockade.

Once when we were struggling to get a fire going in the pouring rain, two ladies suddenly appeared before us and reproached us for breaking the rules of the forest. "One spark, and the whole forest is ablaze!" And we had been trying to get the water to boil for at least an hour! After the two angry ladies had gone, we wondered where Luz had got to. We found her in the end under a ground sheet, half suffocating with laughter. Those two ladies were teachers at her school!

In the summer we would often go out for one-and-a-half days, which meant sleeping in the hay on a farm. We usually paid a little, and we could also buy potatoes, milk sometimes, usually fruit. Sleeping in the hay is not nearly as pleasant as you might think: very scratchy, and in the morning we were often shaking with cold. Then we had to wash at the pump in the farm-yard. In the summer we sometimes enjoyed good weather and slept in the open by the River Nuthe: meadows right and left – a perfect place to get sun-burnt. We were usually very lazy by the Nuthe, sliding back into the water again and again, lolling around in the flowery meadow and talking end-lessly about our inner, spiritual experiences.

But we went on very long hikes, too, for which we used the word "klotzen", which meant walking till one was totally exhausted. Then Luz would start singing, accompanying herself on her guitar, which made it much easier. Those marching songs really consisted of nothing but rhythm; but at other times we sang old folksongs from the Zupfgeigenhansell[1], the sadder the better. We always sang slowly and tragically.

The original idea of the Wandervogel was to escape from the city, and to make one's country one's own by rambling through it. And I think it worked very well. When I look back, I always see the villages, the paths, the hills and woods and fields through which we walked. I remember one evening in late autumn. We had lit a fire, it was dark, and it was raining. But we were sing-ing some of the songs that still run through my mind and often come out aloud as I do my housework, much to some people's annoyance: songs

---

1   A collection of traditional songs published for the Wandervogel at the beginning of the twentieth century.

praising the unique beauty of Germany and our deep sense of companion-
ship as Germans. Now that is 53 years ago. But my homesickness is as strong
as ever.'

*****

'On the first day of Advent we had a ceremony: when it began to get dark we
would look for a little tree somewhere in the forest, fix candles on it, and
spread Christmas goodies and apples and nuts on a groundsheet in front of
it. Then in the light of the candles a Christmas story was read aloud, and we
sang Christmas carols, although most of us in our group considered ourselves
to be "atheists". Another great festival was at the summer solstice. Later one
hardly dared to admit it, because it was so abused by the Nazis, and turned
into a völkisch, in other words an anti-Semitic festival. Until that happened
we enjoyed it enormously. We would meet with other groups on one of the
hills by Potsdam, which consisted of sand, so there was no fire risk. I think
there were about a hundred of us, boys and girls, and the bonfire was very
high. There was singing, dancing round the fire, a speech, badges were given
out. There were no grown-ups, and there were no arguments or fights. When
the fire had burned away we lay down and slept. The next day was mainly a
sports day, which I always kept away from, but there were singing contests
too.

I took part in two longer excursions. The first was to Möser, near
Magdeburg, in the flat, sugar-beet country. We thought it was glorious. We
had to work for our keep in the garden and also on the fields. The house
belonged to the parents of one of our leaders. We ate in the servants' room,
which was very cosy. We were always hungry, but there was always enough,
sometimes just soup, sometimes, on the Sunday, a dessert, some sort of jelly.
Divine! We all slept in the attic on a communal heap of straw. Will you
believe that we never quarrelled, were always discussing profound psychic
problems? The second excursion was to East Friesia. We walked from
Oldenburg to Oberhammelwarden. Unforgettable. The River Weser is very
wide there, flowing through flowering meadows stretching as far as the eye
can see. This was at the height of the war, and as we approached the coast we
saw airships. We walked across a big meadow for hours, the larks were singing above us, and there were flowers and cattle everywhere. But it was
tiring, and very monotonous. Then we saw a ridge in the distance which I
could not account for at all: it was the dyke. We climbed up it, and expected
to see the sea – but it was low tide, and there was no water to be seen far and
wide, only a warning sign telling us not to go any further. So we went back,
and came to a village where we wanted to spend the night. The only food we
could buy in the village was a sack of very small new potatoes, intended for
the cattle. I myself ate 80 of them, and the consequences did not take long to
reveal themselves. We were all ill. So we decided to go home early. The town

we were travelling from was Esens. Transport was very difficult during the war. There were many long stops in the middle of nowhere, and we could not get to a toilet. It began to be urgent, and in the middle of the night, when the train was once again stationary in open country, we climbed out laboriously, only to climb back again rapidly, as the train chose that moment to start moving again. Then we came to Hanover, where a train of soldiers on leave from the Western Front had just pulled in. Soldiers poured into our compartment, where there was not even enough room for all of us girls to sit. In despair, I screamed: "Stationmaster!" and he came and expelled the soldiers. Then he locked the door to our compartment and handed us the key through the window.

It took 30 hours to get to Berlin! But there was no one at home: they had all gone to Ferch. So I set out for Potsdam and sat on the jetty, dirty and despondent, got on the ferry to Ferch Neue Scheune (New Barn), and struggled up the raspberry hill in Ferch with difficulty; but again no one was at home, they had all gone to Brüggemanns to buy butter. So I went there, and how glad I was to meet Mother and Aunt Hedchen on their way home! After that there were some glorious weeks in Ferch before school began again.'

My mother never lost the semi-mystical love of nature which was such an important strand in the life of the Wandervogel. Those young people were so well organised that they published not only the Zupfgeigenhansel collection of folk songs, but books of Germanic myths, and also periodicals in which they described their hikes and their meetings – called 'nest evenings' – and above all their feelings. Here is an example from a pamphlet, *Deutscher Wandervogel* 1917, which I found among my mother's papers:

'… What a lot there is to be heard in the soughing of the wind in the forest! In Spring. There is calm, and there is storm. It is the forest, and it is the sea. It is life. It is everything. Joy and beauty and sorrow and longing. Everything except ugliness. Not ugly.'

'And that's just now. Often there is far more. When everything is green at last. When the birds sing. Such happiness. And the sun shines. Or in the evening, when everything goes to sleep. Only the soughing is awake. Watching over the sleep …'

But the magazine also reveals those other strands in the Wandervogel – medievalism, paganism, racism and sexism. The girls in their dirndls and pinafores and braided hair were to be 'brave and hard working, to guard the stronghold of our noble culture. Hail to them,' as one young soldier-Wandervogel wrote from the trenches. The movement was, generally speaking, not only nature-loving, romantic and idealistic, but also opposed to liberalism and democracy, which were considered to be 'foreign' to the German soul; and anti-Semitic, for 'The Jew', it was said, could not respond to Germany's culture, nature, landscape, since 'he' lacked the 'atavism' which enabled proper Germans, whose forbears were, without exception of course, decent German peasants or else troubadours, or perhaps noble knights, to be truly at home in Germany …

In fact many of Mu's Jewish – or partly Jewish – relatives fought in the war. But there were compensations. Growing up in Berlin, she was never far from affectionate aunts, her mother's sisters, such as:

'My Aunt Hedwig – Tante Hedchen – who lived round the corner from us – had a very strict sense of duty, and self-denial was second nature to her. Her self-discipline was steely – she was a true Prussian in that respect. She had four sons. The first died very young, possibly, as rumour had it, because his father, Ernst Nelson, had tossed him up into the air too high so that his head hit an iron chandelier. Then came Hans, Fritz and Erich. The three boys had to share a room, always getting on top of each other.

Tante Hedchen always comforted me when my schooldays were too depressing. When I got a bad mark at school I did not dare go home, but went to Hedchen instead; and she would comfort me until I felt able to go home.

Her son Hans was a painter, and the most beautiful man you could imagine. Tall, blond, blue-eyed, an angel of light in my eyes, and a totally free spirit. He enjoyed life. He played the violin and the guitar, and hiked through Norway, playing in lonely farmsteads in return for a night's sleep in the hay loft. Small girl that I was, I looked up to him as if he was a being from another world. He gave us a drawing of a girl, and when he came to see us after a journey, I said: "I thought of you every day when I looked at the picture." (I was about six years old.) He was so pleased that he blushed. He kissed me and said: "Every day? You thought of me every day? How can I ever thank you?"

Hans Nelson

He had a Norwegian sweetheart, Gertrud, and they would surely have married, but the war came instead, and he had to go to the Eastern Front as an officer. His letters showed that military life was intolerable to him. He hated every moment in the army. The last time he visited us I sat and listened and looked at him. I had just been given a penknife, which I was holding, and did not notice that the blade was cutting into my finger, ever more deeply. Suddenly Mother noticed the blood and screamed. I could not explain what I had done. I still have that scar on my finger, and every time I feel it I remember him.

I never saw him again. He fell in 1915. I have a picture of his grave in Russia – a little wooden cross. It is incomprehensible that this radiant person had to die like that.'

*****

The family visited the non-Jewish, Hempel relatives in Saxony from time to time. Mu tells us that:

'*...just getting there seemed like a journey to the ends of the earth, changing trains again and again, and missing connections. The last part was by the little local train, straight through the villages. The grandparents' house was right beside the railway line, and they would be standing at the window waving as we trundled past. I have never seen a table so heavily laden, with gherkins in mustard, gherkins in vinegar, gherkins with dill, butter from the farm, ham, sausage, cheese .... It was impossible to eat everything, but woe betide you if you could not manage any more: your pleas were simply not accepted, and your plate was filled again. For breakfast there was honey and home-made jam and fresh bread rolls; masses of everything. I can't remember lunch; but in the afternoon the sisters-in-law would come by horse and cart with baskets full of apple crumble and plum and cherry cake; the baking trays were a metre long! We sat and ate and drank. There was not much talk.*

We usually went there for Christmas, when the snow was deep. We slept in the attic, which had one window and one skylight. Of course the skylight had to be left open so that we got sufficient fresh air – and once I woke up to find my bed full of snow. It was fearfully cold, but we had big stone hot water bottles and featherbeds up to the ceiling. Wonderful beds!

My mother was afraid we were still not getting enough fresh air; so we had to put on our winter coats and sit by the open window in the reception room, which was called the "cold splendour", like in Danzig. Every house had one of these parlours, and they were very uncomfortable, only heated for special occasions, and with white dust covers on all the furniture; and everything was terribly valuable, so you had to be ever so careful.

My grandmother was almost blind. She wore a little lace cap and always sat by the window at her sewing table. My father, being her youngest, was her favourite. I cannot remember anything she said, but she was warm and affectionate. My father loved his parents, but being a moral coward he did not dare to go to his mother when she was dying. My mother had to go instead, while he stayed in Berlin, crying like a child.

My father was one of nine children, five girls and four boys, so there were plenty of relatives round about. Lina was the oldest daughter. She married a farmer in Leuterwitz who drowned in a flooded cellar. She was left with three children: Osmar, who was to inherit his father's farm; Herbert, who was studying to be a dentist; and Luise. When the First World War started, both boys joined up. I was sent to Lina at Leuterwitz to be fed – city children were being given such country holidays because of the blockade and the shortages in the cities – and I slept in Herbert's room. He was reported "missing" at Langemark and no further information was ever received. It was a regiment of students that fought at Langemark, and they went into the attack singing. It was comparable to the "Charge of the Light Brigade", and the officer in charge should have been shot, for most of those young men drowned in the swamp. Luise loved Herbert dearly and could not bear losing him; Lina found her hanging from a roof beam in the attic when she was seventeen years old. Among his belongings, in heaps of cardboard boxes, I found a dilapidated copy of Tolstoy's "Resurrection", and read it: an unforgettable experience. But on the whole I cannot say that I enjoyed my stay in Leuterwitz.

One of my father's brothers, Karl, was a doctor too, and his wife, like my mother, was Jewish. But there the similarity ends. Karl was a good, kind man, deeply in love with his wife and loyal to her, and she to him. When the Nazis sent her to the concentration camp at Theresienstadt, he wanted to go with her. In the end she was allowed home to die near her husband.

✳✳✳✳✳

Many years later, in 1972, David and I visited the ancestral farm in Saxony, in the German Democratic Republic, communist East Germany. It was now part of a collective farm, or LPG – Landwirtschaftliche Produktions-Genossenschaft – called Frohe Zukunft: Happy Future. We sat at a long table in an upstairs room, the windows wide open to let in the stench from the midden, and feasted. It was like having one meal after the other, non-stop, like the meals with Lina that Mu described: as soon as we had finished one large helping of meat, vegetables and potatoes, another one was placed before us; and finally the yard-long plum and apple cakes, just like the ones my mother remembered from half a century before, possibly baked on the same baking tins. There were at least sixteen relatives at the table, ranging from babies to grandparents. It was interesting to talk to them. For some of them, collectivisation meant life was a good deal easier. Work was more interesting, too, and they even had holidays abroad – unheard of in my mother's time. Some had visited Czechoslovakia, others the Black Sea, even China, but several were hostile to the communist regime and resented the lack of freedom, especially the closed frontier to the West.

We visited the farm again in 1995, six years after Germany's reunification. With the abolition of communism, collective farms like Frohe Zukunft had been divided up again. 'Our' farm was now an independent dairy farm, with a hundred cows, whose milk was sold to Müller, of yoghurt fame. The farmer had a familiar name – the same as Mu's brother's: Reinhardt Hempel. His wife, the village schoolteacher, had a lot to tell of the difficulties reunification had brought; the increased bureaucracy, the reduced social security, and the immensely hard life of an independent farmer. None of their four sons wanted to follow in their father's footsteps, working a fourteen-hour day with no hope of a holiday, just like the bad old days, before collectivisation. Most of Reinhardt's free time, and his wife's, was spent phoning or waiting to talk to some official and filling in forms for benefits that had come to them automatically in the GDR.

I showed my grandmother's memoirs in the three black exercise books to Gerlind, a young relative who had just qualified to be a doctor, and Reinhardt's mother, Oma Irma. She was over 80 but still getting up at four every morning to help with the milking. She told us about conditions in 1945, when waves of refugees arrived begging for food and shelter: first from the concentration camps, then from the army, running away from the advancing Russians. Even six members of the SS, five men and one woman, came, and vanished in the night, leaving parts of their uniforms behind, to avoid identification. Irma's husband, Alfred Hempel, was not in the army, since farming was an essential occupation, and he was also the village mayor. When the Russians arrived and demanded a pig and some eggs, he denied having any. They took him out into a field and shot him through the head.

Now Irma was left alone with four young children; more refugees came from Poland and other East European countries. Some would stay a while and work for their keep. They replaced the PoWs and other foreign men and women who had worked on the farm during the war. Under the communists, Irma counted as a grossbauer or kulak – a large-scale farmer. This meant that her children were not allowed to study anything beyond the age of sixteen except agriculture. In 1952 the LPG Frohe Zukunft incorporated the farm, along with a hundred others in the area.

But now, communism had been replaced by West German capitalism. Another relative, who worked on a fruit farm, gave us a basket with twelve different species of apple. But they could not sell their produce. West German supermarkets, with their huge imports from abroad, were destroying small scale local production. Under the previous much-criticised communist government, they never had to worry about marketing, the State took care of that. Now many of the workers on the fruit farm were redundant and the future looked bleak for the few who were left.

Another, older relative, Heinz, had lost his left hand during the war. He had spent his eighteenth birthday in a hospital train. Two months later, the war ended, and he made his way home. The Americans had reached a point well to the east of Zschoppach, but withdrew, in compliance with the Yalta agreement. Heinz, a man of volcanic energy, told us all this and much more in an enormously loud voice, gesticulating with the stump of his left arm, neatly enclosed in a knitted grey tube. His wife, Elfriede, was a typical Hempel: short, plump, blue-eyed, fair-haired, with a low brow, thick eyebrows, a retroussé nose: features which recur in later generations of our family. She and her sister Luise, who lived with them, kept up the old customs: they bottled fruit, grew and pickled gherkins, produced a purée of plums by stirring a copper full of them day and night for 72 hours, with pebbles in the bottom to prevent it catching: the stirring must never stop, even during the change-over from one pair of hands to the other. They made an excellent elderberry 'soup', slightly thickened with flour and sprinkled with toasted breadcrumbs. They regaled us with superb Kaffee und Kuchen and blackberry juice and much more besides and told us the story – already familiar to me – of Karl, who must have been so different from his brother Hugo, my grandfather.

Perhaps it would have been better if Hugo had stayed in Saxony, and never studied medicine, or met and married Oma. Or perhaps, as Oma herself thought, he should have been a country doctor in rural East Germany. His violence and crudeness may have been a reaction to being uprooted and transplanted in such an alien environment as upper-middle-class Berlin.

✴✴✴✴✴

As soon as the First World War started in September 1914, Hugo left to join the medical corps, which, Mu writes,

'…*was a great relief to us, but a disaster for him. His initial Hurrah-patriotism, which we all shared, soon turned into a deep depression. All his letters had phrases like "… if the war ever ends…" At first he was proud to be in the army; he sent us toys from France. He was a medical staff officer and had a horse and a batman; but none of the horses was strong enough for him. In the end he was found a Belgian farm horse that could take his weight. But he was so fat and clumsy that he could only mount it if it stood in a ditch and he stood on a milestone and was helped up by his batman.*

He felt no hate or hostility for the French. As a farmer's son, the senselessness of the War was very clear to him. Devastated fields, trampled gardens! In his free time he would ride for miles into the farmland, looking for an unspoilt field. The sentimental side of his personality was revealed when he sent us some violet plants from the park of the Prince of Monaco, which later flourished in Ferch. He had found them crushed under the wheels of a munitions column. He kept Goethe's "Werthers Leiden" in his knapsack all through the war and insisted on reading it to us when he came home on leave.

But he also spent a lot of time in a field hospital, voluntarily dissecting corpses for "research". Leo Zuntz, who was stationed nearby and rode over to see him one day, found him in a blood-soaked shed, with hacked off limbs everywhere, and my father in the middle, with staring eyes, up to his elbows in intestines. Leo was convinced that he was insane. He came home for a "gas course", and was completely deranged. Things got even worse when the military defeat came at last in 1918 and he came home. If he saw us girls with a book, or gossiping with friends, he would go wild. "Germany is lost, and my daughters gossip!" We had embroidered a collar box for him as a birthday present (men still wore stiff collars in those days). He looked at it and threw it on the floor. "Germany is lost – what am I to do with a collar box?" And so on and so on. He became increasingly brutal. When Germany was humiliated and economically ruined by the terms of the Versailles treaty, his patriotism turned into a virulent nationalism. He concurred with the "stab in the back" theory – that Germany was only defeated because of the socialist uprising in Germany itself: and a number of the socialists' leaders were Jewish. Moreover, and on the other hand, some of the war profiteers and black marketeers were Jewish. His nationalism was permeated with anti-Semitism, often directed at his own wife and children (though Judaism played no part in their lives). He was grossly overweight and self-indulgent and promiscuous. And he was increasingly violent against us children and the servants.

Mother had not expected his homecoming to be like that and was not willing to put up with his bad moods. She had been leading a good and useful life without him, like many German women; her conscience was perfectly clear, since she had managed everything by herself and had moreover helped many other people. And he beat me more than ever, so much so that our nice maid, Anna, threatened to report him to the police. His behaviour was disgusting. When he used the lavatory in Marianne's presence, it was the last straw, and Mother decided to leave him, taking us with her, of course. For the last few weeks I was sent away, for my safety, to Mother's brother Heinchen and his wife Flora in Bernau, so I did not witness the final scenes. I was told that he begged Mother on his knees to stay, implored Marianne to help him, but all to no avail.

Reinhardt was the main problem. Legally Father had a right to all us children, since Mother was leaving him of her own free will; his behaviour was not life-threatening, just unbearable, and there was no suggestion that he had been "unfaithful". Reinhardt was only ten years old, and he was tormented by both parents alternately begging him to stay or go with them. But finally he came with us.

As soon as we had left, Ida returned. She cared for him, worked as his receptionist, and put up with all his moods. The house was overrun with women from a class much lower than his own. He behaved like a Pasha.'

*****

I believe Germany's defeat in 1918 was as traumatic for my mother as it was for her father and many Germans, who had confidently expected victory. Decades later, in Oxford, she described, vividly, how she had watched the German army march through Berlin in December 1918, in uniform, in rank and file, in step. They were not a defeated army! They had defended the fatherland, the homeland, die Heimat, against enormous odds, and not one foreign soldier had ever set foot on German soil! I could see that she still felt proud as she described the scene. Her eyes blazed and her voice shook when she spoke of the humiliation, the grotesque injustice, of the Versailles treaty, when all the responsibility for the war was piled onto Germany, and she was obliged to pay crippling reparations – 5,000 locomotives, 150,000 railway carriages, and so on and so on, while the blockade was maintained for another year after the end of the fighting.

But there was no excuse for her father's appalling behaviour in those immediately postwar months. His crude vulgarity was unbearable. The very eroticism which Oma had welcomed when they first married now took the form of totally unrestrained promiscuity, involving servants and patients. After a year of this, Olga could not live with him any longer. In 1919 she took their three children – then aged ten, fifteen and sixteen – to Freiburg, in the Black Forest, the scene of her happy student days.

Chapter 10

My mother remembered that journey across Germany from Berlin to the Black Forest – the flight from her father Hugo – very clearly. It can't have been much fun. Here's what she wrote in her memoirs:

'The trains were not running according to any timetable in that chaotic postwar period, and we had to stop at a tiny place no-one had ever heard of, which gloried in the magnificent name of Weil-Leopoldshöhe. Mother was worn out and kept crying, which was very uncharacteristic for her. My brother had brought his guinea pigs in a cage which stood on the little table by the window and filled the whole compartment with their stench. The liquid from the cage ran out over the table, on which we had rested our heads to go to sleep. So we were not in very good spirits. The train stopped for hours on the station at Naumburg; finally it set off again, at a snail's pace. It was hot, and we were all apprehensive of the future. But we were fascinated when we saw the mountains of the Black Forest – at first we thought they were blue clouds. While we sat in our stuffy compartment, we imagined vividly how cool and shady it must be in the forest, what berries one might find to eat there, and we could "hear" cool little streams purling through.

We reached Freiburg about ten hours late, and so we missed Aunt Hedchen, who had been waiting on the station for hours with a huge pot full of rice pudding (her oldest son Fritz was then an assistant at the eye hospital there). But we knew there was no accommodation for us in Freiburg and went on to the spa town of Badenweiler. The country grew more beautiful by the hour: the mountains of the Black Forest higher, and the Vosges could be seen on the other side. We had to get out at Müllheim and into the local train to Badenweiler. We were enchanted to see open country, green meadows with fruit trees laden with fruit – it was reassuring to see that there was fruit here, not only in Ferch. In Badenweiler we were met by Mother's old friend "Pieter" – Pietrkovski – and his wife Evi, who had found us a little flat and led us to it. All the windows looked out into the hills, and to Mother's joy the living room faced the west, where the valley opened out into the Rhine Plain, and we could see the most glorious sunsets, with the Vosges looking like a Promised Land. We had three rooms like mouseholes, and had to cook in the cellar. Our landlady was particularly hostile to north Germans, and even more so to children. We called her Frau Serpenz, Latin for dragon, which she luckily did not understand, so we could talk freely about our dislike of her. She watched us all the time, and was of course dissatisfied with our cleaning of the kitchen. She would move the table to see if we had washed the floor under the legs, and woe betide us if she found dry spots there. Still, things worked out more or less. She even invited us to her vineyard at harvest time. We were allowed to eat as much as we wanted, which was a lot.

Mother's most urgent task was to settle us in school, and we joined quite a crowd of Badenweiler children who went to school in Müllheim, in the valley. There was a train which went bim-bim-bim through the villages to collect children for school and travellers to or from the spa. School was fantastic. Everyone spoke a dialect which was incomprehensible to us at first. It was a mixed school, a great change for us, as boys and girls were strictly segregated in the north. Of course all the boys sat on one side and the girls on the other. Recreation was also separate. The yard was divided by a cement wall, on which a teacher walked up and down, ensuring that boys and girls did not talk to each other. The lessons were not very interesting; still, Marianne managed to come top in everything, while I trailed far behind. Marianne got private lessons in Latin, which she needed to enter the grammar school and get the qualifications to start studying medicine. Her Latin teacher was an elderly retired professor. She had to make up sentences to show she had understood a rule. On one occasion she very daringly came up with: "I went for a walk with my friend", using the masculine form for friend. The professor blanched, so my sister accepted his recommendation to use the feminine form.

After the winter, Mother found she could no longer pay for the train fares and our lodging. She found an even more modest place, but in the most wonderful part of the country, with an unobstructed view of the Vosges. Now we had to walk to school, it took about three quarters of an hour each way, over green meadows, far from any streets, but very close to fruit trees. We were really very happy. On some specially fine days, Marianne decided she did not want to go to school. She would settle down under a cherry tree, or a peach, or an apple, depending on the season, and send Reinhardt and me on to school, to report that she had to stay at home with a sudden headache. We were always believed, for, was she not top? On our way back we would collect her from the tree, where neat piles of cherry stones and the like showed what her activity had been while we were slaving away at school.

I cannot tell you how wonderful south Germany was, especially in spring and summer, when the abundance of fruit and flowers and mushrooms was overwhelming. Life seemed much easier here. The small towns and hamlets all had their own style and cheerful atmosphere. Everybody had a vineyard, the gardens were full of flowers and superb vegetables. Everything seemed to grow of its own accord, not like in the north, where you had to fight for each harvest.

Behind Badenweiler was the Hochblauen, a wooded mountain. It took about three hours to get to the top. I had so much energy in those days that I went straight up the hillside, ignoring the official paths, jumping over

*streams – and never meeting a living soul, apart from rabbits, deer, birds.
All the time the views kept changing, and I really felt on top of the world.'*

The Black Forest near Badenweiler

But they had to move again. Marianne, who wanted to study medicine, needed to get into the sixth form of the Freiburg Grammar School; so for a time they stayed in a boarding house in the town, and then with Pieter and his family. Oma started waging war with the Freiburg housing office for a whole bitter year. She went to the housing office every day and raised Cain. no one was ever pleased to see her there! She threatened to kill herself and her children if she was not allocated a three-room flat. Of course nothing was further from her mind than suicide.

Finally she heard of an attic with a number of small rooms intended for the maid servants of the flats below, and a large open area above it for drying laundry. There was a space under the stairs which could be used as a kitchen. Oma told the landlady that she would have to get permission from the housing office first, as she was not entitled to unfurnished accommodation with cooking facilities. When the landlady went to the office, they agreed at once, and when she asked if they wanted to see Oma again, they declined, vehemently, dreading more dramatic scenes.

They called their attic die Erwinhöhe – the Heights of Erwin; the street is called Erwinstrasse, and their house – number 39 – was still standing there in 1995, despite the bombing of Freiburg in the war years.

'We could hardly believe our luck (writes Mu). From all the windows we could see treetops and glimpses of mountains. Our furniture arrived, and into one of those rooms Mother managed to fit a four-seater sofa, a book case, a piano, a baroque wardrobe which took up a whole wall, a sideboard, an antique writing table, a sewing table, a tiled stove, and several chairs. The

kitchen was a gas cooker under the stairs leading up to the laundry drying attic above, plus a tin bath for all of us.'

Now for the first time in her life, Oma was having to keep house and cook meals. Hitherto she had always had housekeepers and maids and servants. But she told herself, once again, that if other people could do these things, then so could she, and applied her intelligence to the matter. To save time and money and gas, she cooked just once a week, a large pot full of rice and meat, and placed it in a hay box to keep warm. When she made a cake, she offered the mixing bowl to the children to lick. Observing how much they enjoyed it, she didn't bother to bake any more – just gave them the uncooked cake-mix to spoon up. She saw no need to clean the outside of pots and pans and crockery, only the

Erwinstrasse 39

inside; so everything got very greasy and grimy to the touch. And she got the children to do as much of the housework as possible.

In summer, when the attic got stuffy, she, being a fresh air fiend, would sleep on the roof that jutted out over the flat below. It was four floors up, and there were no rails. One day a young man who lived opposite called and begged her not to sleep up there any more, as she might so easily move in her sleep and roll off, and he was having nightmares. This had never occurred to her; but out of sympathy for the young man she took to sleeping on the windowsill, extended by a table.

She needed to earn some money. Freiburg was full of doctors, so she didn't even try to get a practice. For three years she took on any work she could do that would pay. She spent her nights writing out addresses for companies; translated scientific documents for chemical and pharmaceutical companies for 4½ pence per word; gave English lessons to an American woman who had lived in Germany for 30 years and was afraid of forgetting her English – she paid her 50 pence an hour to go for walks gossiping in English. She translated, into English, a detailed description of the composition, but above all the effect, of a new sexual stimulant for bulls and stallions. She had never come across many of the expressions in German, let alone in English. Once, when she was brooding over it despondently, her friend Pieter called, and offered to help. He knew a professor of pharmacology who had lived in England: if Olga would make a list of the expressions she did not understand, he would ask this friend to help. When the two men studied the list they were almost prostrate with laughter at the demands being made on a respectable lady.

She accepted a temporary job arranging the scientific library of a pharmaceutical company, Rosenberg's, which had just moved into a new building. It was a big job; but she had two hours off at midday so that she could have lunch (from the hay box) with her children. As soon as she came home in the evening she had to make the supper, with the help of the two girls.

'Once the Rosenberg library was organised, the professor of Roman Law, Professor Levy, asked her to "index" certain basic Latin and Greek books. Without having the faintest idea what it involved, she agreed immediately, true to her principle: "If other people can do it, then so can I." This meant she had steady work for months. She had to cut up the books, word by word, stick each word onto a card, and then define it – grammatically, legally, and so on. She had help: two elderly ladies dealt with the cutting and sticking, and a junior barrister with the legal side. If the paper was very thin or the print too small, whole sentences had to be cut out as often as the number of words in it, and a different word underlined each time. It all seemed completely pointless to her, but when it was finished Professor Levy was very satisfied, and so was another professor who came from Heidelberg specially to examine the work.'

Old Mr Rosenberg of the pharmaceutical firm engaged her again, this time to catalogue the company's papers and its correspondence with doctors all over the world. The man who was doing this work before her had got it all into an unholy mess. He stowed everything he had not dealt with in some files that were not in use. This came to light when the said files were dusted and shaken out of a window, and their hidden treasures flew out into the street below. Then he had hit on a more radical solution and stuffed the unsorted papers into the lavatory; this led to his being discovered again because of flooding, and finally to his dismissal. That was when Olga took over. She had to look through all this material, rearrange it, and record it in a new card index. She was also put in charge of the commercial registry, which was chaotic, with the

Oma in the office

information about doctors in many different languages. She coped, and got the reputation of being a polyglot; even Spanish letters were entrusted to her to translate, which she managed to do with a dictionary and her knowledge of Latin.

This was full-time work, with a reasonable salary, and at last she was free of pressing financial worries. The 'Erwinhöhe' (Heights of Erwin) were soon famous, and they had many visitors. One rainy day Mu brought home a very bedraggled group of about eleven young people. They were from the Odenwald School – a famous experimental, co-educational boarding school with which our family got quite involved later – and had been refused accommodation in the Youth Hostel for some reason. When Oma came home from her job, where she had been climbing up and down ladders all day 'like a squirrel', and wearily trudged up the four flights of stairs to her attic, she found the entrance filled to overflowing with rucksacks and wet blankets and all these people, while a young man stirred a huge pot full of porridge in the kitchen – the space under the stairs. She was not in the least upset. The group leader confessed that the reason why they had not been allowed to stay in the Youth Hostel was that four of the children were bed-wetters. Mother offered the laundry-drying attic to the bed-wetters, with iron mesh mattresses, washable blankets on them and a lot of newspapers. The rest of the group went to the Youth Hostel.

She also looked after a series of foster children, or rather, young adults. One was a student, Fred Rickert, who was epileptic. His fits were usually in the evening or the night. She always looked into his room before she went to bed, and sometimes found him on the floor – once, naked, wet and holding a sponge: he had fallen while he was washing. It was winter, and the window was wide open. She could not lift him alone, only cover him to keep him warm, and lay a pillow under his head, which was flinging wildly from side to side, and wait till he was able to get into bed with her help. It was a nerve-shattering time; but he was such a good, gentle, lovable person, that she had no regrets. Later, after he had left the Heights of Erwin, he became violently insane and died in a lunatic asylum a few years later.

Another foster child was Vroni Berfels, who was about the same age as Olga's daughters. Vroni had lived with her grandparents most of her life and was happy to be among young people at last. Sonja Traube came for a time; like Vroni, she had no mother, and her father, a professor, was exceedingly unpleasant. They called her their Lily, because she was so beautiful, so gentle, quiet and graceful – yet she could be as stubborn as a mule. Before the divorce she had stayed with them at Ferch sometimes, and the famous interchange came when the children had all been making mud pies and Oma told them to wash their hands before lunch. Sonja refused, saying it wasn't necessary. Oma, indignantly, demanded to see her hands – and they really were clean: "blütenrein" – as clean as blossom – was the expression always used when this anecdote was repeated to me. Oma's cousin Lutek's daughter Lisa, who was to study medicine, like Marianne, stayed with her for many years; she was like another daughter to her. Lisa, like Sonja and Vroni, had been frequent visitors in Ferch before Olga left Berlin. To these and other young people, Olga was a motherly friend. They had a lot of fun together, putting on plays, going for outings in the Black Forest, and so on. But when Schubert asked her to take in his son, when he reached university age, she refused. She felt her full-time work and her other commitments were more than enough. This boy was very similar to his father! Highly talented, in too many different directions, unbalanced, a slave to his moods. A few months after Schubert's death, when he was aged twenty and studying at the polytechnic in Danzig, he killed himself by throwing himself under a train.

As for Mu: for the first time in her life, she enjoyed school. She writes: *'For my last year at school I attended the old girls' school on the Holzmarkt in Freiburg. It was really very nice. I had the never-to-be-repeated experience of success. There were only four girls in the top class, and I was the best – probably because Marianne was in a different school. I had two young teachers with whom I got on very well, and my final report was brilliant in comparison with previous ones. I realised that I was not stupid. This went to my head. I wanted to go in for the Abitur – the university entrance qualification. I was entitled to transfer to a higher school, and did; but it was a science-based one, and I was struck down by mathematics. Maths was always a mystery to me; moreover the teacher, Ludin, was a sadist, later a prominent Nazi, and he annihilated me in a few short weeks. So I left at Whitsun, instead of sticking it out to the end of the school year and went back to Berlin.'*

Reinhardt wasn't doing well at school. In accordance with the German system, he had to pass tests before he could move up from one class to the next; but it was only with Oma's help that he managed to scrape through. He didn't have the slightest interest in school. Farming was the only thing he had ever been interested in. Hugo was going to buy him a farm as soon as he had the basic school leaving certificate and started agricultural training. But one day, to her alarm, Oma received a message from the school saying that he would not be moved up into the top class, which meant he would not be eligible even for the basic certificate. She went to his form teacher.

"Why won't he move up? What's the trouble?"

"The French pronouns!"

"The French pronouns?! Right. If I make sure that he knows the French pronouns forward and backward, will you let him move up?"

"Do you think you can do it?"

"I promise you I will."

"All right – it's a deal."

They shook hands on it. Then, night after night, she drummed the French pronouns into the poor boy's head – me te se le lui leur and so on.

Everything went according to plan: he got his certificate. But it meant that she lost her son when he was fifteen; he became a stranger. His father bought him his farm – it was at a place called Mellensee, near Berlin. One of Hugo's brothers looked after it until Reinhardt was old enough to take over. He went to Zschoppach to learn to be a farmer from his grandfather and uncles. Here is one of Reinhardt's rare letters from Zschoppach, which Oma copied out and sent to Mu:

'*Dear Mum,*

Sorry and please don't be cross with me for not writing sooner, only the drainage people were here last Saturday till late in the evening, so I didn't have any time, last week we were hoeing turnips, so I was dead tired in the evenings. On Sunday I was on the field with Uncle Otto and Aunt Bertha and got back at 10, and yesterday there was no light! So am I forgiven?

I guarantee that this letter will be long, good, and posted tomorrow (and legible)…Let me describe a day to you:

I get up at 4.15, clean 2 horses ,and then have breakfast, an indefinable soup with a lot of milk and bread, till 5. Then I harness up the oxen, while cousin Alfred harnesses the horse, and we go and mow the clover field. We finish out there at 6. Afterwards, until 7.30 or 8, I chop wood or turn the grain. Till 10.45 the women and I cut the thistles (but we get cut ourselves quite a lot). Inside I unload clover and at 12 we have our dinner. From 1 till 6.30 we cut thistles. Then I tidy up the yard, do a few small jobs and get into my comfortable bed. More tomorrow. Good night. R.

You needn't be afraid of me coming home to you de-cultured. Cousin Hilmar is making sure of that, training me to stop sniffing and keeping my hands in my pockets, and Uncle Otto's stopping me biting my nails. Eating with one's knife and scooping soup up is customary in the country (I won't introduce it at home)…

Uncle Otto is very nice. If it was up to him, I'd eat till I burst. When I go to write a letter, he pulls the lamp down for me, pushes the table over and looks after me generally. To celebrate my birthday Uncle Otto got me drunk; Alfred had to take me upstairs and undress me. My hangover was bad, never again! But don't let Papa know, he wrote specially I wasn't to smoke or drink.

Goodnight now, otherwise I'll be dead tomorrow. Love to Marianne…
from your
Reinhardt'

Oma said she was very pleased with this letter; but she knew in her heart that he did not really love her. The gulf between them was to widen even more when the Nazis came to power.

Now she was left with just one of her children, Marianne, and her niece, Lisa; they lived together in great intimacy and happiness, though money was still a worry: Olga was reduced to doing '"stupid housework, transforming the kitchen from a rubbish tip to a jewellery box, sewing and patching – an old sheet is transformed into ten immaculate tea-towels, snow white, hemmed, marked, supplied with hangers, boiled and ironed,' as she wrote to Mu. For now her lifelong correspondence with my mother began – a very regular weekly exchange, resulting in boxes full of her letters to Mu. Unfortunately, she destroyed Mu's to her along with many other papers before she died. In one of hers, Oma describes how she and Marianne would lie in bed together on Saturday mornings having a good cuddle and waiting for the postman to bring Lorchen's letter, which they would then read together. I feel this must have jarred a little with Mu, who always felt excluded from their intimacy, however warm Oma's letters to her were.

Her old friend Pieter was a frequent visitor; he read to her, and they went for walks, watched the sun set, and talked. There was plenty to talk about. These were the 1920s, and the political situation was dire with the inflation, strikes in the Ruhr, where she sympathised with the strikers, and the rising tide of fascism. The Völkische Partei, precursors of the Nazis, published anti-Semitic plans as early as 1924: if German Jews emigrated, the federal state they lived in last was to get at least half of their property; if they returned they were to be hanged; Jews were to be excluded from all public offices as well as from professions like teaching and medicine, which they would only be allowed to practise on other Jews; they were not to work in any theatre, or in any nationalised enterprises like the railways or power supplies; they were not to be allowed to buy land. But at the time this was the hysterical yapping of a small minority, and Oma was not the only person who refused to take it seriously.

Chapter 11

My mother's experiences as a teenager after she left school were rather tumultuous, as she describes them:

> *'So I left school at Whitsun – and decided to go to my father in Berlin, because he had pleaded for at least one of his children to come, if only for a holiday. Marianne refused to go, point blank. And Mother would not let Reinhardt go. I knew that I was the one he wanted least, but that I was acceptable as a bridge to the other two. I was terribly afraid. Mother tried to dissuade me. She was angry, accusing me of "playing the parents off against each other", and no doubt there was a touch of sensationalism there, but that hurt me most bitterly. I did not even try to justify myself.'*

Having heard the rumours about Hugo's way of life, Oma demanded some assurance that he would not expose their young daughter to shocking scenes. He told her he had a wonderful new housekeeper, a clergyman's daughter, very respectable. Oma asked that this housekeeper should be interviewed by her sister Ludowika, and this was done. Ludowika reported that she was enchanted by the housekeeper: no harm could befall Lorchen while she was present. So finally Oma relented. So, writes Mu,

> *'I went. I did not find the parting hard. I had a growing sense of being misunderstood in Freiburg, and after that final debacle at school had absolutely no self-confidence; that short happy time at the Holzmarkt school had meant nothing. I didn't know what I really wanted to do; perhaps to be a gardener. And of course there were still some of my old Wandervogel friends in Berlin. Father undertook to arrange for me to get me some sort of professional training.*
>
> *The new housekeeper was called Helene Meinhoff, always known as Hövi, and she and I became close friends, and she told me all about herself and her experiences –a fascinating and shocking tale. Her father had been a country clergyman in eastern Pomerania, and had six children. In his spare time he had taught himself Swahili. Now there were two things that our Kaiser was terribly proud of, and both led to disaster: the Navy, and the African colonies. In connection with the latter, he founded an African Institute in Hamburg, and Reverend Meinhoff was called from his country vicarage to become the Professor of Swahili there (there was no competition – no one else knew any Swahili).*
>
> *His wife died, and he married again. He had two more children with her; and she was like a wicked stepmother in a fairy tale. She made all her six stepchildren sleep in the attic. They were kept quite separate from the family. They ate separately, were given different – and worse – food; the boys were*

sent away at an early age to learn a trade; most of the girls became deacon-esses. Hövi worked as a governess, and she had been engaged to a theology student who was killed at Ypres. His picture stood on her bedside table with the caption: "If we live, we live for the Lord. If we die, we die for the Lord."

My father had got to know her when he treated members of the family where she was working, and invited her to come and keep house for him. Now that Mother had gone, Ida couldn't cope on her own. The real reason, I now realise, was that the sentimental part of my father was enamoured of Hövi. She was very competent; but soon her relationship with my father was an intimate one, which was of course contrary to her puritanical upbringing. And now the brutal side of my father's nature asserted himself. He would mock her, tell everyone about their affair; Hövi's response was: "I have sinned and deserve this punishment."

She was ash blond, with a sweet little face, very pale and frail – I think she had a bad heart – and terribly thin. When I got to know her she was about 29. We took to each other at once. I didn't realise that she was my father's mistress, although I found them in bed together more than once, which I regarded as one more example of my father's inconsiderateness (Hövi needed her sleep!) and vulgarity. I will never forget how he came into our shared bedroom and flung himself, fully dressed, onto her bed and instantly started snoring loudly. I could not understand how she put up with him, but every attempt to leave failed because she was homeless, and perhaps also because she loved him.

I owe Hövi a great deal. For one thing, we read Goethe together and really that was glorious – how could it have been otherwise. And she had a dog, Trudi, and when she had puppies, she gave me one, called Marielly. I loved her intensely, could hardly bear to be separated from her – she was my comfort and my joy. Hövi and I would go for walks together very proudly in the deer park with our dogs, take them with us to Ferch, and so on.

Then we went on trips together, to Hiddensee and Rügen, Pomerania, and the Sudeten Mountains. In the Sudeten it was still very cold and wet; but she was convinced that Father had promised to come to Hirschberg for Easter. So we spent the whole Thursday on the station at Hirschberg, wait-ing for every train from Berlin. He did not come. We also spent a lot of time together at Ferch, and it was a lovely summer. Nothing bad was ever said about Mother, and my father wrote a letter which infuriated Mother: "To have a young daughter in the house is like having the house adorned with may blossom."

Now Father tried to get me settled in some vocational course. First he suggested I should go to an agricultural college for farmers' daughters; but nothing came of that, because they all had anti-Jewish restrictions. So then Father sent me to a head forester at Neubrück on the Spree. I arrived in the autumn and was wild with joy. After the richness of the Black Forest this was a new world: flat, and sandy, with pines. I thought it was glorious. It was just what I wanted. Everything else was awful.

I disliked the people – I'm sure they were Nazis later. The work was very boring: cooking, tidying, washing up. I was just the cheap housemaid. I wasn't learning forestry. My father was having to pay quite a lot for my "training" and it was pointless. I lost all my courage; I felt that I could not get on with anyone and that everything was false. And I was all alone. This got better when a governess came to teach their daughter, Lotte. The governess and I became friends. She loved Brahms and Schubert, and we sang together, went for walks and talked endlessly. Lotte was always with us.

It was dreadfully cold. Ever obedient to my mother's fresh air principles, I left the window open at night. The water froze solid in the wash basin and broke it. And I broke a lampshade. And I caught a kind of 'flu. Then one day I was instructed to take the young sons' boots to the cobbler to be mended, and I went on strike. I refused, saying the boys could take them themselves. That was it. There was a row and without more ado I left the house, taking my leave only from the governess, dragged my suitcase to the station and sat there for many hours, until at last a train to Berlin came. I was very ill when I arrived. Aunt Lutchen met me by chance and described, years later, how frozen, starved, wretched and intimidated I looked. I was put to bed straight away, there were no reproaches, not even when a letter from the forester's wife arrived enumerating my shortcomings. At Father's behest, Hövi wrote in reply: "Kindly send an account of how much you consider is owing to you for the broken wash basin etc." The account never came.

Next came a sewing course. Father had to pay one month in advance. After one week I fell seriously ill with tonsillitis. When I recovered, I started again, and again I fell ill; the same thing happened three times. So nothing came of that. But I had enjoyed the little time I had spent there. I cannot describe how nice everyone was to me: they were all much older and I was really spoilt. Of course I knew that no one there must ever know that I was a "communist" and a Jew; they were all officers' daughters and the like who were sewing their trousseaus. However, in those three start-ups I did manage to produce a nightdress for Mother.

So then I entered the Brevitz Commercial College and that was another very enjoyable time. Again I had two superb teachers: Frau Unbehagen, from the Baltic, possibly the ugliest woman I have ever seen, but a great, wonderful personality; and Frau Julius Bab. I entered a world which I loved and understood and where I was accepted at once as an "equal", invited to visit Frau Bab at her home, where I met my dear Ina Rüppel, a general's daughter, who was my close friend for years, till the Nazis separated us.

I finished the course at the Commercial College with very good reports (except in book-keeping) – and fell ill again. I had a sore throat; but my father, the renowned ear-nose-throat specialist, refused to look into it and my tonsils became badly inflamed. I was really ill and in great pain. Blood poisoning was a possibility. Hövi was desperate and did her best to nurse me. Sometimes I would wake up to find my father sobbing at my bedside and saying loudly: "I've killed her!" Well, obviously it was not that bad. After some weeks I was well enough to sit up in bed. Often my friend Nina Lachmann or her sister Vera was sitting beside me, quiet, and attentive, helping me to sit up or to have a drink, and disappearing again just as quietly and kindly. They were patients of my father's. Aunt Hedchen came too, and suddenly I felt as if I was not so unpopular after all. Mother wrote, very concerned, urging me to come to Freiburg to recover and, now that I had completed the commercial course so successfully, she would find me a tip-top job. So that was agreed. But a little while before I was to go, I heard that Father wanted to sell Marielly. I felt like Eliza in "Uncle Tom's Cabin". My dear kind Frau Bab, to whom I poured out my heart, offered to have Marielly till I went to Freiburg and to bring her to me on the train. And so it happened. No matter how Father raged, I would not tell him where I had hidden her. When I called to see Frau Bab, how often I would find her lying on her sofa with Marielly fast asleep on top of her. "Ssh," she would whisper, "she's asleep." Marielly had a wonderful time in that family, though they lived in Potsdam Road with no garden and no park anywhere. But when I left, Frau Bab brought the dog to me herself on the station as promised, in a rucksack.

Mother was not so thrilled to have the dog; after all, we lived up four flights of stairs, and she was the one who would be looking after her most of the time. I planned a week's cycling tour with Marielly in the Black Forest, but I had hardly been going for half an hour when she was run over and killed. Only those who have had a dog can understand what that did to me. For her it was a very quick end.

Freiburg itself was lovely – the mountains, the glorious nature: everything could have been very nice. Mother had managed to set up a really good home for us, and we generally had friends staying with us – Sonia, or Lisa, or Eva Berg. And I started working in an office. But I was absolutely useless at work, could not type a single word without making a mistake, and was in a chronic state of panic. It was no bad thing for me when I was very soon dismissed, along with many others, because of the economic crisis. I got another job straight away, in a very dubious outfit, but there too I was very soon sacked, for insubordination, I think it was. It dawned on me that I could never live in the commercial world, and one night it came to me like a revelation: I had to be a nurse.

What a row that caused! I was told in no uncertain terms that I was absolutely unsuited for nursing, I would be overwhelmed with pity for the suffering of the sick, but this time I stuck to my guns. I had a passionate desire to work for "society", to devote myself to an ideal. I was too young to start the nurses' training course, and I had to earn some money to get myself some underwear — so I got another job. This was 1923, the time of the great inflation after the war. At first we were paid by the week, then daily, then twice daily, and had to run off at once to buy something. In the lunch break I could afford to get two vests; if I left it till evening it would only be two handkerchiefs. This was the way the German state got out of paying back its war loans. It ruined the middle classes, the pensioners and so on – savings were wiped out. There were no end of suicides. My grandfather died, and in due course I received my legacy of 25000 marks – for which I could buy – in midsummer in the Black Forest – just two pounds of cherries.'

*****

'Then I met Günther Zuntz again – the boy I had played with at Walkemühle, son of my mother's friend Leo, who had studied medicine with her for a time. He became a gynaecologist and had a successful clinic in Berlin, where all the rich women went to have their babies. He was a kind and generous man, and visited the poor in the dreary flats in north Berlin and would often treat them for nothing, caring, comforting, helping; he was loved and respected by everybody. His father, Nathan Zuntz, was regarded as the founder of physiology in Germany – though, being a Jew, he was not able to become a professor, but was officially only a veterinary surgeon. Still, despite these restrictions, he did pioneering work on high altitude physiology, using his own body as a guinea pig, and worked out many things that were important during the war, such as the maximum load a soldier could be expected to carry while marching. Leo was his only son; he also had two daughters. Leo married Edith, who was not Jewish. They too had one son – Günther – and two daughters, Dora and Leonie. Leo had an affair with a nurse, and when he was at the front in the 1914–18 war, he sent all his letters home for safe-keeping – including the ones from the nurse. He was a bit naive. Of course Edith read them. The result was a suicide attempt by Edith;*

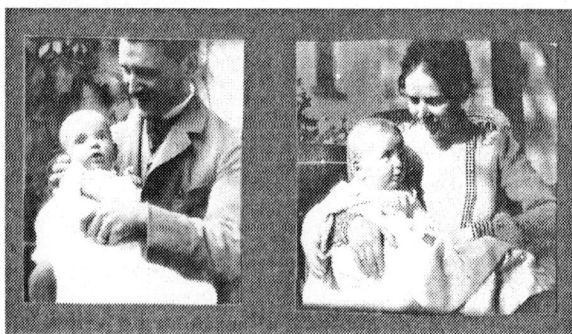

Leo and Edith Zuntz with baby Günther, 1902

Günther, still a young boy, had to run through the streets in the night to find a doctor. For years she did not speak to her husband, who lived on bended knee. But in time Edith came round.

In the end, when the Nazis made him, like all Jews, wear a yellow badge, she insisted on wearing one too: this required great courage. He had made no secret of being a Jew by his ancestry, but felt himself to be a German, a Christian, a European. Like all the liberal Jews, he got his full share of insults. He was no longer permitted to have a maid or a receptionist – who were more friends than employees – because he might rape them; he was no longer permitted to treat his poor patients because they were "Aryans" and therefore too good for him to touch; he could only treat Jewish patients. Thank God he died before the worst happened, and Edith came to England as a widow.

Günther was not only the only son and the eldest child, he was handsome, athletic, highly intelligent, and exceptionally musical. He was the apple of his parents' eyes. He was given everything imaginable: books, visits to the theatre and the opera, travel, music lessons, and love, love, love. Edith taught herself Greek, so as to be able to read the classics with him, and held "philosophical mornings" with him in the Tiergarten at 6 a.m. One of his teachers in Berlin once said to her: "Your son is a genius! He does not need to work: he knows it all." Edith took him out of that school without more ado and entered him in the most demanding classical grammar school in Berlin, where he had to work hard; but was soon top there, too. Her dream was that he would be an eminent classical scholar one day.

Why was he in Freiburg? He was staying in a sanatorium, really a kind of mental hospital, called the Rebhaus. He had been making such heavy weather of puberty that his parents thought he must be disturbed. His mother could not understand why her adored son should be so difficult: clearly he needed treatment.

We had known each other since our earliest childhood, but had never taken much notice of each other. Now we fell in love with each other, quite suddenly: both of us were overwhelmed by a great passion. We wanted to get married, at once. There was a deafening outcry – his family were outraged, and my mother also thought it ill-advised, too, less because I was unworthy of this genius, as his mother thought, but because he, and I, of course, were much too immature and flighty; moreover she felt we were temperamentally unsuited to each other. However, he decided not to go back to Berlin, but to continue his studies in Freiburg. This was ascribed to my evil influence and never forgiven. In Berlin he had the most famous Greek teachers and was their star pupil. Still, he got his Abitur with top marks in everything at school in Freiburg, in due course.

When Günther and I decided that we were in love, he wrote to his girl friends and I to a certain Wandervogel called Klaus Peter, telling them of *our decision. Klaus Peter was the son of a very rich family. One day I had received a love letter from him. At first I was not sure – was this a love letter or not? I showed it to various girls in the Wandervogel, and they were not sure either; but when I showed it to one of our leaders, Lizi, she flew into a terrible rage and told me I was unworthy of such a great and pure love. Thereupon I decided that I was in love with Klaus Peter too; but that was as far as it went. In all those years I only saw him about four times and only spoke to him once when we were alone, and then neither of us could think of anything to say.*

So now I wrote to him, to tell him that Günther and I were in love, and to my surprise I got a most beautiful letter in reply from him, though I had not seen him for months, full of platonic love and tearful renunciation. I showed this letter to Günther – who felt that he ought to be the generous one and leave me so that I could "return" to Klaus Peter. This made me feel certain that Günther was the only one for me and that Klaus Peter and I could only bring each other misery. So I persuaded Günther not to give me up.

I loved Günther more than I can say, believed in him, and made a sort of fetish of him, rather as his mother did. He was so gifted, so blessed with understanding, so beautiful, that there could be no doubt that one day he would be a revelation to the world. I did not really want to marry him, feeling instinctively that it would be catastrophic; yet I sensed that it was unavoidable, and being in love, of course I hoped all would be well, despite my fears. We started to have sex rather early and I daresay without any enjoyment, tormented by the constant fear of pregnancy. We were both virgins, which was not good: our previous affairs had been platonic, and it is always better if one partner is experienced in love-making; better still, both.'

Nurse and Student – the young lovers

'I reached the age required to start nursing training, and got a place at Dortmund. It was a great and wonderful experience, but I was torn between my loyalty to the work, and to Günther.

We spent a "honeymoon" by Lake Constance, in ravishingly beautiful country, but I was tormented not only by the fear of pregnancy, and of being discovered to be unmarried, but also of being inadequate for this brilliant man, sexually and generally. He was very downcast too. If only we had realised that a trial marriage should be just that, and leave one free to choose, being wiser, if not happier, by experience. But we felt we had committed ourselves; if one of us was deserted by the other we would lose all our self-esteem.

In Dortmund I developed a serious boil and had to be operated on. I was told later that when I was under the anaesthetic I had smashed the glass instrument table and "said terrible things". As soon as I had partly recovered the matron – who had always been nice to me before and had taken an interest in me – told me curtly that I had to leave at once. My ward sister was as amazed as I was, and I wanted to die. The matron was a friend of the matron in Günther's father's private clinic, and I feel sure now that my disastrous exit from the Dortmund hospital was thanks to Günther's mother Edith's machinations. She was passionately opposed to my relationship with her adored son. However, I did not die, and the assistant matron, who did not understand why I had to leave either, got me another place in Berlin Lichtenberg. She arranged everything for me, even got me my ticket for the train, as I did not have enough money. I earned one mark a day, the same as in Dortmund, but I got free board and lodging and managed very well, except when big expenses came along.

Lichtenberg was a very strict hospital, and some of the ward sisters were demons, but I enjoyed nursing, and I had a very nice room-mate, Hermine. She was engaged to a friend of Günther's (they tormented each other for years but did not marry in the end). Then Günther came to Berlin, to spend his vacation with his parents, and I was desperate, knowing how much I loved him, but convinced that our parents were right and that we should not marry. Death seemed to be the only way out. I did not want to kill myself outright as this would have been such a shock for Günther and for my family; but I wanted to die. I was working on the TB ward, and I tried to catch TB. To weaken myself I drank morphine, not that I was addicted, just a desperate girl.

I was ill, and wretched. But I did not get TB, I got pregnant.'

Chapter 12

Oma's letters to Mu at this time show that she knew Mu was feeling ill and unhappy at the hospital. She begs her to come home to her in Freiburg to rest and recuperate. But clearly she has no idea what the real reason is; because, as Mu writes in her memoirs:

'Of course we did not tell anyone that we had sinned and were expecting a child. Günther was very good and did not hesitate for a moment: of course we must get married at once. He told his parents that we were getting married, though not the reason why. They were furious and tried to forbid it. When I told her my mother, in August 1925, she too advised against it; but if we were determined, I should come home to her anyway and prepare my dowry, or "bottom drawer".

She told me that she had had no money from my father for seven months; in fact, Marianne, who was studying medicine, was going to take him to court, as he had a legal duty to pay for her professional training. Since he had paid for my secretarial course, and the other interrupted courses as well, I had no further claim on him; and certainly if I married before I was of age, without his permission, he would not be under any obligation to me. So Mother urged us to wait until things improved – and we agreed.

But I was so distracted and absent-minded that my ward sister noticed and I was told to go and see the director of the hospital. Probably everyone guessed that I was pregnant, but I was sure that nobody knew anything. The professor was very kind and asked me why I was in such a state. I could not answer, just broke down in floods of tears. He asked me to explain my state, but I could not say anything. When I managed to stop weeping I got up and said I would leave at once.'

They waited to get married until Mu's 21st birthday, 25 October 1925, when she was of age and did not have to ask anyone's permission. Then she joined Günther at the Odenwaldschule: he had started teaching there and was feeling very happy. It was a progressive coeducational boarding school, founded in 1910 by Paulus and Edith Geheeb, who still directed it: a school which was also a community, run on completely democratic lines, with a profound belief

Part of the Odenwaldschule

in humanity, dedicated to help each child develop his or her unique personality. 'I am living among gods' Günther had written to Mu. Here he could
expound the lofty ideals of classical antiquity, which the Geheebs acknowl-
edged were the source of European culture.

Twenty years later, I spent a year in the school the Geheebs had founded
in Switzerland in 1934, refusing to stay in Germany when the Nazis were in
power; and I think I understand my father's enthusiasm for the
Odenwaldschule. I shall have more to say about this later in the story (I
hadn't been born yet!).

Marriage did not make Mu happy. She felt deeply ashamed, in fact:
guilty, sinful, for having become pregnant out of wedlock. She was well
aware of what happened to single mothers not so long ago – the tragic fate
of Gretchen in Goethe's *Faust*, which she had read with Hövi, for instance –
and neither her mother nor her mother-in-law left her in any doubt as to the
shamefulness of her condition when they were finally told about it at
Christmas. So though they had two lovely rooms in the Odenwaldschule,
with a wide view over the hills and woods, her heart was desolate. But her
mother-in-law (who had refused to come to the wedding) mellowed
enough to send her a book, *Our Child in Wool*, and she started knitting.
And never stopped for the rest of her life. Then another disaster struck, as
she describes in her memoirs:

*'Günther and I went skiing when the snow was very thin, and he fell and
tore the meniscus in his knee. Little did we know then that that torn meniscus was to dominate our lives for years to come. It was very painful and, at
the orthopaedic clinic in Heidelberg, his knee was opened and the loose
meniscus was removed. The wound would not heal, and I was told that this
probably meant that he had TB. That was a very miserable time. I visited
him every week, leaving the Odenwaldschule in the early morning when it
was still dark to walk to the station, which took three-quarters of an hour,
and not returning until after dark. Otherwise I stayed in my room, so that
none of the children might see that I was pregnant – because what would the
parents say, said Edith Geheeb, if the wife of one of their teachers was so
obviously pregnant so soon after marriage?*

*When it became apparent that Günther would not be well for months,
and could not work, his parents took him home to care for him. And in January the Geheebs told me that I would have to leave, as they needed the
rooms for another teacher. Where could I go? My mother refused
point-blank to have me stay with her: what would the neighbours say? I
wished I was an elephant and could be pregnant for eighteen months and
protect my child from this cruel world. Mother arranged for me to go to stay
with her friends Lilli and Julius Ehrlich at a farm called the Winkelhof, near
Lake Constance, lovely people, who were caring for fourteen homeless street
children from Berlin.*

I travelled to the Winkelhof alone with my heavy luggage and even heavier heart, feeling guilty towards my unborn child, for whom I had no secure nest. I was to stay in a hut that Lilli had built in the grounds for her mother, when she came to stay with them in the summer. Fine in summer, but not when I arrived. Sometimes the snow was so deep that I could not open the door and had to climb out and in through the window. I had my meals with Lilli, but most of the time I was alone in the hut, or gathering wood for my stove. The wet wood did not burn well, and it was heavy. The stove had a chimney which zigzagged through the whole hut so as not to waste any warmth. A good idea, of course – only at every bend, liquid soot leaked out. I collected it in old tins all over the floor; and as I had no mirror I did not know for some time that the liquid had dropped on my hair and everything. When the snow began to melt, the mud was ankle deep, and on my way to the house in the dark I often lost my shoes and could not find them again till the morning.

Children at the Winkelhof

When spring came, and the daphne was in bloom, things looked up a bit. I felt sure that everything would turn out all right, although we had no money. Günther was well enough to start a two-year practical unpaid teaching course in Marburg; his father and my mother were going to have to provide for us. I was happy at the prospect of living in that lovely town. Friends from the Odenwaldschule rented a flat for us, and in March I was summoned to go and get it ready. Günther was still in Berlin with his parents. Julius Ehrlich took me to the station in his horse-drawn cart – the road consisted of ruts and puddles – and he looked at me anxiously. "Don't have your baby here on the road!" Peter – the unborn baby – was sensible and stayed put.

I arrived in Marburg late at night and almost penniless, as usual. I carried my luggage to Uferstrasse 12, where there was no electricity and no heating. I stumbled about in stygian gloom until I found something that felt like a bed, fell down on it, and slept like a log – Peter still being sensible.

Morning came and revealed a scene of utter desolation: dirt, torn curtains, cobwebs – evidently the place had not been lived in for years. I counted my money and went out to buy soap powder, a scrubbing brush, a saucepan, a kettle, two cups, and some bread. Then I set to work. For the next four days solid I was on my knees, scrubbing away at the ingrained dirt. When it was more or less done, the landlord appeared and told me that I had to move out at once or the rent would be trebled: the university term was beginning, and he could easily let the flat to students for much more. (He didn't say: now that I had got it clean!) I did not know what to do, and sent a telegram to Günther. He came promptly.

I shall never forget the moment when, hanging over the banisters, I saw him approach, a cripple, pale as death, on two sticks, evidently in great pain. He had to go to bed at once, and I set out to find another place.

Luckily I had two Wandervogel friends in Marburg, and one of them, Elsbeth Braun, got us a small room in the small house on the Schlossberg where she herself was living. Elsbeth was romantic and completely crazy and one of the most beautiful people I have ever known, with a classical Greek profile and long chestnut tresses. All the boys, including Achim, my sister's intended, were in love with her at one time or another. Her father was a very conservative Lutheran pastor in Berlin who disapproved of the Wandervogel and tried to prevent her meeting any of us. However, she managed to find and marry a communist leader in Berlin, who was in and out of prison, which, she said, was fine in winter, as it meant she could save on heating and lighting, but she got quite frantic when she had to be without him in the summer too. However, when I met her again in Marburg, she had just discovered that she was a lesbian. Her communist husband Braun had gone to Russia and disappeared, so she felt quite free. She had been taking a course in rhythmic gymnastics, which were in vogue at the time, at Loheland near Fulda, and she told me about the elated and superior emotions she had experienced there, especially with one girl called Dorle. She and Dorle had evolved some kind of telepathy, so when for instance she went to the toilet she always made sure to sit there very decorously in case Dorle happened to look in just then from Loheland…

There was only one bed in the room she let us have, and a very narrow sofa. Günther was really very ill and went to bed at once, while I – with Peter still inside – had to sleep on the sofa, fenced in with chairs to prevent my falling off in the night. However, this room had been promised to a student, so we soon had to move out. Now my mother came to our help. She knew a professor in Marburg, who was spending a year in France, and she arranged for us to have two rooms in the attic of his very big house for a moderate rent. Günther spent nearly all his time in bed, but as the school term approached he had to crawl out and practise using his stiff and very painful leg. He was visited regularly by a masseur.

I had the use of a gas cooker in the cellar, so you can imagine how often I had to go up and down all those stairs carrying trays. On one occasion I brought up a boiled egg. Günther wanted it mashed in a cup – a "Russian" egg – and expected me to go down again to fetch a cup and a spoon. I demurred. Then he said I was ungrateful and selfish and forgetting how much he had sacrificed on my behalf. My heart was heavy. I hoped Peter would wait a few more weeks. He did.

The masseur saw me climb onto a table to fix a lampshade and advised me not to do so any more. The following night I went into labour, and Günther had to go to a neighbour's house to call an ambulance. The ambulance driver was the masseur! He laughed and said he had expected this.

Peter was born on 21 April 1926, in the afternoon, healthy, strong, and entirely angelic. I was overwhelmed with happiness. I looked at him as into a deep well reflecting heavenly light. When we came home, and he cried at night, I was desperate. What is making my child cry? What grief is in his mind? I had worked on the maternity ward at Lichtenberg, but I was an utterly incompetent mother, trembling with fear that my child could be unhappy. But Günther was furious whenever Peter cried, and threw his shoes against the door – I can still feel the shock at this display of unkindness to my child.

Günther considered his work at the grammar school as a student teacher degrading (he wanted to be a university professor), but soon he was greatly admired and loved by his pupils. I still believe teaching was his greatest gift. When the summer holidays came, his parents invited him to join them in their newly acquired summerhouse in Bavaria. I did not mind. It meant I could concentrate on my incomparable child, who stood outside in the fresh air all day, while I stood by the window listening for the slightest sound from him. I would dash down to take him in before the other house occupants could complain. I could hardly ever go for a walk with him, for I had no pram, only a lovely crib lent to me by a friend's mother. Later an aunt of Günther's sent me an old-fashioned pram which had no tyres and made a terrible noise in the street.

Günther had left me with a long reading list. He had discovered how uneducated I was when we were in the Odenwaldschule and had started teaching me the rudiments of grammar. He was very pleased when I developed an interest in history, so now I had to read twelve volumes of medieval history and summarise them, to show I had read them properly. I cannot describe how tired I was, but it did not occur to me not to do as Günther expected, so I trained myself to sleep for half an hour, read for half an hour, and so on, and I managed to get through my task in time. And I enjoyed it; my thirst was not sated; I wanted more and more history books. Meanwhile Günther was working on his PhD thesis. It was about Hölderlin's translation of Pindar's odes, and in this way I was introduced to classical literature, which I also enjoyed immensely.

But the professor who owned the house was returning from France in the autumn, so we had to move again. We found a place with tall pines by the window and a wonderful view across the Lahn valley and "straight into eternity".

I cannot tell you how cold it was that winter. The hot water bottle froze solid in my bed. I had to do a lot of coal carrying, and had to cook in the cellar, so I was taking things up and down the stairs all day again, and was soon in a bad state. One morning, when I had laid the fire, I found I could not get up off my knees, and I had to wait for someone to pass on the stairs outside to help me up. Once I was on my feet I was all right again. But it got worse, and I was so unsteady that I was afraid I might drop Peter, so I washed him on the floor and did most of my work on all fours.

The wife of Günther's headmaster heard of my helpless state and came to visit me. I sobbed as I told her that I was afraid Peter was not being fed properly and so on. So she told me about her firstborn, a sickly child. The doctor told her that she had to sterilise everything the child touched, plates, pots, everything – which she did, obediently. Then one day she heard a gurgling noise in the corridor, and found the well-sterilised child gulping the dirty water from the floor bucket which the maid had left there. She rushed him to the doctor, who had a good laugh and said: Well, if he survives this, his clothes and cutlery do not need to be sterilised any more. And he did survive. It was a great comfort to me to talk with that woman, who then arranged for me to go to hospital, where I was diagnosed as having encephalitis. At first Peter was in the room with me, but since I was unable to look after him he was taken to the children's hospital, just two streets away. In the night – the first night without him beside me – I thought I could hear him crying. I decided to go to the children's hospital, tumbled out of bed, crawled to the door, which was ajar – I could not have reached the door handle – and along the corridor to the stairs – and fell down them headlong. I was found there and taken back to bed, but all the time I was screaming that Peter was crying and I had to go to him. Hallucinations was the diagnosis, and a psychiatrist was called in and had a long talk with me, and also with Günther, who really saved me from the lunatic asylum, because when he was asked if he had noticed that I heard voices he replied innocently: "Yes, of course, her hearing is quite normal."

While I was in hospital, Edith came to Marburg to look after her son, and she also hired a daily help for me. She came to the hospital with Günther to fetch me, and then we went to the children's hospital together to pick up Peter. Of course he was looking well, clean and well-fed, but seeing him I had another fit of weeping. I felt he had changed; that he was reproaching me for leaving him with strangers; that he no longer cared for me. Sheer nonsense, of course, as I dimly realised myself, but I was so distraught that I could not control myself.

Edith left the next morning and I tried to cope. The daily help was extremely autocratic and I feared her almost as much as the ward sisters at Lichtenberg. In the end my mother invited me to Freiburg to recuperate. Frau Rohde, whose flat was below our attic, the Heights of Erwin, expressed her surprise that the child was so big when I had not been married long, and left me with a knowing nod of disapproval. While I was there, Günther got a *new job in Cassel.*

I was too shy to go out, except to take Peter for a walk. This meant carrying him down four flights of stairs. Once I was sitting on a bench, exhausted, and shivering in the cold wind. Peter of course was well wrapped up and warm in his pram – but an elderly lady scolded me for letting the child stand outside in such cold weather; and I cried and cried, having once again been found wanting in my care for this precious and unique child. I stayed in Freiburg for a couple of weeks, not feeling that I belonged there at all. My mother worked in an office all day, my sister was studying for her finals, my brother was away studying agriculture. However, when I returned to Marburg I felt much stronger and more competent. Günther went to Cassel, and I stayed in a room in a village with Peter. There was forest all round, and I spent my days walking with Peter. He was a toddler by now, very demanding, and as I had nothing else to do, I became his slave.

After some months Günther found us a three-room flat in Kragenhof near Cassel. It was incredibly beautiful. The River Fulda was just under our windows, and all day and night you could hear the rushing river and the rustling trees. I became pregnant again, and this time there were no scathing comments – even Edith only said: "As expected." Long silence. "Better not to have an only child." I caught a kidney infection and was in hospital with it when Maleen was born, a little prematurely, but strong and healthy, and at least as lovely as Peter. She was the only one of my children whose birth was not greeted with reproaches and dire warnings. But I was ill for quite some time, and my mother came to look after Günther and Peter. She found Peter's whining and his difficult temperament trying. In her eyes he was just terribly spoilt, and surely he was, and very demanding. But she was delighted with Maleen. She visited me in hospital – no reproaches, no complaints, just pleasant. I relaxed and took my time getting well again.

The summer in Kragenhof with my two beautiful children was perhaps the happiest time of my life. Maleen was an exhibition baby, beautiful, healthy and peaceful. Günther took her to his heart. She spent all day on the vine-covered veranda and every bit of sunshine was for her. I was afraid that Peter was being neglected.

When she was about a year old, we had to move into Cassel, and found a hinterhaus, a back house, very ugly, but with a tree in front of the window, a large kitchen, one large room and three smaller ones, all along a wide corridor, ideal for the children to romp. All the big boys from Günther's school who came to see us fell in love with little Maleen. We even had a swing in the corridor. Our respective parents must have given us the money to buy furniture, second-hand, of course, apart from a few things my mother gave me: my grandmother's beautiful writing table, a large table, an easy chair. Everything seemed just perfect to me, except there was no bathroom, and the toilet was half way up the stairs, which was embarrassing at times.

Irene Gill

Günther's appointment at the Friedrichsgymnasium, the grammar school, was quite well paid. It was a famous school: our revered Kaiser had been educated there. In fact, this was one of the high points in Günther's life. Contrary to his expectations, he found he loved teaching the classics, and he inspired his pupils so much that they decided to perform "The Persians" by Aeschylus, in Greek.

This play deals with the war in which the Greeks had defeated the much more powerful Persians. But it is not a triumphalist celebration of victory. The defeated Persians, the enemies of the Greeks, the aggressors, are honoured, and the whole emphasis of the play is on the Persian women suffering the loss of their loved ones. The play shows Greek civilisation at its best; and it was just what Germany needed. Remember that Germany had lost the war, and the victorious powers heaped abuse and shame on us – even today I tremble when I think of the humiliation we suffered as a nation. That gave rise to the hyper-nationalism of the Nazis.

For about a year we lived and breathed "The Persians", everything was subordinated to the play, costumes and masks were all home-made – there was a very gifted art teacher at the school. The boys were in our house all the time, always welcome, always pleasant and agreeable. For them, it was one of the greatest experiences of their lives; several, like Boehncke and Agricola, got in touch with us after the war, and told us so. In 1982 Günther was invited to Germany for a class reunion.

"The Persians" was performed in the City Theatre. There were reviews in all the papers; it was transferred to Düsseldorf to one of Germany's leading theatres, and met with a tremendous response everywhere.

When it was all over, I said, optimistically: "Now we can live a normal life for once." "Not at all," Günther replied. "Tomorrow we start rehearsing Seven Against Thebes."

This is a very different play. It is about hostile brothers fighting for the possession of Thebes. It consists of fourteen long speeches describing battles, and was not a good choice – but Günther felt like Faust, never satisfied, always striving. In order to work with the boys without distraction, he rented a youth hostel called Tannenburg, near Cassel, for the summer, where they lived a Spartan life, and the forest echoed with Greek verses. Their enthusiasm never flagged. I stayed with the children about an hour's walk away with the Reemans at their house, the Engelsburg: another excellent couple.

Felix Reeman came from Estonia. During the war he had been in the Russian army, but he was a pacifist and got through the war without ever firing a shot. Just before the war he had got engaged to a girl from Holstein called Dora. As soon as the war was over they got married and used all Dora's money to buy the Engelsburg, a rambling old house without water or electricity, overgrown with clematis and roses and far from human

115

habitations. Here these two townsfolk, with no experience of rural life, started to scratch a living from the soil, gathering wood from the forest, milking their two goats, and leading a primitive but spiritual life. Felix looked like a scarecrow, haymaking all by himself at five o'clock in the morning, or tending his exemplary vegetable plot. Dora was very energetic and practical; it was an ideal marriage, and they managed. They had two sons, Olev and Ivar.

Peter in particular loved the Reemans dearly and when the holidays were over he implored me to let him stay. I was quite glad to do so – he had not yet started school – knowing that the atmosphere would do him good. One night I cycled out to see him. It took six hours, but it was wonderful. The corn was tall, the meadows smelled of hay, the moon and stars were bright, birds made sleepy sounds in their dreams. When I arrived, Peter was in the garden, playing with a little cart. He shrank from me. "Have you come to take me away?" "No, you can stay here." "Then you can come in." I stayed for three hours and cycled back.

We spent all our holidays there, in a room with a big veranda, where we slept in the summer. One of the schoolboys, Agricola, came to see us, climbed up from the outside and found us all asleep on the veranda; so he lay down and slept, too; we were all very surprised to see him there when we woke up. For a time Peter attended the village school in Süss with the Reemans' son Olev; but my attempt later to repay the Reemans for all they had done for Peter, by having Olev to stay with us, so that he could go to the grammar school, was a total failure – he could not fit in or keep up with the work, though I tried to help him with his homework; so at Whitsun he went back to the village school.

The performances of the "Seven Against Thebes" were another resounding success. After some time, Günther was offered, and accepted, a permanent and pensionable teaching post in Marburg, so we moved back there. For a short time, we lived in a lovely flat with a view from each window, of trees and hills. But not for long.'

Chapter 13

From Mu's memoirs:

> *'In 1932 I was pregnant again for the third time. Günther was simply horrified. Not because he did not want any children, but because the times were so terribly threatening, with the hordes of unemployed and the Nazis going from strength to strength. He wanted me to have an abortion; I refused. I said I would leave him rather than destroy an unborn child.'*

Well, in 1932 it was not unreasonable to argue that that was no time to be having babies, and half-Jewish ones at that, in Germany. It was foreseeable that the Nazis would win the next election. Anyway, I'm sure that was not the only reason why my parents split up. My father's knee was very bad again: so bad that he could not work. He went back to his parents again to have it looked after. They gave up their flat. My father started collaborating on a major edition of the writings of the Church Fathers (people like Origen), the Prophetologium, with a Danish professor called Carsten Hoeg. This was far from his true ambition: he was not a Christian, and though Greek was used in these writings, it was not the classical Greek of his deep love. However, Hoeg was a very good friend, and later made it possible for him to get out of Germany and live in Denmark.

As for my mother, left alone with two children and a third on the way, she took the children to stay with her good friends, the Reemans, again. She writes:

> *'My mother paid for us, as I was penniless. The children were happy, and I was glad to be with such good friends. As autumn approached we had to leave; there was no heating in the room and I was getting closer to the time of the birth; so it was back to Mother, back to Freiburg. Mother found a three-room flat for us near her own place in Freiburg, and we settled in quite cosily.*
>
> *Peter went to school and Maleen to a nursery school — until the Nazi influence, already very strong in Freiburg, led to her being ostracised as a "non-Aryan" by both teachers and classmates. When the school went on an excursion, she was not allowed to go. She begged and begged me to let her go, thinking it was my decision; so I took her on a private excursion in the woods, with a picnic, but she was not to be comforted, especially as unfortunately her whole class passed by the spot where we were. I tried to rivet her attention with a story, but nothing helped. The only good thing was that she could speak about it, while Peter became more and more silent. He was attacked in the street, he was no longer allowed into the church, where he had been an altar boy. You have to understand that the Nazis were already*

out and about everywhere, with their flags and their barbarous shouting; you could not forget them for one moment.

Our refuge was the convent of St Lioba, on the outskirts of Freiburg, with its beautiful Italianate garden, roses, clematis and wisteria over marble staircases, white doves nesting in the little house where the priest lived. Maleen was accepted in the kindergarten, with a splendid nun, Sister Gregoria, in charge. Both children were now receiving Roman Catholic instruction, which was quite contrary to my principles; Peter became quite a fanatical Catholic, threatening me with hellfire if I did not join the Church. I didn't; but I helped them to attend mass at St Lioba, where the best kind of Catholicism was to be found, and true civilisation: it was the only "clean" place in the whole of the Nazi-besotted town.

St Lioba

One evening — it must have been 16 December, 1932 — when I fetched Maleen from St Lioba, I had a long talk with Sister Goswina, who under-stood the political situation better than I did, and she said she hoped very much that we would soon be in safety abroad. I had told her that Günther was in touch with a professor in Denmark, and might be able to go there. Then surely it would be possible for me and the children to join him there, she said. I was not so sure; but I did hope.

When we got home – our flat was on the third floor – I had a mountain of ironing to do after the children were in bed. And then the labour pains began. I just managed to get the ironing done when I realised it was time to go to the hospital. So I went down the three flights of stairs and asked our very nice landlady if she could look after the two children during the night. She agreed very kindly, and moreover her husband insisted on taking me to the hospital in his car (quite a rarity in those days). I was quite embarrassed to accept so much. I still feel grateful to those good people. I did not want to disturb my mother, who lived quite near; of course she had no car, and by now it was the middle of the night, and no one had a telephone.

I was afraid they would not let me into the hospital, being a "non-Aryan", and in fact I had to leave two days after the birth instead of staying in bed for at least a week, which was the custom in those days. The nice landlords had informed my mother, who then visited me faithfully the next day and cared for the children. She was working full-time herself, so it was very necessary for me to take over again as soon as possible.'

Well, that baby was me. I was called Gabi (among other things). My mother heaps compliments on me in her memoir: I was a good baby, Peter and Maleen were very nice with me, I hardly ever cried, and I thrived. I was used as a hot water bottle, keeping her warm while she read all ten volumes of the *History of the German Reformation* and I slept. If she had not been so dreadfully afraid of the future, that would have been a happy time.

*****

Only a few weeks later, in January 1933, the Nazis came to power, and set about implementing their programme immediately. My father, and my uncle Achim, were dismissed from their posts: no "non-Aryans" could remain in state employment. Achim found work in Persia. The fire in the Reichstag – the Parliament building in Berlin – on 27 February 1933 was held to be the work of Communists; this led to emergency measures of great brutality being taken against all Communists and their sympathisers. The triumphant Brownshirts marched through the streets, waving their swastika flags and bellowing their militaristic, anti-socialist and anti-Semitic songs; walls were daubed with their slogans; on 1 April, at the government's behest, Jewish shops were boycotted, and all papers that did not support the Nazis were banned in the interests of Gleichschaltung – switching the whole country to the Nazi line. Everyone's chief concern was to get my father out of the country as quickly as possible, as he might be called up for the army or for forced labour. It was extremely difficult to go abroad if one had no money. One simply could not get a visa – not even for a place like Bolivia – unless one had a job to go to, and even then only provided no native of that country could take the job. He was very lucky to have the work with Professor Hoeg, who made it possible for him to go to Copenhagen. And he went. It seemed wonderful. Not only was he abroad; he was actually earning money, and not as a tram conductor, but working in something not too far removed from his own field. Mu wrote and asked him to take the necessary steps to get herself and the children out as well, and to find them somewhere to live. But it took a long time. A very long time. Was he really trying? He seemed to be suffering from writer's cramp. And there was a beautiful Swedish woman. Meanwhile, Mu writes:

'Conditions became worse and worse. By 1936, Jews in Germany were no longer regarded as German citizens. They couldn't vote. They couldn't occupy any public office. A Jewish teacher couldn't teach non-Jewish students, a Jewish doctor couldn't treat non-Jewish patients; a Jewish man couldn't employ any German female under 45 years because he couldn't be trusted not to rape her. Jewish businesses were "Aryanised". Jewish passports were to be marked with a red letter J. Jewish emigrants had to pay a swingeing tax to leave Germany. They all had to adopt Jewish names, whatever their religion: Israel for men, Sara for women. The Nuremberg Laws made it a crime for a Jew to marry a German, as both my mother and my father-in-law had: in both families, Hempel and Zuntz, Aryan blood was defiled by the vile Jewish blood that was irremediably mixed up in the children. There were hideous anti-Semitic caricatures on walls and even on the ground and scratched into the sand: I could not prevent the children seeing them, and Peter stared at them, pale and serious. As yet, no one knew just how much worse the situation for Jews would get; but the need to get out of Germany grew more and more desperate.

One day I plucked up my courage and went to the priest and said: "We are in great danger here. What can I do if the mob comes for us?" He replied: "If or when you feel the time has come, come to me with your children. I have a car. In less than an hour I can get you to Switzerland." I am sure he would have kept his word, had it been necessary.

For a time we shared a little house with my mother, but in the end we found a house in Günterstal, a suburb of Freiburg, where we had the basement, Mother the ground floor, and the landlady the top floor. Gabi was developing into a happy and very pretty child; everybody liked her. She was a great comfort and a joy to me, while all the time I was so very worried about all three of them. Continuing her career as a hot water bottle, she was put into each of the beds in turn, never waking up.

Of course the landlady asked where my husband was, and when I said "Abroad", she became suspicious. Then she invited me to go to the National Socialist Women's Group with her, which I had to refuse, of course, and so the terrible secret came out. We knew we could not stay much longer. The children had to go to school, but their homework was no longer taken in; they were not allowed to look into the schoolbooks; they had to walk in the gutter, not on the pavement; Peter, who was a devout Catholic at that time, was not allowed to enter a church, and when the class were taught about the Crucifixion, he had to stand outside in the corridor: when the boys came out at the end of the lesson, they cast baleful looks at him, as if he, personally, was to blame for Christ's suffering and death...

Only a garden lay between us and our neighbours. In the evening the old woman used to stand by the fence with a copy of "Der Stürmer", the Nazi paper, tucked under her arm and yell: "Jew brats, I'm going to burn your *house down tonight," and the like. I had to put up thick curtains in the children's room, and sit on the floor, so that my shadow could not be seen, with a candle, and read stories to them out loud so that they could not hear the shouting. When I took them to school in the morning they would run ahead, but our neighbour would come out with a big broom to sweep the road, because Jewish children had been walking along it.*

Our only relief was in the convent of St Lioba, where manners were still civilised; in fact it was absolutely lovely. The nuns refused to consider the "Jewish Question" in any way. They could still see individual human beings, not just racial types. Of course they were in great danger themselves; they never put up any Nazi flags; but they thought, like most people in Germany, that the Nazi nightmare would soon pass.

I decided to have the children baptised as Roman Catholics. I said to myself that no matter where the children go, they will always find a Catholic church and in it a point of contact. I did not want to be baptised myself, which upset Peter who was, as I have said, very church-minded at that time. After school Peter and Maleen generally came to the beautiful convent garden, and Peter had met a very nice Catholic priest, who ran the youth group and accepted Peter as a member straight away. So before we left Germany, all three children were Roman Catholics.

I said to myself: Günther had better get a bit of a move on so that we can get out of here at last. But he did nothing. I would have to go to Copenhagen to persuade him of the urgency of the problem. My mother had gone to Persia, to visit Marianne and her family. It was not easy for me to find somewhere for the children to stay while I was away. In the end I found a Protestant orphanage which was willing to look after all three of them, although they were half-Jewish; but no one must know about it, or the home would be closed down. I knew that that was not idle talk.

I arrived in Copenhagen alone, and was not met, though Günther knew when I was coming. Many people in Denmark speak German, so I was able to ask my way to Charlottenlund, where Günther was living very comfortably with a nice elderly Jewish gentleman. Günther was very pleased to see me since, he said, this meant we could now go to the German Embassy to start divorce proceedings; he wanted to marry his Swedish lady friend. I was shattered. I told him he was living in cloud-cuckoo-land if he really thought we could risk going to a Nazi authority, and suggested we might have somewhat more urgent problems to discuss. I assured him I would not interfere in his Swedish idyll, provided the children did not know about it. The thought that my children, in a foreign country, might see their father in the street with another woman was intolerable. He complained bitterly about my bourgeois petty-mindedness. He did not believe that our position in Germany was really dangerous, but in the end I convinced him. He promised he would have everything ready for us in a few weeks: papers, permits, and somewhere to live.'

*****

As for Oma – she seems to have been totally unconcerned by the rising tide of Nazism; as if it did not affect her at all. She hardly mentions it in her memoirs, or her generosity to my mother and us children. I think she may have been a fairly stern grandmother – Peter remembers her waiting for him at the top of the dark stairs from the basement and scaring the life out of him by giving him a resounding slap as he emerged for riding his bicycle across the garden. But she was certainly very affectionate to me, and somehow in those first few years of my life implanted a deep love of her in my heart, which time and distance did nothing to weaken.

When the opportunity arose to visit Marianne, who had gone to join her husband Achim in Persia with her two little girls in 1935, for a holiday, she seized upon it. Mu urged her to stay in Persia, in view of the Nazis' increasing persecution; but she had no intention, yet, of leaving Germany permanently, just because a pack of contemptible thugs had temporarily got into power. She never thought of herself as a Jew. So she set out to travel by train, an immense distance, via her own Danzig and Warsaw and across Russia, to Baku. She does not mention how Danzig affected her; but she recalls the journey itself vividly in her Memoirs:

'The railway journey seemed endless to me. I shared a compartment with a Dutchman who was allocated the bunk above mine. We got on extremely well. He would wait tactfully in the corridor while I got ready for the night, and then he would undress on his bunk. His trousers, dangling over the edge, served as a sign that he was still up there. Then, in accordance with our agreement, he had to get up first and go into the washroom along the corridor, so that I was not embarrassed as I got washed and dressed in our compartment. During the day we sat together peacefully on the lower bunk, talking, eating, and looking out of the window. I have never seen a more melancholy, desolate, bleak landscape than Russia outside the cities. It was completely bare, covered with reddish sand or dust. Not a tree, not a bush, not a village or a house, no animals – as far as the eye could see: nothing. Now I understand why Russian folksongs, both the melodies and the words, sound so sad, lonely, monotonous.

In Baku, on the Caspian Sea, we passengers enjoyed a huge meal, with lots of caviar, up on a hotel terrace, while we waited for the ship that was to take us to Pahlevi in Persia. My Mariannchen was to meet me there, and I had at her behest to wear a certain silvery-grey silk dress, visible and recognisable from afar, and to stand leaning against the ship's bulkhead so that she would know me at a distance. And so we fell into each other's arms. We had not seen each other for about two years. We sat talking in a restaurant garden for hours, and only remembered to charter a car when it started getting dark. I shall never forget the sunrise as we approached Teheran.

I spent some happy weeks with Marianne, Achim and their little girls, Hetta and Dudu, and then set out on the return journey. I travelled by car to Hamadan, through endless expanses of desert, to Baghdad, where I spent a few days in the home of a German doctor, until the desert, which had been softened by rain, became passable again for heavy buses. So at last I came to the Promised Land, first to Haifa, then to Jerusalem. Friends drove me all over the country, and always and every-where I saw how sharply the land inhabited and cultivated by Jews contrasted with that of the Arabs. I watched an Arab ploughing: he looked regal in his long white robe, push-ing his primitive wooden plough slowly, slowly through the sand, and at each step he trod on the hem of his robe. There was not a tree, not a bush to be seen, far and wide. I turned back to the Jewish land: orange groves laden with fruit, chicken farms, clean habitations, swift, busy hands, chil-dren's homes where dedicated carers looked after happy, well-dressed, well-fed children, while their parents worked in the fields. I

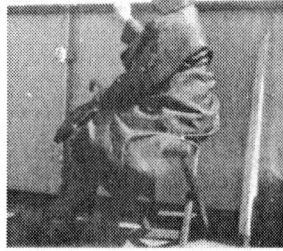

Sailing across the Caspian Sea

came to a village that re-echoed with the clucking of hens. Dignified men were riding on donkeys with baskets of eggs or milk cans attached right and left, and again and again I heard them greet each other: "Good morning, doctor!" So many of the Jewish immigrants were university people, who embraced the agricultural life without demur. I saw women who had been students in Germany climbing up ladders with hods full of bricks, or earn-ing their living as window-cleaners with a ladder and a bucket. I felt quite cheered. I believed that now Judaism would build a model state. Now, about fifteen years later, these hopes are beginning to fade. What I hear about the orthodox Eastern Jews, who still cling to medieval, even Old Testament customs and attitudes, and are now dominant there, makes me shudder.'

So her childhood prejudices prevailed!

She returned to Freiburg, where we – my mother, and my brother and sister and I – were still dependent on her and living in the same house. My father was now safely in Denmark. Oma wrote to her old friend Leo Zuntz and asked him to persuade his son to have his wife and children rejoin him and to provide for them himself – a task he had quite cheerfully left to her, Oma, all this time. Perhaps this nudge via his father had the desired effect on my father. In 1936 we left for Copenhagen at last. Now Oma moved again, to a small flat, and lived quietly, and got on with her work, as if the Nazis, who were making life more and more intolerable for her Jewish relatives and friends, had nothing to do with her. But she developed painful arthritis in her ankles.

Old Dr Rosenberg, being Jewish, had to hand his pharmaceutical company over to the chief clerk, Dr Kaiser, an 'Aryan'; he moved to Basel in Switzerland. Now Oma was the only Jewish employee among about seventy 'Aryans', who were all very friendly – though they had the usual official spy, charmingly named Betriebszellen-Obmann (works-cell-overseer): a man called Strub. He used to work down in the machine room, but now he had a place more in keeping with his new rank in the big room next to the registry as supervisor of the twenty women who filled the medicine bottles, packed them up, and so on. There was a hatch in the party wall which enabled Oma to use the telephone in there. This Nazi Strub was, until the Hitler era began, devoted, even grovelling to the Jewish directors and indeed most of the staff. Now his behaviour changed radically. For instance, he would not greet the secretaries until they had given him the Heil Hitler salute. And they did, as everyone, the entire German nation, without exception, did. No one had the courage not to use the Hitler salute – no one except my Oma (she says). People only said 'Heil Hitler' to her by mistake, and if one of the packers let it slip out accidentally she always apologised straight away: 'Oh I beg your pardon, Dr Hempel!' But Strub – who could not humble himself enough to her in the past – Strub walked past her silently. She did the same to him. But one day, when he had attended to the heating in her room, and was walking out silently, Olga called him back.

'Oh Strub' (he always had himself called Mr Strub these days) 'Strub, just come back a moment, will you?'

Dazed, indignant, he returned, and she laid into him.

'Isn't it about time we introduced a slightly more courteous tone into our dealings with each other?'

'But Dr Hempel, you won't give me the Hitler salute.'

Then she let rip.

'In the first place, I am a lady, and a lady does not greet anyone first. I have never even greeted the directors first! And as for you – remember how polite you were to me just a few months ago – and now, because someone else is in power in Berlin, you dare to insult and humiliate me! You must be mad! You are still the same man you were, and I am still the same woman, so let's try to be a bit more civilised, shall we?'

'Oh Dr Hempel, I had no idea – please – let me shake your hand. I do apologise. You are quite right, of course – we are still the same people, and I'll be more careful in future. If ever you need anything doing, you have only to open the hatch, and I'll be at your service.'

And so it was: from then on he was like a devoted page to her. Yet he could easily have had her sent to a concentration camp. But evidently her fearlessness impressed him. A little later the registry had to be spring-cleaned, so she opened the hatch.

'Strub!'

'Yes? What can I do for you?'

'Could I have some women to help me clean the registry?'

'Certainly – how many would you like?'

'Say ten. Or six would be enough.'

'Did you have any particular ones in mind?'

'Well, yes – I'd like the ones who are best at singing – for instance –'

'Oh, Dr Hempel, it would be better to ask for one from each table, otherwise they'll get jealous. They all think it's a privilege to help you clean.'

The reason for this was that while they worked she taught them new songs to sing in harmony. But all by Mendelssohn! Once they had learned the song she said:

'All right, my dears, that was fine. But from now on you mustn't sing that song any more. The composer is Jewish. I can sing it, but you can't.'

'Oh, but that's such a shame – it's a lovely song!'

'Well, there you are – you see how stupid it all is.'

Another person in the company who liked to come whenever he was free to join in the singing with her was a young man called Zeissler. He had a beautiful voice and was very musical. He joined the SS, but this did not prevent him loving and honouring Oma. She had the utmost difficulty to deter him from visiting her in her flat. She could see that he was honest and sincere, and simply did not understand the true nature of his party; so she tried to enlighten him. He listened with smiling incredulity.

'But Dr Hempel,' he said, 'You're such an intelligent woman, how can you believe all this nonsense you've been told!'

However ...

He was injured in a motor-cycle accident and had to stay in hospital for weeks. When she heard of this, she sent him a nice little parcel of good things, and was surprised when she did not get a word of thanks. When at last he was discharged he came to the company – on crutches – and his first visit was to her.

'It was very kind of you to send me those lovely biscuits and chocolates. I...I'm terribly sorry I didn't thank you for them then – but I was very grateful – and now I'd like to say thank you ...'

'You could have spared yourself feeling as embarrassed as you obviously do by sending me a little letter or even a postcard with your thanks.'

'But Doctor – you don't seem to understand – I couldn't possibly put anything in writing there ...'

'Oh, I begin to understand. You couldn't be seen to accept anything from an old lady – or rather you couldn't be seen to acknowledge receiving it – because she is Jewish?'

'Yes, you see –'

'Right, that's it. This is the end. You are a coward. I don't want to have anything to do with you any more.'

'Oh, please don't say that – I – '

'Get out!'

'Try to understand!'

She opened the door.

'I understand perfectly. Out!'

This made her understand what made this intelligent, educated, gifted people submit unquestioningly to the Nazi criminals. The national failing of the Germans, she believed, was their passion for commanding and obeying, cutting out all individual, independent thought when confronted by Authority. That as why they all bellowed 'Heil Hitler!' so merrily, even those who did not approve of the aims and the nature of National Socialism in the least.

❖❖❖❖❖

In 1936, the papers came at last that enabled my mother to go to Denmark with us children, and we went. Reinhardt was on his farm at Mellensee; Marianne and Achim and their two little girls in Persia. Oma's sister Lutka was settled in her 'eyrie', her rooms in an old tower in Positano, a village in Italy near Sorrento. The story is that she arrived at the local railway station and looked for a porter. Finally she found one, lying asleep in the sun. She poked him with the tip of her sunshade to wake him up and asked him to carry her suitcase. 'No,' he replied, 'I have already eaten today,' and went back to sleep. This, thought Lutka, is the place for me! And there indeed she stayed for the rest of her long life.

So the diaspora continued, as more and more of Oma's friends and relations were caught out by the race laws: teachers and lecturers were pensioned off, then their pensions were cancelled; if they had started their own business, that was taken from them. 'Aryans' got divorced from their Jewish partners; Aryan housemaids left their Jewish employers for fear of racial contamination; Jewish companies, like her own Rosenbergs, were 'aryanised' – taken over by non-Jewish Germans.

On 27 May 1938 she was summoned to the boardroom, where the three new, 'Aryan' bosses were sitting. They got up, introduced themselves; seated her in the only armchair – the director's – at the table; there were long speeches; greetings from old Mr Rosenberg were read out. She was to stop working on 1 July, but would get her full salary until December. She was quite happy at the prospect of being free though – after December –

penniless. She was almost 68 years old, and as soon as she was retired, in July, she set off on her travels, first to Berlin – where she met Hugo's latest partner, for whom she felt very sorry – her sister Hedwig and her cousin Jula Wolfthorn, then to Reinhardt and his fiancée at Mellensee, and finally to Denmark, where she stayed with us for some weeks. Not in the least concerned for her own safety, she returned to Freiburg. She felt confident that there would not be a war. She decided to visit to Marianne and her family in Persia again. As she wrote in her memoirs:

'In 1938, in the autumn, having been dismissed from my job in Freiburg for being Jewish, I locked up my flat, left all my possessions without a second thought, slipped the key into my pocket, and set out for what was to be about a two months' visit to Teheran.'

She was going to fly this time, from Berlin. But she and the other passengers had to wait till late at night for the departure:

'This was the night of "Munich", the second meeting between Hitler and Chamberlain with his umbrella. Everyone was waiting with bated breath: War – or (temporary) Peace? Well, it was Peace, so-called, that is to say, poor Czechoslovakia, prepared to defend her freedom to the utmost with the help of the Allies, was shamefully betrayed and handed over to Hitler.

Which meant that our little plane could take off at about 2 a.m. It was a lovely, comfortable journey. Apart from the pilots, there were only four or five of us on board. I will never forget the flight across the Balkans, the Mediterranean, Rhodes, Athens, Damascus. I saw rivers flowing from mountains into the sea as on a map. The islands looked like green leaves floating on the water. The light kept changing; everything looked unreal. And then there was a comfortable bed in a tiny room, closed off from the corridor by thick curtains. I fell fast asleep and did not wake up until the sound of the engines stopped. I looked out of the window – and there was Teheran airport, and there was my Marianne with the two little girls, waving! I hardly had time to get dressed before we disembarked. It was 1 October 1938. I was not to see Germany again. I stayed in Teheran for eight years.

Of course, I didn't know that then. I was a visitor, enjoying my daughter and son-in-law and my grandchildren, fully expecting to leave again after some weeks. But then came news of the Grünspahn murder in Paris, when a young Polish Jew killed a German diplomat, which the Nazis used as a pretext for unleashing the nation-wide pogrom known as the Kristallnacht, because so many Jewish windows were smashed. Synagogues were burnt down, many Jews were murdered, businesses ransacked and their assets confiscated – clearly I could not rely any longer on my charmed life and risk returning to Germany. So I stayed in Teheran.'

Chapter 14

The name I was given soon after my inauspicious birth was Vera Irene Gabriele Beate Zuntz, no less. My mother, whom I always called Mu, had wanted many more children and had selected names for all of them; but when I came along, five years after my sister (Elisabeth Maleen) and seven after my brother (Hans Peter) she had good reason to think that I was the last; so she gave me the cream of the remaining girls' names. That's why I have four first names. Gabriele was the one used most, soon abbreviated to either Gabi or Ele; this last was then lengthened to Elüx, Elüxel, Elüxelchen, which in turn got abbreviated to Lüxel, or lengthened to Lüxelinchen, while Gabi was elaborated into Gabi-Gax-Galine, which was then shortened to Gax. It all depended on the mood of the person addressing me. I accrued many more names in the course of my life, and am not at all sure who I am. But I have my stock of memories to help me: here's the oldest.

I'm lying on a bed in a shadowy room with light filtering through the blinds of a tall window. There's another bed between me and the window. There's a nun lying on it. Her name is Schwester Permina. She wants me to go to sleep. After a while she turns her head to look at me. I quickly shut my eyes. She gets up and moves silently to the door, her pale grey veil and gown floating behind her, and out of the room. She thinks I'm asleep! I feel triumphant. Fooled her!

That's my earliest memory. Soon after, we went to Denmark – my father, whom I always called Fe, had sent the necessary papers. Mu recalls that we first went to the island of Bornholm,

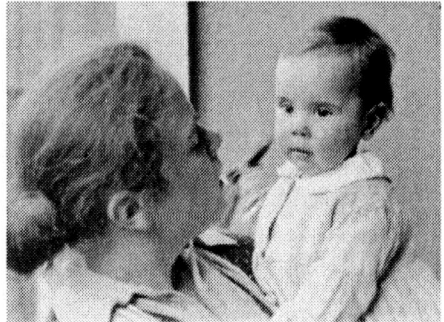

Me with Mu

'...*where we got a room in a stable. The children slept in a crib, and my sleeping arrangements were not much better. Günther came a little later and immediately demanded a proper bed – and got one; but it was so full of fleas and bedbugs that he was no better off than me. Every Sunday Peter insisted that we had to go to church. This meant a walk of about two and a half hours to the capital, Roenne. I had to carry Gabi on my back almost all the way there and back. I cannot remember the church at all. The priest was not in the least interested in the children, so my dream that as Catholics they would always and instantly find "contact" proved to be so much "froth". I was terribly depressed, so Günther suggested I should walk round the whole island; he would look after the children meanwhile. That was my salvation. The countryside was glorious, the sea clear and blue. I was overwhelmed by the beauty and the solitude; everything was easier to bear afterwards.*

Not long after my return we moved to Copenhagen and found a fourth-floor flat in Jyllingewej in Vanlrse. From now on, there was no more talk of divorce: we had to stay together if we were to have residence permits for all of us. We lived together – but not "as man and wife". Günther had a study with a bed, I slept on the sofa in the living room, and there was a room for the three children. In due course our furniture arrived and we were quite comfortable.'

The flats in Jylingevej

My second memory: I wake up in the night and scream: my thumb has swollen and looks like a purple ball. I scream again in terror and Mu comes. She discovers the elastic I had wound round my thumb and forgotten about. She gets it off by snipping it with a small pair of curved scissors and promises me that my thumb will soon be normal again. But because I am still sobbing she lets me come downstairs and sit in what we called the 'Mutter-coupé' – the space behind her in the armchair. My favourite place. There are various grown-ups in the room. Mu has explained about my thumb and they have made soothing noises. Now they go on with their conversation: a background murmur which soon has me asleep again.

*****

Maleen and Peter had to go to school. Mu comments wryly in her memoirs:

'*So here we were in a 99 per cent Protestant country with our Catholic children. That had been a clever move! But I found a Jesuit school for Peter, and a French one for Maleen. On the 14 July the little girls were dressed in white with red sashes and sang the "Marseillaise" in the presence of the French ambassador, in the midst of charming, smiling nuns – stamping their feet to the words "Le jour de gloire est arrive". I felt desperate at this display of French nationalism, just as bad as any other nationalism. I hoped Peter would get a good education from the Jesuits, their schools being renowned. One day when I was waiting for him outside the school, lost in thought, a boy came tearing out pursued by a Jesuit in a long robe flourishing a cane. I don't think he caught the boy. But I was not at all sure that that was the right school for Peter.*

In 1938 we learned that Günther's father had died. Günther could not go to the funeral in Berlin because he would have been conscripted, or worse, so I went. I saw how many people wept for Leo, what a great hole his death tore in all our lives, though only Jews were allowed to come to the funeral.'

That must have been the night I remember waking up and discovering that Mu was not there. In a panic, I ran to the window and looked across to the tram terminus: she must have got into one of the trams over there, that went screeching round the circular rails. I had to find her! I rushed out of the flat, down the stairs, in my pyjamas, and across to the terminus to look for her. There were numerous trams there, and I got more and more confused as grown-ups bent down to me and said things I didn't understand – I hadn't had time to learn much Danish. Suddenly Maleen was beside me; she took me by the hand and led me home, explaining that Mu would be coming back some time later. Mu continues:

'*I cannot remember much of that day in Berlin, with the Nazis everywhere, except for a deep sense of gratitude for his death before what was to come: by then I knew, we all knew, that there was much worse to come. Edith, despite her hatred of me, thanked me for coming. I really felt that our fight was over and we could be friends. She visited us twice in Denmark, and then went to England, where her daughters were already living, Dora in London, married to a journalist, Leonie in Oxford, studying Hittite and Turkish.*

In Copenhagen I made friends with a family called Larsen, who lived two floors below us. They were very sincere Christians. Their oldest son was shot later during the German occupation because he was a member of the resistance. The second son went to Korea and married a Korean woman. Fru Larsen, now a widow, was left with her daughter, who was mentally handicapped. All the families I got to know in Denmark had at least one mentally ill member. Perhaps this was due to inbreeding. The whole country only had three million inhabitants, and about one and half million lived in

Copenhagen. "Everyone" was called either Larsen or Jensen.

One evening – it was after the outbreak of the Spanish Civil War – Günther and I were discussing what we would do if Denmark was occupied, since every newspaper was screaming WAR. I said: "Don't worry, I've got enough Veronal to kill us all if the Nazis come for us." But Peter had heard me and came rushing in in a terrible state of despair. It was very bad. I tried to comfort him, saying no Nazi would ever touch any of us, and that I would only use the poison in the most extreme circumstances. Not very comforting; but I thought it best to be open and honest.

Once, when I was by the window looking out for Peter to come home from school, he called up to me: "Come down and fetch me." — "Why, no," I said, and laughed; "I don't enjoy going up and down the stairs." So he came up, very slowly, and I could hardly believe my eyes. He was red in the face and crying: the knee he had fallen on the day before at football hurt so. He had a high temperature; evidently it was blood poisoning. He was taken to hospital by ambulance, where he stayed for several weeks. He was in some danger, and I reproached myself, because though I thought I had washed out the wound thoroughly, there was still a lot of grit in it, and I should have taken him to the doctor straight away. So now I visited him every day with a bag of cakes – smaakager – and he got so fat that he couldn't get into his trousers. I went to the biggest gentlemen's outfitters, but they had nothing big enough. They had to make a pair specially, and promised to deliver them in three days, so poor Peter had to go home in gaping trousers concealed under a coat. The new trousers came, but for a time Peter could not sit at the table because his stomach had become so fat. All because of the smaakager. And whose fault was it? Mine, of course, as usual.'

I can remember visiting my big brother Peter in hospital. A nurse comes along with a roll of toilet paper. I am fascinated. Is she going to wipe out the poisoned blood? I want to watch, but Mu hurries me away. Something quite straightforward is to happen — but it's rude, I mustn't watch.

And then there's the time I locked myself into the bathroom. I couldn't turn the key to unlock the door again. Mu is on the other side, encouraging me to try again. My big sister Maleen joins her; she tells me I can't be too weak to turn it, since I'd managed to lock it in the first place; but I cannot. My father, Fe, comes home. He tells me to pull the key out and push it out to him under the door. But I can't pull it out. I'm panicking. Mu fetches the concierge. There they all are outside and me a prisoner! There's talk of taking the door off its hinges. Then Peter comes home from school. He pushes his penknife, unopened, under the door. I'm to push it through the ring at the end of the key and then use both hands to turn it. And it works! The door opens and I am free! Tears streaming down my face I collapse into Mu's arms.

That bathroom was the scene of the only physical punishment ever meted out to me. I have no idea what I had done wrong; but Fe, sitting on the lavatory, had me across his lap and looking round I saw his hand, as big as a spade, coming down onto my unprotected bottom and was terrified.

The grown-ups were living in a far more alarming world than I was. Mu records:

'The Spanish Civil War was lost, and that was a turning point for Europe. There were some terrible revelations: Stalin's betrayal of the idealistic fighters in the International Brigades, for example. None of those who fled home to Russia after the debacle were free a few weeks later. It was like the Decabrists after the Napoleonic War, who returned to Russia – of course, unlike the International Brigade in Spain, they were victorious – and though they were obviously enemies of Napoleon, still, they had picked up various Western ideas, which meant they were a threat to the Russian state, which was an autocracy and practised serfdom. So the Decabrists were received with hostility, and those that survived were sent to Siberia, first to a penal colony and then as settlers. Their wives, mostly aristocrats like them, followed them into the wilderness. So when after the Spanish war a new influx of exiles came to Siberia in chains, they were received with love and kindness by the descendants of the Decabrists. In many respects Siberia is one of the happiest lands: so many highly educated, cultured people were settled there, who treated poverty, and even the merciless climate, with contempt. There are some good, fruitful areas; and certainly there has never been any serfdom in Siberia. In the past the peasants always put bread and water outside their houses for the "unhappy people", i.e. escaped convicts. Under Stalin no one could risk being so charitable.

Günther was able to go to England, where he taught at a public school, Repton, for half the year. We moved out of the city to the village of Kajerrd, to save money, and lived on a big farm in what was called an "inspector's cottage" – five rather small rooms, but with a wonderful view of forest, lake and meadows. We lived there for two happy years. We all spoke fluent Danish. A friend, Frrken Meier, invited us to a macaroni meal from time to time. The desperate cries from Germany were muffled, and for hours at a time I was able to forget it and just inhale the air, the green shades, and enjoy the little house in which we lived. The children were happy in their schools, especially Maleen, who had a very kind teacher, Frrken Dorothea Andersen.'

I remember that house vividly. On one side there was a big gooseberry bed, with a hedge round it. It was in this hedge that my admired big brother Peter created a stable for my toy animals. They were made of a kind of rubber. I also had a wonderful doll called Kirsten, who shut her blue eyes when she lay down and opened them when I raised her blonde curly head. But mostly

Kajerød

Nearby Sjaelsø

I played with my little farm animals –
the brown mare with her beautiful foal,
the sheep, the hens with their cockerel,
the cow with pink udders, and the old cow, not nearly so plump and nice,

The house in Kajerrd

being made of metal,
not rubber like the
others – they all had
to be looked after,
taken out for fresh
grass and fresh air, and
led safely back to their
stable in the evening.

*****

There was a patch of
gravel behind the
house, and one sunny
day, when we were sitting there for coffee,
with the shadows of
leaves fluttering over the cups and jugs on the table, I was told the story of
'The sun will reveal it': *Die Sonne bringt es an den Tag*. A man robbed and
murdered another man in the forest. no one else was about, so he thought
he was absolutely safe. But the dying man looked at the sun through the
leaves and said — these were his dying words – 'The sun will reveal it'. Years
later – the murderer had prospered with the dead man's money — he was
sitting just as we were here, having coffee, and smiled to see the shadows of
the leaves which the sun cast onto the table and shook his head. The dying
man was wrong, no one had ever found out. He murmured the fatal words:
'The sun has not revealed it.' But his wife heard him – and questioned him
until he told her why he had said those words – and so the sun had revealed

it, after all. I can still see those fluttering shadows, and feel the chill of the story.

When Oma came to visit us, we had to observe an evening ritual. In a procession we carried a chair, cushions, a rug, and her writing things to a gap in the hedge so that she could sit in comfort to watch the sunset, as she did every evening, wherever she was. There was a double row of hazels on our side of the fence, and on the other, a field belonging to a farm where Prepen lived. He was a boy of about the same age as me, and he liked to make me feel inferior, for instance because I could not – however hard I tried – emulate the fountain of urine he sent up behind a certain great oak tree. I did realise that our games were rude and told no one about them until now.

We went for walks with Oma – very slowly, because of her bad knee and ankles – along a path beside a green field and up a low hill. She was clad in black, and had a furled umbrella which she used as a walking stick. Her silver hair was gathered in a bun on top of her head. At one point, she stopped and swung the umbrella round in a circle and sang in a low vibrant voice one of those homesick German songs about wide valleys and hills and the green forest. Later in our slow progress she pointed up into the sky, and her grey-blue eyes looked at me over the top of her glasses.

'See the skylark there?' she asked. 'Hear it? It's going up and up. If you turn round three times it will be out of sight.'

I did so – and she was right: the skylark had vanished into the sky. She knew everything.

Soon after, we started getting wonderful letters from her from Persia.

*****

We often cycled out to a nearby lake. I would sit in a seat on the handle-bars of Mu's bike while Peter and Maleen, being seven and five years older than me respectively, had their own cycles. I remember a curving road towards some woods; a grassy embankment rising on our right. In the shadowy wood, the path split round a massive tree. Maleen and Peter raced each other round either side. Further on we came to the lake: Sjaelsr.

*****

When Fe came home from England I would feel the family was complete, not realising how profound was the rift between him and Mu. I have an indelible memory of him, on one occasion when he had just reappeared, tall and slim, and – as I suddenly recognised – beautiful, stretching up his right hand to pull a flowering twig down from a tree to sniff at the blossom. There was a large sepia photo portrait of him as a boy indoors; he was looking up with a dreamy expression from a book open on his knees, his shoulder-length hair resting on a large lace collar: Little Lord Fauntleroy we called it, thinking it was a bit silly and effeminate. Fe deplored Mu's slap-dash energetic ways; she despised his fussiness and hypochondria. But that was not the only trouble between them, as I gradually learned as I grew older.

*****

I begged to be allowed to go to school, like Peter and Maleen, and so one morning I was walking along to the Komuneskole, clutching Mu's hand, in a state somewhere between excitement and panic. The brick buildings – huge in my eyes – surrounded an asphalt playground, where drinking water fountains bubbled from the edge of a circular basin. Some of the big boys – so daring! – would sit on one of these fountains and then holler 'Ma! Ma! I've wet myself!' They would spit their chewing gum out onto the ground which was blotched with the flattened pink shapes. I was not above secretly peeling these off to find out what they tasted like. When the bell clanged we trooped up the wide stairs to the classroom, where I sat next to a beautiful fair-haired girl called Inge with fascinating ridged finger-nails. There were tiny white flecks in them; these, she told me, were supposed to appear every time one told a lie. Inge did not deny having told so many lies; she looked at me through her silky lashes and said nothing. Sometimes the wicked boy sitting behind her dipped the end of her pigtail into his inkwell – and she did not tell on him; just gave him a stony stare and wiped off the ink with a blotter. The classroom seemed huge to me; somewhere up in front the teacher sat behind a desk on a platform. Sometimes I was allowed join the Big Girls, and I would sit under the table at which they were sewing, and run my finger nails up and down the teacher's stockings. She shrieked with laughter because it tickled so, but no one was ever angry with me. I was a sort of mascot. And presumably I was still picking up the Danish language and didn't understand everything that was said.

Peter would sometimes walk home with me. He tried to teach me to whistle. At last I learned it, and hurried to demonstrate it to Mu. But when I got home, I was as always in urgent need of a toilet – so urgent that Mu said I need not go up to the bathroom, but might squat down behind the hazels. By the time I got into the house, the ability to whistle had left me. In fact for a time I could only whistle one note, once a day. I tried to save this one whistle till I got home, but could not resist using it up on the way. It was Peter I most wanted to impress. And Prepen.

I was given a warm blue winter coat, which I wore on one of Mu's visits to a nearby farm. While she and the farmer's wife talked, I played in the yard. My ball rolled out onto a flat brown area. I ran out after it – wondering why the surface was so brittle. It was actually a pool of slurry, but I pursued my ball till I was waist-deep in the stinking liquid. Mu was appalled: the coat was ruined.

That visit of Mu's was probably a farewell visit. It was 1939, and as she wrote:

'A German invasion of Denmark seemed likelier than ever. Günther decided to stay in England, and found work as a college librarian in Oxford. We were to join him there. He promised he would get us a visa to come to England. I dreaded going to that country, not only because Günther's mother and sisters lived there, but because England to me was the land of class distinction, snobbery, the industrial revolution and all the human degradation it had caused, and colonialism. Still, I sold nearly all our belongings, and sent books and some furniture to England.

When our little house was empty, Peter, now aged thirteen, had a sort of breakdown, with a high temperature. He cried all the time. He didn't want to leave Denmark when it was in danger; he wanted to fight and perish with the Danes. I was at the end of my tether. Frrken Andersen, Maleen's teacher, came to the rescue. She called to see us; and when she saw the state we were in, she invited us to stay with her. Four extra people in a tiny spinster's flat above the school. I accepted gratefully, and we spent peaceful days there. Every day we looked out for the postman with bated breath, but in vain: the visas didn't come. We could not stay with Frrken Andersen any longer. We were to move even further away from Copenhagen, and go into hiding on Samsr, the little island between Sjaelland (Zealand) and Jylland (Jutland), from where the steamers went to England, hoping the Nazis, if they invaded, wouldn't find us there. Frrken Andersen and the headmaster did all they could to help us, finding out about trains and boats and so on: Peter recovered and even began to look forward to life on an island. At that time he still wanted to be a farmer.

So we went to Samsr. How lovely it was! The children went to school in Tranebjerg – and it seemed incredible that I could send them off on such a long walk to school without any anxiety: everybody knew them and was kind to them. When Peter and I visited the island after the war we found pictures of the three children in several farmhouses. A woman called Kirsten Holst in particular was kindness itself, and I saw her quite often. But I was desperately lonely in our little house – a converted stable – with the terrible news coming out of Germany. It became obvious that Denmark would soon be conquered by the Nazis. I was terrified.'

But for me, in my memory, Samsr is a blessed island, an earthly paradise. Our tiny house on the road between Tranebjerg and Ballen was surrounded by hollyhocks, and had an outside toilet with a warm, wide wooden seat, which I liked so much it became my domain: Gabi-Privat.

*****

At the end of the lane behind the house was the farm to which it belonged; along the road to one side we quickly came to the beach, where tall blonde brown-skinned women took a liking to me and bought me ice creams. Mu would help me pile up a hill of sand, patting it firm, adding handfuls of water to make it even firmer. Then we would start tunnelling, she with two fingers from her side, I with my whole hand from the other. Sometimes the hill collapsed before we had reached the middle; sometimes we had misjudged the direction of the tunnels and came out somewhere at the side; but occasionally our hands met in the middle and we laughed with the pleasure of touching each other – warm and smooth and alive – in the gritty depths of the sand-hill.

'When I was your age,' Mu said, 'my mother – your Oma – played with me just like this in the sand in Ferch. And she told me that she learned to make sand-hills and tunnels like this from her grandfather, when she was a little girl.'

'Her grandfather!'

'Yes – my great grandfather, and your great great grandfather!'

'Where did they do it?'

'A place called Zoppot. If we went on and on towards the sunrise from here we'd get there. Some of this same water has probably been by the beach at Zoppot.'

*****

In Samsr, we all always felt perfectly safe. Everyone was kind and friendly to us; and the weather seems to have been perfect all the time. We were happy there, and it is lodged in my consciousness as Ferch was in Mu's, as the place that encapsulates the innocent time of childhood, the place for which one is homesick all one's life.

The papers came at last. and we had to leave. As Mu remembers:

We were all sad to leave this lovely place and the kind people we had got to know. In fact, Peter did not want to come with us. He felt, again, that it was an act of betrayal to leave Denmark when it was in such great danger. I had to explain that our very presence would enhance the danger for all the people who befriended us: as if we had the plague. Of course this made him despair. He threw himself on the floor and was not to be persuaded to get up. I was quite worn out. For a long time I pleaded with him: he was too young to help Denmark now, but perhaps, once we were settled in England and when he was old enough, he might be able to fight the Nazis. At last he agreed, and we

Me on the beach

went to Kolby Kas for the ferry across to Jutland. From there we had to go to Esbjerg by train.

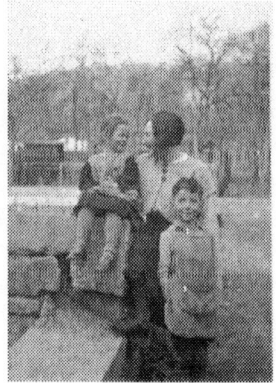

Peter and Maleen with a Danish friend

The journey was not devoid of comedy. The little train across Jutland had to stop because 1.) there were cows lying on the line, and 2.) because Gabi had to go to the lavatory. There was none on the train, and so, as we were the only passengers, the train stopped at a small station where there was a toilet and waited for her to relieve herself. This made the train late at the junction where we were to board the express to Esbjerg. Railway officials came running towards us to help us and hurry us along, because we were so late. However, the express was waiting for us, because the driver of our local train had telephoned. So at last we got to Esbjerg harbour, and boarded the Harwich boat.'

✵✵✵✵✵

I didn't return to Denmark until 1988, when I went there with my husband David. Of course there had been a lot of changes, but we managed to find Jyllingevej in Vanlrse, Copenhagen, and the block of flats on a corner in which we had lived. It all looked much smaller than I remembered it. But there on the other side of the road was a plot of waste land with the circular tram lines still visible, and I could almost hear the screeching noise the trams used to make there as they turned to go back into the town, and the night of panic when I had looked for my mother there.

We also visited Birkerrd, which had become a suburb of Copenhagen. The place was completely engulfed in nice new houses – small bungalows embedded in lilacs. Finally, after scouting around on hired bicycles, we found the junction of three roads that I remembered; but the shop in the angle of the junction where I used to get morehrved – a divine mass of some creamy substance on a stick, coated with chocolate – was now a veterinary surgery, Dahlgaard's Dyreklinik; the short steep road up to our house had been paved and led to a long terrace of town houses. But going through a gap in the terrace, and across a patch of waste land where some boys were playing football, and past some allotments, some beehives, some ponds – there, suddenly, was our house. Utterly charming. Behind that window was the living room, with the big black wooden settle against which, trying to retrieve my satchel that had fallen between it and a chair, I hit my head so hard that blood poured out. Mu scooped me up and got me to a doctor somewhere, somehow; I still have the scar. Beyond that room would be the kitchen, where we had our meals, with a window looking out onto the two rows of hazels.

And as we cycled along the path with the Sjaelsr gleaming through the trees on our left, I suddenly recognised the huge tree in the middle of the path, and a little further on the spot where we used to bathe: Mu swimming out slowly, head up to keep her hair dry; Maleen and Peter having water fights. But I had quite forgotten the round shallow pond just the other side of the path where little streams falling down through the forest had been dammed and diverted into a modest fountain: I remembered it as soon as I saw it.

At the local library we found photographs of the Kommuneskole, which had been demolished years ago. But where was the flowering fruit tree by our house? The gooseberry patch? The hedge where Peter made the stable for my toy animals? Prepen's family's farm? All vanished, except in my memory.

David and I explored Samsr too, in 1998. We crossed the Kattegat on the ferry – the sea was calm despite a strong cold wind, and some fine yachts, even a schooner, were sailing in the sunshine, all sails set – landed at Kolby, and took the one and only bus, mysteriously numbered 131, through the rolling green land. Many places looked familiar to me: cows and calves and a few horses in the lush meadows with ponds, little houses like toys with corrugated iron roofs painted red, or thatched. We passed through Kolby, Permelille, Ballen, and got off at Tranebjerg, where we stayed with Asta Rasmussen, a big, warm, welcoming woman, her English – which she was keen to practise – about as hopeless as my Danish. Mrs Rasmussen went in for knick-knacks, hundreds of them, on highly polished surfaces, from tiny china dogs to model bonsai trees. She served fabulous breakfasts, organised a couple of bicycles for us to hire, on which we explored the island, and introduced us to one or two people who had known Kirsten Holst. She had been a good friend to Mu, but was now buried by the white, red-roofed church.

In the night I had a strange dream: a calf approached its mother to drink milk – no – it sprawled on the ground; she lay beside it; its legs disappeared into her, then its body, then its head; she got up, walked backwards, lowered her head and gently spewed out grass …And my grey hair turned dark, my six-year-old shape returned, and I was a small child again, on Samsr, with my mother.

I woke up early and walked along the road toward Ballen, exploring some of the farm tracks, looking at the small houses and wishing for some strong sense of recognition, for the present to coincide with my memories; but it was not to be.

Chapter 15

This is how Mu remembered our arrival in Harwich:

'We were not allowed to disembark; the authorities wanted to send us to Hamburg. I had been afraid this might happen. I explained the situation, they listened politely, then went to telephone London. Meanwhile I took my pills out of my bag and ordered tea. If the reply from London was "to Hamburg" I was going to slip a pill into each cup of tea. I held those pills – our salvation — in my hand for many hours while we sat there in Harwich. But we were allowed in, and I buried the pills in my bag.'

From Harwich the journey continued by train to London – I have confused memories of the deafening hiss in the black vaults of Paddington as clouds of white steam were let off – and thence to Oxford. It was night time when we got to the house Fe had found for us in Oxford, in Thorncliffe Road, one of the series of streets that lie between Woodstock and Banbury Roads like the rungs of a ladder. While Mu sat wearily on a chair and spoke with Fe, we children rushed around exploring the house excitedly, vying to discover details that the others had missed. But soon I was exhausted and half asleep, which had the curious effect of making everything look a tenth of its normal size. In the pile of luggage stacked in the hall, Mu found a folding bed, which was opened for me in a small room upstairs. I knew nothing till the next morning, when I sat up and looked out of the window at the yellow brick wall of the next-door house, and long, narrow gardens separated by brick walls and containing apple trees, their blossom veiled with a soft, gentle rain. I got out of bed and opened the door to a corridor leading to stairs. A slanting door near the top of the stairs opened into a bathroom with a cast iron bath standing on lion's feet. Two steps up led to more closed doors. I descended the staircase, and found myself facing the front door, which was partially glazed with ornamental green glass leaves and red lozenges. I turned and went along the side of the staircase till I came to a step down and a door to the kitchen. That was where everyone was.

This house was the seventeenth and last address in Mu's married life; it was to be her home until she died. She moved sixteen times in the first fourteen years of marriage, and not at all (except for visits) for 54 years thereafter; and she came to feel very possessive indeed about the house; it was to be a refuge and

Beamsend

a home for the family first and foremost, but for all sorts of needy people in the years to come.

Yet she did not like the house at first. It belonged to a Mrs Monk, who lived in the next street, Beechcroft Road. My parents could have bought it, in 1939, for £400; but they didn't have £400, so for decades to come paying Mrs Monk the rent was a priority. It was – and is – a late Victorian end-terrace tunnel-back house, of yellow brick, facing the street and the north, so that the front rooms never got any sun. That only shone on the back garden, when the high brick walls surrounding it allowed, and onto the scullery, the small bedroom above it, and an outside toilet. The rear of the house consisted of the kitchen and the scullery; the 'tunnel'– a narrow sunless passage – ran along the side of it, and the back room window looked out on it, as did the bathroom and two bedrooms upstairs. The 'tunnel' could be reached by a door from the corridor that ran from the front room to the kitchen, or another one that opened from the scullery, beyond the kitchen, to the garden. One corner of the scullery was taken up with a 'copper' for boiling laundry; there was a gas cooker beside it, and a sink under the window. There was an outside toilet which backed onto the pantry in the kitchen. Above the kitchen door there was a panel with curious numbered tags which corresponded to bell pushes in all the rooms: the house was designed for servants. Of course we tried all the bells, but none of them worked.

Upstairs there was a large front room which had been claimed by my father for his study; his big black bookcases and his leather-topped writing table were already installed. A fair-sized back-bedroom overlooked the tunnel, as did a small bathroom with a cast-iron bath on lions' feet, a toilet and a wash basin, a 'box room', where my father slept, and a small bedroom overlooking the garden. In the long years that followed, these rooms were allocated and re-allocated, furniture was moved from one to another – which was almost as good as moving house, said Mu, who, for a long time, would have liked to. We reproached Fe, who could have got a much nicer house in Bainton Road with a back garden that ran down to the canal; but he feared that rats might emerge from the canal.

The Brookes family lived on one side. Mr Brookes had a small square car. Mrs Brookes looked like a hen and was soon an enemy. There were two children, Mary and Malcolm. They were all deeply suspicious of 'ruddy foreigners', especially us next door. Mrs Brookes believed that the only reason why Oxford was never bombed was because we were sending secret messages to our people in the Luftwaffe; she told us so once. When we were too noisy, she would bang on the adjoining wall, and Mu would retaliate in kind. On the other side was a deaf family, the Harrisons: elderly parents, their middle-aged daughter, all deaf; their booming voices could be heard almost all day. They were all intensely property conscious – so were the Brookes – and old Mr Harrison would laboriously lean his ladder against the garden wall and demand to speak to 'the professor' when he had a complaint. None of them ever came to the front door. One complaint was because of an apple core which I had thrown over the wall. He waved it indignantly as he boomed his complaint to the 'professor', teetering at the top of his ladder. Another time we saw him at dawn climbing over the wall into our garden to pick up some apples that had fallen from his trees. Their daughter would hang out of the window to comb her few grey locks; then she would reappear downstairs with a dustpan and brush to sweep up whatever had dropped from her head onto the concrete paving.

My father's beautiful sister Leonie was living in Oxford, studying Hittite and hoping in vain for a university post; but she did not make any attempt to befriend us. His other sister, Dora, and her English husband, Brian Roberts, a night editor on the *Daily Telegraph*, once invited Peter to stay with them for a short time in London; thereafter there was no contact with them, either. Their mother, Oma Edith, came and lived with Leonie for a time, but she never called on us, though Fe spent a good deal of time with them in Norham Gardens.

❖❖❖❖❖

September came, and Germany invaded Poland. On the 3 September, Britain and France declared war on Germany. The streetlights remained unlit at night. We got ration books, and we had to put up blackout curtains – sometimes an air-raid warden would knock at the door in the evening and warn us that there was a chink of light showing. We were now enemy aliens and had to go to the police station and report to a friendly policeman with a walrus moustache at intervals. We were not allowed to travel more than five miles from the house, so when Fe took me for Sunday morning cycle rides into the country, we would hide our bicycles in a hedge at a certain point and walk from there, through the fields and woods round Elsfield and Woodeaton. Walking was not travelling. Once we came to a water-filled ditch which Fe, with his long legs, crossed easily, but was too wide for me – so he flung himself down across it as a human bridge and I crawled across him to the other side.

❖❖❖❖❖

We children had to go to school. Peter went to St Edwards, a minor public school a short walk from Thorncliffe Road. It was not easy for Peter to be a day boy. The boarders looked down on day boys, and he was made to feel that he was an outsider, and moreover he was a 'bloody foreigner', with a funny name, speaking broken English, a Jew, and a 'Jerry' — an enemy. He was bullied and humiliated, and reacted by working incredibly hard to master the language and the curriculum. Soon he was getting top marks. But that did not help: now he was maligned for being a 'swot'. He burned to be accepted and realised that sporting prowess was the only thing that impressed these boys; so it was a great relief when, being slight, he was chosen as cox of a rowing eight. As he grew and put on weight, his dread of losing his one toehold in the world of sport was so great that for months he deliberately starved himself. Possibly because of this he was often ill with a high temperature – it may have been jaundice. Some years later, in the sixth form, he was more or less accepted by a small gang of rather loutish young men who were also day boys, and went out with them in the evenings, getting drunk. Things were no better for him at home, where he was in a state of open conflict with his father. They clashed over everything, even at mealtimes, when they would both stretch out their legs under the table and complain if – as was inevitable – their feet collided.

St Edward's School

Maleen and I were sent to Rye St Antony, because we were nominally Catholic. The Hastings family, devout Catholics, took us under their wing. Mrs Hastings, a short, stout woman with a large nose and blue-tinted glasses, had six children – her husband was usually away, being in the Diplomatic Service – and the youngest, Susan, and I played in a bedroom with a big rocking horse at the foot of the bed. Once we played at hairdressers, and Susan cut off my hair, hiding it under the rocking horse, where the maid – they had a maid, who wore a white apron and cap – found it. In the evening Mrs Hastings drove up in her Austin with Susan, who was sobbing and red eyed, to apologise. But Mu, absorbed in the News, had hardly noticed that my hair looked as if it had been ravaged by mice, and was certainly not upset. 'It will grow again,' she said. In the summer, Susan and I decided to establish an aquarium. For this we needed a large blue bowl from Woolworths, which was then a '3d and 6d store'. Susan asked her mother for sixpence. 'Take a shilling, dear,' she replied. When I reported these words at home, the family could hardly believe that we knew such wealthy people. Sometimes we would go out on the river in a punt with the Hastings; at one point this meant passing through the men's swimming pool called 'Parsons' Pleasure'; since men were allowed to swim naked there, Susan and I would have to lie down in the punt and be covered with towels, lest we saw some unmentionable sight.

Rye St Antony School was then in two large houses in Woodstock Road and, on our first day, totally bewildering to me, I found myself sitting at a table in a crowded basement room with a large piece of paper in front of me and a woman circling her hands over the paper. I was fascinated by the rings on her fingers. She was saying something, but of course I could not understand: I only understood Danish and German. Maleen came to the rescue. She managed to divine the meaning of the English words. In Danish, she told me the teacher wanted me to cover the whole paper with a drawing. So I set to and drew cows and horses and houses and trees. School was fairly pointless for me, since I couldn't understand a word; but I had just learned to stand on my head – a skill I was keen to practise, since I intended to be an acrobat when I grew up – so my first school report ended with the comment: 'Gabi must not stand on her head when the teacher is talking to her.'

I was an outsider here in school, behind the language barrier. No one who has not experienced it can imagine what it is like to live in a country whose language you do not understand. You feel as if your brains are wrapped in cotton wool; a dense fog shuts you off from the rest of mankind; you are stupid, deaf and dumb, invisible; you keep making silly mistakes – not only linguistic ones – and feel mortified; you are so ashamed you want to kick yourself. Of course we were all learning the language all the time, and found relief in sharing our experiences, and laughing at 'refugee jokes' – such as:

A: Spring in the air!
B: Why should I?

– or the story of a refugee woman on a crowded bus, whose husband has gone to the upper deck; she says to the conductor: 'The Lord above us will pay.' 'Refugiese' became our language, a mixture of German and English. My own contribution was to point at the mist rising over St Edward's School grounds, and exclaim to my father: 'Kuck mal der reisende Mist,' which was German for: 'Look at the travelling manure.' During those walks, he was getting me to recite multiplication tables. He took my schooling very seriously.

Mu christened the house 'Beamsend' – because she had seen a poor man trying to sell matches with a sign hanging from his neck saying: 'I AM AT MY BEAM'S END'. Whatever that means, so are we, she thought. She was struggling to learn the language and sometimes got it wrong. There was a notice in a dark corner between buildings in Oxford with a rather odd notice saying: 'Do not commit a nuisance'. So when I brought home a girl I had made friends with at school, Mu asked her: 'Will you commit a nuisance?' – indicating the toilet door, and pronouncing the word: nooeesants. The butcher – a stout man – was asked: 'Please give me a pound of your flesh,' the German word fleisch meaning both 'meat' and 'flesh'. She could laugh at such incidents later. Since she had virtually no English friends, and insisted on our speaking German at home, lest we forget the language, her English was derived entirely from books and newspapers, and it was vivid, sometimes baffling, often funny – unique. Years later, telling grandchildren at a bus-stop the story of Paris and the three goddesses who asked him to say which of them was the most beautiful, Venus, according to Mu, said, 'My foot! I will give you a real good time', having misinterpreted expressions like, '£10 my foot, I'll give you five.' She often had us all roaring with laughter, and she was quite capable of laughing at herself; but she often wept. She said she had a high water table. When she was reading aloud – a Grimms' Fairy Tale, a German ballad, a Dickens novel, Dostoyevsky, she would at certain points hand over the book for someone else to read as she knew she was coming to one of the places where her tears would flow irrepressibly. And they invariably did. Her imagination threw up lurid images of the suffering of the helpless and she wept. As the tanks rolled into Danzig, her emotions could not bear it, she had to do something to help, and if there was nothing else to do she would scrub the floor or clean the windows, furiously. Her contribution to the 'War Effort' was to open her house to fellow refugees; every room had a family, or several children; we had to queue for the bathroom and ate in shifts at the kitchen table. A home for refugee boys at High Wycombe, run by an English couple, Mr and Mrs Bolton, was closed by some orthodox Jewish organisation because the boys should not be brought up and indoctrinated by Christians. Three of these boys came to us, though there was no religion of any kind in our family, certainly not Judaism: Stefan, Erich and Kurt.

Kurt, thin, pale, sad, clever, kind, stayed and became to all intents and purposes my brother. On Saturday mornings we all queued outside Oliver and Gurden's cake factory in St George's Street (now called Middle Way) to get bags of broken cakes and buns: we were allowed a bagful each. The chocolate-coated shortbread was the best. On Sundays we cycled out into the Thames valley beyond Godstow to pick blackberries. Here Kurt invented the Iwnicki patent thirst quencher: a large handful of blackberries thrust into the mouth and crushed. Finally Hitler broke his pact with Stalin and attacked the Soviet Union. Everyone was surprised – it

Me on Erich

Kurt

seemed a crazy thing for him to do. It meant that the dreaded invasion of Britain was off. Fe said it was enough to make one believe in miracles.

The Winter War of 1939–40, when the Soviet Union attacked Finland, and that heroic little country was fighting back against the Soviet giant, had Mu in rain and wind at the corner of Thorncliffe Road, rattling a tin to collect money to send aid to the Finns. It was always the underdog, the victim, that stirred her to the depth of her being. At the same time she had a deep love of Russia and believed that communism was the only possible way forward for mankind: 'Workers of the World, Unite! You have nothing to lose but your chains!' she would shout, fists clenched. 'To each according to his need, from each according to his ability! That's communism! And what did Jesus say? "Love each other!" It's the same!' But attacking Finland … the alliance with Hitler … these things were hard to accept. Stalin was one of her heroes. She had quite an array of heroes over the years; they included, at various times, Tolstoy, Lenin, Trotsky, Mao, Haile Selassie, Nehru, Gandhi, Kenyatta, Tito – and Stalin, the 'little father' of his country. It was almost a relief for her when Germany attacked the Soviet Union in June 1941 and she could revert to her reverent love of Mother Russia and her brave, simple peasants and her wise, benevolent leader so heroically fighting the Nazis. Even after the murder of Trotsky, after all the show trials and the blood-baths and the revelations concerning the prison camps and the 'gulag' – somewhere in her heart she retained that image of Stalin.

In 1940, in March, Finland surrendered to the Soviet Union. Soon after, our beloved Denmark and Norway were occupied by the Nazis; in May, the Netherlands were overrun. Would Britain be next? The word went round that these countries had fallen so rapidly because German parachutists had been able to link up with Nazi sympathisers inside. Now Britain feared the same might happen here – and who more likely to keep them informed than we refugees from Germany?

One afternoon, when I got home, Mu greeted me with the dramatic announcement: 'Your father is in prison.'

We refugees were now 'enemy aliens'; the adults had been questioned by special tribunals, and assigned to different categories, A, B or C; some women and most men, including Fe, were interned. Place names were obliterated on station platforms, and the German parachutist and the German spy became bogeymen – though jokes were made about them too: one cartoon showed a bowler-hatted Briton, lost because there were no sign-posts, asking the way from a German parachutist, who had a map. Now Mu had a new cause. She assumed that, since Fe was in an 'internment camp' on the Isle of Man, he must be suffering terrible hardships, and sent him regular parcels of home-made biscuits and any other goodies she could lay her hands on. She included daffodil bulbs in one, to beautify the camp in spring: but he was not grateful: 'There was something wrong with the onions you sent,' he wrote, 'they tasted awful.' In fact he was as happy in internment as he had been at the Odenwaldschule. The 'camp' consisted mainly of seaside boarding houses; he was among some of the most learned men Germany had produced, and they very quickly organised themselves into a kind of university – a truly 'universal' one as professors and experts in the most divers fields happily lectured to each other on their subjects: Schumacher (of *Small is Beautiful* fame) on economics, Paul Maas on Greek metre, Professor Welleszc on Byzantine music, while Rawicz and Landauer gave concerts, as did the four musicians who later formed the world-famous Amadeus Quartet.

While Fe was away, Mu naturally used his room for another family of refugees – the Rosenbergs. Ludwig was a teacher at Dartington Hall School, and must have been interned; his wife Anna, who had two children and was expecting the third, had to leave Devon as the fear of invasion had led to the coastal areas of the country being declared 'protected areas' where no refugee – no potential spy or collaborator – could stay. Anna worshipped her son, aged about five, and one evening at supper time, when he deliberately poured his cocoa over the white table cloth, and Mu asked Anna to tell him to stop, she said dreamily: 'No, he must not be stopped. Can't you see how artistic he is? He mustn't be frustrated!' The three Jewish boys, Ernst, Erich, Kurt, shared an upstairs bedroom; and there was a Jewish couple, but they did not stay long: when Mu asked them what their profession was, they said, quite coolly: 'We are terrorists.' Mu though she had misheard, but no: 'We believe Israel must be won for the Jews by terrorism.' At that, Mu asked them to leave her house, at once. They were quite surprised at her reaction, but went quietly enough, once they had found somewhere else to stay.

I would like to try to convey what it was like living in the refugee community in north Oxford. I was only six years old, but I have vivid memories of those people who came and went in the house. Quite a few of them were academics who hoped to resume their careers at Oxford University; there were women like Frau Borcherdt, who bowed down to me and smiled archly and said: 'Your grandfather brought me into the world.' That was Fe's father, Opa Leo, in whose clinic in Berlin women went to have their babies – including the mother of this Frau Borcherdt. But Opa Leo, I knew, was dead now. There was Frau Kann, who lived in a flat in Woodstock Close and made a lot of fuss about making coffee; there was an elderly couple, the Slutzewskis, who lived a little further along our road; having been actors they kept using high-flown quotations from plays all the time: 'Emil, my hound of heaven, please pass me your cup', or: 'Oh thou my only child that I bore in agony, where have I left my purse?' The Liepmanns had a big house in Rawlinson Road, and lodgers. Herr Dr Liepmann had a little goatie beard which he would thrust out horizontally from time to time. This made him look like a fierce gnome. His thin, puritanical wife, a pastor's daughter, would scoop the last remnants of egg white out of the shells with her finger when she was baking. She always looked as if she was exercising her Christian forbearance, as I daresay she was; her husband was as aggressive as a small dog and I can remember him saying sharply: 'Elizabeth, I would like to draw your attention to the fact that you have just interrupted me for the third time.' No doubt she had, inevitably, as he – a professor of economics before Hitler – did not *speak*, but *lectured*, non-stop, and if she needed to say something she had to interrupt in her somewhat croaking voice. But she was absolutely loyal to him, and had not hesitated to emigrate with him, though she was not Jewish. She was extremely kind and gentle and a good friend to Mu; and her husband was one of the small group that founded Oxfam a few years later.

When we went to the dentist, it was of course to a refugee dentist: Dr Pick, in St John's Street, a small man in a white coat with a lamp on a ring round his bald head. He insisted on speaking 'English' –

'Gut morrning, pliss tek a sit.' His word for 'rinse' was a version of the German 'spülen': 'Spill pliss,' he would say. He gave me an injection which made my lips so numb that I could bite through them without feeling anything. I did this a lot, and it led to an inflammation of my mouth; for ages, just at Christmas, I could only eat strained porridge, charmingly called haferschleim – oat slime.

Old Mrs Rosenberg – Ludwig's mother – lived in St John's Street, too. She had managed to get into England on the scheme which had English people engage refugees as domestic workers. Her employer was a Mrs Gerrard, a professor's widow, a pleasant, easy-going old soul who lived in St John's Street and kept a fine library in her toilet, which had a window overlooking the garden. I know, because years later, when I was transferred to a secondary school, I needed to catch up on a year's French, and Frau Rosenberg undertook to teach me: 'Voici Toto, Toto entre,' and so on. Frau Rosenberg was a highly intellectual and intelligent woman, gentle and generous; but she looked like a haggard old witch, with a long purple nose, usually with a drop hanging from the end of it, so we only ever called her 'hexchen' – Little Witch.

The Meinhardts lived on Woodstock Road, and had a daughter, Marianne, who was my age, and a younger son. Marianne developed a passion for horses, and taught me to ride on Port Meadow: or rather, she taught me to sit on a horse, gallop, and fall off without hurting myself, still holding the reins, during a short period when my pocket money shot up to half-a-crown a week, for reasons unknown. Another family was the Hammerschmidts: Herr Hammerschmidt had been a pharmacist 'Vor Hitler' and now did almost nothing all day except sit in their house in Museum Road and pontificate. He believed any argument could be settled if he raised one finger and intoned a quotation from Goethe, whom he called 'Der

Altmeister von Weimar' – the Old Sage of Weimar. He almost fell off his chair once when I was not silenced, but said, 'I disagree with Goethe there.' That was blasphemy. His wife came from a very rich family: she had fur coats and all sorts of expensive tailor-made clothes and hand-sewn shoes in the fashion of the 1930s. They had a housekeeper, Irma, who had a round, Slavonic face and light blue eyes. Their daughter, Gretchen, was mentally disturbed, and their son, Hans, was not like other boys: tall and gangling and cruelly bullied at school.

A frequent visitor – and long-term friend – was Professor Maas, a brilliant classical scholar. He had taught Greek at the University of Königsberg (then part of Germany, now Russian, and named Kaliningrad) until April 1934, when the 'Gesetz zur Wiederherstellung des Berufsbeamtentums' (law for the restoration of the professions) passed by the Nazis soon after they had been elected, purged all academic posts, the entire civil service, in fact all the 'professions', of Jews, who had for too long been cheating 'Aryans' out of these privileged and desirable positions. Clearly it was intolerable to have a Jew lecturing on Greek and Latin prosody, so Paul Maas, then aged 54, was forced to retire. In 1935 the Nuremberg Race Laws made him give up his house to a Nazi family – though he did not go willingly, but fought a fierce legal battle, believing that Germany was still a 'Rechtsstaat' – a country under the rule of law. He still had some money and travelled extensively. He attended the biennial International Congress of Papyrology in Florence in 1935, where a brilliant young British scholar, Enoch Powell, read a paper. Powell was then only 22, and already a fellow of Trinity College, Cambridge. He and Paul Maas discovered shared interests in such academic fields as textual criticism and became fast friends. After a lively exchange of letters they met again at the next Papyrology Congress, which was held in Oxford in 1937. Maas stayed at the house of Professor Gilbert Murray on Boars Hill, and also at Enoch Powell's parents' home in Sussex, and at Trinity College, Cambridge. Powell described the relationship between Maas and himself as one of the greatest intellectual romances of his life. He went to Sydney, Australia, where he became a very youthful Professor of Greek, and Maas returned to Germany.

In July 1938, Jews in Germany were obliged to carry identity cards; then they all had to adopt the name Israel or Sara; none of this deterred Paul Maas. Like so many others – like Oma – he was a staunch German patriot, and regarded the Nazis as a temporary aberration; and he seems in some respects to have led a charmed life, though he was imprisoned for eight days in connection with the 'Kristallnacht'. Powell, on his way back to Britain from New Zealand, had stopped over in Berlin. He heard that his revered teacher was in prison and managed to get him out by persuading the British Consul to issue a visa for him to go to England. Powell went to Königsberg to visit him, and tried to persuade him to go to Britain. But still, Maas was not impressed by the antics, as he saw it, of the Nazis, and stayed. His Danish wife went to Denmark, where she spent the war. Paul Maas did not set out for Britain via Hamburg and Harwich until August 31 1939 – the very day when the Nazis staged their phoney 'Polish attack' on the German radio station at Gleiwitz (Gliwice) near the Polish frontier, which triggered the Second World War: it began as Maas reached Oxford.

He used to visit us quite often to discuss classical topics with my father. Powell, now in his smart major's uniform, sometimes came too. The three of them were able to converse in classical Greek: there were few other people in the world who could. When Powell shook hands, he stared into your eyes and gripped your hand so tightly you almost screamed with pain. Maleen was quite flustered by his powerful masculinity. He seemed to be fascinated by my mother, as quite a number of our visitors were, sitting talking round the metal 'Anderson Shelter' which served as a table in the kitchen, and under which we were to hide in case of an air raid – which never came in Oxford. I can remember various men, including Powell, watching Mu at work rather intently. But she would play the part of the traditional German 'hausfrau', urging the men to go and talk in the front room while she prepared their coffee and brought it in to them.

After the war, Powell went into politics. Mu followed his well-documented career with interest and growing misgivings. There was little further contact with him. He moved further and further to the Right, culminating in the notorious 'Rivers of Blood' speech, which unleashed an ugly upsurge of racism. Yet he had helped to rescue Paul Maas from the Nazis.

Professor Maas worked for the Oxford University Press. He had a room on the top floor of a house in Beaumont Street. Guided in all things by pure reason, he kept his water supply in a large battered watering can, as his room was some way from the nearest tap, and he needed water from time to time for his tea and coffee and for washing. He rode a large bicycle which he would mount from behind with a dramatic leap after a vigorous run to get up speed – necessary for balance, as he maintained. He was fond of trenchant sayings like: 'My principle is to have no principles.' He was a keen gardener, but he drew the line at plants with shallow roots, unless they were to be eaten. He was knowledgeable about pruning roses, which have deep roots; but when I brought him a bunch of flowers, he threw them angrily into his bin: 'Do you think I want to be surrounded with these dying things?'

Our visitors would often start singing. Schubert's *Der Lindenbaum* was their favourite, sung with enormous feeling, elderly refugees mopping the tears from their eyes. Before and after internment, my father and Professor Maas would try to take charge, Fe on the piano, Professor Maas by striking a tuning fork against his own bald skull and giving us all our notes; we would sing a Bach chorale in four parts. Sometimes Professor Maas took the top line, falsetto, which had us doubled up with suppressed laughter. Fe would try to get us to sing correctly, rather than emotionally; he got Maleen and me to sing songs and duets by Mendelssohn and Mozart, or to listen while he played a Haydn sonata. And we knew countless German folksongs which Mu sang as we did the housework.

*****

The talk was all about the threatened invasion. We were given gas masks. Mine was in a square cardboard box with a string to go round my shoulders, and it kept it bobbing up and down on my back as I walked along the Woodstock Road to and from school – except that I very often forgot it. I would notice half way to school, and then be faced with the dilemma: to go back home and fetch it from the hook by the front door – and be scolded for being late – or go without it, and be scolded for forgetting it. To this day, I occasionally experience the old lurch of guilt as my hand goes round to my back and finds no gas mask there.

What a gas attack would entail never dawned on me. But the Nazis' victorious progress was apparently unstoppable. The Channel Islands were occupied by the Germans; France collapsed; the little boats crossed the Channel to rescue the troops from Dunkirk; the German word Blitz – lightning – came to mean the Luftwaffe's bombardment of London; the newspapers showed warning pictures of 'Firebomb Fritz'; the grown-ups' talk was full of English expressions: the Battle of Britain, 'The Few', and the name of Churchill. Once again, Mu was assuring us that she would never let the Nazis get hold of us alive.

Since I could hardly understand what people were saying, I would slip out through the steam-filled scullery to the garden, to play with my toy animals. I half believed that they all came to life in the night. The metal cow looked too old to produce milk; but I thought that maybe the other, rubber one was milked by elves when I was asleep. During the day I patiently fenced in tiny meadows with bits of stick, and found titbits like daisies or apple blossom petals for them to eat, especially my favourite, the little foal, who always kept close to his mother.

Chapter 16

Maleen and I did not last long at Rye St Antony School, and here is Mu's account of the reason why:

> 'One day Maleen and Gabi came home and told me that the whole school had assembled to give thanks to St Teresa, because an old gentleman had died and had left his palatial house in Headington to the school. I told them that St Teresa had nothing to do with it: the old gentleman had died because his time was up, and not because St Teresa had killed him off in order to help the school: besides, cheques come from the bank, not from Heaven. Gabi had already told me that she must not slide down the banisters at school because it would distress this same St Teresa. Next day Maleen proclaimed in school: "My mother says cheques come from the bank and not from heaven." Then I received a letter from the bishop asking me to sign an undertaking that I would never again interfere in the religious education of my children; and I was to ensure they attended mass regularly. Of course, I could not do so. Instead, I went to see Mrs Hastings, and told her about St Teresa and the cheque, and sliding down the banisters, expecting her to laugh. But she said quite seriously: "Didn't you know that St Teresa takes a particular interest in girls' schools?" No, I did not, so the only thing I could do was to take both girls out of that school at once.'

So we were transferred – Maleen to Milham Ford, and I to St Denys, an elementary girls' school in Winchester Road.

Sister Constance and Sister Catherine, Society of the Holy and Undivided Trinity

My new school, St Denys, was a primary school for girls. It was founded in 1854, at the height of the Oxford Movement, as I learned many decades later, by the Anglican nuns of the Holy Trinity Convent in Woodstock Road. The convent building still exists and is now St Antony's College. The school in Winchester Road has vanished; but in those days there were five classrooms – Standards One to Four and the Remove – and a cloakroom, with rows of pegs on stands and little washbasins along the wall where a narrow staircase led up to Sister Constance's tiny office. She was the Headmistress, and reminded me of Churchill. The toilets were outside in a separate building always referred to as

'The Offices'. Mrs Silcox was the teacher in Standard One, a thin woman with bulging eyes who impressed me greatly with her artistic skills: for Christmas she produced a frieze of the Holy Land, and helped us to cut out camels and wise men and shepherds and stick them onto it. Sometimes Miss Bamwell was in charge, a large, lumpish woman whose grey hair was twisted into a row of snails in the nape of her neck. Miss Wright was a glamorous young woman who played the piano so brilliantly in our singing lessons that she could make us positively hear how –

the wind whistles cold on the moor of a night.

I would teach Mu the songs I learned when I came home, to add to her repertoire. 'Swanee River' had her in tears:

When shall I hear de bees a-humming
All round de hive –

and 'Poor Old Joe' made her weep so much we tried to cheer her up and make her laugh (which was also easy) by putting in actions:

I'm coming, I'm coming
For my head is bending low

…'to my toe' we would growl, repeatedly, bowing down as we plodded through the kitchen, and she would laugh as helplessly as she had been weeping before.

When the American soldiers came to Oxford in large numbers later in the war, Miss Wright was seen one evening *kissing* a Yank in Friar's entry. Shocking! Very soon afterwards, she was no longer at the school. She was replaced by a shy young nun, Sister Catherine, whose teeth protruded.

Behind the school there was an air-raid shelter which had been built 'for the duration' of the war, like so many things: the phrase was used for closed shops and factories and many other privations. It was a dank, dark, windowless brick building in which we spent many hours, though there were no air-raids in Oxford, either for an 'air-raid practice', or because the warning sirens had howled – perhaps a German bomber had lost its way and had been seen approaching Oxford – and no one had heard the 'All Clear'. Here we sat on narrow benches, getting very bored, and the teachers would try to keep our spirits up by singing 'Ten Green Bottles', endless verses of 'One Man Went to Mow', 'Old Macdonald had a Farm', or 'Underneath the Spreading Chestnut Tree'.

Near the shelter there was a patch of gravel where we had PE, standing in lines and jumping and flapping our arms. This was difficult for me at first as I was wearing heavy knee-high boots, which I detested. They were totally un-English. But when we twisted, arms akimbo, and the teacher called 'AND left left left AND right right right', I learned those two important words. For years I had to imagine myself back on that patch of gravel when I needed to remember which was right and which was left. Behind the convent there was a field where we played rounders – at which I may say without undue modesty that I sometimes excelled, hitting the ball as high as the tall trees.

There were prayers every morning, and soon I had memorised Sister Constance's favourite bible reading: 'Behold ye the lilies of the field ...' as well as the Lord's Prayer. We put on extraordinary plays: in one, I was a banana in a fruit salad ('But nothing's as nice as fruit salad and cream'); in another, I emerged from Pandora's box wailing: 'We are the TROUBLES!' and was startled when the audience laughed, instead of being frightened. There was one in which my friend Anne was King Canute, and I one of her flattering courtiers. For this I had borrowed a toy sword from Malcolm Brookes, the boy next door, and thrust it through my belt. But while we were flattering the King, culminating in: 'Even the waves of the sea will obey you!' my belt came undone and my sword started slipping. When Anne said: 'We'll see about that! Meet me on the beach tomorrow!' we were supposed to walk off the acting area. I felt I had to maintain the fiction of my sword being in my belt and must not hold it with my hand; so I clutched it unobtrusively between my knees and inched along in such an awkward way that Mu, who was in the audience, assumed I needed to go to the lavatory. In the next scene, all the girls who did not have speaking parts were ranged in rows in front of us, representing the waves of the sea. When Anne pretended to challenge them to obey her, they ran forward and backwards, a little nearer each time, just like breakers, until they knocked Anne off her chair – thereby proving a point about flattery.

There were quite a lot of outings from the school, which meant long walks in a 'crocodile' before and after: to Tumbling Bay for swimming (but I learned to swim at 'Dames' Delight' in the University Park, the opposite number of 'Parsons' Pleasure') and once to the gas works, a hellish place with huge, ugly structures, clouds of steam and smoke, clanking and hissing noises, coal and coke fragments crunching underfoot, and a pervasive, sour smell. There was a metal staircase winding up the enormous gasometer, and I started climbing up it. After a time I was noticed and a terrified teacher implored me to come down. I lingered. It was rather nice, frightening a grown-up like that. Then I ran down, and was 'told off'.

*****

The more I learned English, the more I forgot Danish. At first my brother and sister and I only spoke Danish to each other; but soon we started using English. I would lie in bed trying to remember Danish. I would try to count in Danish. More and more numbers vanished. It was like watching holes appearing in fabric, and growing larger, till it had all gone. With our parents we spoke German. Outside, the English language made me feel as if my brain was wrapped in cotton wool: I lived in a blur of incomprehension. It seemed essential to learn perfect English. I collected words and phrases as if my life depended on it. I did not want people to know that I wasn't English, and I was terrified lest I betray my origin with a wrong word. One that gave me particular trouble was 'flicker'. I remember standing on the wooden drawbridge over the canal at the bottom of Frenchay Road, cudgelling my brains. The German for the same phenomenon was flimmern. Or was that the English? Which was which? (I hadn't heard of dictionaries.) If I got it wrong, people might realise I wasn't English. It was even worse when I was asked me my name 'Gabbi? (or Garbi?) Ooh, that's a funny name. Where are you from, then?' And then, the game was up; my whole shameful life history would be revealed. German! Half Jewish! Refugee! Enemy alien!

Of course the girls at school had great sport with my name: 'Gabbi's scabby' or 'Gabbi's got the gift of the gab'; or 'Garbi's garbage.' I envied the true English girls with names like Susan and Jane, their fluency, their natural patriotism and straightforward hatred for the Jerries. I wished that my hatred of the Jerries was not complicated by the fact that I was a Jerry myself, speaking their language. How could a simple English girl, whose fathers and brothers were fighting the Jerries, ever understand such a tangle? I was deeply ashamed of my knowledge of German. When I went to Devon to stay with the Rosenbergs at Dartington Hall for a holiday with a German book (*Hannibals Schwert*) to read on the train, I wrapped it in brown paper and tried to hide it from the friendly guard and his, 'What's that you're reading, then?' burning with shame and fear.

It all came to a head one day in the asphalt playground at St Denys. There was one desirable wall to bounce a ball against – between the back door and a window – so we had to take turns at that wall. But Eunice Coghill would not give way, though she had had a long turn, and the argument became heated. Suddenly Eunice shouted:

'You're just a dirty little German rat!'

At this, a gaping void seemed to open under me, into which I was falling helplessly, in floods of tears, unable to do more than gasp

The desirable wall

'And you're an English rat!' realising as I said it that a proper English person could not be a rat, like a Jerry, and that I was not only unacceptable to the Germans, who wanted me dead, for being half Jewish, I was not acceptable to these English girls either, for being half German, or to anyone, anywhere, ever.

Some of the older girls ran to fetch Sister Constance, who soon stormed onto the playground, her veil flying in the wind, looking more Churchillian than ever; she ordered everyone into their classrooms, stood in front of us, glaring, muscles in her jaws pulsating; made me sit on a chair facing them all; and said: 'I'd like to flog every one of you.'

I fervently wished I could cease to exist, while she harangued the girls, most of whom had nothing to do with the case. She was giving them a lesson in collective responsibility. Finally she insisted on every girl getting up from her desk and coming to me to apologise. It was extremely embarrassing. After all the others had left to go home, Sister Constance pushed Eunice and me – both of us sobbing again – roughly into each other's arms. 'There now,' she said. 'Kiss and make friends.'

Which we both found rather difficult.

Anne was waiting for me; so was a fat girl called Gillian Kirby, who lived in Hayfield Road. We discussed what had happened as we roamed home, and agreed that Sister Constance had been unfair to demand apologies from all the girls – like Gillian and Anne. They said they hadn't known what to say, and had mumbled 'I'm sorry Garbi, I hope it won't happen again', wondering if that was right. But when I got home and told my parents what had happened, they expressed their admiration for Sister Constance, and told me a few of the things some German headteachers were doing to Jewish children, and had done to Peter and Maleen.

*****

It was while walking along Woodstock Road four times a day that I started worrying about time. I could not see or feel or touch it, yet nothing happened without it. I would look along to the next lamp-post. Soon, however slowly I walked, I would be there, looking back at this one. What was it that pushed everything into the past like that?

When I got home, I would fling open the door, shout to tell everyone I was home, slam the door, drop coat and gas mask and satchel on the floor and run along the corridor, jump down the step and slam into the kitchen door – so hard I once broke a pane of glass in the door. Then Fe – who had been released from internment by now — would fling open his study door upstairs and shout – Jupiter thundering from Olympus – about the need to be quiet, because he was having his necessary rest. I forgot this almost every day. Mu would shoo me out into the garden and start shouting back up the stairs at Fe. After a while Mrs Brookes next door would bang on the wall in protest at the noise; Mu would seize some heavy object and bang back. Fe would go rumbling back into his study and slam the door.

The reason why he needed this afternoon rest was because he did his real work at night. This work was his raison d'être. He would sit hunched at his big desk, several books propped open on it, peering at photographs of

156

ancient tattered papyruses through a magnifying glass, smoke curling up from his Wild Woodbine cigarette, working out what words or bits of words had been written in the missing parts of the papyrus. He could only do this during the night because during the day he had to do 'coolie work' in the Mansfield College library – to support us, as he often stressed. So his prolonged after-dinner naps were sacrosanct.

Sometimes he took me along to the library, housed in New College, and gave me big, boring books with pictures of old buildings to look at, while he arranged books on the shelves and sorted out the catalogue. Afterwards we would walk round the College garden. It was sometimes used for military exercises, and the word 'BLOCKED' had been chalked on the wall beside the archway to the front quad. This produced one of Fe's witticisms: 'Add just two letters and what do you get? BLOCKHEAD!' He laughed uproariously.

Fe joined the ARP (Air Raid Precaution) and spent chilly nights standing round in the street ready to spring into action if bombs started falling – as they never did on Oxford. Once there was a major training exercise for ARP wardens on St Edward's school grounds. A real wooden shed was set on fire and my tall, gauche father had to take a turn pumping water from a bucket into a hose with a stirrup pump. In vain – the shed was reduced to a pile of ashes and we all had sandwiches and tea in the gathering dusk before going home.

*****

I was enrolled in the Brownies, and spent hours walking, or rather rambling to their meetings in Wolvercote or, later, St Ebbes. Again I was fascinated by the lamp-posts: each one had 'City of Oxford' embossed near the base, and the emblem showing the 'cow in a puddle'. And this at a time when all road signs, station names, and so on, had been obliterated, so that German spies, dropping down by parachute, should not know where they were! The authorities had not noticed that the information was on all these lamp-posts! So I wrote 'This is BRISTOL', with chalk on the brick garden walls along the Woodstock Road. I'm ashamed to say it was not only to mislead the German spies, but to get them to direct the Luftwaffe to bomb Oxford. I thought air raids were exciting; they were reported in the newspapers, so I wished we could have some in Oxford – so well had the grown-ups shielded me from knowledge of the horrors of war.

Such activities, and picking up bits of rubbish, examining old bus tickets to glean more English words, making bracelets out of the long inflorescences that lay on the ground under the edible chestnut trees, pondering over notices to elicit their meaning ('trespassers will be prosecuted' took me a long time), stroking cats – meant that I was often very late arriving at the Brownie meetings – 'Just in time to go home!' said Brown Owl cheerfully.

✼✼✼✼✼

My early years in Oxford were brightly lit by my friendship with Anne.

Anne

The war, troubles at home, school, were all less important than our private fantasy world of ships and aeroplanes and all sorts of adventures. We would roam down from her house in Polstead Road, across Aristotle Bridge, to the playground, where the swings became the whirling propellers of a Spitfire we were repairing in mid-flight, which involved my raising my feet and holding on only with my hands when she whistled. Alas, on one occasion I let go with my hands too and crashed down onto the cinders and was rather badly hurt. Or we would go to the railway and place a penny on the rail, hoping a train would flatten it so that it could be used as an identity disc (which everyone was supposed to carry, in case of air raids, but we had lost ours). We never found the flattened penny. Near the railway was an abandoned dump of builders' materials, where mounds of gravel and sand, overgrown with weeds, produced a wonderful terrain for exciting games of hide-and-seek, which we played with some boys. But when they started playing football, we were told that as girls we could not join in. We were furious. As we walked sulkily back along Polstead Road, we decided that there must have been a war at one time between men and women which the men had won, so that now they were the bosses. One day soon, we promised each other, there would be another war, and this time we would win, and then the boys would be the inferior sex. Secretly, I thought that probably I was a boy, and had always been dressed as a girl by mistake.

Me

Usually we would go across the railway bridge and down onto Port Meadow and tell each other stories of the kingdom as it actually was, with the children in charge and the grown-ups having to do as they were told. At times we practised tree-climbing on a willow in preparation for a career as sailors on tall ships, when we would need to climb up and down the rigging: my favourite book was *A Girl Before the Mast*, and I had memorised the names of all the sails and rigging of a four-masted barque. High in the branches on a windy day we could almost see the heaving ocean waves come rolling across the grass. Once Anne's delicate little sister Clare came with us, and we picked cuckoo flowers and made a wreath and crowned her Queen of the May. If it rained we had to stay in Anne's house. Once we decided to put on a play. Having never noticed that plays had plots, ours was simply a succession of ideas. One was 'Autumn comes whistling overhead', enunciated by Anne, at which point I leapt off a table outside the door into the acting area in the basement kitchen with my arms outstretched. Our audience – Anne's mother, aunt, and grandparents – were very polite, but puzzled. We also had a go at cooking, and decided to see what happened if one cooked opposites: sugar – and salt; cheese – and jam; marmite – and honey. The result was such that a certain smell which occasionally reaches my nostrils still makes me feel sick.

Every morning, Anne would be waiting for me at the corner of Polstead Road to go to St Denys. We walked so slowly, stopping to discuss everything we saw and thought of, that by the time we reached 'Phil & Jim' (St Philip and St James' Church) it was often late, and we would start concocting our excuses. Anne's best one was: The clocks on the four sides of the church all said a different time, so we 'didn't know which one to go by'. The reason why they said different times was, of course, our incredibly slow progress round the sides of the church.

One day Sister Constance sent for me to come up to her little office. There sat a large woman with a large folder of papers and a stop-watch. Sister Constance explained that I was to have my intelligence measured. As an enemy alien I was not entitled to sit for the scholarship which enabled a few girls to go to a grammar school; but this test should have the same effect. I found myself answering strange questions, such as: could this triangle fit into this square? The upshot was that I had to leave St Denys and enter the secondary school, St Faith's, its sister school in the Woodstock Road, which I hated: at St Denys we resented the girls at St Faith's in their pink, maroon and grey uniforms and told each other 'St Faith's girls are stuck up.' Now I was to go over to the enemy, because I was brainy. I wished I wasn't.

Far worse was the fact that Anne had to leave Oxford, because her mother had to work and didn't have the time to look after her two girls, Anne and Claire; so they went to live with an aunt at Twickenham. My friendship with Anne had meant that the 'dark days of the war', the fear of a German invasion, the fear of the Nazis, had meant almost nothing to me. Now we only saw each other when she came to Oxford during school holidays, when it would take us quite a time to get over a sense of strangeness and back into the swim of our symbiosis.

I spent a lot of time alone, now. I lost interest in my farm animals when my favourite, the little foal, disappeared and I couldn't find him though I looked under every leaf in the garden. I was keen on practising my acrobatics, head-stands, hand-stands, cartwheels, forming a bridge, or playing ball games against the windowless yellow brick wall of Mr Goldsworthy's shop in Oakthorpe Place, or skipping – how I longed for a skipping rope with wooden handles and ball bearings, instead of my piece of washing line! – and playing hopscotch in the road (there were virtually no cars) – again, wishing I could have a proper marker made of blue glass, instead of having to use a pebble – but we were too poor.

In the holidays I sometimes went to North Wales with Fe, to a village called Brithdir, not far from Dolgelley. We travelled by train and stayed in a grey stone house crammed with furniture – I could just find enough space on the floor between my double bed and massive wardrobe to lie down and read *Three Men in a Boat* and laugh myself silly. That was when it rained, as it very often did. In fact we were often overtaken by rain on our day-long hikes along the torrents in the valleys, up Cadair Idris, round the crater high above the mysterious lake. Once I slipped on the wet grass and got my pants muddy. Fe made me take them off and washed them in a stream and continued down waving them on the end of his stick. I was hideously embarrassed as we entered the village and had to walk past a group of boys. They had a dog, a collie, with whom I had fallen in love; I could hardly bear to leave him.

Once we got up before dawn to see the sunrise up in the mountains. We sat on a rocky ledge, and Fe held me and wrapped his 'Lodenmantel', his loose green woollen coat, round me, for it was bitterly cold. As the sun rose we lay on the edge of a precipice, looking down, and a fierce wind blowing up the rock face distorted his features. I learned to love mountains, and I still love them, giants on whose knees and shoulders we can clamber, on whose massive torsos we can lie. The only bad experience was crossing a steep slope of scree. I was terrified as the rough stones slid away from under my feet; but Fe only smiled as he waited, and when at last I got there, took my hand and assured me that I had not been in any danger.

On hot days we took the train for the short ride to Barmouth and swam in the sea. This was where Fe expounded his views on true Jews and Levantines, and where, after some hesitation, he discarded his woollen bathing trunks and pranced happily across the sand and into the breakers. Later, he told me that as he sat on the warm sand watching me he realised that I was getting into the grips of a current and was in danger of being carried out to sea and drowning. I noticed him after a while, gesticulating and entering the water – I couldn't hear his shouts because of the noise of the water – and swam back reluctantly, convinced his fears were unfounded – but a little pleased to see how anxious he was.

Apart from our landlady (who would call: 'Dinner is ready if you are!') we got to know two other women. One kept the village shop. She was extremely fat and greasy. Her tiny shop was packed with everything imaginable, from bacon to corsets, notepaper to boots. A huge cylinder of butter stood on the counter, next to a similar round of cheese, and she would hack pieces off with a big knife and slap them into pieces of newspaper for you. On warm days bits of butter would slither down onto the black, greasy floor. The other woman was English, and profoundly deaf: her face was pale and twisted, and she spoke in a curious honking way. She was an author and showed us a children's book she had written and illustrated. It concerned a friendly dragon, who helped people carry water by letting them hang a bucket on each of the spines on his back. She had a tiny two-seater car, and took us to Port Meirion, that fabulous Italianate seaside town: Fe sat in front with her, while I was behind in the open boot, somewhat nose-out-of-joint.

*****

I did make some friends at St Faith's: Jocelyn, a tiny girl with long plaits, and Joy, huge and short-haired, who would invite Jocelyn and me to sit down among the damp coats in the cloakroom and 'meditate on the futility of life'. I was still building up my English. At the beginning of one play-time, I heard a teacher ask a prefect to go out and see if it was raining. The girl came back and announced it was 'more like a penetrating drizzle'. Two new words! I rushed up the steps to see what a penetrating drizzle was, missed my footing, and fell with my face on a higher step. In fact I had landed on my front teeth, which left two white marks on the step, and were – and still are – slightly chipped. Never mind! I now knew exactly what penetrating drizzle meant.

I did not stay long at St Faith's; my father, perhaps remembering his own transfer to a more prestigious school in Berlin, when his mother felt he was not being stretched sufficiently, transferred me to the Oxford High School, with its navy blue uniform, which I hated: just as St Denys girls resented St Faith's, so St Faith's girls resented the High School girls, who were stuck up and always won all the inter-school competitions. Once again, I was obliged to go over to the enemy, and once again regretted having brains. My chief trouble at that school was boredom.

Miss West, the buck-toothed games teacher, would stand at the entrance to the hall for Prayers every morning and note any girl whose back was not straight, or who was breaking the 'no-talking-in-the-corridor' rule. Then we would sit on the floor in silence, the teachers on chairs alongside; Miss Stack would pace in and onto the platform, followed by the head girl carrying her books. Later I was in Mrs Archer's choir and stood by the window overlooking the Banbury Road to harmonise the hymn singing. After prayers we would file out to our lessons. Chemistry was best, because we actually did experiments – though they usually went wrong, so that we would write up what should have happened, not what did. Jumping around in PE was all right, and running up and down the hockey and netball pitches, and swimming. But clause analysis in English with Mrs Thomas, long division sums slanting interminably down the page in maths with Miss Jackson, sentimental French songs with Old Ma Webb, copying drawings of the life cycle of the frog in biology with Miss Brown – I simply had to do outrageous things to make life more interesting. One of my chief aims in life was still to frighten the grown-ups, and I remember enlivening a tedious wait for a French conversation lesson at the top of the building by climbing over the banisters and dangling over the four-storey stairwell. When an anxious, angry teacher ordered me to come back at once, I teased her by moving my hands from one banister to the next for a while, before swinging back over the handrail onto the staircase. Such misdemeanours meant being 'sent to Miss Stack'. We sinners would queue up outside her white-painted door feeling rather frightened, although in time I was aware that all that would happen once I was in there would be: 'Oh Garbi, not again! What is it this time?' followed by a pleasant chat about this and that – my future, for instance, maybe as a doctor – sitting in a comfortable armchair opposite her. Once I was sent to Miss Stack because of an opera Liz and Lillian and I were making up. I was the tenor. Since Miss Tait was always late for Latin on Friday afternoons, we would continue our lunchtime rehearsals while we waited. But Miss Southwell was teaching French in the room next door and asked us repeatedly to make less noise. One Friday, as we entered the classroom, singing a passionate trio, we discovered that Miss Southwell had tried to pre-empt us by writing a message on the blackboard: Please do not make a noise as the girls in the next room are preparing for an examination. Still singing my tenor part, I rubbed the message off the board, which led to the glorious moment when Miss Southwell – a thin, yellowish woman – flung open the door, pointed at the blackboard with a quivering finger, and cried: "Can't you READ?" Of course, there was nothing there to read, so I burst out laughing. This time Miss Stack took a very serious view of the matter; I was given several detentions, and at the next parents' evening Mu was asked if she knew the dreadful thing I had done. Mu, probably mindful of occasions in her own childhood when teachers and parents had seemed to gang up against her, replied: 'Yes, and I supported her very much in this.' She told me this, proudly, in the evening, and of course I was grateful, though I had a sneaking feeling that she should have been angry.

Chapter 17

All the time these things were going on in Oxford, we were getting letters from Oma in Persia and Hedchen in America. During the war, these letters were often delayed for weeks or even months, and many were no doubt lost as ships were sunk. For a time a special kind of airgraph was available: these were photographed and carried as microfilm, by air, to be printed out in the country of destination – stiff little documents they were, with tiny writing, about half the size of the original. Everything was censored. One of my airograms to Oma was rejected by the censor because I had drawn a palm tree – he must have suspected some secret coded message was concealed in it.

Oma's letters were brilliant. They conveyed an impression of sunshine, peace, fun. For instance, here's part of her letter to Mu dated 7.2.39:

'Achim and Marianne are profoundly shocked at the low level of my educa-tion and my hedonism, only reading what I enjoy, instead of improving my mind. They sit there in the evenings reading each other something educa-tional, fat tomes, sometimes in French, sometimes in English, yawning fit to break your heart. From time to time one of them sighs and murmurs: "God, how boring!" but still they persevere. What must be shall be. Meanwhile I sit at the other end of the room with my back to them so as to hear as little as possible of the educational tripe and write letters. Those two discover new gaps in my education every day and are indignant at the serenity with which I accept that. I have not the slightest ambition to improve, except in English, partly because I'm good at it, and want to speak it perfectly, and then because I'm a conscientious teacher, and have started giving English les-sons.'

Looking back, years later, in her Memoirs, she reflects:

'Having spent so many years in complete independence, my own mistress, "lord and master" in my own house, it was not easy for me to adapt to the family. It may not have been easy for the family, either, to accommodate such an intractable being as me. I was accustomed to deciding everything for myself rather than waiting modestly in the background to see what the others decided. I daresay I was hypersensitive. A word emphasised rather more than necessary, for instance "TUESday", to correct a misunderstanding, could easily make me livid, which was unfortunately always visible as my ears would go red. My little Dudu, my youngest granddaughter, who always sat next to me at table, would know if something Achim said annoyed or offended me, and would stroke my knee under the table with her plump little hand and whisper: "He doesn't mean it!" Meanwhile Marianne would

warn Achim: "Careful, her ears are going red!" These were little things, and my anger would evaporate quickly, because all in all Achim was the best, most chivalrous son-in-law anyone could have wished for. Only once did he raise his voice, in fact, he shouted at me. I went out at once and started packing my suitcase, intending to rent a room for myself somewhere else. But when the whole family, including the son-in-law, begged me to stay, I relented.

Then they added a lovely room to their pretty little bungalow for me. It had its own door to the garden, with a high hedge separating my private part of the garden, beneath my window, from the rest. Soon I managed to earn enough through private language lessons to keep myself; it was a great relief to me not to be a burden to my children, at least financially. The American mission school sent me all the little Arabs, Iraqis, Syrians etc to be taught English, so that they could enter the classes appropriate to their age. Some of them knew no English at all, and of course I had no Persian or Arabic, but we managed. Most educated adult Persians at that time spoke fluent, elegant French, far better than I had ever heard in Germany; but as the American and British influence grew, the need for English got stronger and I had many upper-class adult students. Many foreigners whose English was faulty, especially Czechs, but also Poles, Germans, and French, found their way to my small domain and had lessons either in my bit of garden or in my room. I got to know many interesting people, some of whom became real friends, and have remained so.'

From Oma's letter to Mu, 15.7.39:

'... Today I had a great pre-birthday treat: Achim, this dream of a son-in-law, hired a pianino for me. I had no idea, and suddenly, there it was! And while the six Hamale (porters), the transport boss and our gardener still filled the room, I was already sitting there blissfully playing and singing – the clever reader will have guessed it – the four folksongs which constitute my entire repertoire without music. ... I will accompany Achim on his flute, Enge in the "Winterreise", with Hetta (the older granddaughter) I have already played some pieces from a borrowed book of American hymns and children's songs, so now she will really work at her violin-playing, with accompaniment. I'm going to write to Miss Buff in Freiburg and ask her to send me my music. There's to be a great to-do for my 70th birthday – 25 people are expected!'

From Oma's Memoirs:

'Because of the intolerable heat in Teheran in the summer, we moved to Shemran, near the mountains and much cooler, where there was a park owned by the American Embassy with several swimming pools and some houses. That was where my 70 th birthday was celebrated in a most

164

charming way: Achim and Marianne told my life story in humorous verses with big illustrations, and performed it like a couple of buskers to the audience in the garden. Everything I had told them was shown: my gloriously free childhood, my first shy love affair, my year in England as a teacher, my escapade in Paris in 1892, and so on – my whole life, right up to my arrival in Persia.

Life was good in Shemran. One only spent the night indoors, with the doors wide open. All day one was out in the garden, or going for long walks – the landscape, with strangely shaped mountains, folded, and coloured amethyst, amber, purple, lilac, is unforgettable. The stony fields were cultivated by wooden ploughs and little hand sickles. Threshing was carried out by a cart pulled by a donkey, mule or cow, and loaded with stones and children, driving round and round on the sheaves lying on the ground. Afterwards the trampled sheaves would be tossed into the air by hand, so that the grains fell onto the ground and the chaff was blown away by the wind. The Arabs in Palestine used similar methods.'

*****

Oma had had no dog after Harras, her constant companion in Danzig and Zoppot, died. But in Teheran the family had, she writes:

'...a beautiful long-haired Airedale, non-pedigree, called Aloys, with legs slightly too short for perfect beauty, not in the least house-trained. Now I undertook to train him. But I broke three sticks on him, my heart bleeding.'

This dog featured in many of her letters to us. Here's part of one to Peter, dated 21.1.40:

'The other day Aloys attacked a smaller but cheekier cur. I tried to defend the little dog – and fell into a ditch, luckily without water, but very dirty, where, on my knees, I thrashed away at Aloys, but in vain. Finally I handed my stick to a man who was stronger than me and I took advantage of a moment when Aloys was going for the man, snorting with rage, to grab him and – still on my knees on sharp stones – to hold him until the little dog departed. Then I picked myself up out of the dirt and stones and saw that all around people were watching the inglorious battle of the old woman and the beasts from their windows and balconies ...'

And to me she wrote:

'So now at last I'm going to write you the long-promised Aloys letter, since you are so interested in this bosom friend of mine. He is not prone to bite; he confines himself to barking furiously, where Harras

would have bitten. He is filled with love and tenderness up to the brim of his soul. He always wants to sit hand in hand with me, resting his head against me, gaze meltingly into my eyes and then groan with happiness! Wherever I sit, he has to lie beside me. If I get up from my grandmotherly chair by the stove to go to the piano he gets up immediately to lie down beside it. For the night his couch is an armchair, whose cushions are turned over for him. He understands that perfectly. If he feels I am occupying the chair for too long, he will sit in front of me, and look at me pleadingly: "Do please go to bed," and pat my knee again and again until I relent. Since my door to the garden is wide open at night, he gets a screen on that side – a plaid that I hang up – which he appreciates greatly. Before he climbs up onto his armchair, he always comes to my bed first to say goodnight, gives me his paw, rests his head against me, gazes at me lovingly, and then goes off to snore peacefully. During the hot part of the year he prefers to lie under my bed, which is so low that he has to crawl under it on his belly. It's bad for me when he needs to scratch, which he can only do with vigorous blows against my mattress, which of course invariably wake me up. But what doesn't one do, or suffer, for one's love, right?

In the morning he observes my toilet closely and knows precisely when I have combed my hair and got my dress on, then there is a good chance of a morning walk. If I put on my outdoor shoes, then he howls with anticipation. But woe if I take my coat out of the wardrobe! Then he is wild with joy, dances, leaps, barks – the whole house knows: there's going to be a walk. He is quite an elderly gentleman really, eight years old, but out of doors he is as high-spirited and wild as a puppy. His experiences are: interesting corners, trees, crates etc with "visiting cards" from other dogs; rubbish carts full of rotting garbage, the smellier the better; cars rushing past and especially motor cycles; dogs whom he approaches, blissfully wagging his tail at an angle, which is a fine affectation, because he is bitterly disappointed if they are just as friendly to him. He never starts a fight, but of course, if the other one starts biting him, then he bites back vigorously, for the sake of his honour. He has two favourite pubs: an Armenian shop where people, soldiers, etc., often eat sandwiches – he runs in there straight away every time I pass that way and sits down with a companionable smile – and gets a good feed. And – a favourite place – the Canteen or Service Club for British soldiers, where Aunt Marianne helps serve one evening a week and where Uncle Achim then calls for her in the evening, with Aloys. Then Aloys runs straight into the kitchen, where everybody knows him and feeds him. Sometimes I pass that way at six or seven in the evening; he immediately disappears into the kitchen and comes home two, three or four hours later, well fed and satisfied. I take him for a walk two or three times a day and he expects me to. On more than one occasion I spotted his four legs stretched up vertically: that meant that he had found a cadaver, a dead donkey or horse, and was rolling around on it on his back voluptuously. He would return to me, beaming, enveloped in the stench, unspeakably disgusting. As soon as we got home I had to wash him in a tub of warm water. He can conceive of nothing worse than this and tries to escape by hiding under my bed, so that I have to drag him out by the tail or by one leg and tow him to the bath house, where I bolt the door. Then he sees that there is no way out and accepts his fate with a tragic mien. But on Fridays, which is like Sunday here, he has no time for me, follows me unwillingly for a few minutes and then runs straight back. Because on Fridays the family goes for long outings without me, and he trembles with the fear he might miss the start! How does he always know it's Friday? Firstly, because Uncle Achim is at home in the morning; secondly, because a lot of rucksacks are being packed; thirdly – the surest, most convincing sign: Uncle Achim is wearing shorts!! Then he goes berserk. Our whole district knows me and Aloys very well (like in the past, "the little miss with the black Satan" = Harras!). If I stop anywhere and look round for him, some beggar or someone else comes at once and tells me where "sag" (dog) has run to. Sometimes I tell Mashallah, our servant, that Aloys is hungry, he should give him some food, but then I am told he is not gurusneh (hungry), he has left some bread uneaten, and shows it to me, lying on the ground. Then I give it him, bit by bit, and he eats it, whereupon Mashallah shrugs his shoulders and says "Dust" (love). A proper dog has to be fed with love! Harras, my childhood friend, was just the same. He would never touch his food until I had put it back on the cooker, added a few drops of water, stirred it and sniffed at it and said: "Ah, lovely!"– So now you know my Aloys.'

And the end of the story? This is how she tells it in her Memoirs:
'When I left Persia in 1946 with the family, since it was impossible to take him to USA, I had him killed the day before my departure by lethal injection. I held him in my arms, so he suspected nothing and kept still. But my knees were trembling when I left him, dead.'

*****

Aloys was not her only animal. She had a jackdaw too, and she wrote about this bird:
'One day my grandchildren brought me a little featherless jackdaw which they had bought from some children who had taken it from its nest. I reared the poor creature, and she became very big. Like Aloys, she became my constant companion and would sit on my shoulder at meal times and snap the cheese or egg off my bread.

As soon as I opened the mosquito net in the morning she would swoop down elegantly from the highest tree, straight into my room; then suddenly she was all helpless and pathetic, fluttered her wings, opened her beak and screamed blue murder for food; she even pretended she couldn't eat alone. But if I stayed firm and ignored her babyish helplessness she was quite capable of finding her hidden bowl and eating everything in it. If a piece of meat was too big, she would hide it: under the carpet, on the wardrobe, in my slippers, even in my bed – and fetch it out later to deal with at leisure. If I lay on my bed for a nap – whoops, there she was, seeking insects on my head, pinching my ear, poking my nostrils, and I had no rest until I pressed her to me and stroked her; then she would purr contentedly and fall asleep. So all this was quite charming and I was quite pleased to have Jacko and Aloys beside me wherever I went. But – she was a thief. She stole pencils, pens, rubbers, even my precious notebook from my writing table and hid them on the roof; she stole bits of food not only from our kitchen, but from neighbours' as well; she was keen on brooches, rings, scissors, hairpins, and hid them in the most extraordinary places. Once she laid a toothbrush at my feet as a gift which turned out to belong to a neighbour, Miss Rowlie, and of course she left her souvenirs everywhere, preferably on books. I tried to educate her, gave her some hard smacks left and right on her big beak with one finger when she tried to take my fountain pen out of my hand while I was writing. That made her scream, but it didn't stop her.'

I am amazed that she believed so strongly in corporal punishment – under which my mother had suffered so much as a child – that she even administered it to the jackdaw. Of course it didn't work!

'So it was decided, to my regret, that she must be expelled. The children took her along on an evening walk and put her on a tree a long way from our house. And there she stayed as long as it was dark. But very early the next morning she flew into my – her – room. After a second attempt had also failed, we took her by car to Golhak, where the British Embassy had a summer house. At the entrance to the dark garden my poor jackdaw was thrown out of the window. Later I asked a member of the Embassy whether they were missing any shiny objects such as silver spoons? But no, nothing was missing – my poor jackdaw was lost.

We had gone to Golhak for a concert, and during the interval an elderly gentleman in a shabby angora jacket came and sat beside me. Soon we were having an animated discussion about Dickens, whom he admired as much as I do. Much later I discovered that he was Sir Reader Bullard, the British ambassador, an extremely likeable man, erudite, devoid of pretensions. He visited us sometimes in his patched grey jacket, and once I heard him give a talk on the changes in the English language during his lifetime. He spoke a very pure English himself, which I much prefer to American English, which always irritates me with its sloppiness.'

*****

'Mashallah, the cook, housekeeper and moral guardian of the family, had a different relationship with each of us. For Achim he felt deep respect, with some distance; he was jealous of Marianne, fearing for his sovereignty in the domestic sphere; he was hypersensitive to the slightest criticism. Several times he appeared in my room unexpectedly and asked me if I had any wishes: if so, I was to tell him straight away, as he was leaving in the afternoon. That always meant he had been deeply hurt and was giving notice to quit. Then it was my task to soothe him and calm him down – all with my vestigial Persian. But he was so intelligent that he adapted to my Double Dutch, which had virtually no verbs. I would say something like:

"Tschera, Mashallah? Sahib – chube. Chamum – chube. Batschi – dust. Mau – chube. Tschera?" ("Why, Mashallah? The Master – good. Woman – good. Children – you love. I – good. Why?")

Then I would stroke his rather bristling cheek, coax a liberating smile from him, and he would stay. If ever Marianne, the chamum, was not available, he would do his approximately weekly accounts with me, in the following way:

"Sibsami" (taking a potato out of his pocket) "– x rial. Gusht" (showing me a scrap of meat) "x rial", and so on, with vegetables, fruit, etc: he used visual aids. Occasionally there was no money in the house, as Achim's salary was not always paid regularly, and Marianne might be in her laboratory. Then Mashallah would come energetically to me, the chamum busurg or Big Woman, and say curtly: "Chamum busurg – pul!" (money). If I appeared surprised, he would say: "Sahib – pul hitsch" (no money) "Chamum – pul hitsch. Shuma" (you) "kar" (work); "shuma pul". And he would repeat sternly: "Pul!" and I would have to hand over.

Mashallah was concerned for my well-being. If I had been teaching for some hours in my part of the garden he would bring me some refreshment, a piece of water melon or some grapes (angur) saying: "Shuma pis, shuma chaili kar" (You old, you much work) – "indsha kam angur" (here some grapes). In general he was averse to spoiling us with little extras on weekdays; but sometimes he would surprise us with a chocolate pudding and in reply to our astonished "Tschera, Mashallah?" he would turn his head bashfully to one side and say: "Chamum Suzan!" Suzanne – Dudu – was his weak point. When she came home from school she often ran straight into the kitchen to express her urgent desire for chocolate pudding, and he could not resist her – and we all benefited.

He strongly disapproved of the visits – too frequent, in his opinion – of a certain German Dr Mayer, whom he called "the big white one" because he generally wore white clothes. Mayer was undoubtedly courting Marianne, which she thoroughly enjoyed, even occasionally going for a walk with him. Mashallah clearly regarded this as an infringement of sahib's honour, and disapproved of "the big white one": Achim and the children could have done *without him, too. Sometimes, when Marianne was out for a stroll with Mayer, Achim would come to my room, downcast and resigned, with his book or newspaper, for comfort, as it were.'*

*****

'I had a "bodyguard" of five or six little beggar boys, of whom there were large numbers in Teheran, spending their childhood in the streets, begging, playing, hungry, in rags or half naked, even in winter. They would pursue a potential donor relentlessly, even onto the running-board of a cab, till they were given something. They regarded me as a promising case from the first day, with psychological acumen, and after I had bought them some sweets one day they besieged me as soon as I went out onto the street. At least one of them would always be on guard outside our door, and would look at me enquiringly. If I nodded, his whistle would assemble all the scattered friends, and they would escort me to the nearest baker or cake shop, and wait outside till I came out and handed them, or rather, the smallest of them, a bagful. Then they salaamed politely and ran into the nearest side street, crouched in a circle on the ground, and the smallest one shared out. I often observed them secretly – never any quarrelling, never any unfairness in the distribution! I educated them not to beg from me. I told them that from time to time I would give them something nice of my own accord; the signal would be my nod. But if they saw me shake my head they had to go away. And this was adhered to strictly, on both sides. Once they surrounded me hopefully when I was in a cab. I shook my head, and they jumped down, salaamed, and disappeared. The cabbie asked me how I had got them to behave in such an uncharacteristic way. The boys slept in a niche in a wall in the Embassy Road, just round the corner from us, even in the cold winter; there they tended a little charcoal stove, and consumed whatever they had got through begging. We gave them a few blankets, and sometimes one of them would show me – without begging – his tattered trousers, or his non-existent shirt, and would be blissful if I bought him something of the sort.'

*****

She wrote serious letters to her only grandson, Peter. This one is dated 29.3.40:

'...I grew up in a completely rationalistic epoch and environment, so I didn't think much about religion in my early years. I think Christianity is a significant advance on the other religions, especially Judaism, and every word supposed to have been spoken by Christ seems wonderful to me in its goodness and mildness. And I have always tried to live in accordance with his teachings, not because the religion and the church demand it, but because a voice within me wants me to. But as for what the church has done with his

teachings – starting with the pointless schisms – I can't go along with that. I can't pray, because I think that if there is a God, then the earth and its so wretched mankind must be no more than a grain of dust to him, and I would be just the tiniest fraction of that and therefore infinitely insignificant to God, however important I may seem to myself. I do know what it is to feel devotion, most strongly when I look out into the infinity and eternity of the stars, or at the sea, the distant horizon, in fact Nature insofar as it is free of mankind and our works. I sometimes feel devotion in church, too, when the organ plays and I see pious, relaxed faces all round me. But as soon as the preacher opens his mouth it all vanishes and all I want is to get out quickly. ... But this godless old grandmother of yours has more than once, in deepest emotion, wept during the St Matthew Passion.'

She also wrote to Peter about her political ideas on 14.1.43:

'All my life I have keenly felt the injustice and cruel selfishness of capitalistic society, and I feel sure that very much has to be changed before there can be any real peace in the world. I dearly love my little comforts, my privacy, my freedom to live just as I like, yet I think even these modest privileges of mine are an injustice to the greater part of mankind and their wretched conditions. I feel rather happy to be so old; it means I shan't have to live under, say, Bolshevism, which would mean giving up my personal freedom and independence. But I see no alternative if mankind is to get out of the mess they have made of life. If I were young (fortunately I am not!) I would be quite willing to submit to all the hardships, mental and physical, that will have to be imposed until people have learnt to do their duty, by themselves and by each other, voluntarily, without being forced to by any kind of dictatorship. Until that goal is reached, life will be pretty disagreeable and uncomfortable for such self-willed people as me; so I'm glad I shan't live to experience it.'

Many of her letters to my mother describe their idyllic lives in Persia, with plenty of sunshine, friends, and everything they needed. A recurrent topic was the contrast between their well-being in Teheran with Mu's hardships, living in Oxford. Even when the war came close, with the British and Russians invading Persia in August 1941, it led to more enjoyment. On 26.9.41 she wrote:

'...we have had a tiny bit of war here, three days of it, but still we heard a few bombs dropping somewhere. We spent about three days as "guests at the British Legation", camping in the garden with a lot of other people of all nationalities, all harmless and anti-Nazi ... it was rather fun.'

*****

Oma often describes how she has arranged the photos of us on her table and how much pleasure she gets from looking at them. But like Hedchen, she returns again and again to anxious speculation about friends and relations still in Germany, their wretched lives and increasingly desperate attempts to get out. For a time she was able to send them – and us – little parcels of coffee and other good things like halva; but then that modest relief had to stop. Soon even sending letters became problematical. A friend was questioned for hours by the Gestapo because she was getting so many letters from overseas: best to stop writing to her. People in Berlin were only allowed to send one letter abroad a month. Certain names recur: Flörchen, her brother Heinchen's widow, the Little Wolves, her dear cousins, the painter Jula Wolfthorn (to whom she had paid that memorable visit in 1892 in Paris) and her sister Liese, who were to perish in concentration camps.

'*What will the spring bring?*' she wrote on 2.2.40. '*I shudder to think, and yet – there will have to be an end, one way or the other. Recently I read something by H.G.Wells about what is to be done with God's country when it has been defeated: division into lots of separate little states – just what I have long considered to be the only possibility. Once it's all pretty little princely courts, centres for a revived Blue-Flower-Culture, then this demoralised, lost, barbarised, megalomaniac nation could turn from being the best-hated to being a lovable one again, with real poets, musicians, dreamers. That's what it's good at. Bismarck's great deed was a disaster.*'

It was a forlorn hope. The continuous stream of bad news dented her cheerful optimism. When Finland surrendered to the Soviet Union in March 1940, she wrote:

'*So Finland is done for, and will soon be forgotten, like Abyssinia, Albania, Austria, Czechoslovakia, not forgetting Poland, Spain. Life goes on, no matter what is trampled underfoot. We're waiting patiently for our turn to come. Everyone is trying to get to the U.S.A., even I, though because of my German-Polish-German quota it's probably hopeless.*'

✻✻✻✻✻

Two people still in Germany were her ex-husband and her son. And for her son, Reinhardt, his farm at Mellensee was the most important thing in the world; more important than his mother. Because of her Jewish ancestry, he was in danger of losing his farm: the Nazis could not have anyone whose blood was tainted with Jewishness owning sacred German soil. He therefore denied that Oma was his mother. He claimed he was the result of an extra-marital affair between his father and an 'Aryan' peasant girl, and his father cheerfully confirmed it. This was accepted by the Nazis and duly entered in the booklet every German had to possess, showing his or her ancestry and racial purity (or otherwise). And so he kept his farm. On November 15, 1940, Oma wrote to Lorchen in English:

> *'...Reinhardt I try to eliminate from my thoughts. Somehow I cannot feel any real grief and sorrow because of his unpardonable behaviour. I feel sure that his attachment to me – what there is of it! – has not changed, and that, if we meet again, he would be exactly the same as when I last saw him. Those fellows, or criminals, at home seem to strangle every natural feeling in the poor slaves they all of them have become by now...'*

However, she did not succeed in eliminating her son from her thoughts. Again and again she wonders: 'Is he married? Does he have any children?'

In 1944 news reached her that Hugo – she calls him, very sarcastically, Engelshügchen – Little Angel Hugo – had married for the third time, aged 67; she felt sorry for the 35-year-old wife, but hugely grateful that she herself was free from him.

After the atomic bombs destroyed Hiroshima and Nagasaki on 6 and 9 August,1945, she wrote to Lorchen:

> *'What do you say to the Atomic Bomb? We envisage some idiot one day fiddling around with it a bit and suddenly the whole world is done for. Perhaps that would be quite a good solution to the problem: Mankind... Wouldn't it be quite good if ... it ceased to exist, along with all its modern and murderous achievements? I don't believe that the manufacture of the atomic bomb can or will be controlled. The Russians will find the necessary Uranium in the Urals ... and so, when everything has been reconstructed nicely, everyone will use it against everyone else. I'm glad I won't be here to see it. '*

Chapter 18

7 May, 1945: VE Day – Victory in Europe: how we had all longed for it! Now we were all wild with joy. American soldiers in the Clarendon Hotel in Cornmarket set loudspeakers in the windows playing jazz and danced in the street. At some point we were in London in the huge crowds surging towards Buckingham Palace, where the Royal Family and Churchill stood on a balcony and smiled and waved. Mu went out in the night when, for the first time in years, the street lights were switched on, and helped herself to armfuls of blossom from trees in front gardens, confident that no one would blame her on such a day. Now, she said, everything will get better, you'll see. We will become naturalised British citizens. Fe will get a proper job at a university and we will move from here to a bigger place somewhere and we'll have enough money ... 'We'll get onto the green branch,' as she put it.

How wrong she was.

✵✵✵✵✵

9 September: and the war in Asia was over, too, at last; Peter would be coming home from his two-year tedium in the army in India, safe and sound, spared the horrors of the war with Japan. Anne and I, on holiday at South Cerney, near Cirencester, where one of her grandmothers lived in a home for clergymen's widows, joined the villagers celebrating VJ Day – Victory over Japan – round a huge bonfire with a small figure of a human on an old chair at the top. 'That's Hirohito,' we were told; but, though we had seen plenty of cartoons of that evil little man with huge teeth and glasses, we found ourselves unable to cheer when the flames licked him to pieces. We were not then aware of what had been done to Hiroshima and Nagasaki, and the worst cruelties of the Japanese had been kept from us; and our imaginations were too vivid to rejoice in the replica of a human being burnt. We felt the same on Guy Fawkes Nights.

Back at school one day, I was walking across the grass to the hockey pitch in Five Mile Drive with my friends Liz Cairns and Lillian Lake, and decided to tell them a momentous piece of news:

'I'm being naturalised.'

They made a joke of it. 'You seem quite natural as you are.' So I replied, 'You don't understand. It means I'll be English, like you!'

'No, I think not. You can't be naturalised English, or Scottish, or Welsh. You can only be naturalised British.'

'Oh,' I said, crestfallen. Seeing this, Lillian said, 'And does it please you to be British?'

Her question made me realise how great a gulf existed between us. Was I pleased? How could she ask? What did they think it felt like to be stateless, and an enemy alien? I resolved that if possible, no one in future would know of my dark origins. As soon as I was grown up, I would change my name to something thoroughly English.

*****

Peter was still languishing in India. He had one good friend, called Jock Beveridge. Mu exchanged letters with his mother. Whenever either of them heard from her son, she would write and tell the other; so they became friends by letter. After Christmas in 1946 Mu sent Maleen and me off to Kirkcaldy in Scotland to visit the Beveridges, and to experience the Scottish New Year, Hogmanay. We hitch-hiked, getting lifts in lorries and private cars, and sleeping in cheap bed and breakfasts in Doncaster and Newcastle. Kirkcaldy smelled of linoleum, the town's chief industry. Mrs Beveridge was a small, energetic woman, about Mu's age. Her second son, Tony, a medical student, and his friend Ian, nicknamed Tubby; made sure we understood Hogmanay: we both got very drunk. After a few days, we had recovered sufficiently to return home, by bus.

Maleen started working in the English Speaking Union. The American soldiers organised dances there, and my pretty sister soon had numerous admirers. My mother insisted that she should always bring any man who wanted to go out with her home first, so that he would know that she was a respectable girl from a good home; so Beamsend was often overrun with Maleen's Americans. There was a whole Negro Spiritual choir once, huge men who seemed to pack the kitchen full when they sat at the table for tea. After tea they strolled into the front room and sang 'Swing Low, Sweet Chariot', and other spirituals, in deep, rumbling harmony, bringing tears to Mu's eyes.

One day Maleen was invited to a party. Mu records that:

'I was worried, as I had never met any of the people who had invited her, nor had she; so I made her promise to meet me by a certain lamp post at 9 o'clock. Unfortunately I was about 10 minutes late, and when I dashed down Queen Street and into New Inn Hall I could hardly fight my way through the crowd. This was nothing unusual, as Oxford was full of soldiers on leave. Turning the corner, I saw Maleen standing under the street light, and all around her – gaping soldiers. I could not have chosen a worse place to meet my daughter. From time to time a soldier would venture forward and ask her to go home with him, but she always answered: "No, I'm waiting for my Mummy." "Mummy my foot!" was the response from the laughing crowd. Using my elbows I fought my way through to her, grabbed her by the arm, and we flew away as fast as possible, as the English police were

already beginning to show an interest. I trembled for a long time after-wards.'

There was nothing simpler than getting an American boyfriend. I got one myself, by joining a busload of girls going out to the camp, I think it was at Brize Norton, for a dance. This particular Yank – I've forgotten his name – danced with me a lot, and met me in Oxford several times, when he would shower me with chocolates, nylon stockings, and the like. But he seemed to have nothing to say except asking for kisses and something called 'nookie', which I didn't understand but suspected it meant sex – a subject I knew practically nothing about. He embarrassed and bored me. I despaired of get-ting him to call me Gabi with the correct pronunciation, so I chose another of my names: Irene, with the English pronunciation. This led to the Ameri-can loungers in Cornmarket and Queen Street, when I rode through on my bicycle, intoning a dreary song that was popular at the time:
Goodnight, Ire-e-e-ene
Irene, goodnight...

In vain did I ask for a three-syllable version of the name. Some people even shortened it to a single syllable: Reen. This sounded like a shampoo, Drene, so I settled for two syllables – the last two: Re-ne. Now people thought it was a French name and put an accent on the last e, making me a re-born man. Others, to show their erudition, gave me a second e to make me a re-born French female. So my identity continued to be doubtful. As there was no glory in having an American boyfriend, (anyone could have one), and mine was so unsatisfactory, I ended the affair, such as it was. Maleen, however, continued to collect boyfriends. She started working in Tap-houses music shop, and then university students were trooping in to Beamsend, as well as soldiers.

We often queued up in the Town Hall for 'British Restaurant' lunches – food was still rationed – and here Kurt introduced me to a tall, rather swar-thy man: Jacky. I found out very little about him – he was a refugee, like us, but from Czechoslovakia, though he had studied at the famous Bauhaus school of art and design in Germany before the war. I was smitten. Tall and slim, handsome, even the crinkly hair – he reminded me of my frequently absent father. I say that now with hindsight. At the time I did not know what drove me to visit him so often in his small, neat workshop on the second floor of one of the old houses in Broad Street. He would look round when I came in, put down whatever he was doing, smile expectantly. I would wander around, looking at the magnificent, life-sized marionettes he had carved – he was planning to open a marionette theatre on Gloucester Green, but nothing came of it. Sooner or later I might think of something to say. He would listen, never comment, hardly ever say anything significant himself, and I would leave feeling baffled. But I went back again and again for these almost silent encounters, and he seemed pleased when I did, or when we met in the queue at the Town Hall.

*****

In the spring Anne, her friend Liz Whitaker and I spent ten days cycling round Wales, visiting parts I knew from holidays with Fe. I wrote home, of course:

> '...We walked up Cadair Idris; I recognised it partly, but not all. It was terribly steep, and I got to wondering *how* I could have done it when I was only ten or so; Anne and Liz found it even harder. All the time we could hear the stream in the valley, once a proper waterfall; and the sheep bleating. We went on up, Anne and Liz thought they'd die, kept resting, I was OK. I persuaded them to go to the lake. It was worth it.'

*****

I returned to a Beamsend redolent with impending change. My cousins, Hetta and Dudu, were to come from Persia to live with us for a year and go to school in Oxford. Their parents, and Oma, were planning to leave Persia as soon as possible and go to live in America. And where was Fe – he was seldom at home?

There were a few interesting documents which my mother kept in one of the small drawers of the elegant writing table that had belonged to her grandmother, Rose Fajans, back in Danzig. One was a notebook containing her account of Peter as a toddler, completely illegible to me, with a few paragraphs in Günther's handwriting which I can read: he tells how little Peter called him Fe-ti-ti-ti, from Väterchen, a diminutive form of Vater, soon abbreviated to Fe; how he strayed from the path they were walking along, dawdled and dropped behind and had to be called repeatedly; and then Fe (as we all came to call our father) indulges in a pipe dream: one day, when Peter is grown up, they would walk together along a path like this, discussing some intriguing point of scholarship. But in his teenage years Peter wanted to be a farmer, not a scholar; and it was only when he came back from his two stultifying years in the army in India and was demobbed and offered a place at Oxford that he began to follow in his father's footsteps.

But by then, our father had gone. The two of them never strolled along that path together. Because one of the other documents in that little drawer was a letter from Fe, telling her that he had found the one person who could make him happy, to give him a miraculous spring just when the autumn of his life was due to begin, and begging her to let him go.

When she got the news, Oma wrote from Persia:

'*4.5.46*
My dearest Lollelorchen!
*Your letter of 8 April came today and has made me very sad. That you
should have become so joyless and bitter, when once you were such a merry,
pretty little bird, really high spirited! I can still see you as you were when you
were three or four years old, with your blonde curls, your dark, shining,
laughing eyes! Oh this thrice damned, accursed marriage, it was bound to go
wrong! But who ever accepted advice or interference from others in such
matters. My family, too, could see from the beginning that dear Hugchen
was not the right man for me, and still I married him. After your wedding
you were walking to the station, and I watched you from the bedroom
window, and at the corner of the street I saw you take the rucksack or whatever it was from him, and he let you, let you carry it! Then I knew. But I
don't want to make your heart still heavier ... Let G. go, the sooner the
better, even if he fails to contribute to your upkeep, as I believe he might
well, remembering how he did when you were in Freiburg with three children – still, you will be better off without him. Peter and Maleen will
manage to get along all right on their own, and you're quite capable of earning enough for yourself and Gabi. Only peace is what one needs, no quar-
rels, no hurtful incidents every day, great and small: they are deadly.*'

No doubt about it: the marriage was accursed. Not just because of his frequent infidelities and absences, not only because of his mother's and his sisters' hostility. Each was bitterly disappointed in the other, and they brought
out the worst in each other. Separately, both my parents were actually
rather nice people. Together, they tormented each other.

Fe and Mu. A bad marriage

And this must have started quite early, when the first fine flush of passion
that led to the pregnancy and the wedding – when that heady hectic rosy

dawn, when they ran to meet at a certain street corner at a certain time each day to kiss and caress, as she often told me – when all that faded into the grey light of common day, and the shimmering vision each had of the other fell away before the reality of their short-comings. Mu's amazing humbleness, that she describes in her memoirs, her gratitude to Fe for marrying her, making a respectable woman of her, and her admiration of his intellect, gratefully accepting reading lists to study while he was away on holiday, or convalescing with his bad knee, with his parents – that soon gave way to exasperation. When he was at home, he would recline on a sofa, and Mu would wait on him hand and foot, with increasing resentment as the years went by.

They both suffered a lot of illness in those early months, as well as poverty, ill health, parental disapproval, and all around them the rising tide of political chaos. But such difficulties might have drawn them closer together. Why did they not?

Perhaps because of the unrealistic nature of their love. Mu saw herself as a Gretchen – the simple country girl in Goethe's *Faust*, who is swept off her feet with wonder at the man's intellect, the magical flow of his words – and physical desire. Fe was highly talented, mentally, and musically; he was tall and slim and good-looking, whereas Mu had had a real struggle to get by at school – not for lack of intelligence, but because she was guided more by intuition and emotion than by logic. She could only think laterally. Where he had been worshipped by his family, she had a grinding sense of inferiority towards her sister Marianne, who was always top of the class and always their mother's favourite. She knew, from an early age, that her birth had been unwelcome. She was self-conscious; ashamed of her small plump body, the partial curvature of her spine, her somewhat misshapen feet; she stuttered; she bit her nails.

In fact, she was beautiful, with her arched eyebrows, her large hazel eyes, which could look blue or green or brown, depending on her mood, a mane of tawny hair, and a tip-tilted nose; she sang beautifully, she was eloquent, her mind was full of songs and poems and stories; but all this, she felt, counted for nothing, because of her lack of success at school and her successive failures in the world of work. Yet here was this tall, slim, handsome, gifted Günther, and he loved her.

For six months, she reckoned later, he loved her. Still she clung to him, even when with another part of her mind she despised him. After she had insulted and annoyed him, and he her, for decades, after he had left her for good – years later she would sigh: why oh why did he not go to Greece when she urged him to? As if that was her greatest regret.

*****

Classical studies were the pinnacle of academic life in Germany; his mother Edith recognised this and wanted him up there on that cloudy peak of academic success. His admiration of the Greeks rose to mystical levels. He would put it to me on our walks: How was it possible for that culture to reach such heights so quickly? Where did those people come from – tall and fair-haired, with the nose and the forehead one smooth shape ... He left the question hanging in the air, and when I hazarded guesses, culminating in: outer space? – he did not dismiss it out of hand as childish nonsense.

Of course Athens became an area of conflict between them, like everything else. Mu would shout, eyes blazing, fist pounding the table, that that fine civilisation rested on slavery and the subjugation of women, and that that nullified its worth. And he would hunch his shoulders and go back to pore over his books, smoking his Woodbines; and she would feel penitent.

It was when the Nazis came to power and he lost his job that she had urged him to go to Greece, and wander alone, with a rucksack, among the great ruins and the mountains and valleys of his obsession. She would stay behind with the children, she would manage somehow, knowing that his dream was being fulfilled. But he refused, perhaps because of his knee, probably because the 'reality might interfere with his imaginative picture of the country in ancient times', as another scholar – Lloyd-Jones – put it. But she said this proved he cared more for the stuffy indoor life of Germany than for the glory that was Greece. She never forgave him. (In fact when he did visit the country many decades later he was not only disappointed – he was disgusted.)

He undoubtedly regarded the ancient Greeks as a superior race. Classicists tend to be racists. Indeed, Professor Maas, earning a pittance at the Oxford University Press, turned down the chance to earn some extra money by teaching Greek to an adult beginner, because the man was a Negro. Let them first develop some sort of civilisation of their own, he said. Perhaps after a few hundred years they may be ready to study Greek. And one day Fe, when he and I were on the beach at Barmouth, told me that a true Jew was tall and slim, with slender ankles and wrists and a straight nose: very different from Mu, but just like himself, in fact, as I observed a few minutes later when, after a brief hesitation, he discarded his black woollen bathing costume and ran naked across the sand to leap into the breakers. The ugly Jew of the Nazi caricatures, fat, small, swarthy, with the famous big nose – was actually a Levantine;: the true Jewish race, like the Greek, had been adulterated by centuries of proximity with Turks and Arabs. Despite all their suffering because of the Nazis' race theories, many refugees could not divest themselves of a racist mindset.

❖❖❖❖❖

Married life consists of millions of tiny recurrent elements. Fe was fastidious, Mu was rough and ready. He spent ever longer in the bathroom, enraging the other members of the household, fixing his metal shaving mirror to the window to get the best light, and shaving meticulously, standing on two pieces of dowel (to avoid getting flat feet). He maintained he had a delicate skin – unlike the rest of us – and therefore needed his own private Pears Transparent Soap (which my wicked sister used, secretly – he found her out when he spotted a few flakes of foam on it, and there we had another row). He would emerge from the bathroom at last, his face glistening with Vaseline, and a curious net cap on his head to press his hair down which, left to its own devices, tended to be fuzzy. He grew ever more fussy. He had to have his own ration of butter kept separately on a high shelf, as he suspected he wasn't getting his fair share, and his coffee cup had to be heated in the oven before the coffee was poured into it.

Mu also believed in cleanliness; but in her case this entailed a great deal of muscular labour and discomfort, not to say violence. *Furor domesticus*, Fe called it. Most clothes and linen were boiled, at first in the old wood-fired copper built into a corner of the scullery, later in a zinc tub on top of the gas cooker, then rubbed energetically on a washboard – when it was not infrequently discovered that some had got singed – and finally lugged upstairs to be rinsed in the bath. It was then hung out to dry in the garden on ropes which broke from time to time, dropping everything into the mud, or, if it was raining, it would be left to drip from string criss-crossing the kitchen. When things were more or less dry, they all had to be ironed on a folded blanket on the kitchen table, when further singeing might occur. Creases in trousers were particularly difficult to achieve, and if Mu noticed that one of the boys was going out with trousers that looked baggy, or concertinaed, she would hold him back, and endeavour to iron better creases into them while he was wearing them – to save time – pressing brown paper against one side and the hot iron on the other, while he gibbered with fear. Carpets, however, were not ironed. They were washed in the bath, having been cut into manageable sizes with scissors first, and then dropped from the bathroom window and manhandled onto the washing line. The kitchen and scullery floors were washed with plenty of soapy water and some old vest or pants and a scrubbing brush. Then newspaper was spread to soak up the wet. The soggy papers were pegged out on the washing line to dry ... Waste not, want not! Every room, the stairs, the corridors, were cleaned every day with broom, dustpan and brush, mop, duster, and floor polish. Door knobs and taps were polished with Brasso. Windows were cleaned with damp newspaper. Anything that looked like rubbish was stuffed into a sack that hung outside the scullery door. Periodically, this had to be tipped out on the kitchen floor, when some important documents, even cheques, had been lost, and we rummaged through the rubbish to find them.

While she worked, she sang. She had a clear soprano voice and an enormous repertoire: folksongs, Lieder, operatic arias, hymns, patriotic songs, even Nazi hymns like the 'Horst Wessel Lied', followed, as often as not, by the communist 'Internationale', in German, with great vigour. Her day-long singing got on Fe's nerves, especially as she tended to simplify melodies, and to slow down. It distracted him from his work. 'I have music going through my head all the time,' he grumbled. 'No need to sing it out loud.' So here was another row.

They must have started early, those rows. She confessed to me, in her old age, quite shamefacedly, that when they were first married she had wanted to rub his nose in one of his short-comings: his untidiness. He left things lying around instead of putting them away. So one day she placed one thing on each step of the staircase – she really had to hunt around for things to put on the last few steps, she admitted – so that when he came home she could point to them, quivering with indignation. 'It was wrong of me', she conceded.

Yet she never expected him to help her with the housework. She would paint walls and woodwork, even, most memorably, the bath, during the night, without any silly fuss over preparing surfaces or ensuring that she was using the right sort of paint. The result was wrinkled wallpaper drooping off walls, doors knobbly to the touch where drips had hardened – and one was sometimes stuck to the paint in the bath tub and had to be pulled off and have the paint scoured off one's bottom painfully with turpentine.

Such things did not amuse our fastidious, aesthetic father. The worst problem was food. She considered cookery books and recipes a ludicrous affectation, like gardening books. One just **knew** how to do these things. She would buy huge quantities of the cheapest vegetables, meat and fish from the stalls that surrounded the cattle market every Wednesday – going there on foot with a baby or two in a pram or pushchair. Back home, she would tip them out on the kitchen table next to a newspaper, which she would read while she prepared the vegetables, leaning on her elbows, sometimes blinded with tears at the awful events in the war, occasionally cutting a finger, or confusing the parings to be thrown onto the compost heap with the bits to be cooked. These would then be slammed onto the cooker at whatever time of day, for any length of time – rather like the cauldron in the Wandervogel – so our meals consisted of tough bits of meat, either bloody or singed, gritty vegetables, either soggy or underdone, potatoes half raw or burnt, semolina puddings with lumps in them like ants' eggs, and cakes which were often 'sad' because she neither knew nor cared about the difference between 'plain' and 'self-raising' flour. It never occurred to her that cooking might be worth thinking about. You used your brains to find out about the war, about Finland, about Socialism, colonialism, communism, the evils of capitalism and shareholders, big business and the arms trade, and about history and politics, and literature, Dickens, Goethe, Dostoyevsky …As for food, hunger is the best cook, no one had ever been poisoned by her, and what could possibly be nicer than a big bowl of boiled spinach with a hunk of bread, sawn off a loaf pressed against her bosom? One of her friends had been given a cookery book as a wedding present entitled, 'Cookbook for the Feeble-Minded' – what a laugh! She quoted from it: 'Don't worry if it gets lumpy, but go on stirring calmly' – who needed to be told that? So her gravies were always lumpy.

Her gardening methods were equally eccentric and laborious. A knife from the kitchen drawer would do for weeding, shopping bags and a pram to fetch horse and cow manure from Port Meadow, ordinary scissors to cut grass. Plants were allowed to spread and multiply freely; a vine that reached the scullery window was invited in and trained along the edge of a shelf; the stone of a delicious cherry was planted and grew into a huge forest tree spreading its branches over several gardens. Its cherries – the few the birds left – were not the splendid black miracles she hoped for, but never mind! It was a splendid tree and had every right to live. Her apple tree bore little or no fruit, year after year; her plum tree was infested with silver leaf virus. It was a shame, but their right to life, too, had to be respected.

Fe, for his part, battled to fulfil what he regarded as his destiny. He resented having to earn money for us, his children, and for Mu's protegés; he resented the noise in the house and on the street – he would lean out of his window and shoo children away to play elsewhere as they were disturbing him. Such was his devotion to his work that he could see nothing wrong in telling Kurt one day that his presence was burdensome to him and he would like him to move out – since this fourteen-year-old orphan was bound to be unhappy, he might as well be unhappy elsewhere. He was wide-eyed with surprise when I told him that this must have hurt Kurt, and came downstairs to tell him he was sorry, and that he could stay. It never occurred to him spontaneously that there might be a different point of view from his own. His egocentricity was total. So he always had a perfectly clear conscience. 'Am I a monster?' he would expostulate, laughing at such a preposterous idea. But he was.

✳✳✳✳✳

In 1946 Hetta and Dudu arrived, after an exciting voyage from Persia. In age they were between Maleen and me. Hetta was extremely intelligent and competent. She had already decided to be a doctor, like her mother and our grandmother, and threw herself into her studies energetically. Dudu, just a year younger, was quite different, vague and easy-going and fond of painting. Hetta would pick up her knitting the moment she had finished eating, making good use of the least fragments of time. She organised energetic bicycle tours for us and our friends. One day after school we cycled all the way to Stratford, 'saw' a play (slept through most of it), and cycled home again in the final stages of exhaustion in the dark. During the holidays we cycled to the Lake District and back, staying at youth hostels on the way. York was memorable for bananas – the first we had seen since before the war. We bought all we were allowed on our ration books; they were wrapped in newspaper and we tried to hold them on our handlebars as we rode through the narrow streets, the Shambles, dropping bananas right and left. As soon as we got out of the town we sat under a hedge and gorged ourselves.

The next bike ride took us all round the south of England. The youth hostel in Winchester was an old water mill; to wash, we plunged into the racing mill stream; there were chains at the side to hold onto – if you let go, you would be swept naked into the middle of the town. It all got too much for Maleen – she disappeared somewhere along a steep uphill ride. We were alarmed – had there been an accident? In fact, she had gone home by train. I rather envied her. I could not assert myself like that against Hetta. Nor could Dudu, though it often rained, and one night was spent in a cowshed.

'The door to the cowshed' (I reported to Mu) *'was cunningly arranged so that you first hit your head and then caught your foot on a high step behind which were heaps of turnips. I stumbled back across the wet field to fetch the jam from my bicycle bag – and dropped it. It broke; I scooped up as much of the jam as I could and tried to carry it in my hands; the rain made it dissolve and trickle through.'*

But Kent was a revelation. We had sunshine and cloud shadows running along the road ahead of us, and saw oast houses and hop fields for the first time. There were anemones and primroses everywhere. We heard evensong in Canterbury Cathedral and stayed in the youth hostel – which, I wrote to Mu,

'...is lovely, and quite new. There is a party of young Chinese men here, Dudu talked loudly and vigorously with them, Hetta watched from a distance.'

These students were also on a cycling tour with an English friend and also came from Oxford. One of them, Cheng Chen-Chiu, homed in on me. From then on, he was a frequent visitor at Beamsend, which suited Mu, with her passion for the China of Mao Tse Tung and Chou En-lai – Cheng was a communist. Mu followed the news from China passionately, and would often describe how the communists were doing deeds that were both heroic and humane in the villages. So she was quite keen on Cheng; but I found him boring. He was always tongue-tied with me, would sit and stare at me, and I wouldn't know what to do. Sometimes I suggested going on a bike ride, and on one of these, when we were sitting by the roadside for a rest and to eat some cherries, he suddenly seized hold of me and started kissing me. I found it most disagreeable – he had such thick, rough lips – and wished he would stop. I pretended to go to sleep, and he did stop kissing me then, but clutched me instead. When that got too much for me, I pretended to wake up and sleepily asked for some cherries. But he had crushed the bag containing them with his leg and as we looked at the sorry pulp he said: 'Not crushed, but melted by our passion.' This was just daft. Fortunately he went away quite often – to Communist Youth gatherings in Prague, or on sight-seeing or cycling tours on the Continent with his friends, which led to numerous letters; he described places in the language of a nineteenth-century guide book – impressive only in that he was after all using a foreign language with almost impeccable accuracy. I have these letters still. Of a photograph taken of him carrying the flag for the Chinese delegation in Prague, he writes:

'You might be interested to know that this photo will be sufficient to send me to prison if it comes into the hands of the government's secret agents.'

Many of his letters contain political essays such as he was probably writing for his tutor at Christ Church; but one, triggered by the British troops fighting the Jewish terrorists in Palestine, ends:

'Sometimes one feels so dreary and empty. At such times one ought to look at – nay, stare at – you, and let your freshness, youth and poetic idealism revive one's Hope in Life!'

This was really the only declaration he ever made, apart from a poem which he wrote in Chinese. He explained that it meant:

'Rose, rose, you must smile for me alone or I will die!
But the rose still smiled at everyone.'

Yet he really believed that we were lovers and that we would soon go to the New China together and produce a tribe of staunchly communist children! He spoke to Mu about it, not to me, and was devastated when she assured him that since I was only fourteen this was out of the question, and that he could continue visiting us as a family friend but definitely not as a fiancé. He was dismayed, indeed furious. He wrote to Mu:

'You have won and I have lost ... Call at Thorncliffe? Certainly I'm allowed to. But the time is likely to be inopportune and besides, could I really be so inconsiderate as to interrupt her study just before the exams? ... What do I get out of coming? A stealing glance at an idol who has ceased to care? A terrible feeling of non-existence in her presence? ... The sense of

futility to recapture the past? And the future – what can one expect from a future where separation will be no less final than Death?'

I was kept totally unaware of all this. For me, he wrote only travelogues and political essays. Finally, after endless delays and difficulties, he got back to Peking (now Beijing) where he worked at the Teachers' College and wrote letters to me about such things as:
'the Communist plan in fifteen years' time to make 30 – 40% of our entire economic life devoted to industrial production.'

His last letter to me was a description of the Forbidden City. Then I heard no more; but many years later he visited Mu in Beamsend. She told me that when she opened the door to him, his first words were: 'Greetings from the People's Republic of China!' He was then some kind functionary in the communist hierarchy and, she felt, completely lost to normal human relations.

❖❖❖❖❖

In the summer of '47 we went to Cornwall for a seaside holiday. While the others went by train, Dudu and I hitch-hiked, and met up with the family at Par, where we were staying with a Mrs Tregaskes. One day I had wandered along the curving beach when, looking back, I saw some figures in the distance. There was Mu, and – I realised as I sprinted back across the sand – Hetta and Dudu's parents, Onkel Achim and Tante Marianne, and to my unspeakable joy, Oma. I clung to her throughout her stay with us.

We went back to Oxford together. They spent some time with us, Marianne sewing, Achim sometimes playing the flute, sometimes talking and joking, swapping quotations and detailed reminiscences, and often all singing together in harmony from memory. A little later, Oma and Marianne and Achim went to America; our cousins followed after the end of the school year. I never saw Oma again.

❖❖❖❖❖

Fe did get a proper university appointment at last, in Manchester – not that it was what he really wanted: ever dissatisfied, he found himself 'teaching Greek to the Theology students' (which meant Hellenistic instead of Classical Greek) 'and Theology to the Greek students' – Christianity, that 'crazed product of primitive half-starved desert tribes', as he described it. However, he was an assistant professor. Only it wasn't with us that he was going to enjoy a more prosperous life.

One day he brought Stella to have tea with us: a woman as tall and thin as Mu was short and plump, much younger, very English, with a somewhat horsey face and glasses and a shy but friendly smile. She had been the producer at the BBC when Fe gave a talk there; they had spent a good deal of time together, and now they wanted to get married. It all seemed so improbable that none of us knew how to react. We ought to protest, to leap to Mu's defence, to hate or scorn or mock Stella; but it was hard to rouse such feelings to someone so gauche and harmless and common-sensical.

But not long after, when I came home from school, it was to be told that Fe had left, for good. Mu wept, I hugged her, and felt terribly sorry for her.

I was devastated. The hole he left in my life was huge. I tried very hard to hate him, as Peter and Maleen did, but I kept remembering him, and longing for him. I believed that he loved me, that I was important to him. Now I had to face the fact that I was not, since he had left me without a word.

Once, just once, when I was walking along the Woodstock Road, I saw him walking on the other side of the road, a little smile on his face, a spring in his step, quite oblivious to me, and I wondered if I actually existed. For years I could see no point in anything I did, since he was not interested, and as I developed thought myself fat and ugly, trussed up in suspender belts and bras, and definitely not a boy.

His departure reinforced our refugee complexes to make us feel totally unwanted. Every setback, every failure, every rejection that we suffered subsequently outweighed any successes. Even when Peter, years later, had become a professor, he was hag-ridden by the sense, the panic, that he was being overtaken by others on the escalator of academe. Maleen suffered serious depressions. As for me, any mention of a party to which I was not invited, or just seeing two acquaintances talking to each other, but not to me, almost anyone simply walking away from me, could throw me into a pit of despair. Later, every reject slip from an editor, every failure to get a good part in the theatre, or any other job, devastated me. I was convinced that there was something repugnant about me, like a bad smell, which was obvious to everyone else, but no one would tell me what it was.

*****

Peter came home and was demobbed in 1947. In April, Mu sent him and me on a cycle ride round Scotland, to get to know each other again. As we pedalled along, I tried to get him to sing some of the songs which Mu and I would sing in two-part harmony; but it was impossible. We had mainly bad weather, as is normal in Scotland, but some uplifting sights when the purple mountains were streaked with sunshine and shadows. We stayed in youth hostels, and went up to the strange formation called Pap o' Glencoe. A very handsome man came part of the way with us, and I was smitten for several days. He was an architect, with silvery fair hair and black eyebrows, tall and slim; for at least 24 hours after we had parted I got quite a thrill from thinking that his feet were on another part of this same mountain as mine. I did not mention this when I wrote home from Birnam:

'Our bikes really weren't made for this – at first we were terribly embarrassed when other cyclists on lovely bikes spun past us and said "hello" ... because, well, a toothbrush sticks out of the side of my kit-bag, and socks and tins of condensed milk dance about in my basket; Peter has a haversack on his back-carrier held down with sundry straps and bits of string, and an ancient basket that groans and creaks and nearly collapses under the weight of a huge rucksack resembling a bulging parcel of dirty laundry ...

Then, suddenly, about five miles from Birnam, the road dipped down between lots of weird conifers we'd never seen before. It looked like an enchanted wood. You could believe that these trees could suddenly get up and walk to Dunsinane.'

We saw many more wonderful sights ruined cathedrals, stone bridges, waterfalls, before we returned to Beamsend.

*****

Peter took advantage of a scheme for ex-servicemen to go up to Oxford University; he studied Russian, living in his college – St John's. Maleen started a course for gymnastics teachers in Denmark, then went to London to start nursing. Kurt left. Anne was in Twickenham. Many members of the refugee community had dispersed, and Fe's mother, Oma Edith, had alienated most of the ones who were left against us, with just a few exceptions: Professor Maas, the Hammerschmidts, the Liepmanns. But mostly, Mu and I were alone, apart from paying lodgers. Mu did her best to occupy my free time, with cycle rides, swimming in the Thames, and reading aloud – German poetry, lots of Dickens – and telling me stories about her own childhood. I pitied her, and believed I ought to make up for all her past suffering; but however hard I tried, there would always come a moment when she indicated with a shrug of the shoulder and a twitch of an eyelid, or walking silently out of the room, that I had not fully understood her, had shown that I didn't really care by yawning, couldn't think of anything to say to her. She kept taking offence where none was intended. She sometimes said she thought there was something wrong with her chemistry which repelled people. This added to my own gloom, as I thought I had the same problem – no one could ever really like me, except odd-balls like Cheng who didn't count.

My obsession with time melted into an obsession with death. I was terrified of it. How could all my being be extinguished, blotted out, my consciousness disappear? I painted pictures of drooping autumnal birches, and worked on a long poem about death. I was miserable, so much so that Mu took me to our GP, Dr Herrin, who found nothing more serious than short-sightedness and a weak circulation.

Cycling home from school along the Woodstock Road one day, I decided I would be a doctor. A gynaecologist – I had just learned this impressive new word. I would be following a noble family tradition: My father's father, my mother's mother, and her sister, and now Hetta, my cousin, were all doctors. I saw myself, a plain, bulky figure, sitting by a hospital bed, wearily helping one more woman cope with her nether parts.

When I was fifteen, I took School Certificate, and did well. I was a year younger than the rest of my class, so Mu, to cheer me up, sent me to the Geheebs' École d'Humanité – the successor to the Odenwaldschule – in Switzerland for a year.

Chapter 19

How Mu managed to scrape together the money to send me to the École d'Humanité in 1948 is a mystery. At that time she was having to call on lawyers to get any money at all from Fe. It was finally settled in January 1950 at £250 less tax as alimony plus 19 shillings and 3 pence per week maintenance for me. She was working as a domestic in an Old People's Home for 30 hours a week for 1 shilling and 8 pence per hour. Yet somehow she did it; only there wasn't enough for a taxi – we had to walk to the station before dawn, balancing my suitcase on the saddle of her bike. She looked very small as she stood on the platform to wave goodbye. As the train began to move, she suddenly remembered something and hurried to keep up. 'Don't worry if you get a baby. I'll look after it.' I was fifteen!

So I set out on a long, long journey to a new life, and I was wide open to new impressions. From Paddington I had to go to Victoria, where I got on the boat train to Dover. On the ferry across the Channel, my old dream of being a sailor returned. I watched the white cliffs recede, hung over the rail marvelling at the turquoise flowers of foam rising up and opening out at the surface. Then came the long, long train journey through the night, up the Rhine valley to Basel; I was sleeping uncomfortably. But I was bewitched by all the new sights and sounds. In my first letter home (preserved by Mu, of course) I wrote:

'Basel is a lovely city. When we were there (before 6 am) it was very quiet …The streets are fairly wide, beautifully clean, and with little traffic. Wherever two roads meet, there's a grassy triangle with trees and flowers. The shop windows were beautiful, with wonderful wares – esp. most heavenly cakes and chocolates. The porters in Basel wear little bright blue smocks; some carry buckets on their backs (polished silver) and waddle around spraying the platforms clean.

My train went on the dot of 6.24, through long, rolling hills, with a great deal of forest and meadows rippling right up to the forest edge. The sun came out and tore up the blanket of cloud and blew the bits away towards England until the sky was a burning blue. There were scattered red-roofed chalets with a lot of white and brown on the walls; they all have a very narrow paved walk right round them, and seem to grow out of the emerald green. The hills grew higher and steeper, with more forest, and here and there a tooth of pale rock showing. Then I saw peaks with soft clouds coiling round them and their tips whitish against the blue blue sky. In the valley a mist rose and caught the sun till it was blindingly white; a haze gave the mountains a weird look.

I had to wait almost three hours in Lucerne because I wanted to get hold

190

of my luggage and the Zoll didn't open till eleven, it being Sunday. So I had plenty of time to walk around.

Even in the station there was a strange smell in the air, and when I got out it was like cold clear water. I saw a great rock of a mountain called Pilatus, very black against the sun. There was a wide river of fairly green water and across it was a most beautiful wooden bridge; it had a roof, and wherever there were pillars of wood to hold it up there were triangular scriptural paintings. I leaned over the parapet and the clear sunny water swirled round the posts, while the warm wood breathed a delicious innocent wholesome smell at me. The houses all had their windows open and bulging feather-beds in them, hanging out to air.

Finally I got my case – the lock had broken off, and some kind person had put a leather strap round it – and the journey continued. There was some festival that day, shooting and archery, and from the train I saw lots of people wearing national costume at each station, and there were flags everywhere. At Brienz we had to wait for an hour for a connection, so we, a friendly fat German fellow-passenger and I, went into a little station hotel, she to eat, and I to telephone the school. After I had got through, despite the tremendous complications of the Swiss telephone system, I found the German woman had ordered me some dinner. (I paid for it.) It was just wonderful. First a glorious soup from a big pewter pot with some little pasta letters and numbers floating in it, then a most beautiful salad, and a cool, sweet drink called Grappillon. We ate outside with a view of densely wooded slopes very rarely baring their rocky fangs. Then we took a little cogwheel train very steeply uphill right through the greenest meadows and woods, with a view down to two lakes, and the sound of cowbells whenever the train stopped (Swiss trains make a tremendous noise).

At Brünig-Hasliberg the bus to Goldern was already waiting. It was bright yellow, about half the size of an English one, and at first about three times as many passengers – mostly families – who talked loudly and unintermittently.

Switzerland is very musical; when a train approaches a station it starts hooting melodiously; then bells join in; when it comes in with a huge crescendo, there's a sudden and dramatic pause in the concert, until the guard blows a little trumpet and the driver rings a little bell; all the bells in the station joining in, and the train chuffs rhythmically out. As for the bus – well, you don't, on a slender little road slipping along through shadowy woods, clinging to the sides of cliffs, through tunnels, serpentining through alpine meadows, or running alongside a stream – on a road like that you don't want to hear some ugly "parp-parp" or "honk"; so here, the buses send out a clear arpeggio as they approach blind bends.'

And then I came to the school, which had been the Odenwaldschule, where my father had taught in 1926, and my mother had lived for a short time just after they got married. The school was imbued with ideas and ideals which were anathema to the Nazis; so in 1934 the founders, Paulus and Edith Geheeb, closed it and moved to Switzerland. Here they founded a new, much smaller school in the French-speaking part at Lac Noir, and called it École d'Humanité. During the dark days of the war, the school suffered great poverty. The children and the teachers were mostly penniless refugees, and they depended on the support and generosity of a few Swiss citizens. They had to move several times, coming to rest in what had been a holiday home for protestant clergy at the village of Goldern on the Hasliberg in the Bernese Oberland. After the war its numbers grew a little, but many teachers and children were holocaust survivors from the Third Reich who could not pay at all.

École d'Humanité

The school I came to consisted of two large chalets: Haupthaus and Turmhaus, and a small wooden house called Stöckli. It was afternoon when I arrived, and the hot sun elicited that special smell from the wooden walls. A number of children and adults were standing idly chatting on or near the wooden steps up the side of the Haupthaus: among them Paulus, looking like an Old Testament prophet with his long white beard and deep-set eyes, and Edith, his warm, friendly wife. She asked a girl of about my age, Sabine, to look after me; she led me past the front of the Haupthaus and across a small grassy area to the Turmhaus – the Tower House – so called because it did indeed have a tower at the corner. The ground floor consisted almost entirely of a large hall, which had been used for religious services by its previous owners, with two tiny rooms, or cubicles, in two of the corners, one labelled Sakristei. We went up the stairs to the room I was to share with her, which had an uninterrupted view across to the snow-capped Wetterhörner.

I dumped my suitcase as a gong sounded. We hurried to the Haupthaus, passing the small boy who was enthusiastically banging away at the huge gong, and found ourselves in the throng entering the dining hall. We sat at

Paulus and Edith Geheeb

tables allotted to each 'family' – each grown-up or Mitarbeiter had a family consisting of between three and seven Kameraden – the words children and grown-ups were never used; anyone who was not a Kamerad was a Mitarbeiter – a colleague.

I belonged to Paulus' family, along with Piet, the oldest boy in the school, and his Dutch sweetheart, Elnis from Israel, and Peter from Germany; so I sat with them. The noise was deafening. When everyone was seated, Paulus went and stood by the entrance and silence fell while he read a short Thought for the Day, as he did every day; it might be a passage from Pestalozzi, or Tagore, or one of his other mentors. I was

The P;aulus Family

reminded of Sister Constance. As soon as he had finished, and was walking back to our table, hubbub arose again. One or two Kameraden from each table went to the serving hatch to fetch the food, and we could eat.

After this my first evening meal, or Vesperbrot – bread and jam and lime blossom tea – many of the Kameraden were milling around the front of the Haupthaus, talking, and I felt a bit shy. I was referred to as the 'English girl' – ironic, when I recalled how being the 'German' had made me feel excluded in my English schools – so I was quite pleased when a tall French boy came up to me and asked if I would like to go for a walk with him.

We strolled across a meadow behind the school which had a great rock in the middle, and into the forest. It was beautiful, with a golden sunset gleaming through the branches. But this boy was rather odd: he kept talking about trains, or rather, train timetables. Flapping his hands excitedly, he informed me of the departure time of some train from Berlin, its route across Europe, and the time of its arrival in Rome. We wandered on through the trees for a while, until I noticed that it was getting dark. I suggested we should go home. He seemed to agree quite willingly, and proceeded to detail another long train schedule. But which way should we go? It soon became apparent that he had no idea, and was not, in fact, quite normal. I caught sight of the rosy evening light on the snow-covered peaks of the Wetterhörner through the trees and thought that must be the direction to go, with Danny behind me still babbling on about trains; but in the gathering darkness, I lost the path, and found myself in an impenetrable thicket.

'Surely you know which way to go?' He was silent, raising his shoulders. I felt angry now, as I backed out of the thicket and stomped ahead. It got quite dark, I had to hold out my hands to avoid crashing into trees. Then the moon, hanging between two peaks, lit up the tree trunks and what I thought must be a clearing ahead. But it was not a clearing. Suddenly, I saw lights, far, far below. It took me a while to understand that I was looking down a precipice into a deep valley; the lights were in the windows of houses, tiny in the distant depth. One more step, and I would have fallen hundreds of feet. Panic stricken, I turned round, and clung onto the boy as if I was in danger of falling. That was a big mistake. He immediately put his arms round me and grunted and chuckled happily. 'I'm protecting you, aren't I?' he said. 'Am I your protector, little girl? Can I call you little girl?' I struggled out of his grasp and scolded him: didn't he realise how dangerous our position was? But all he wanted was to embrace me again. I walked as fast as I could away from the precipice, the boy pleading: 'It was so nice! Let's do it again! Just once, please, just for a little while!'

At last, at last, we emerged from the trees onto the meadow with the big rock behind the school. I ran to my room in the Turmhaus, and there was Sabine, looking at me slyly. It was midnight.

'Have you been having a nice time with Dani?'

'Dani – is that his name?'

'Why did you go with him? All he knows is train times. Surely you must have noticed. He's nuts!'

'Why didn't you warn me?'

'Didn't think I needed to. So obvious. Anyway, everyone's been rushing around looking for you. You'd better go and tell Edith you're all right.'

Edith gave me a hug. She didn't seem to be in the least angry. But Dani kept boasting and wouldn't leave me alone, as if he had done something heroic. I was mortified. What a dreadful beginning!

*****

I wrote letters home almost every week, some in German, some in English, detailing everything, like the food: extremely simple, mainly vegetarian, Bircher muesli for breakfast, boiled potatoes with Quark, a kind of cream cheese, or thick soup, at midday; bread and lime-blossom tea in the evening. Nevertheless, Beckmann, the cook, was disgusted at our gluttony. All you needed, he grumbled to me once, was a piece of bread and a few grapes; quite enough to keep you going throughout a day's mountaineering. One of his jobs was slicing loaves of bread for the evening meal; as he turned the handle on the slicer and flung the slices into the bread baskets, I heard him furiously saying: '*Immer fresse, immer fresse* – nothing but eat, eat, eat…'.

After the midday meal, we went to our rooms, or out of doors, for a quiet time, until the gong sounded again; this was the signal for everyone to go about their allotted tasks of tidying or cleaning or washing up or weeding or window cleaning. There were no servants. Beckmann was the cook and his wife Julie the house keeper; a small bevy of young Dutch women helped them; but the bulk of the domestic work was done by us, and organised by one or two of the older Kameraden. We were responsible for our environment: if anything was wrong, we had to put it right ourselves. Here's part of a letter I wrote home:

'The other day Elnis, who comes from Israel, and I had to scrub a floor, and we were both dog tired afterwards. But then we went to a limestone cave with Sabine and a little thirteenyear-old called French boy called Pierrot who talks non-stop; it sounds quite intelligent, but it's all rubbish, quite funny for a while, but in the end it gets on your nerves. And Axel and Nicki, two lovely Austrian boys who tell you the funniest stories all day long in soft, melancholy tones. They look identical, but they're not twins. And a boy with the charming name Walter Zwieback, who looks quite nice, but is extremely dull and stupid; he whistles the most frightful modern dance tunes non-stop. The cave was interesting because it was dangerous, and my first ever cave – but unfortunately it was rather small. We had a candle.

So now I was very tired, but then a boy called Deretzki suggested going to the sports field, which I find irresistible, so we went. Herr Kool, the Dutch maths teacher came; there were just five of us big ones, and several little ones. This sports field is just a muddy, sloping clearing in the forest. So we played a kind of rugby, but it was hard, just Deretzki and me against three others. I got into a hopeless position on the ground, clutching the ball, and the others throwing themselves on top of me; so I tried to throw them off by heaving myself up – and hit my head against Kohl's knee, so hard I thought my head was broken, and everything was whirling round. Next thing I knew I was looking up at a ring of faces, but I couldn't see them properly, because something like pieces of jagged broken glass seemed to be flickering in front of my eyes.

Well, it's not worth going into all the details, but I'm writing this in bed, recovering from a slight concussion. Everybody is being very sweet to me. Herr Lüthi, who teaches music, and Kohl carried me home (which was hellish, I almost fainted), and they and the Dutch girls and Sabine and Julie Beckmann and especially Paulus are all being so kind to me. I have been ill – I didn't eat anything for 48 hours and am beautifully slim (tell Maleen – starvation works!) but kept feeling cold, though they piled feather beds onto me and gave me two hot water bottles. Every time I woke up there was somebody like Willy Aebersold, or Lüthi, sitting beside my bed. I got up yesterday, but was dizzy and my head ached so had to go back to my blasted boring bed. There's a vase of gentians beside my bed, which the Dutch girls gave me. I wrote a poem in German about them.'

So the last days of the holidays passed rather dramatically. Once I had recovered, I took part in a bunter Abend, a fancy-dress party, when Sabine and I dressed up as gipsies, using the knitted patchwork covers from our beds, and Elnis, as an Arab sheik, danced with me, until Walter, in lLederhosen, intervened, asking pointedly if Elnis and I were getting married. He tried to monopolise me for the rest of the evening – only he couldn't dance, and he is so boring.

✻✻✻✻✻

School began, and was totally different from the schools I had attended before. There were just three one-hour lessons – Kurse – every morning; extra subjects, art, languages, dance, drama were evening activities after the domestic chores were done. No tests, no grades, no set homework. We made up our own timetables. In leisurely gatherings, the teachers, Mitarbeiter, explained what they proposed to deal with; we listened, asked questions, and finally chose just three subjects. Since I wanted to be a doctor, I chose the sciences at first. Each course-period lasted six weeks; after that we were free to continue with the same subjects, or change. The groups were small, about half-a-dozen learners with one adult, and lessons were informal and extremely stimulating. The teachers were not having to stick rigidly to a syllabus or prepare us for exams; they were free to go into their subject as deeply as they wished. In my previous schools, I had often been bored, waiting for the slower ones to catch up; here, if one had grasped something, one tried to put it into words, to tell the others, and lively discussions would often continue after the course.

One of the teachers, Wackernagel, owned a hut on the nearest mountain meadow, above the tree line, called Balisalp, and sometimes small groups would stay there overnight. Four of us who were native English (or American) speakers had supper and breakfast up there once and provided an English-speaking environment for a student of English. Or we would discuss philosophical and political ideas with Kool and Wacki. Mathematics, which I had always hated, burst like fireworks in my mind when a friend of Paulus, Martin Wagenschein, got an unusually large group to spend a whole week considering the question – 'Is there a highest prime number?' It fascinated us. Suggestions darted to and fro between us and were checked out. Gradually we approached the solution; it finally came to me in the night when I had been sleeping in the mountain hut, and I was so excited I had to sit in a trough of cold water outside to calm down.

For once being brainy was not a handicap; others enjoyed debating with me, the teachers did not slap me or anyone down, but urged us on to find out about topics ourselves. Leibniz and his monads was one; another time, when I had asserted that a poem by Walt Whitman could not be translated into German, I was told to go away and translate it – and I did. In art, we did not have to paint still lives or illustrate poems; Willy Aebersold would give us paper and paints, or a lump of clay, and let us get on with it, only intervening when we needed practical help or encouragement. A lot of girls and women were in love with Willy, who had a fine head of black hair, large brown eyes, and great warmth and charm despite his rather short legs. His room was the Sakristei, the cubicle in the corner of the big hall, with a ladder leading up to his bunk bed – in which, he told me, he had once found one of the Dutch girls lying in wait for him. He said he had had great difficulty in getting her to leave, and thereafter had a lock put on the door of the Sakristei.

The Mitarbeiter could be seen as consisting of two distinct groups. The one, which was closest to Paulus – people like Wackernagel and Kool – spent their free time mountaineering or in organised games or in rational discussions and scientific pursuits. Willy was one of the other group: they were not as health conscious as the others; they smoked, drank wine, and sat around talking and enjoying the company of Lulu – Susanne Rolo, a psychologist, who had been married to an Englishman, and Nini Bausch-Willens. Nini was undoubtedly the greatest teacher there. She had been a ballerina, and had married some very rich financier, who divorced her when Hitler came to power, since she was Jewish. She had escaped to the École with two half-Jewish nephews, Thies and Hanne, who were students now but came back to the École in their vacations, as it was their only home. Nini was teaching literature and cultural history, dance and drama. Where previously I had chewed and swallowed gobbets of information, and regurgitated them in tests and exams, Nini opened the world of ideas up to me. A word like 'Renaissance' came alive, a movement I could almost see spreading slowly from Italy across the countries of Europe in many varied manifestations. With the help of pictures, recordings and texts, we gained a feeling for Baroque and Rococo, in art, music and literature. She got us to perform Goethe's *Die Laune des Verliebten*, culminating in a minuet, for which we girls had to wear crinolines which were so wide they prevented us from going out through doors: we had to drop them inside. Taking part in that performance left us with an indelible understanding of the nature of the Rococo. The hall in the Turmhaus was packed for the three performances with parents and friends, and the applause was exhilarating.

Nini made us aware of two modes of being, for which she used the titles 'Apollonian' and 'Dionysiac'. Using many examples from the realms of literature, art and philosophy, she showed us that we had a choice: to submit to the instinctive, exhilarating, passionate, or to be guided by reason and intelligence. Alas, she herself, in later years, sold her soul. The last time I saw her, she was plump, bedizened with jewellery, heavily made-up, and with an entourage of men, one, much younger than her and extremely handsome, quite possibly, it seemed to me, her lover, her 'toy boy'. It was all a far cry from the Nini I had known just a few years before, in shapeless black slacks, getting us to perform pirouettes and arabesques the length of the hall. How, she asked us, could one express 'pursuit' and 'escape' in dance? After much debate, we settled on Orestes pursued by the Furies. She got hold of a recording of Gluck's music and soon we were Furies, dancing to and fro with outstretched arms, dressed in rags and crowned with wire snakes, to prevent Orestes escaping. We read the whole play and rehearsed many of the scenes – I memorised Cassandra's lines of prophecy and doom. The performances we gave of the *Oresteia* were tremendously exciting, and the unbelievable relief when Apollo lifts the curse from Orestes and the Furies withdraw seemed to illustrate what we had been learning about the Dionysiac and the Apollonian.

These alternatives became meaningful to me. Goethe's dismissal of Romanticism as exemplified in Kleist as 'das Kranke' – the sick – reminded me of my father's dismissal of Mu and all of us, insisting that he could and should run his life rationally, rejecting us as factors that disturbed his inner harmony, embracing cool, reasonable English Stella – a perfect contrast to my mother, whose intelligence was always subservient to her tumultuous emotional life. Both my brother and my sister suffered breakdowns in late adolescence, largely brought about by their being totally rejected by Fe – who saw their condition as the sick – from which he felt quite justified in distancing himself, as it would interfere with his work, his priest-like service of Athens. He felt no responsibility for them, no guilt. He felt himself to be totally innocent of causing my siblings' depressions: they were due to something innate, hereditary. He was 'Apollonian'.

I wrote a letter to him, in Manchester, and received a reply. Quite a correspondence ensued, and he kept all these letters, and often drafts of his replies, and gave them all to me in a carrier bag a short time before he died; I have them now. Here's something I wrote to him:

'... I'm often "desperately unhappy", I suppose that's my nature. Firstly about Time and Transience, human suffering and human ignobility, the suffering of animals. ... And secondly about myself ... I seem to be a sort of lump that exists without deserving to; I'm so inconsiderate and forgetful and inefficient. But what I grieve about most is you. I often wish I was dead or had never been born. After all, I know you are a totally inconsiderate egoist, and have made the life of the best person a hell. So why do I still love you? ... Knowing what you are like I want to have no contact with you, yet here I am writing a letter which is bound to lead to contact.

I don't feel very well, it's true. I often feel dizzy and unreasonably tired, my heart beats so after every exertion. I could see a doctor, but I don't want to be a hypochondriac, after all, I've seen too much of that in you.'

I don't know if Fe took offence at this. But he did not immediately cast it aside as another instance of das Kranke. He wrote to the Geheebs, the directors of the school, to ask whether I appeared to have the same depressive tendencies as my brother and sister. In her reply, Edith Geheeb (her letter is in the carrier bag too) told him that there was no sign of ill health or depression in me. He told me in one of his letters that he wanted to be free of those dark clouds, to build up a new life of balance and sanity. He also wrote that I was the only one of his children who appeared to have developed 'straight'. Soon I felt it was unforgivable of me to communicate with him. But he kept the letters I had written – for decades.

*****

At the weekends, when we were not rehearsing the next play, we would go for long walks up the Hasliberg, sometimes with Paulus or other adults. Above the forest belt there was a string of 'Alpenwiesen', mountain pastures, where the cows spent the summer with one or two peasants who lived in small wooden buildings and made cheese. I often walked up to one or other of these meadows with a tall, quiet Estonian boy, Andreas. The air was clean, the only sounds were the liquid notes of the cows' bells, there were many flowers in the grass, harebells, gentians, dianthus; troughs – hollow tree-trunks – with spring water continually flowing through, and wonderful wide vistas across the valley to the Wetterhörner and down to Meiringen and Brienz.

::*:*:*

Nini decided to stage a medieval nativity play for Christmas, and I was to be the Virgin Mary. But my birthday comes a week before Christmas. And I celebrated it. It was my sixteenth.

The school was extremely democratic: not in the sense of having elections and committees – that would have led to dominating majorities and oppressed minorities; no, in the Quaker sense: problems were to be discussed by everybody for as long as necessary until the best solution was found. From time to time we would all gather in the dining hall, from the smallest six-year-old to Paulus and Edith, to deal with any problems that had arisen. That was the theory; in practice, it was often a case of Paulus and Edith reading the riot act to us. And in fact there were three rules: No alcohol; No going out at night; No lighting fires in the forest.

So Sabine, Andreas, the Estonian boy, and I decided to celebrate my birthday by breaking all three rules. With the knitted patchwork blankets from our beds, bottles of wine and matches, we set off for a midnight party in the forest.

We were soon drunk. We did what people always do when they are drunk – laughed, talked nonsense, veered from maudlin self-pity to absurd high spirits and back again, and finally felt extremely tired. We stamped out the remains of the fire and started blundering through the forest. I felt absolutely confident after my bad experience with Dani on my first night, and loudly called to the others to follow me. Why did they hang back? I knew the way to go! Then I stepped over the edge of the precipice and started flying through the air.

I heard someone screaming in the distance. After quite a while I hit the ground. It was a steep slope, and I rolled down it, ending up curled round the base of a tree. The scream came closer; in fact, it was coming out of my mouth.

Well, Sabine and Andreas came down by a more circuitous route and in due course found me whimpering, still curled round my tree trunk. They got me back to the school and I was driven down to the hospital in Meiringen where the same doctor who had diagnosed my concussion now diagnosed a broken arm and badly bruised knees. Duly bandaged and plastered up I returned to the Brünig by bus and from there to the Ecole on foot, and as I approached the school I saw a knitted patchwork blanket hanging from the top of a tree halfway up the slope to a rocky outcrop. I was dumbfounded to see how far I had fallen. Did I have a guardian angel? No, said Willy, when he heard the whole story: you were drunk, so you were relaxed and just let yourself fall. You might have been killed if you hadn't been drunk and had tried to save yourself.

The three of us went back to retrieve the blanket, and the others shared my feeling of awe when they saw it hanging from the tree. But Nini was beside herself with rage: how could I be so thoughtless as to injure myself just days before a performance? Did I know my lines? And my bruised knees – as the Virgin Mary I had got to kneel!

Well, duly chastened, I learned my lines; and in the performances of the play, I kept my broken arm, draped in the loose sleeve of my costume, upstage, with a cushion wedged in under my elbow. When I had to kneel, I slipped the cushion under my knee. 'I am the servant of the Lord,' I declared piously, 'May it be according to his will.' Perhaps because I was still feeling unreal, the performance was deemed to be deeply sincere, and I came in for a lot of praise.

*****

Those children who could went home for the Christmas holiday – mainly the Swiss; the rest of us waited impatiently for snow, which was phenomenally late that year. Some Old Boys came to the school, their only home, for the holiday. When at last the snow came, those who could ski, young and old, rushed to the store room for skis and disappeared into the white wonderland. The few of us who had never skied – Elnis from Israel, Hope from America, a little Belgian girl, me – were left to our own devices. We worked out how to buckle skis onto our shoes and after many minor mishaps learned to step sideways up the slope opposite the school and slide down it, stopping at the bottom by sitting down in the snow. We enjoyed this; but after a few days Kool felt guilty towards us and decided to take us on a mountain tour: by the time we had spent a whole day on skis we would know how it was done. Strips of fur were attached underneath the skis to prevent them slipping on the snow, and we set off up the mountain, through the forest belt, and onto Balisalp. So far it had been fine, though strenuous, pacing sideways up, following a zigzag route, learning how to rest one ski after the other vertically while we turned at the corners of the zigzag Coming down through the trees was a different matter. I did not know how to steer, and crashed into one tree after the other, until I was quite hysterical, crouching in the snow and not wanting to feel the skis sliding away beneath me uncontrollably any more. It was like my panic on the scree in Wales, and it took Kool a long time to coax me back onto my feet. He steered me along gently descending lines, so that I slid over the snow so slowly that I could not feel afraid. That was all the skiing I ever learned, though I envied the experienced skiers flying down the mountain sides in wings of flying sparkling snow.

On Christmas Eve everybody in the school walked a short way into the forest after dark and found a small fir tree covered in candles. It was just like the Christmas custom of the Wandervogel that Mu had described to me.

Here Paulus, the agnostic, read out the Christmas story. Then we returned to the school and found an unusually festive meal prepared, even better than the usual Sunday evening treat: each of us got a plate with a silver-paper triangle of cheese, a boiled egg, fruit and so on, and some Christmas goodies. The fourth candle on the big Advent wreath hanging from the ceiling was lit, there was singing and talking, the Old Boys – huge fellows, like Nini's nephews – reminisced about the heroic, hungry days at Lac Noir, and how they had stolen food from the cellar. Suddenly, looking across the room, I was smitten with love for a young man with curly black hair and a profile that reminded me of some Roman emperor's. I soon got to know him, and listened to him as he talked about his studies in Zurich, and about skiing and swimming, entranced by his brown eyes and silky lashes. His name was Stefan, and when I told Paulus and Edith that I wanted to hitch-hike to Ticino with him in the Easter holidays, they raised no objection: this Old Boy was perfectly safe.

At New Year the local peasants, in accordance with an ancient pagan custom, hung cows' bells round their necks and, consuming only beer, walked round the villages on the Hasliberg for 24 hours, to drive out evil spirits, then for the next 24 hours, round the individual houses, and for the last 24 hours, they entered into houses, ringing their bells, in the final stages of exhaustion and drunkenness. Naturally they thought our school, being a foreign entity, would harbour most evil spirits. We were warned that they would come in and that we should keep out of their way. As luck would have it, I was having a shower in the basement when they entered the Haupthaus; but I turned off the tap and kept the door locked and – shivering with cold – did not make a sound, so they did not find me.

❖❖❖❖❖

In the Easter holidays I set out to visit Ticino with Stefan; but we had hardly walked for twenty minutes before I was totally disillusioned with him. He was not quite as bad as Dani, but nearly. His conversation was trivial and boring; he never stopped talking, except to sing silly little ditties. After another twenty minutes I found him intensely irritating – he was petty-minded and timid and fussy and kept sniffing, and he kept his money in a silly little purse and kept counting it. Still, we got a few lifts and were not far from our destination when we got into a fierce argument about the best way to go on. I left him and headed straight up a grassy slope, while he continued on the road. My steep climb was richly rewarded – the brow of the hill was a mass of wild crocuses that caught the sun, and as I approached it, more and more of the scenery beyond became visible, until I had Lago Maggiore spread out below, the little islands in it like jewels, and the square towers of the village churches rising in front of it.

Lago Maggiore

It was my first taste of the Italian, and I responded in true German manner: ecstatically. I turned to look at the lake again, and there was Stefan, like a beetle, coming up after me, wiping his nose with the back of his hand. I was cruel to him. I tried to get him to understand that though I had for a time had a crush on him, I no longer did, but he could not accept this, and stayed with me, occasionally making little sentimental remarks.

The cobbled streets in the steep lakeside villages were at times more like stairs, and the stone houses, designed for shade in that bright sunlight, with geraniums on the sills of their shuttered windows, the slender cypresses – it was overwhelming.

We slept in the hay-loft of a very cheap hostel, and next day visited Professor Schmied, who had a beautiful house right at the water's edge outside Locarno, with life-sized carvings of naked boys and other works of art. We knew him, because he came to the École from time to time, where he was warmly welcome, especially with Nini and Willy. He was a rich man, owning some chemical factory, and took them for rides in his car and restaurant meals. He gave talks on various cultural topics; once he showed a silent film he had made; some handsome boys running through a wood and out onto a hill top where they hoisted a flag as the sun rose ... I felt I was getting an inkling of something. Fascism? Homosexuality? He came to all Nini's theatrical performances; he had been lavish in his praise of my acting. It was exciting: he seemed to think I was brilliant. He also believed in Willy's exceptional talent as an artist, and had given him a large sum of money on condition that he should get his next sculpture or image, no matter what it was or when it was completed (he had already been waiting for some years). Schmied was a suave, wealthy, middle-aged man; his hospitality was lavish. At one point he was reproaching me for being vegetarian.

'If you told me', he purred, 'that you were vegetarian because you feel you are too passionate by nature, and must avoid red meat for that reason, I might understand. But because you pity the animals – that's no reason. You are a human like me, a carnivore; you need to bite into meat. Here, bite my thumb.' He held it by my mouth and would not stir until I bit it. 'Harder,' he said, 'much harder. There, that's more like it. You liked doing that, didn't you?' There were a few drops of blood on it; he wrapped a handkerchief round it, smiling. I took my leave nervously, and found a quiet place to write my weekly letter to Mu, in which I described what had just happened. She wrote back a letter full of dire warnings against this man. She wrote to Paulus about him, too, who replied gently that he did not like him much himself, but he did enrich the artistic life of the school, and he did not think that I would be in danger from a homosexual...

✵✵✵✵✵

Nini's plays dominated the life of the school: everyone was roped in to make costumes, rig up stage lights, organise the performances, or take part. During my year there, I played the lead in five plays. It was my performance as Melanie, in Robert Ardrey's *Thunder Rock*, with Willy Aebersold as Charleston, that brought me so much praise that it quite turned my head. I was told I had to be an actress. The world would be a poorer place if I wasn't.

Not the sort of thing a sixteen-year-old can ignore. Obviously, I wasn't going to be a doctor. But an actress.

Chapter 20

The world would be a poorer place if I didn't become an actress! But how was I to break the momentous news to Mu? Best to write a long, eloquent letter, hoping to win her over with a nature description:

22.5.49:

'On Saturday four of us had a "philosophical evening" with Wacki in his hut and spent the night there. Next morning I got up when the others were still asleep, washed in the ice-cold trough and set out for a day's climbing by myself. It was cloudy, but when I got to the forest belt below the Balisalp the sun broke through, and a farmer was letting his cows and calves out – the whole Hasliberg echoed with the sound of their bells, and the beautiful animals stepped out into the sunlight one after the other, like the members of a Greek chorus getting into position in an amphitheatre. Coming round a bend in the forest path I was confronted by a giant pine, dripping wet, with the sun shining on it; it looked like a luminous mist, and big raindrops, glowing green and red and blue and yellow, were hanging from its twigs; great slanting shafts of sunlight were falling through the trees onto cushions of moss, from which twirls of mist rose ...

I wanted to go up to the summit. But great, ragged clouds were flying around, and sometimes a wall of mist rose from a valley; I could hear the thunder of rock falls. Soon, I was surrounded by mist. There were lots of flowers by the path, but when I came to a steep rock face, common sense prevailed and I turned back.

The reason why I set out alone was that I wanted to think. Here are my conclusions:

I don't really want to be a doctor. I want to be an actress. ... Nini can take charge of my training for one or two years, and then send me to theatres here and in Germany: she has connections. So please, dearest Mu, let me stay here for another one or two years!'

I had not expected the vehemence with which Mu opposed these plans. In letter after letter she insisted that I must return to the Oxford High School and get the Higher School Certificate which would make it possible for me to go to university. I owed it to the school. I owed it to Miss Stack, who had been so kind and forbearing. I owed it to my British passport, somehow. She would not insist on my actually going to university, though she could not see that a degree would prevent my becoming an actress afterwards. But I had got to finish my English schooling properly.

In letter after letter, I argued that at the Ecole I could take the Swiss Matura, or – if the High School would send the syllabus – prepare for

Higher there, with the help of the teachers. I argued that if I did not stay with Nini now, my acting gift would wither and die. I appealed to Fe: would he help pay for me to stay? He would; but he too thought that if one had brains one should go to university. Once again I cursed my brains. I got both Paulus and Edith to write to both Fe and Mu; they even said that money, or the lack of it, would not matter: all to no avail.

I think the truth is that Mu was jealous of Nini, and suspicious of her friendship with Schmied. I felt 'shades of the prison house' closing in on me, and submitted. All I achieved was permission to do the Higher School Certificate course in one year instead of two. But I felt sure it would make no real difference: my chance to be a great actress would be done for.

My last morning in Goldern was damp and overcast. After packing, I went for a short stroll along a familiar path above the village. The skies do weep to see me go, I thought. I went back to the school, said my tearful farewells, and then I was on the musical yellow post-bus again, heading for Brünig, Zurich, Paris, and home.

In Zurich I spent a few days sitting under the lime trees dreaming of Danni, the current object of my love, aching and writing poems to him. Alas, after a very brief amorous walk on the Hasliberg (he was an Old Boy of the Ecole) he had written a gentle letter of renunciation. But I was chronically in love in those days; the objects varied, but the condition was the same.

I met Maleen in Paris. She had just spent three months as an au pair, to improve her French: we were to travel home together. She introduced me to an American student, Norman Ramsdell, who had offered to book a room for me near his own. I spent a long evening strolling in the Latin Quarter with him and talking: he was particularly interested in my falling off the mountain, wanting to know exactly what it was like to come so close to death. At about 3 am he remembered that he had failed to book a room for me; I was going to have to sleep in his. We crept up the stairs of his Hôtel Excelsior in Rue M le Prince, and he gave me a coat and a cushion to sleep on on the floor, while he got into his bed. I did not think this very chivalrous of him. But worse was to come: the flabby old concierge who sat in a glass box at the bottom of the stairs raised Cain when she saw us descend next day, loudly accusing me of immorality, prostitution and dishonesty, and demanding money. We fled, and I hurried to meet Maleen at the Gare du Nord. I was a little early, so, seeing a sign for Café Exprés, which I thought must be very quick, I sat down at a small table on the pavement and ordered one. But when it came, it turned out to consist of

a small container from which the coffee dripped slowly into a cup. While I waited, the boat train – with Maleen on it – had gone. Fortunately there was another one shortly afterwards, and when I got to the ferry in Calais I saw Maleen, standing on the deck, looking out for me, tight-lipped, and shaking her head despairingly when she saw me.

*****

Now a dreary year began for me. I was back in the navy blue uniform of the Oxford High School, back in the old building on Banbury Road, and even the fact that Anne was in a parallel class did not help much. I was made a deputy prefect and was expected to enforce the school rules. One of these seemed foolish: talking was forbidden in the corridors even in the lunch hour, when there were no lessons to be disturbed. Sitting beside the deputy head at lunch, I said as much, and suggested we should have a meeting with a view to changing that rule. She stared at me, as if she could not believe her ears. Finally she said, in strangled tones: 'We have very few rules in this school, but those there are must be obeyed.' Suddenly I recognised the huge difference between the Ecole and this school. The only nod in the direction of democracy was the mock elections, when I stood for Labour and got two votes (the Tory candidate got hundreds).

At Easter, Anne and I went to Paris together for three weeks. We had about £10 each, and stayed in Rue Monsieur le Prince, lived almost exclusively on bread, oranges and coffee, which we brewed over a candle, walked a good deal, pencilling in the streets we traversed on our street plan, attended some language classes at the Sorbonne, and went to the theatre almost every night – the cheapest standing places in 'the Gods', of course. Here we were among old women whose whole life was centred on the Comédie Française. All through the play they would comment excitedly – 'Oh là là! Tiens! Il va tirer l'épée, vieux sot!' – and were quick to clap and squeak 'Bravo!' when an actor, a speech, an exit had pleased them. As soon as the lights went up for the interval or for the end, they would start discussing the play animatedly, comparing this with other performances. 'Comme elle tourna la tête et parlait a travers son épaule – cette geste etait pleine de poésie,' said one old woman, remembering Sarah Bernhardt, 'comme ça:' and she demonstrated the movement by resting her own hairy chin on her bony shoulder.

We were very shocked by some plays and curtain-raisers – 'Marlborough s'en va-t-en Guerre' was one – which were immoral. We walked out, indignantly, in protest at any erotic and lavatorial humour. (My reaction was similar to Oma's when she visited Julie Wolfthorn, her artist cousin, half a century before, but I didn't know that then.)

We got extremely hungry. We would stand outside restaurants, drooling as delicious odours reached our nostrils. On our last day, we counted our money, studied the menu displayed outside one restaurant, and entered boldly, to order the one dish we knew we could afford. The waiter gave us a funny look, and returned after a while with two large plates. A small dead fish lay in the middle, complete with eyes. That was it.

✳✳✳✳✳

Maleen had gone to America, Peter, now a student at St John's College, was living in a room some way away, Kurt was in Israel, so Mu and I were alone together, apart from lodgers. It was hard for me not to be resentful: I didn't want to be there, I was bored and bitter. I was writing long letters to Switzerland, particularly to Willy Aebersold, who replied from the TB sanatorium with beautiful script in Indian ink. I got affectionate letters from several of the other children. Poor Mu, she was convinced she had done the right thing for me, had saved me from her own fate: having no qualifications at all, she had to work as a cleaner in an old people's home to make ends meet, coming home to more housework, and a sullen, silent daughter. She would ask me to tell her something from my day at school, which exasperated me, as I couldn't think of anything worth saying. Mu would talk about the book she was reading, and that was almost always about the concentration camps. At least once a week she would walk to the City Library in St Aldates and bring home more heavy tomes full of horror. She felt she owed it to all the people who had suffered that dreadful fate, especially those she had known personally. Chief among these was her aunt Julie Wolfthorn, the painter. She knew now that Julie and her sister Liese had been dragged off to Theresienstadt when they were both in their 80s – what made the Nazis fear them? – and had died there. Mu had an irrational feeling of guilt, because she had escaped, had led 'a charmed life', as she often said, although it couldn't be described as 'charming'.

The Higher School Certificate exams came and went, the results were good, and at last, in accordance with our bargain, I was to return to Nini. But she had left the Ecole and was trying to run a theatre school in Zurich: I was to be one of her students, though I knew in my heart that this dreary year had killed any flair or gift for acting I had possessed. Officially I was to register at the university so that money could be sent to me legitimately.

I found a small attic room at Hirslanderstrasse 26. It had a big bed with a huge feather mattress, a dormer window, a table with a bowl and jug for washing, and nothing else. My landlady was a severe-looking spinster who seemed to spend her life cleaning. The only other inhabitant was her fat old uncle, who spoke to me once on the stairs when he was going out with an equally unattractive friend. 'We're going to catch birds, but the sort that don't have feathers' he said, and both of them laughed greasily. But when the friend started leering at me, the uncle said: 'No no, this is a very respectable young lady – e ganz seriöses Fräulein.' I was so appalled to be called e ganz seriöses Fräulein that I resolved never to be in before midnight, even if it meant walking round the house for half an hour.

*****

Nini was living in a modern flat in Balgriststrasse; her nephew Thies was with her, and Lulu, who had also left the Ecole, had the flat opposite. Lulu wanted to earn her living as a psycho-analyst. Several ex-Ecolianers beside myself were Nini's students; but in fact she earned most of her money, as she said once, bitterly, by massaging and doing exercises with rich Swiss women to help them get over their constipation.

My first lessons confirmed my fears: I wrote home that I was *'stodgy, stiff, clumsy, and heavy, my voice hard and pressed and Nini won't let me do any real acting until these things are under control.'*

Nini had me doing gymnastics, breathing and ballet exercises in the confined space of my room, and writing and performing sketches, as well as learning and practising parts. I earned a little money by giving English lessons, which I enjoyed doing. One of my students, a nurse, fed me chocolate throughout the lesson. I attended a few art history lectures at the university, and enjoyed them, too. But I spent many long hours alone in my room, writing poems, dialogues, plays, stories, and drawing in a tatty old exercise book. Whole days would lie in front of me with nothing to do.

I loved the days I went to the Balgriststrasse.

'Nini takes herself so seriously (I wrote home). *She's always having these infuriating illnesses which are usually gone in a matter of hours; but before they've gone she's absolutely in despair. "Why should I go to the doctor," she cries with flung hands every time Lulu suggests it, "when I know exactly what he'll tell me? Stay in bed and don't go outside in this atrocious weather – but I've got to." Whereupon she leans back in agony, looking perfectly healthy. Sometimes it's sinus trouble, and she holds a hot water bottle across her face with great sighs of relief. She gets into an absolute rage if there's a mess in the kitchen, or if she's kept waiting when the food is on the table. The odd thing is that while I find many little everyday things about her quite absurd, I still admire her.*

As for Lulu – she's always fishing for compliments. "I think this blouse is perfectly lovely on me, what do you say, Nini?" and Nini, of course, says: "I'm sorry, Lulu, I don't. I think it makes you look old and fat." Lulu: "But I am old and fat." She seems to be making her mark: quite a lot of people come to her for treatment, and she gives lectures and goes to conferences and so on. Of course there are lots of Swiss psychologists, but they're all rotten, she says.'

*****

I think it was Poldi, another of Nini's ex-Goldern students, who introduced me to Bebbi – a thin bespectacled man in his 50s, nicknamed Bebbi because he seemed as harmless and innocent as a baby, and his eyes were such a milky blue. He lived, with other artists and craftspeople, in a converted farm on the outskirts of Zürich. The city had made a number of studios there available to such people, hoping that they would produce works that would put Zürich on the artistic map of Europe. We spent many long hours sitting on his dilapidated sofa, drinking tea and talking, while his brass plates were being etched with abstract patterns in an acid bath, or he was painting one of his strange, dreamy paintings – one, which he gave me, shows a girl's face almost disappearing under a flood of tiny human and animal figures. Sometimes he gave a party, and then there would be crowds of people drinking wine and talking, playing the guitar and singing. Willy Aebersold appeared in this studio quite often, having at last been released from the sanatorium. I called him Charleston, and he called me Melanie, after the characters we had played in *Thunder Rock*. At first I was quite dismayed at the sight of him, and wrote home:

'He isn't nearly as charming as he was in Goldern; he's pale, a bit puffy, looks dissatisfied with himself, can't stop smoking. He hasn't got enough self-discipline to get started in anything. So he still lives with his parents (he's 26), gets into debt, exploits everyone who likes him, and wiles away his time with dreams and card tricks. Perhaps it will get better. Just now he's working properly, eight hours a day, as a commercial artist, but nobody thinks he'll stick it out.'

Bebbi was as welcoming in his studio as Jacky was in his workshop in Oxford. Often I was alone with him, drinking endless cups of tea until the small hours. Showing me the blackened interior of his teapot, before brewing up yet again, he said earnestly, 'You and me, we're just as black inside.' He was kind to me – a bit like Kurt. He got me to talk. He took me seriously, so I was able to confide in him – my feelings of guilt, my fears, my self-doubt. He was the first person who tried to explain me to myself, saying I had built a protective wall around myself, not letting anyone guess at my innermost doubts, 'and now you're sitting there in your tower,' he said, 'and don't know how to get out of it.'

And in return he confided in me. Gradually, I got to know his whole story.

He had been brought up by a Swiss peasant couple near Zürich who received money monthly from someone in Germany right up until the assassination of Crown Prince Franz Ferdinand and his wife in Sarajevo in June 1914. Then the money stopped coming. Always aware that the people he was living with were not related to him, he became obsessed with the wish to find out what his true identity was. As he described it to me: 'This thought, who am I, went round and round in my head all the time; I couldn't think about anything else. Nothing else was real. It was a never-ending nightmare.' Still, he did well at school and got a job in Zürich city council. After the war, he went to the German town from which the monthly cheques had been sent, and looked for the address, and tried to find out who his mother had been, but he was baffled at every turn. This convinced him that some important and high-born person wanted to conceal his parentage. Who could it be? When had the money stopped coming? He became convinced that he was an illegitimate son of Crown Prince Franz Ferdinand.

When he was in his twenties, he learned that an unmarried niece of his foster parents had become pregnant and that the child was to be given away for adoption as soon as it was born. Bebbi was appalled: another human being was to be subjected to the nightmare of not knowing her true identity! Without having any feelings for the woman, he married her so that she could keep her child. When she gave birth to a girl, Bebbi's whole life focused on the child, and for years he was happy. But now she had grown up, and married, and his life seemed meaningless. He had given up his job, left his wife, and spent all the money he had on a trip to Africa. He got no further than Algeria, and discovered that – like other Mediterranean countries – it is cold in the winter. He showed me a snap-shot of himself standing in front of a stony desert and my heart went out to him: he looked so desolate in his beret and rain coat. All this had happened a few years before I got to know him. When he returned from Algeria, he set up as a craftsman, etching brass bowls and plates and ashtrays and making a scant living.

✳✳✳✳✳

It was on 28 March that Willy informed me that he and I were now a pair. He had invited me to join him in an old, elegant wine bar, where he also introduced me to Rioja wine, and showed me the correct way to hold a cigarette and to let the smoke curl out of my mouth and nostrils. 'Du und ich, wir sind ein Paar,' he said. I took his word on it, though I was rather surprised; so now he was the object of my love.

The effect was electrifying – for a time. He started carving a small wooden figure. Wherever he went, wherever he sat, he would pull it out of his pocket and continue whittling away at it with his pen knife. He pared away more and more, until the whole figure seemed to consist of a few interwoven bands of thin wood. We called it a Noodle Figure. (I think it ultimately ended up in Professor Schmied's possession, in payment of that ancient debt.) Meanwhile, I lost my inhibitions in acting and dancing; I wrote little dialogues and acted both parts, gaining praise from Nini at last.

After long sessions at Bebbi's, Willy would walk me home – and at a certain corner we would sit down on a bench under a street light. He might lay one arm round my shoulders, and caress me with the other hand, more as if he was trying to sculpt me than in any erotic way. He said he thought he was born to be platonic. We talked a little – this was at the time of the Korean War, and we were both appalled at the horrific news that reached us occasionally. I toyed with the thought of going to the Red Cross and volunteering to go to Korea as a nurse for a year. Willy's reaction was different. 'Every soldier,' he opined, 'should be obliged to eat every enemy soldier he had killed. That would put a stop to war.' Every time we met he seemed to be a different person. He was the focal point of a large, loose group of people, who called him Bö, and now that I was accepted as his girl, I got to know many of them, usually in one of the inns in the Altstadt, the old centre of Zürich. There was one veteran of the Spanish Civil War, and one night I dreamed that I shot Franco with a small jewelled revolver, escaped in an aeroplane, which crashed into the sea, but swam ashore. Another in Willy's entourage was a young man of great beauty, Carlos: he looked like a Greek statue. Others were working men, or would-be artists and actors, or tram drivers; they all gathered round the table where Willy stage-managed them, smiling, his long fingers holding a glass of red wine – as I wrote to Mu:

'Everything I told you about him and his unreliability is true. However, there is the other side to him. Everything that was "terrific" about the Ecole – brilliant people, the creative atmosphere – it really emanated from Willy's Sakristei. And he still has this power; I can't explain it, lots of people depend on him.

And he himself? He disappoints everyone who believes in him. People, his family for instance, say: "He should have done an apprenticeship, he's 26, he should have a proper job, help to support his family, he shouldn't drink and smoke and sit around talking all the time, he should have a bit of self-discipline." People get commissions for him, put themselves out on his behalf, talk to him for hours, and he agrees with everything they say, admits it all, and stays as he is, lets them down, every time.

I like him best when he smiles through his fingers and fantasizes and plays games with people and chats idly.'

I had to go back to Britain for a time: Peter was getting married in August, to Brenda, a petite, shy, sweet Welsh student nurse (could he have been unconsciously emulating his father's involvement with a petite, shy, sweet student nurse quarter of a century ago?) and I was to be a bridesmaid. It occurred to me that it would be very nice to go to the wedding with Willy, since, as he had informed me, we were a pair, and introduce him to the family. I dropped a hint to Mu, and she promptly sent him an invitation. He responded with an exquisitely worded letter, penned in Indian ink:

'... Please do not take it amiss if I now write that I cannot come to England this summer. The reasons for this lie in a deeply rooted feeling of not-yet-having-the-right and not-yet-being-qualified to occupy any

position in your vicinity.

During the coming months I have to work for the most elementary necessities and will only be capable of doing so if I use blinkers, as it were, which permit me only to look towards my immediate goals. So I think it will be better to use the period of separation from Gabi to find a path to reality and only to come to England when I am sufficiently consolidated, inwardly and outwardly, to give my great attachment to Gabi a calm and absolutely appropriate outer form.

Believing you will understand this my attitude I offer you as a sign of my affection the most sincere greetings
Yours
Willy Aebersold.'

This letter had no connection with reality. However, at that point I wanted to believe it.

But only two days later, I was writing a long letter to Mu, thanking her for money and chocolate, and announcing that I would be leaving Zürich on 12 or 13 July, and staying in England before and after Peter's wedding to see if I could get work in a theatre. If I couldn't, then Nini was prepared to have me back.

What had happened?

One evening, as I was watching the rain sweep down past my window like a silver curtain, the phone rang. It was Bebbi.

'Can you come? Can you bring some money? We're in trouble.'

I went to the inn he named, and there he was, drunk, grinning, and Willy, drunk, grinning, and saying, 'Thou art fallen among thieves.' I emptied out my purse on the table. Willy said it was to pay the month's rent for his family's flat in Rotwandstrasse; his sister Erika, a secretary, would get paid at the end of the week, and on Friday evening he would meet me and give me back the money.

Now I had no money at all. Mu's last remittance was finished. I had a collection of empty yoghurt pots, and took one back to the shop every day; the rebate was just enough for a bowl of soup at a friendly restaurant. Friday came and went, but Willy did not appear. I went to Rotwandstrasse, found the Aebersold flat, rang the bell, and an old woman appeared: perhaps his mother, rumoured to have been a Rumanian gipsy. She did not understand me; then a younger one, who looked like Willy and was in fact his sister, hurried out, giving me a cynical glance in passing: she didn't know where Willy was. I drew a large question mark on a postcard addressed to him and posted it through the letter box. There was no response. Days passed. I visited Schwester Annie, who gave me a book of vouchers for the Zürcher Frauenverein restaurants, which kept me going for another week. And the little nurse I was teaching must have been amazed at the speed with which I wolfed down the chocolate she always gave me.

I thought about my future with Willy: it was going to be a life of drudgery. I could see myself scrubbing floors somewhere to keep us both going; he would never fulfil his promise, any more than I would. He was a cheat and a lay-about. So, as I wrote to Mu:

'A certain distance from Willy seems desirable (one of our future discussion topics, Muttchen!) – and this "end of the chapter" feeling has been with me for some time.'

*****

It was a cold, wet August. As Peter and Brenda knelt at the altar in the Newport church the entire congregation could see the holes in the soles of his shoes. Afterwards there was a reception with what seemed like a host of Brenda's relatives, and finally we returned to Oxford, to find Kurt sitting by the blazing kitchen boiler, complaining of the cold.

I applied for an audition at RADA and at the Central School of Acting and was offered a place; but then I had to apply for a 'discretionary grant' from Oxford City's Education Department, who did not see that the world would be a poorer place if I didn't become an actress, and failed to give me the grant. But they would give me one to go to university. I then rather grimly agreed to apply to Somerville College to read English. I got through to the interview stage, and had lunch with some high-powered women there, and was offered a place – but only to read Modern Languages. This I refused: English or nothing, and preferably nothing, had been my attitude from the start, so I got out of that one.

Next I went to see Peter Streuli, the son of that English clergyman who had made Oma so happy when she was a student at Freiburg. Peter Streuli had quite an important position in the Royal Shakespeare Company. I didn't know quite what I was meant to be doing or saying to him, so he didn't know what exactly I wanted and gave me a few rather general pieces of advice, such as reading *The Stage*, but nothing concrete.

So I returned to Zürich, stopping off in Paris, where I stayed in Rue M. le Prince (of course) for a few days. I roamed around, and tried to convince myself that one day I would be a famous actress with my name up in bright lights and the world eager to know my every thought. I sat on benches, and scribbled thoughts in pencil on scraps of paper:

'I'm forgetting – forgetting – slowly, vaguely, unconsciously, everything is being borne away from me on the river of time.

In the Eglise St Germain des Prés – I stumbled in during a service – the priest spoke very quickly in a hard falsetto, the small congregation put in a 'Priez pour nous' every so often. All the time, tourists were walking up and down, talking, shuffling, dragging back a chair... Everyone got up for their bread and wine with the tourists standing there, watching them, as one watches animals being fed in the zoo. In an alcove there was a Victorian-style Pieta. One after the other, old, lonely women came up, kissed the parted lips of the stone Christ, his forehead – stood back and looked – laid their hands on his wounds, on the holes in the stone hands and feet, that is, one by one, for a long time each, to make them hurt less.'

*****

Many things had changed during the few weeks of my absence from Zürich, and I did not stay long. Nini had given up her dream of starting a theatre school, and was resigned to massaging constipated Zürich women. She said there was no point my staying as her sole pupil for more than a few weeks; she would prepare me for auditions, and then, as English was my language, I had better try my luck in Britain. I realised she felt she would gain nothing for herself by introducing me to old friends in the German theatre (if indeed those contacts really still existed) and her enthusiasm for my great gifts had quite obviously waned – as had the great gifts themselves. Nevertheless, I persevered, and kidded myself that one day I would be rich and famous.

I found another attic room; this one, in Nordstrasse, belonged to a red-haired policeman and his wife Margrit. They had two small children, and were extremely kind to me, inviting me to join them for meals, letting me cook in their kitchen and invite friends, lending me a bicycle; sometimes we went out together. They wanted to introduce me to fFondue, but unfortunately the melted cheese had got too hot and was like chewing gum in texture, which led to an apoplectic rage on the policeman's part, and tears on Margrit's. Soon she and I were spending a good deal of time together, pouring out our hearts to each other. One of us would go to a nearby shop and buy a delicious sort of macaroon; while we consumed them and drank coffee, she would try to teach me the local, Zürich variety of the Swiss dialect. I was not good at it: when I dared to use it to ask a passer-by the way, the answer came – not in Swiss German, not even in German, but in English.

At a rather sordid alcoholic party Bebbi tried to kiss me. I was horrified, and fled. I realised that his devotion to his adoptive daughter, now married, had led to his finding young girls irresistible, and that his kindness to me had not been entirely avuncular. Not long afterwards I heard that he was proposing to marry a little housemaid in Schaffhausen, and to travel all over the world with her.

Most of the old friends from the Ecole had scattered; Poldi was about to go to Canada. But Willy was still there, and as usual, was full of big plans – once again, or still, to go to Paris. I was half in love with young Carlos, the beautiful, who was also an artist; but at the same time I felt I was still in love with Willy, despite everything, and still believed that it was my destiny to spend my life with him – a dreary prospect, in view of his unreliability. But one day when I was cycling through the city I chanced to see him, looking plump and buttery, in a pavement café, with a beautiful girl, a teenager from the Ecole called Doris. I soon learned that she was pregnant – so much for his having been 'born to be platonic!' – and that her family had presented him with an ultimatum: either he should marry her, or, if her father was to pay for her to have an abortion, Willy was to make a bronze portrait head of her. Under this pressure, Willy got to work, and produced a fine piece of sculpture – proving once again that he really was both gifted and able. But now it was obvious to me that I must finally part from him. For a long time afterwards, for years, my mind held an image of his face, his black hair, his large, liquid eyes, his smile, revealing his poor little teeth, his long fingers holding a glass of red wine and a cigarette, and I ached with sorrow as I contemplated it.

Chapter 21

After their short stay with us, Oma and the Leppmanns arrived in Chicago in October 1946. In one of her last letters to Mu from Persia, Oma had written quite apprehensively about her future:

'... I'm not really very keen to go on living, now that I can't plot my path ahead myself, but have to sit around passively and wait to see what will happen to me. All my life I have set myself targets and reached them; action is in my nature. And now I don't know what lies ahead. USA? Will I work and earn my keep, or will I have to depend on someone's grace and favour? That would be far worse than death. I always have managed, so far, to make myself independent, in Freiburg, and here, too. If I could hope to give Aunt Hedchen a few carefree and happy years with my work, then I would be entirely content.'

Hedchen with Nelson family

Hedchen had been living in Colorado Springs with her son Fritz, the eye specialist, and his wife Thilly almost all the time since she got out of Germany in the early 1940s. Fritz was suffering with cancer, and their son Peter had married a deeply depressive woman who committed suicide, leaving him with three small children. The relationship between Hedchen and her daughter-in-law was not a happy one. Hedchen longed for Olga to come and 'make her happy'; so now Oma did set herself another target: to earn enough money for both of them by teaching German, and

'...living in two small shabbily furnished rooms, perhaps with a bathroom, no kitchen, just a little table and a gas cooker – Voilà tout! But Fritz is quite seriously urging me to learn to drive, because life there is supposed to be impossible without a car!!! How does he think that could be??'

So as soon as Marianne and Achim were settled in Chicago, Oma set off for 1121 North Tejon Street, Colorado Springs, and for some weeks she and Hedchen indulged in an orgy of reminiscence and news. She had written to us about:

217

'...the ghastly condition of the displaced Germans, the East and West Prussians, Silesians, Sudeten Germans, who have been driven out everywhere and are pouring into Germany, some packed into cattle wagons, or on their roofs, or walking for 100 or 180 miles, sick, starving, with children and old people, carrying wretched bundles, in the probably forlorn hope of finding somewhere to stay. After all the terrible things the damned Nazis (not to say Germans) perpetrated in Poland and Czechoslovakia it is not surprising that they are not tolerated anywhere.'

By now they must have known that those 'terrible' things had been done to their beloved cousins, the Little Wolves, and to their brother Heinchen's widow Flora, and many others.

She decided that their shared home should be in Berkeley, California, near her old friend Pietrkowski – 'Pieter' – and she begged him to find her something. Finally, in November, he told her of a live-in job, at 2810 Kelsey Street, near his own home: she would have a rent-free room in exchange for looking after a woman even older than herself who was confined to bed with a broken hip for a few hours a day, and to be on call at night. She agreed to take this on with alacrity. Life in the Nelson home was not harmonious. She felt confident that once she was in Berkeley, she would find a place to share with Hedchen, and would be able to teach a few students so that she could pay the rent. She was also trying to get her money out of Germany, including her alimony from Hugo since 1936 – 150 marks a month for ten years.

In Kelsey Street, she had a very small room which did not have a proper door, only a curtain, opening onto a porch. So she had no real privacy. The bed-ridden woman had a severely handicapped daughter who careered round the flat in a wheel chair. Oma had always hated any kind of nursing; now she was having to do everything for the poor woman, including heaving her onto a commode, or pushing a bedpan under her, several times every night.

In February 1947 she managed to realise her plan in part: Pieter made a small flat at 2355 Hilgard Avenue available to her until May, when he and his wife would want it for themselves. Hedchen came, and there they lived together for five months. Oma's foot was so painful that she had splints made up to the knee, which were only moderately helpful; and she did not get as many students as she wanted. But the climate of California delighted her, even when it was cold:

'It looks as if all the plants were delirious. There's a vacant lot opposite which must have been a garden at one time but has now run wild; uncared for, unwatered, but with a veritable orgy of blossom: great thickets of man-sized red and pink geraniums, and all sorts of other things I don't know yet flowering so profusely that you can't see a leaf or a square

centimetre of earth – just flowers in such brilliant colours that they dazzle your eyes when you look at them.'

However, the idyll with Hedchen soon ended: her Puritanism and pessimism did not harmonise with Oma's unconventional ways. She was, for instance, embarrassed when Oma sat down on the pavement with her feet in the gutter to rest her painful ankles. In August she went back to Colorado Springs. The Pietrkowskis were returning from a long journey and needed their flat, so they had to move anyway. Now Marianne and Achim arranged for Oma to live in Forest Avenue, paying a Frau Maas $70 for full board for her. Things looked up: her favourite granddaughter, Dudu, now a student of anthropology, came to live with her, and for a time, she wrote to Lorchen, she was inundated with invitations. Two young men, Laurin and Fulton…

'… can't do anything without dragging me along. So I was out with them from 12.30 till 6.30 in San Francisco, by the sea, in exhibitions, organ concerts, etc. Then they brought me home for dinner and picked me up again for a lovely Caruso film, with ice cream to follow … Apart from my foot, which gets worse and worse, and backache and stiffness in my arm and shoulder, I am better than anyone I know – in the pink of health.'

When Marianne came from Chicago for a short holiday, to recover from retaking her medical exams, Oma introduced her to no fewer than 25 of her friends. According to Dudu:

'She would sit on the stoop and wait for the mailman to come by with his dogs, for whom she saved titbits. Then the neighbour kids would come home from school and sit down and talk to her. Her two young men, both quite gay, whom she tutored in German, would happen by and see if she had time to take a spin in their old jalopy so she could watch the sunset from some vantage point. Or the kids on the street would plan a theatrical for which she was the audience or had to fill in a bit part.'

She enjoyed being alone, she wrote, mostly sitting on the sunny porch, darning and patching second-hand clothes to be sent to Germany. Fewer people in America wanted to learn German than had wanted to learn English in Persia; but she was pleased when she earned enough to make up parcels to send to Germany, especially the Russian zone (which was, she was convinced, as bad now as it had been under the Nazis), and to us in Oxford. She was as trenchant and forthright as ever:

'I have no wish to talk about politics. I hate them. They bore me. And I don't believe a word of all that drivel.'

These were hard times for my mother: divorce, poverty, difficulties with us teenage children, isolation, and her failure to find satisfactory work. I wonder how much pleasure Oma's long, frequent letters can have given her. Again and again Oma asks her **why** she has no friends, **why** she feels unhappy, **why** her children are not purposefully pursuing careers; and she holds herself, and the Leppmanns, up as shining examples. **She** had felt nothing but relief after **her** divorce, the pleasure of getting rid of 'Hugchen' still glows within her; **she** has made plenty of friends; the Leppmann girls are doing so well in their studies, and have such nice boyfriends ... all this must have been painful reading for my poor mother.

In fact, much of it was a façade, perhaps a clumsy and ill-advised attempt to cheer Mu up. As time passed, Oma's world emptied. Dudu got married and left. She had more or less finished her memoirs, and used her third black exercise book more as a diary, to pour out her heart. What she wrote in her diary was by no means always happy:

29 September 1950: 'Today there is a football match which means the street is full of parked cars – boys yell and shout to drivers to use their parking spaces for dollars. Every third word here is "dollars". There is so much here that I don't like, so much seems more vulgar here than anywhere else in the world. The newspapers are full of pictures of wide open grinning mouths with dazzling teeth, you can look right down into their gullets. There's no such thing as a closed mouth, everyone, men and women, laugh with bared teeth. And all the naked women. And the bras. And all the girls look the same. And the frightful children with their uncontrolled screaming. And radios blaring all over the place, dispensing either football with a passionate commentary, or else the most sentimental, banal music.'

This was the era of McCarthy and his 'Un-American Activities' witch-hunt against the supposed 'reds'; she asked Lorchen not to send her any Leftist newspapers or to express any radical views in her letters, and believed her lack of success in England might be due to her foolishly airing her socialist opinions.

'And Palestine', she wrote, *'that so many, and I, too, dreamed of as the paradise of freedom, is my dream no longer. Medieval conditions are in force there now, a theocracy, antediluvian laws, hostile to anything that is not strictly orthodox – frightful. We here are still the luckiest, freest.'*

Nonetheless, she was increasingly despondent.

'Today is 1 April 1951,' she wrote in her diary, *'and a Sunday – which is, as usual, a depressing day for me. I am utterly alone. Not a soul has bothered about me today, asked after me, thought of me. All of them have their full lives, go off on trips into the lovely spring world, in twos, or in groups. But I am old and alone; my life has been loved; there is no more to be hoped for, expected, striven for ...'*

Hugo died on 11 July 1951. Oma was not moved by the news. His third wife had made sure that he was completely cut off from all his relatives, including his second wife, and his and Oma's son, Reinhardt. Oma had the satisfaction of receiving a few friendly letters from Reinhardt after so many years of bitterness and silence, and at last the family learned what had befallen him. His hand had been injured in an accident with a horse, which meant he was not called up; moreover his farm at Mellensee was a valuable food production unit, and he was able to stay on it all through the war. He left his common-law wife and their son and got married to Annemarie. They had two children.

Reinhardt, Annemarie and children

When the Russians came, they had hidden by the lake, and left the house wide open. It was soon occupied by Russian soldiers. When their supplies ran out, Annemarie went back to the house and pretended to be an idiot, dribbling and mumbling, to collect whatever they needed: the Russians were true to their tradition of kindness to those 'whose wits are with God'. But as time went on, they saw through her pretence: 'You're not an idiot – you're the housewife!' and laughed at her cleverness. So for a time they all lived together – these Russians happened to be Jewish – until they were called to take part in the attack on Berlin and were replaced by a very different group from Siberia, who amused themselves by shooting the dogs and other animals in the legs, until they too were drawn into the battle for Berlin. Wave after wave of Russians came, some of whom burned and smashed whatever they could lay their hands on in revenge for what the Germans had done in their country. After the war Reinhardt rebuilt and restocked his beloved farm, but under the communists of East Germany he counted as a kulak, a big landowner, and they did their best to make his life difficult: they drew a chalk line across his yard and expected him to show his passport every time he crossed it; if he failed, perhaps because he was in a hurry and had forgotten it, they arrested him and put him in prison in Zossen, or got him to sweep the streets for a few days. This happened again and again. One night the village mayor came to him secretly to warn him that his name was at the top of a list of people to be sent to Siberia. Without hesitating, he got on his bike and cycled to Berlin. He was not unprepared – he had made Annemarie the sole proprietor of Mellensee, hoping to return to it one day. But now he spent some time in a refugee camp in West

Germany, until he found work on an aristocratic estate near Hamburg, in Schleswig-Holstein, where Annemarie and the boys eventually joined him.

Oma justified his behaviour – denying that she was his mother, and failing to communicate for years – quite vehemently: his farm meant more to him than anything else. His first child, Jörg, lived with his mother, Reinhardt's first, common-law wife, and was later adopted by her husband. But the fact that through Reinhardt she had three grandchildren never really seemed to register with Oma, though she must have known. She only ever refers to her five grandchildren, four girls and one boy.

The year 1951 was a 'marriage epidemic'; Hetta, Dudu and Peter all got married. On Marianne's birthday of that year, 12 August, Oma confided to her diary:

> '48 years ago today my dearest wish, ever since I was a child, was fulfilled: I gave birth to a child, my Mariannchen was born, and was from then on the dearest being in the world for me. So long as she was only my daughter, not yet a wife and mother, we were closer than is perhaps usual ... Giving and receiving was evenly balanced. We needed each other for pleasure, for sympathy, for consolation. Inevitably this has ceased to a large extent. She has a loving and beloved husband, she has her two daughters, who love and honour her, she has her work, her life, quite separate from me. She is always good to me, by the work of her hands she provides for me, and came to visit me for two weeks again this year for my birthday. But I am such a demanding, greedy person, so thirsty for love – that her visit did not satisfy me. All the time I felt a faint, piercing pain and I cannot get rid of it. I meant so much to her once – now I am only a task for her, a duty, a worry, or an object of worry, of practical concern. In this she is unsurpassable: I lack nothing ... But she is not interested in me any more, not in my thoughts or in that which still, under my apparently calm exterior, seethes so painfully, so longingly, so hyper-intensely. ... It has been so for a long time.'

In addition to this lifelong hunger in her (its object first Schubert, then Marianne) there was her deeply wounded feeling about Mrs Maas, the woman who was looking after her:

> 'There is something artificial about Mrs M that repels me. Her superabundant expressions of love, to me and to her four children too, and her four children-in-law, and her grandchildren, don't seem sincere, seem forced, seem to spring from principle, from intention, from conscious decisions ... I found her oldest daughter Eva profoundly unlikeable from the first day, and she evidently reciprocated in kind. The second daughter ... has not spoken ten words to me during a week-long visit ... The son and daughter-in-law do not consider it necessary to greet me when they come to visit or take their leave as they pass my door or get into the car ten steps away from me sitting on the porch. None of them ever invite me to join them. It never occurs to

them when, as today, they go for a drive in the glorious surroundings, to ask me to go with them, though they know how I yearn to get away from my permanent position by the road, with the same house opposite, with the narrowly circumscribed view, to get away and to look into the distance. No, they go past me unheeding, and leave me in my desolate loneliness with a casual "goodbye". How can they leave a lonely old woman all alone so pitilessly, again and again? ... Every few moments Sunday strollers pass by me, hand in hand, merry, affectionate. But here I sit alone, sad to death, with only one desire, to die, now, this instant ...'

Achim and Marianne decided that they could not allow her to be so depressed. They decided to leave Chicago and move to California and have her live with them, as in Teheran. Marianne would have to take her medical examinations again, and they would have to find a house which fulfilled three criteria: they could afford it, it had the kind of view that Olga craved, and enough space for the three of them. They finally settled at 449 Spruce Street in 1952, and my mother went over to help with the move. Her affection for her mother was so evident that there are no more snide criticisms in the letters that started to flow between them again after she returned to Oxford, but a true warmth.

Pretty soon the old depression returned. Marianne had her work, her family; she and Achim had joined the Quakers and took part in their good works – and Olga was once again alone for much of the day. Marianne was often tired and irritable when she came home. Olga realised all too clearly that she was no longer needed.

'You're somewhat better off than me,' she wrote to my mother, *'as you are the giving one, you are a place of refuge for your children, the master of your house, in full command of your faculties, and with not inconsiderable powers – indispensable. But I? A mere appendage ...'*

Later, when she learned that Maleen and Bob had asked Mu to come and help look after their baby daughter in Chicago, while Bob was finishing his thesis and Maleen working in a bank, she wrote:

'How reassuring it must be for you to be needed. To be needed, to be useful, to be able to help – what can be more reassuring!'

Even better, in 1952, Mu was invited to America by one of her dearest lifelong friends, Vera Lachmann. Vera, and her sister Nina, had been among the faithful few who sat by her bedside when she was so very ill as a teenager, living in Berlin with her dreaded father. Vera had got to America some months after the War had started. From 1944, for 27 years, she found fulfilment in running an annual summer camp for boys at a place she called Catawba, near Blowing Rock in the mountains of North Carolina. It was unlike most summer camps in which American children spend the long summer holidays: it had elements of the Wandervogel, of the Odenwaldschule, and of Vera's own love of classical Greece, every bit as strong as my father's. The days would begin with physical exercises, continue with an assembly where all plans and problems were aired demo-

Morning assembly at Catawba

cratically, followed by the singing of folksongs; then organised games, swimming and riding when the weather was fine, music, arts and crafts, games of chess and cards; weekly hikes in the mountains; treasure hunts; lots of music, sung, played on recorders and other instruments as well as on the gramophone. Vera told stories from Homer's *Iliad* and *Odyssey* every evening, and a play was rehearsed and performed every summer – Aristophanes, Shakespeare, Molière, Chekhov ... Would Mu come and cook for them?

Of course, Lorchen went. And felt at home immediately. Charles A Miller included the following piece she wrote in his book, *A Catawba Assembly* (1973):

'I am glad that Catawba was one of my first impressions of America. In these sadly disturbed times, when one may despair of the American image, I do not forget that there is also Catawba. That means peace and clean air, mountains and trees. When I first came to Catawba I felt overwhelming gratitude. It was cool. Great trees sheltered me. Sunlight filtered through leaves on green meadows. The tender wind brought messages from glades full of flowers. I heard the rustle of the pine trees. I understood that here one could bury the searing homesickness.

The house smelled of wood. Through the window I saw the Old Man – the pine tree, leaning in a precarious angle across the path. I hear the Old Man is still there; I think he will forgive me for doubting that he could live on, being so battered.

The Flat-top was my daily goal. I still remember certain twists of the path, wide views of the countryside, and especially the stillness, except for the voices of the forest. I remember a night lying on a rock, watching the moon rise and filling the valley with silver light. Or another path which leads you through thickets onto an open glade. Green velvety grass, untrodden by human feet, the forest all around. Only one sad dissonance: dead chestnut trees stretching their naked arms to heaven, like a premonition of things to

come. It was frightening. Vietnam was still far off.
May Catawba live serenely as before, a refuge for us wanderers between two worlds.'

Years later, she reminisced about Catawba:
'The organisation was very loose and impractical. Every morning I had to make toast: this meant shutting the oven door and slowly reciting Goethe's verse:

Gottes ist der Orient	*(The Orient is God's)*
Gottes ist der Okzident	*(The Occident is God's)*
Nord und Süden aller Enden	*(North and South of all lands)*
Ruht im Frieden seiner Hände.	*(Rests in the peace of His hands.)*

Then I had to open the oven door, turn the toast over, shut the door and recite the verse again. This was how about 100 slices of toast were perfectly browned every morning. Then there was fruit juice, milk, porridge and so on. Vera would tell the boys stories from Homer, from the Bible, Icelandic sagas and many more. There were long hikes, which those miserable little city kids soon learned to cope with. It was a glorious time for everybody. Only the money was an everlasting problem. Many children could not pay – well, they were the ones who needed Catawba most. Charities were supposed to pay for some, but did not. That was the chief reason why Vera was so anxious to get more work at Brooklyn College. She could and did give any number of unpaid private lessons – but then how was the grocer in Blowing Rock going to get paid?'

However, those solitary moonlight walks, communing with Nature, culminated in a terrible fall, when she lay helpless, her back broken, for some 24 hours. Search parties went out looking for her, even a helicopter. Finally she was found, carried back to civilisation on a stretcher, covered in plaster in a hospital and returned to England by ship. Many years later, she wrote:
'As I lay on the mountain in North Carolina, my back broken, the moon was so bright, I was looking straight into heaven, and was at home.'

This was in 1952, when I was a struggling actress, with time on my hands between jobs, so I went to Southampton to meet her. I was deeply shocked to see her looking so frail, pale and grey as she struggled down the gang-plank, bulky in a plaster cast. She was visibly in pain.

Later, she visited America several times, visiting her mother and sister in Berkeley, Maleen and Bob in Chicago and later in Cranbrook – and Vera at her home in New York. She was highly entertained to see how her old friend – poet, scholar, educator, philanthropist – was living:

'Not very practical, my dearly beloved Vera. She lived in a terrible slum. The flat only had two windows, but four rooms, that lay one behind the other, so that two rooms had no windows at all. This was the palace where Vera lived, with her recorder-playing friend Tui and an old friend from Germany who had heart disease and soon died. Plus six Persian cats, a turtle, and one day a young man appeared with twenty oriental birds. A big aviary was built for these birds in one of the middle rooms. There were cat walks everywhere for the cats; when you sat drinking tea the cats were overhead. The turtle lived in the bath. The young man stayed, because he had a psychological aversion to work. One day he arrived with a raccoon, and that animal went into all the cupboards and chewed up the clothes. That did drive Vera to put it to him, after several months, that he might move on, and then he gave his really wonderfully beautiful birds to a dealer, put his raccoon into a shoe box and set off for California. One winter's day she came upon a young woman with two small children at a bus stop wearing summer clothes. They got talking: she had just come from Brazil and had quite forgotten that New York freezes and now they had nowhere to stay, her husband was hoping to find work. So naturally, they all moved into Vera's flat where another baby was born soon after. The man did find work and came to visit his family. Under his jacket he was holding a small monkey, which he had brought from Brazil, being the most useful thing he could think of, so now it too lived with Vera. There was no room for her; she sat behind a door to prepare her classes.

Vera herself was clothed in rags; there was a loose sole on one of her shoes so it went flip-flap as she walked.'

*****

In 1954, Hedchen was appealing for help again. Hedchen's relationship with her daughter-in-law Tilly was always bad; now it became hellish; she felt she was 'surrounded by hatred'. Oma responded with great warmth for her older and chronically unhappy sister. She must come to Berkeley too. Not to the little house in Spruce Street – there was not enough room – but to Frau Maas in Forest Avenue. Olga knew that Hedchen would not be happy there either – 'that isn't given to her' – still, she would no longer feel she was 'surrounded by hatred'.

So she came. It was some distance away – getting together depended on Achim being able to drive Oma to Hedchen, or Hedchen to Oma – but soon they were in a routine which meant they were together some sixteen hours each week. However, no matter what happened, Hedchen was miserable. In August she fell down the cellar steps at Spruce Street. No bones were broken, but from then on she was bedridden, completely helpless, and increasingly confused, forgetful and repetitive. She died in 1954, as did

Lutka (Ludowika), the oldest sister, who had been living frugally but contentedly in Italy.

Oma could hardly maintain her façade of optimism now.

Lutka

'I've got terribly old and weak in the course of the last year – seeing, hearing, walking, lifting – nothing functions any more; I can hardly read, even with a magnifying glass; and although I am so well off here, God knows, so that I could not wish for anything better – still, like my sisters, who are after all two and four years older, I have a great longing for the final sleep, only out of tiredness, not unhappiness, absolutely not.'

Marianne and Achim were out at work from seven in the morning till six in the evening. Marianne would cook dinner, Oma would wash up, then the three of them would sit each in a different corner of the sitting room, listening to music on the radio. At ten precisely she would go to bed. If they had any free time, Marianne and Achim would spend it gardening, or visiting, or walking – without her. When Hetta's young husband died, she felt it was a cruel irony that death should come to him, who still had everything to live for, instead of her, and her sisters, who did not.

But a gleam of light appeared on the horizon. Her oldest, dearest friend, Pieter, and his wife returned to Berkeley after a prolonged absence in Israel and New York and Chicago. He sensed her need for company and visited her every day. One Sunday at the beginning of September in that same year, 1954, they sat together in the garden, talking about old times. She thanked him for his visit when he left and went to lie down. She fell asleep.

She did not wake up again.

*****

Those last years were arguably the most – or the only – unsatisfactory period of her long life. Her oft-repeated assertions that she liked being alone rang increasingly hollow. During her sleepless nights she would work out alphabetical lists of her male and female friends – so many! – or of all the places in the world where she had been – places where she had been happy; she would recall the men who might have married her, or she tried to remember Persian words, or recited poetry to herself, or ran through the words and music of her favourite songs. In her memoirs, she delved deeper and deeper in the past. Sometimes she mused, 'Did I do anything wrong in my life?' On the whole, she thought not. She may have wronged her husband Hugo; but the very fact that she admitted it, candidly, in writing, to be seen by her children and grandchildren, somehow exonerated her. It never crossed her mind that she might have wronged her second daughter by so blatantly favouring the first. Her supreme quality was always her self-confidence. Her motto was – 'If anyone can do it, then so can I.'

But she returned again and again to the Schubert conundrum. Decades after his death she was still puzzling over the fact that he loved her – as his poems showed – but could not declare it, or take the logical step of asking her to marry him. Despite all her attempts at rationalisation, she was still, I believe, in love with him. She told my mother once, in California: Hinter jedem Sonnenuntergang ist Schubert – 'Schubert is behind every sunset.' This was the great irrational element in her life, in contradiction to her otherwise warm, rational self. She expressed it in a poem

Before, O world, I leave you
Let me see your distant views once more
And once more feel your deepest quietness
And just once more be held in arms of love.
How rich my life was once!
To be one other soul's wish and fulfilment
To be one other person's happiness
And understood without a need for words.
Now you are cold and void
O life, that once so warmly glowed in me!
I am so old, so lonely, and I'm cold
Come death, my friend, take me in your arms.

But thoughts of death were not always so bleak. Not long before she died, she wrote:

'Recently I caught myself – while darning socks, incidentally – feeling a heroic urge for self-sacrifice in myself. I imagined, very vividly, being one of a group shipwrecked on a rocky island, in danger of starving to death: so I proposed that the others should kill me, as painlessly as possible, please, and roast me. The meat might of course, in view of my age, be somewhat tough. But on the other hand all the fat on me was highly calorific and might enable them to survive until they were rescued. All this I thought out most earnestly; it was only later that I laughed. Another time I imagined I was travelling in an aeroplane which was overloaded and in urgent need of being lightened. I, quite naturally, being the oldest and so the least useful of the passengers, offered to jump out, but without a parachute, please. An instantaneous death would be much better. And so on and so on – until I started laughing at myself.'

Chapter 22

On 15 January 1952, I returned to Britain. I was leaving Willy, I was leaving Nini, I was leaving Bebbi and his crowd, I was leaving Margrit and her family; but above all, I was leaving many illusions. I had seen the impurity of Bebbi, I had seen the sloth and corruption behind Willy's glamorous façade – which did not stop me aching for him for years to come; I had seen Nini's greedy egotism. I now said goodbye to the German language and the German theatre and all the high hopes of two years ago. And I had no faith in myself.

Nevertheless, I was determined to get onto the stage, any stage, and was pleased to discover that someone was trying to start a 'Fit-Up Rep' Me company, to tour the villages of Oxfordshire. Soon I was rehearsing *Gaslight*, a Victorian-style melodrama in which I played the part of a wife being driven mad by her evil husband, who terrifies her by interfering with the gas lamps, which grow dimmer and brighter. The husband was played by Jimmy, a cheerful Irish bus driver with very definite ideas of how a play should look. So when we got to the village halls where we were to perform, it was with a complete set of props and Victorian furniture, which had to be squeezed onto the tiny platforms. Real door and window frames were attached to the curtains at the back of the stage for greater verisimilitude. In the end the stage was so crowded we could hardly move, and when Jimmy swung round dramatically his cloak would send little tables flying into the audience; which rarely consisted of more than half a dozen little old ladies. That fit-up rep soon folded.

I then set off for London, the heart of Britain's theatrical world. From now on I was going to be self-sufficient – after all, I was nineteen. First I found myself a room near Paddington, at £3.10s; next, at the Labour Exchange, a job: cutting sandwiches for the restaurant in Dickens & Jones in Regent Street, for £4 a week. This was possibly the most intensely boring job I ever had to endure: most of the day there was nothing to do; then an order might come for a smoked salmon sandwich, or two rounds of cheese and pickle. The white bread was very thin, and I had to cut the crusts off and present the sandwich as tiny squares or triangles. With my first pay packet I paid my rent and bought a copy of *The Stage*, a jar of peanut butter and a jar of strawberry jam and ate them together with a spoon – thereby proving how grown-up I was. Then I went to a Justice of the Peace and asked her to

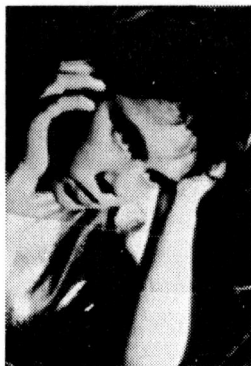

change my name from Zuntz to Henry – the name Peter had been given in the army. The JP was busy baking at the time and invited me into her kitchen to swear the necessary oaths and fill in the necessary form. That done I had to give her five shillings and was henceforth known as Irene, or Rene Henry, and no one need know that I was not a true blue British person.

The job at Dickens & Jones did not last long. To save time, I would prepare a stack of sandwiches, pile them on top of each other and then saw off the crusts. But this entailed pressing rather heavily, and the bottom sandwich, which an indignant customer returned, was decidedly squashed. So I lost that job; however, one of the advertisements in *The Stage* that I had answered came up trumps: I was now a 'Student ASM' – Assistant Stage Manager – at a repertory theatre in Ashford, Kent.

This theatre had opened immediately after the war, as did many theatres during that spell of euphoria when people felt that now that the nightmare of war was over – though rationing and shortages actually continued for years – they could put 'austerity' behind them, and give free rein to their longing for luxury, entertainment, culture. Richard Dale had put his demob gratuity into this venture to bring drama to the little town of Ashford; his sister Marie played most of the leads. Richard and Marie lived with their parents some way away and arrived at the theatre by car, so they must have been quite a prosperous family. However, the theatre did not prosper; nor did many of the other newly opened theatres all over the country, as the postwar wave of desire for a civilised lifestyle broke on the rocks of public apathy, financial problems, and the cinema – which was so much more economical than live theatre (in the fullness of time, because of television, those cinemas had to make way for bingo). Six months before I arrived, the Ashford Theatre had lost three actors, and apart from the Dales themselves there were then only two. Now Richard was recruiting up to four more 'students' like myself, in a desperate and slightly illicit attempt to keep his theatre going.

I now learned just what 'repertory theatre' meant. My pay was pitiful – once again Mu was sending me food parcels and what money she could spare – and the digs, which I shared with one of the leading actresses, Barbara Keogh – freezing cold and sparsely furnished. Only three blankets were on the bed, so I piled coats and jackets on top, and hugged a hot water bottle; but still I froze. Week by week, one play was being performed in the evenings while another was being rehearsed during the day in preparation for the following week. My job was to paint huge posters for each new production, and to assemble all the props required, and to ensure that they were in the right place on the stage at the right time. I was also the prompter, both during rehearsals and during performances, was responsible for 'noises off', and for the lighting, and also had small parts in some of the plays. This meant I had to buy a set of theatrical make-up – greasepaint – and also suitable clothes for my part – usually the sexy maid. I had absolutely no free time, and discovered that I was at heart a lazy person, longing for time to mooch around idly day-dreaming about Willy, and doing nothing in particular. There was no hope of that now. If I was not trying to make paper flowers, or a cake of plaster of paris with a wedge-shaped opening into which a wedge of bread was inserted so that one of the actors could be seen to be actually eating it, I was running round the shops of Ashford to borrow items of furniture and the like; the shop-keepers were promised a free advertisement in our programmes. Sundays and Mondays were the hardest: the old set had to be struck, the new one set up, with all its props, then came the dress rehearsal for the new play, followed by the opening night. Prompting was hard work, requiring great concentration.

I was deeply shocked at the cynicism of the actors. Of course, they did not have the time to do anything except the essentials – and as far as learning their lines was concerned, they seldom managed even that. Certainly no one cared about the art of theatre as I saw it, its lofty role in clarifying our understanding of the great life issues, stripped of the dross of irrelevant coincidences, and so on. This was hardly surprising, since the audience, sparse as it generally was, sat there like suet puddings, only reacting with giggles if there was something sexy. So the actors seemed to regard their work as a rather revolting job without any glamour or even a point: 'the sooner it's over the better' was their attitude. I started feeling the same myself, felt no stage fright before I went on stage, and was haunted by the unspoken question: What am I here for?

One of the plays, *A Mother's Love*, was a psychological piece about the dire effects of too much maternal instinct; most of them were farces; but we also put on the world premiere of *Western Wind* by Charlotte Frank. I wrote to Peter and Brenda about it:

'An 'orrible play, all talk, no action … Nobody knew their parts, one of them kept going round in circles ignoring what anybody else said so that it didn't make sense at all and I couldn't think where I'd better prompt them to. Prompting, they never tire of telling me, is an art … People had to change from pyjamas into full evening dress on stage while someone else was turning down the bed; then a man was waiting for a girl who was getting into a silk nightie. Not knowing what to do while he waited he started bouncing on the bed … I had to laugh.'

A few weeks later, Richard gave us the sad news that the theatre was bankrupt and would have to close. So soon I was back in a bedsitter; this one was in Whitfield Street, behind the Tottenham Court Road. It was one of two at the top of the house; the other one was occupied by an old Polish cook, whom I almost killed. We had gas fires and gas rings, but there was only one meter, into which we had to put our shillings from time to time, and it was in my room. One evening I got home very late and put a shilling into the meter to warm myself up. After a time, I noticed a smell of gas – it was coming from the old Pole's room. I realised that he must have gone to sleep with his fire on; the gas had run out; my shilling had started the gas pouring into his room. I pounded on his door and when at last he opened it, I tried to explain what had happened: but he spoke no English. Still, he grasped enough to turn off his unlit fire – and then we had a good laugh together.

I was once again buying *The Stage*, hoping to get another stage job, and meanwhile looking for any job to make ends meet.

The first job I landed was a rather peculiar one: someone who prepared shop window decorations wanted nails with little metal daisies on them on pieces of wood to be bent by being hit with a hammer. I tried, but failed dismally – the daisies got flattened – so that job only lasted one day. So did my foray into waitressing in a café in the Euston Road. Next I worked for a German couple called Bund who had an establishment near Oxford Circus which supplied hat manufacturers with hat pins of many different designs. My job was to take packets of hat pins to milliners all over London. This involved long and complicated bus journeys, during which I tended to day-dream; on at least one occasion, I had to run desperately after a bus I had just got off, having left the hat pins on board. But that was not the reason why I was dismissed. I was dismissed for lying.

One Monday morning in June I tottered in, and said I felt ill, though in fact I felt fine; and that if I did not feel better soon I would have to go home. The supervisor wanted me to speak to the boss, but I said that would not be necessary. At lunch time, I said that I was still feeling ill; but in fact I was meeting a young South African I had got to know, called Hendrick, and we had lunch together. The next day I went to a hairdresser, and thence to Cambridge, where Peter and Brenda were living. Through them, I had an invitation to a May Ball with an undergraduate called Derek. We danced, drank lots of champagne, and enjoyed some good food. Conversation was limited, but it was all very lovely – the lights in the trees and by the river, the beautiful dresses, the music – this went on until about six the following morning.

The next morning I went to work again. The boss, Frau Bund, a fierce woman whose lower teeth protruded in front of her upper teeth, asked me: 'Vot are you doink here?' 'I've come to work,' I replied, 'I feel better now.' 'Vel, you can go. You say you cannot speak to me. So I vil not speak to you. I sought you are a nice, educated girl. Go now, go.' Her husband, standing behind her, shrugged his shoulders and spread his hand apologetically. I felt a terrible rage mount up inside me, turned and walked out. They still owe me £3 something.

I visited theatrical agents. One was a woman with long grey hair who thought she might get me a part in a film as a 'rather plain girl – you don't mind me saying that, do you darling?' She would ring me if ... but she never did. Another was a short fat man called Hal Moss. He and his friend Harry Lowe had an office on Cambridge Circus; in this shadowy office, behind a screen, there was a sofa. I did a scene from Shaw's St Joan for them, as Nini had trained me to do, and both of them seemed impressed: but Hal went into a long spiel about how difficult things were just then, with theatres closing all over the place and so on. However, he promised to 'go to town' for me – and Harry Lowe told me he would do his best for me once the summer season was over; so I called in at the office from time to time. Barbara Keogh in Ashford had told me that one had to accept that one could only get on in the theatre 'via the bed'. I had only the vaguest idea what this meant, but I was not very surprised when Hal once invited me to lie down on his sofa. By and by he came and lay on top of me – we were both fully clothed – and he started shifting around on top of me. Then he rose and, shoving a handkerchief down his trousers, hurried out to the toilet. This was when I first discovered that sex involved some sort of moisture. A short time later, Harry Lowe told me that Hal's wife had reappeared and they would not be seeing me any more. Whether the theatrical agency was real or not, I never found out.

Meanwhile, another advertisement in *The Stage* led to my becoming a Mayfair Mermaid. Once a week, a dozen girls gathered in a public swimming bath in a fairly distant suburb and were taught the techniques of spinning and surface diving, forming circles and lines and loops, and swimming in time to waltzes and tangos, by an older, rather vague, easy-going woman called Thelma. Early in June the nine girls selected set out by train for Scarborough. The youngest, inevitably called Titch, still had to go to school for a few weeks. I, being nineteen, was the second oldest – the oldest was called Sally.

It was a cold, wet summer, but almost every day we had to go for a practice in the South Bay Bathing Pool, which was an enclosed section of the chilly waters of the North Sea with a tower of diving boards at one end, the top one ten metres high. Twice a week we performed. We dived into the water one after the other and swam in line while the loud speakers blared out *The Blue Danube* and we moved our arms backward and forward more or less in time to it. Then *Jealousy*, a tango, came on; we swam on our backs to form a ragged circle and, at a signal from Sally, performed a 'water wheel', disappearing backward under the water and surfacing, puffing and snuffling, in more or less the same positions; whereupon we would hug our knees and swivel round and round: this was called 'the teacup'. We were not actually very good at any of this; in fact, the director of entertainment, a friendly, avuncular man who pitied us in that cold weather – 'I've got me long johns on today, I have' – told us quite cheerfully that we were the worst water ballet they had ever had.

But Tom Perry made up for it. He, Thelma and a young man called Stan did amazing stunts off the diving boards. The climax, heralded by a long drum roll, came when Thelma poured petrol over her beloved on the ten metre board and set him alight, when he would dive. Pictures of Tom, flying down in sheets of flame, featured on posters and leaflets, and on the sides of the old van in which the three of them lived. It required perfect timing. If he dived too soon, the petrol might not ignite; if he left it a split second too late – well, dreadful scars on his back testified to the very real danger gentle Thelma put her man in at the end of each show. Her vague, patient tolerance must have stemmed from that awful fear. Nothing else seemed very important by comparison.

The midnight show – 'Night Follies' – were the best for us, as these were in the North Bay Pool, which was heated; moreover, it had underwater illumination. We would wait in the changing rooms, tugging at our frilly costumes, until *One Enchanted Evening* surged from the tannoy and we trotted out of the changing rooms to plunge into liquid light. As the music switched to *The Glass Mountain* we felt fatefully beautiful, slinking through the luminous waves slender as fishes, wild perdition following in our wake. We seldom grinned or winked at each other during the midnight show.

We Mermaids were all to stay together at the Lyddon Hotel, which I soon found quite intolerable. The owners were stingy, because we paid slightly less than their normal guests. The girls – apart from one, red-headed Vicky – were childish and silly, and I was hardly ever alone. Sally treated us all as if she was in charge of us; at one point I heard her giving the younger ones detailed sex education. I felt almost as alienated as I had at the High School after the Ecole, and went out as much as possible, finding solitary park benches on which to indulge in my memories of Willy and my sentimental grief over him; and I went to the dances in the Spa Gardens – which meant I came home late, and was roundly scolded by the landlady, rather like the concierge in Paris, with aspersions cast on my morals. So I decided to move out, and asked Thelma if I could have the money deducted from our wages for rent. She agreed readily, and so I found myself living with Mrs Howard in North Street.

Mrs Howard was so fat that when she was seated only the tips of her knees emerged from beneath her belly. She had the face of a Pekinese, frizzy grey hair, and glasses. She was 61, and her daughter, Ada, was a pale little neurotic of thirteen. When Ada went into one of her weeping fits, or got the fidgets, Mrs Howard would roll her eyes at the large photograph of a fireman in full uniform on the wall and comment sagely, 'She's frettin' for her father.' In fact, she had never known her father, he had died when she was born, of a heart attack, or perhaps shock. After all, they had both been approaching 50 when they got married and never expected to have any children. All this I learned within the first two days of staying in her house: she never stopped talking, her little dog perched quivering on the small amount of lap available.

'I done all the cooking and baking for the wedding mysel, 'undred an' fifty fairy cakes I made, two 'undred sausage rolls, and a three-tier cake, with all the trimmings, big enough for nigh on sixty guests. Well, we 'ad a lot of friends, both on us.'

But some time later, she became aware of unfamiliar sensations inside, and went to the doctor, who diagnosed appendicitis and operated on her, without noticing the foetus in another part of that vast belly. Ada was born six weeks later, to everyone's boundless astonishment, and the father, Mrs Howard's 'Loved One', dropped dead.

Like Margrit in that other North Street, in fact like most of my landladies, she was extremely good to me. She would wait up for me after the midnight show with cocoa and cakes. I occupied the back bedroom in her tiny 'two up, two down' terraced cottage at 68 North Street; she and Ada slept in the double bed in the front. I wrote reassuring letters to my mother, who was in America, and sad poems about lost love. I even wrote to Willy once, and received a reply – dreamy, poetic, as if we could still be soul-mates, despite having parted in great bitterness and forever.

The Mermaid shows left me with plenty of free time, and as the weather improved and the holiday makers started pouring in, I earned more money: in the mornings I cleared the tables in a café, and in the evenings sold tickets at the entrance to the Open Air Theatre, where they were performing a musical called *Merrie England*. I saw a good deal of one of the young men I had danced with at the Spa Gardens, Pete. He was a trainee manager in Woolworths, and became very affectionate, wondering shyly if I might marry him. I liked him very much, but put him off with my ambition to be an actress in London. Another admirer was called John, a very different type: big and burly, son of a coal mine owner (the pit had of course been nationalised, but the father remained in charge and John would be taking over later); he too wondered about a future with me when he came back from a nine-month study tour in America. However, apart from a couple of letters, I never heard from him again.

There were often a number of young men hanging round the exit when we emerged from the 'Night Follies', some of whom would shout beerily, while others just stared, probably wondering whether these rubbery-looking girls, their wet hair plastered down, could possibly be the nymphs they had been gawping at. One evening there were a number of National Servicemen there; one of them shouted: 'Hi, good-lookin', what's cookin'?' in a fake American accent. Little Titch knew the answer:

'Chicken!' she piped.

'Don't be silly!' scolded Sally; but promptly, from several of the soldiers came the cry:

'Chicken! Wanna neck?'

'Not with you,' giggled some of the Mermaids. But now several of the men were following us.

'Hurry!' whispered Sally. 'We don't want them to know where we're staying.'

We broke into a run. I was relieved when I came to my turning and slowed down; but after a few steps, I realised I was being followed. Glancing round, I saw two of the men in uniform hurrying to catch up with me.

'Hang on!' one of them shouted, 'We wanna talk to you.'

They were obviously drunk. I started walking as fast as I could. Then one of them lurched across the street and started running: he was trying to get ahead and cut me off. I darted into the first turning I came to, a narrow alley, and heard them cursing: now they were angry.

And I was lost; I had lost my bearings. I started running through the little streets, terrified. One of them crashed into a dustbin and fell, shouting. Lights were coming on in windows. If only someone would call the police! But who would have a telephone in these poor little houses? The soldiers' boots pounded ever closer behind me. At last I caught sight of a pillar box – yes, it was the one near number 68. In seconds I was banging on the door. Mrs Howard opened it, glanced along the street, grasped the situation, shut and bolted the door, and took me in her arms. Or she would have done if her arms had extended further past her bosom. As it was, she held me by the shoulders.

'There now, don't you fret no more. I've got you. Come and sit down and drink your cocoa. You must never go to bed on an empty stomach. Ma Loved One always said that.'

There was a whimpering sound from upstairs.

'They've gone an' set off our Ada an' all,' she observed grimly. She heaved herself slowly up the stairs. 'Don't you fret, our Ada, it's only a couple of drunks. They'll soon give over.'

Ada was standing by the window, shivering in her night dress, sobbing and staring at the two men, who were still shouting and throwing rubbish in the direction of the house.

'An' get away from that window, lass!' Mrs Howard exclaimed, pulling the child back to the bed. The men tired of their shouting at last and left, and we went to bed. While my heart beat slowly returned to normal, I listened to Ada's whimpers next door subside under her mother's growled remonstrances, and my mind returned to its familiar contemplation of the face with the slow smile and the liquid eyes under the thick black hair.

Margrit had tried to teach me Swiss German; now Mrs Howard taught me Yorkshire:

> 'Hear all, see all, say nowt; Eat all, drink all, pay nowt; And if tha dost owt fer nowt, do it fer thysen.'

'An' you'd do well to remember that, 'n all, lass: allus look after number one, as Ma Loved One used to say. I don't know what's eatin' you, but you'd do well to put – it's an 'im, is it? – put 'im out of yer mind.'

'It isn't easy.'

'Oh ah know, ah know, don't ah know it! With our Ada takin' on so, ah'm that worried, ah've lost two stone! Two stone! Ah weighed meself in Boots t'other day – ah'm down to fourteen stone! It's worry what makes you so thin.'

*****

Back in London, I learned that the Cabaret Club was looking for 'Dance Hostesses'. Cabaret! To me, that meant brilliant political satire from stand-up comics and avant-garde music and daring innovative turns by men and women in Germany during the Weimar Republic. I applied immediately, and was duly called for an interview with the owner, a Mr Murray.

It was a night club near Piccadilly, and like all such establishments it looked dusty, tawdry, and threadbare in daylight. A dance floor, surrounded by a ring of small tables with chairs, alcoves with plush covered benches, a piano, and Mr Murray's tiny office, with a desk and a sofa. Mr Murray was a large man who half listened to me as I explained my ambitions, my love of dancing, what I had learned with Nini, my admiration for cabaret, and so on.

'Yes, you'll do; sometimes we have customers who want to talk,' he commented.

I took in that 'sometimes'. What did they usually want?

'I've heard,' I said, blushing, 'that sometimes women who work in this sort of place are, er –'

'Well, you may sometimes get a customer offering to take you home. My advice to you is: Never accept such offers. Get yourself a taxi. OK?'

'OK, Mr Murray!'

Now I had to come in during the mornings to learn the dance routines. The woman who taught us these was a large blonde, who seemed to be intimate with Mr Murray. Soon I was being fitted out with costumes – skimpy green shorts for *Old Macdonald had a Farm*, in which we had to prance around in various ways to indicate farm animals; frilly skirts for the can-can; and flesh coloured body-stockings which gave the illusion of nudity while actually covering us from neck to ankles. After a week, I was considered ready to start work.

This meant wearing evening dress and sitting at one of the little tables with two or three other girls, chatting, until such time as a customer (they were invariably men) sent a waiter over to summon one or more of us to join them at their table. We were then expected to talk with them, dance with them, and accept food and drink, and get them to buy things for us – huge teddy bears, boxes of Black Sobranie cigarettes, bouquets of red roses, boxes of chocolates – which scantily clad girls with trays hanging from their necks brought round from time to time. Most of these over-priced gifts were handed in at the end of the evening to be sold again next day. When the pianist started playing *These Foolish Things* we had to excuse ourselves and go back stage to change for the floor show, which happened twice every evening. It would start with all of us dancing round together; then a contortionist would tie herself into knots, followed by another group dance, then there were some acrobatics, and so on. Afterwards, back in our evening dresses, we rejoined our customers, or, if they had left, sat chatting with the other girls again. So I got to know them quite well. It was quite obvious that they were prostitutes of one kind or another; yet each had her own lover – perhaps a pimp – and despite being promiscuous for money, considered herself faithful to him. I learned a great deal about sex from them. One girl, Yvonne, tried to put into words the sensation of 'coming': 'It's like as if something was being pulled together inside you. I only gets it with my Joe, not with nobody else. 'E's a Jew-boy. 'E's lovely. 'E sells things on Petticoat Lane. 'E says we'll get married once we got enough money.' Another was called Iris; she was very pretty and a brilliant dancer, but dreadfully over-sexed. She saw sex in everything: any round or cylindrical shapes, even in bread rolls, made her think of copulation. One evening she described how she and her boy friend had been trying to redecorate their flat, but had made very little progress, as they had to keep stopping to make love again. These women looked askance at two or three who were 'high-class' prostitutes. This seemed to mean they were willing to go with perverts, who paid far more money than ordinary fellows. My friends pointed out these sleek and very expensively dressed hostesses, and when the opportunity arose I sat with them and got them to talk about perverts. One, it seemed, wanted to tickle a naked woman climbing up a ladder with a feather duster, and was prepared to pay huge sums of money for the privilege. Another wanted her to sit in a cold bath with chunks of ice till she was blue with cold. We laughed heartily at these stories, but then they refused to talk any more; no doubt there were less ridiculous perversions.

I made friends with a large brunette from Oldham called Maggie, who was in love with a man called Derek. He was writing a novel, and she was supporting him: 'If a person wants to write a book or do something like that, they should be given the chance, don't you think?' Maggie and I shared a room for a time, and sometimes took home a box of Black Sobranies

Irene Gill

instead of handing them back, with the result that we discovered just how awful nicotine poisoning is.

After a few weeks, Mr Murray summoned me to his office. He had noticed that I was still wearing the same evening dress – a pink one, from Oxfam; why didn't I get myself a new one? I was astonished.

'I can't afford one – you know I'm only getting £4 a week.'

'Why – haven't you been home with one of the customers yet?'

'Mr Murray! I promised you I wouldn't do anything like that!'

'Well, it's very bad for you not to if you want to,' he said.

Deeply dismayed, I struggled back to the digs through the very last of London's celebrated pea-soup fogs. It was thick and yellow, and so dense that you groped your way along walls, and still crashed into lamp-posts and pillar boxes before you saw them. Even indoors, you could hardly see across the room, and if you ran your hand across your forehead, your fingers were smeared with a black oily substance. It lasted for days, and life in London virtually stopped until at last it lifted again.

I discovered a wart on the back of my hand, and called in at the University College Hospital Outpatients Department to ask if it could be removed. Soon I found myself in a curtained cubicle, my hand anaesthetised, and a nervous Senegalese student doctor asked the nurse to fetch him 'the cut-throat razor'. With this alarming instrument in his trembling hand – I felt I was probably his first patient – he cut out the wart, stitched the wound together with seven stitches, and bandaged my hand. The bus on which I went home jolted; I grabbed a bar – and the stitches opened; blood poured out. Deeply embarrassed, I got off the bus and walked back to Gower Street, and another doctor trimmed the cut and stitched it up again with ten stitches. Later in the evening, at the Cabaret Club, a client shook hands with me – and the wound reopened, and blood poured out, and I was deeply, deeply embarrassed. Early next morning I was back at the hospital; this time the senior doctor in charge saw me and decided a skin graft was the only answer. He sliced a small amount of skin off the back of my arm and stuck it into the wound. My hand and forearm were now enclosed in plaster of paris, to immobilise them, and I found I was helpless: with only one hand I could not even open a tube of toothpaste.

So I went and stayed with Peter and Brenda in Croydon – Peter had left Cambridge and was now working at the Joint Services School of Linguists, teaching Russian to would-be spies; and my niece, little Claire, had been born. We would sit and listen to her crying. 'She'll soon stop, she's just exercising her lungs'. 'But suppose a safety pin is sticking into her?' At that, of course, we would rush to pick her up, to make sure, and the attempt to discipline her was abandoned.

After ten days, I returned to the hospital to have the plaster removed – and lo, the skin graft had not 'taken', it had instead putrefied. Now the

239

doctor said, 'We'll let Nature take her course.' I was dismissed with a bandage, and wandered out into Gower Street. Suddenly I saw the noble Greek front of University College; it looked lofty, serene, clean, reliable – a vision of Academia – and I drifted in mesmerised. I was directed from one office to another with my question: 'Can I study here?' In the end, the answer was almost certainly 'Yes', and I was enamoured with the prospect of escaping from my sordid life at the Cabaret Club.

But when I got back to the digs, there was a letter for me, a reply to one of the many I had written to advertisements in *The Stage*: I was to come to the Tudor Theatre, Bramhall, by the beginning of January. About the same time, Maggie, in despair over Derek's coolness, returned home to Oldham.

A few years later, the Cabaret Club became famous because one of its dance hostesses, Christine Keeler, and her friend, Mandy Rice-Davies, were sharing their favours between members of both the British and the Russian Defence establishment; known as the Profumo Affair, it was headline news for quite a long time. But by then, I was elsewhere.

Chapter 23

When I arrived in Bramhall, in early January 1953, the theatre was still a cinema, and had been for nearly a year. Now another idealist, rather like Richard Dale in Ashford, was determined to bring live theatre back to the people of Bramhall, and the local paper, the *Stockport Advertiser*, did its best to support the venture.

The fog was not as bad as the pea-souper in London, but still pretty bad. I found myself digs with a former ballet dancer, now quite crippled with arthritis, and went to see the last film being shown in the cinema, *Wuthering Heights*. Laurence Olivier as Heathcliff almost ousted Willy in my heart. On the way back to my digs, I came to a telephone kiosk and idly looked at the phone book. We had been resigned, as Zuntz children, to be always the last name on any alphabetical list. Then I had read somewhere that the last name in the New York phone book was Zyz, and since then I had made a habit of seeing what the last name in other phone books was.

It was Zuntz. My own name, though I had not used it for so long. It hadn't dawned on me that Bramhall was in the Manchester conurbation, that I had entered the environs of Fe, now a senior lecturer at Manchester University.

On the spur of the moment, I dialled the number: Chinley 1. A woman answered – Stella, presumably.

'This is Gabi,' I said. She squawked, 'Garbi?' 'Yes. I've just discovered your number in the phone book. I'm at Bramhall. Must be quite close.'

'Wait a minute. I'll get Father.'

There was a long pause. Finally, she came back, 'Father says could you write a letter, please, and explain where you are and what you're doing and so on. All right?'

'All right.'

I copied the address from the phone book. From now on, the Tudor Players took second place in my mind. I prompted *Maiden Ladies*, a farce, and played the maid in Delderfield's *Worm's Eye View*, but my father's proximity outweighed everything else. In the plastic bag containing all my letters over the years, and carbon copies or drafts of his replies, that he presented to me decades later, there is a one which he must have written in response to my phone call. It has been crossed out; presumably a second version was typed and sent to me after he had received my letter, and after some discussion with Stella. But this was his first reaction. He wrote:

'Your telephone call last night was a great surprise. I can only ascribe it to a whim, caused, quite understandably, by the chance of geographical nearness. Otherwise you could not well have concealed from yourself that your

behaviour, during the past years, contradicts your "unproblematical" atti-
tude. If you had had any serious desire to keep in, or renew, relations with us
– there were endless obvious opportunities. These you have chosen not to
use; on the contrary, you have cut off several sincere approaches of ours.' (I
was not aware of any such approaches.) *'I do not reproach you: I merely*
remind you that, in eight years, both you and we have gone our separate
ways &, no doubt, greatly changed. A mere 'nodding acquaintance' between
us is obv. out of the question – &, for the time being, I see little reason to
expect that an attempt at establishing well-grounded relations would not
end in future disappointment. This I wish to spare you and us. We have
made the attempt with your brother – and "have had it".'

I didn't understand what this meant. Later, Mu told me Peter had gone to
their home, and been let in; but other guests were expected, and Peter was
introduced as a friend. No one was supposed to know that Fe had been married before or that he had a previous family; but the guests commented that
Peter's appearance was extraordinarily similar to Fe's, and so the cat was out
of the bag. Peter lost his temper and told them all roundly what he thought
of this attempted concealment or denial of the existence of himself, and our
mother, and all of us. Fe's entry in *Who's Who* mentioned only his second
marriage and the three children of that marriage – as do all his obituaries –
silently air-brushing us out of existence. The draft letter continues:

'I would be less reluctant to renew the attempt were it not that we are
strained to the limit. Carsten has, after six weeks, returned from the hospital;
he has been between life and death with polio (and we with him); now,
partly paralysed and psychol. shaken, he needs our constant and undivided
attention. In addition, we have a new baby, who keeps us on the alert from 5
a.m. every day; besides, we have to keep house and job going without help.
We have not been able, since 1948, to afford a weekend off, let alone a holi-
day; hence we need, and desire, at least the untroubled peace of our isolated,
retired, solitary existence. If you choose to regard this as the heartless egotism
of people living in luxury, you would be more foolish than I expect you to be.
I wish to spare you, and us, a painful experience. I conclude with the sincere
wish that your work at Bramhall may prove a step toward a result that wld
be in keeping with your gifts and promises, & with the outstanding educa-
tion & opportunities which have been lavished on you. ...'

He must have been thinking resentfully of the money he had to send to Mu,
along with the alimony, while I was in full-time education. The letter that he
did send me, in reply to mine, can't have been very different from this draft,
for in my reply to him – which I also found in that plastic bag – I expressed
my concern for my little half-brother, Carsten (named, I assumed, after the
Danish Professor Carsten Hoeg), a polio victim, and continued:

'I do not see why I am not able, or allowed, to be friends with a man I loved & admired a lot before I was thirteen, and who suddenly & mysteriously disappeared out of my life. I am, I will admit, intensely curious to know what he is like, having heard so much about him, & having so sweet and sour a memory of him. I want to see him for myself. It was probably vulgar curiosity that prompted my phone call ...

My vulgar curiosity continues, but I can see that it cannot be satisfied under your present circumstances. I can store it or kill it, as you wish. I have my ambition ... Perhaps it has nothing to do with you, but I believe it has, that these strange & unexplained happinesses and sadnesses that descend upon me, excluding everything else, are yours. I believe we could be friends in the best sense. But it doesn't depend on me.'

He replied:

'Thank you for your letter. It gives us hope that a meeting with you need not end in emotional upheaval as in the case of Peter.'

This was followed by an invitation to come and spend the weekend of his 52 birthday – 28 January – with them. So, about the time when the inevitable announcement came that the Tudor Theatre, too, was bankrupt and would have to close, I made my way for the first time to the village of Chinley, on the slopes of Kinder Scout in the Peak District, and walked a considerable distance along the road that was 'unsuitable for motorists' to the lonely house called Newstead. I found Stella struggling to cope not only with a sick child and a new baby, but also with Fe's familiar insistence on the primacy of his work and associated needs: like the absolute silence, the really hot coffee, the time for playing the piano, the after-dinner sleep, the good food. True he now helped a little in the house and the garden; that was a big change, and he gave outward signs of affection and chivalry to Stella. Little Carsten won my heart immediately; he was improving, though one arm never recovered entirely, and the new baby, Andrew, spent a good deal of time at what Stella jocularly called 'the milk bar'. I made myself useful about the house, went for solitary walks up Kinder Scout when the rain left off for a while, listened to Fe playing the piano, played a little myself. Some time was set aside for conversations.

By now I was disillusioned by the theatre, and felt I ought to do something positive with my life. I dreamed of producing plays – medieval Mysteries; in the weeks and months that followed I wrote stories and plays and poems and collected reject slips from publishers; I toyed with the idea of trying to spend a year in Paris and studying French at the Sorbonne, or of working as a continental tour guide, or of learning Greek, or of studying the history of the theatre world wide; or producing plays in Africa with white and black actors; I entered poetry competitions: I was full of vast, but vague ambitions. Actually I was waiting to be 'discovered'. Was it too late to revert to being a doctor? Then perhaps I should become a social worker: the old dream of an orphanage stirred again. Certainly not, said Fe. Social work and so on was a fine thing to do – but the likes of us should devote our intellectual gifts to higher things. In the months that followed, he took it upon himself – in conversations and in letters – to question my upbringing. Had I not had too much freedom, too little direction; was I not in danger of becoming a dilettante, instead of pursuing one career whole heartedly? It seemed extraordinary that he, who had walked out of our lives, should now reproach Mu implicitly for the way she had tried to play the role of two parents. However, I took what was on offer; invitations to stay at Chinley, to work as a sort of au pair to Stella. I accepted his never-ending complaints about their lack of money, never having enough for a holiday (to make sure I made no demands on his purse, probably), about the extra work necessitated by Carsten's needs and recurrent ill health, about the thankless task of teaching mediocre students and reviewing third-rate books and, in between, he doled out advice for me. In the end I decided to go to university. The memory of the Grecian façade of University College was really quite enticing, and yet at the same time I feared people's 'Told you so' and 'Why didn't you listen to us in the first place?'

By March the Tudor Theatre was a bingo hall and I was back in Oxford, having completed all the formalities to become an undergraduate at University College, London. I was short-sighted, but couldn't bear to wear my National Health Service glasses, so my world was a blur. I found myself a job as a telephonist-receptionist for PJ Jones, who sold cars and caravans in Summertown. I would get a bonus for every caravan I sold. I was not good at this work; the little switchboard was quite baffling and I frequently cut people off, or connected them wrongly. Also I encouraged customers not to buy caravans by warning them of their short-comings like the condensation that formed in them. However, I was tolerated and quite enjoyed myself. Hours would pass by when I had nothing to do and would write letters or poems or stories on company note-paper. Then a customer would enter and I would get to know a new person. I was swept off my feet by one, a very good-looking, very tense young man called Richard Roadknight. He was a salesman for National Cash Registers, and like so many salesmen, he lived on his nerves. He was conscious all the time that everything depended on the impression he made; he was selling himself, rather than cash registers. He treated me to the same vibrant, concentrated attention that he employed in his work. At weekends and in the evenings we travelled around in his car a good deal, and he introduced me to two plump brothers who believed they could make a fortune harvesting a certain water weed in the Thames estuary and selling it to aquarium owners. But there was an additional factor that made him so tense: in the background there was his immediate superior in the area office, a somewhat older man, dark and good looking, who would watch Richard with glowering eyes and pointedly ignore me; I came to believe that Richard was using me as an escape route from an intense relationship with that man. I decided to let the other man win this battle for Richard's soul and detached myself from him with far less pain than from his predecessors.

In the months and years that followed, my renewed but strictly circumscribed relationship with my father did, probably, heal the deeper wounds the divorce had inflicted, and I was not as distressed as my brother, my sister and my mother. Again and again I tried to build bridges between them; and the vehemence with which he rejected them seems extraordinary. In a PS to a letter I had tentatively suggested he might send Peter a card for his daughter Claire's birth in December 1953. His response –

'... *Your post-script re your brother, I suppose, must have come from some sudden whim; otherwise you would have recalled our long talk on the matter. I wish him and his dependants the best – and there it rests. The sphere of instability, unreliability, insincerity, resentment, cruelty – lies behind us and shall never touch ours again. We have tried and been burned once, and more than once – and not again. That's final. Be realistic ... You know that you are welcome here, and more than welcome, for your own sake, and for that only ... We will not be drawn into what is the very negation of the life, and lives, we are building up.*'

I always felt guilty at being thus singled out; and the others must have thought it intolerable of me to continue to communicate with him, and visit him, after his cruelty to Mu, his brutal rejection of Peter, and Maleen, and Kurt, who went on a long cold wet journey once to Chinley to see him, and was left standing on the doorstep, refused entry, and had the door shut in his face. Why did I go back? It was a form of self-preservation: not of my life, but of my inner balance. And I liked my little half-brothers.

Carsten and Andrew

*****

I found a large bed-sitter at 131 Mercer's Road, in Tufnell Park, next to a football field, and opposite a fish and chips shop, with a friendly family called Stanley. Quite often I would find a plateful of home-made scones in my room when I came home. During my first year at UCL I had to learn Latin, Anglo-Saxon, Middle English, Old High German and Middle High

German – which last was the easiest, thanks to the Swiss German I had learned from Margrit in Zürich. It has many similarities with Middle High German. And I was reading Milton, Dryden, Spenser, Dr Johnson, Shakespeare, Virgil, Sturm und Drang literature, and books on stylistic analysis. I also tried to get involved in college dramatics, and joined the swimming team. But as usual, I felt I was an outsider, this time not because I was German in an English school, but because I had not come straight from school, and was at least two years older than the others. I also felt guilty because I had an unfair advantage. Being bilingual, and having been taught by Nini, I found the work easier than they did. I kept my German origins secret.

The German Department was not located anywhere near the noble Grecian portico that had inspired me to enter the university, but in some grubby disused warehouses called Foster Court. Here a charming Professor Forster led a team of mostly quite young men, and one formidable woman, 'the Wilk' (from Wilkinson), teaching and lecturing to mostly young women, with a tiny minority of male students. German has never been a popular subject, trailing far behind French, and even further behind English.

One of the few men was, like myself, a 'mature student', an ex-serviceman called John, and inevitably we became close; I helped him with his studies, he tried to help me to get rid of my haunting feelings of guilt and isolation. But he was unbalanced and found communication difficult; there were hours when he marched through the streets as if in a trance. I would follow him, but if I drew level with him and tried to speak to him, he would be staring blankly ahead and appear not to hear me.

There was another male student a year ahead of me on the course, called David Gill, a tall, slim, brown-eyed fellow, rather shy and gauche. We shared many interests, cultural and political. He co-edited Pi, the student newspaper, for a time. Our first conversation, in the library at Foster Court, was about Nietzsche's lyric poetry, which we both loved. And David wrote good poetry: one of his poems appeared in the magazine, *New Phineas*. Our first date almost didn't happen: we had agreed to meet in a certain café on the Euston Road, where I waited for the best part of an hour before giving up: presumably, he had 'stood me up'. But walking past another café nearby I saw him sitting by the window, absorbed in a book. He was obviously delighted to see me, full of remorse when I

David Gill

told him where we were supposed to meet. So, I thought, he didn't think to look for me; so, he's not a worrier, no good at practical arrangements. This was confirmed when he invited me to have supper with him at a Chinese restaurant in Regent's Street, which his Aunt Edith had taken him to. As the meal ended, he looked more and more distracted and miserable, kept wiping his nose, taking a purse out of his pocket, looking at it, and putting it back. Conversation was impossible, until it dawned on me that he didn't have enough money to pay the bill. Fortunately, I had. A memory of Willy rose in my mind, but I suppressed it. This David was not a lay-about, but a genuine poet. Things came to a head at a weekend which the department spent at Cumberland Lodge, in Windsor Great Park, in November 1955. I could see very clearly that life with John would be dreary and depressing and difficult – not too different from life with Willy, without the compensating factor of glamour. While here was this David, a poet, but also kind, altruistic and sane. Unlike just about all the other men I had known (including my father) he was not absorbed in his inner life; he regarded other people with interest and good will, and literature, the arts, and politics with quite acute insight. And he wrote really good poems.

I was now dividing my time between London, Oxford, Wales, where Peter and Brenda were living, and Chinley. I tried to keep my contact with Fe secret from my family, getting him to write poste restante when I was in Oxford, as I had seen once how bitterly Peter was hurt when I received a letter from him at Beamsend.

Mu threw herself enthusiastically into supporting my studies of German literature; now those long poems which she had memorised as a child, and had recited to her mother when they were picking raspberries in Ferch, came into their own. I listened spell-bound as they came pouring out, fluently, rhythmically, full of feeling and all the power and versatility and musicality of the German language. I particularly remember the terrifying onomatopoeia of Bürger's *Lenore*, where the dead soldier gallops to the graveyard with his bride, or the lofty castle ruins in *Des Sängers Fluch* (The Minstrel's Curse); and of course the tragedy of Goethe's *Gretchen*, which she could never recount without weeping. My father's attitude to my studies was very different. This 'modern' literature was not something one studied; one read it for relaxation in one's free time. The only area he regarded as proper studying was medieval and Old High German and Anglo-Saxon. (But nothing really counted except Greek.)

At the end of my second year, David finished his BA course and went off to do his two-year National Service, spending most of the time in Bavaria, listening to the coded radio messages between Warsaw Pact forces on the other side of the Iron Curtain – and to concerts when nothing much was happening. I took the examinations for my subsidiary subject, English. I had studied Anglo-Saxon poetry with enthusiasm – I was the only person in the class who actually liked it – while the eighteenth century bored me rather. Still, it was a devastating shock when I failed the exam. It was the policy of the college not to discuss exam papers with students; I was not even to be told which of the papers I had done so badly. I would have to take the whole exam again together with the Finals of my main subject, German, the following year. I decided to take a correspondence course, which would teach me exactly what to say in these exam essays and how to say it. Still, I faced Finals with great trepidation. Professor Forster told me that I would either fail, or get a First. I was having little naps at various times of the day, and was afraid I might fall asleep in the middle of an exam. I got some tablets from the college doctor which, he said, each contained the equivalent of four cups of strong black coffee. He did not reveal that they were also laxatives. Again and again, during the five gruelling June days when I wrote nine three-hour papers, I had to raise my hand and ask to be escorted to the toilets. Before I could go in, the invigilator searched the cubicle thoroughly, in case there was some hidden information there (it was all a bit different from my grandmother's medical exams in Freiburg). During the weeks that followed, I was weak with fear and anticipation, back in Oxford, waiting for the result. When I heard that I had got a First, I screamed and almost fell down the stairs.

On the strength of that First, I got a studentship to do research which was slightly more generous than the undergraduate grant, so I decided to live away from the fish and chips shop opposite my room in Tufnell Park: first in an outwardly elegant Georgian terrace near Kensington Gardens, until I discovered that it was filthy, and that mice were eating my butter; then in Kentish Town, in the only clean house in a slummy street. Its neat front garden, gleaming windows and fresh paint work were appealing. Indeed, it was clean, very clean. I would often come home to find that my room reeked of disinfectant, and more than once I looked up to find gaunt Mr Pretty (he had had all his insides out, Mrs Pretty told me) on a ladder outside my window, cleaning it. Downstairs, Mrs Pretty held her cat on her lap like a baby and fed it with a spoon from a dish on the table. Late one evening when I was getting ready for bed, I heard Mrs Pretty shrieking 'Miss 'Enry! Miss 'Enry!' I hurtled down to the basement, where she was standing by the open lavatory door, pointing into it with a quivering finger. I looked in: I couldn't see anything amiss. She drew my attention to the roll of lavatory paper. Still I could not see anything distressing. 'We don't want that many pieces hanging down, do we!' she exclaimed. 'Two pieces, that's all. Don't you leave it all untidy like that again!' I left that house at once and was delighted to find that I could have my old room in Tufnell Park back. The only angry words the Stanleys ever addressed to me came when I offered to pay more rent, as my grant had gone up. They refused, indignantly. After the disinfectant in the Prettys' house, the smells from the fish and chips shop were quite welcome.

I chose a medieval topic for my research, the set phrases or topoi used in connection with courtly love, particularly in Gottfried von Strasburg's *Tristan und Isolde*. I loved this long poem, or rather, fragment. I also enjoyed reading other works in medieval Latin and French, as well as German, that dealt with courtly love or Minne. What I did not enjoy was reading the 'secondary literature' on the subject, which, it turned out, was what this research entailed. Boring, heavy books, often with about three lines of text and the rest of the page given over to footnotes, in which nineteenth century German professors poured scorn on each other's views. My supervisor was a convert to Buddhism who seemed to spend most of his time in Nirvana. I came to detest academic work, in which my father revelled. Peter, too, was a university lecturer now and producing Russian language-teaching books and original research on Russian writers. I found the work as dry as dust and futile. I decided to have **no** irritating footnotes in my thesis; if something was worth saying, I would have it in the text. I typed it out on the typewriter Fe had given me, four copies, using carbon paper, (and I put about every tenth page into the typewriter with the carbon paper the wrong side up and had to do the damn thing again). I loathed this lonely, tedious, fiddly work. Finally I had finished. I got the required three copies of my thesis bound and submitted them correctly, and in due course presented myself to a tableful of professors to defend it.

'Where are the footnotes?' demanded one professor. I explained what I thought about footnotes. 'Can't have a thesis without footnotes,' he expostulated. Then another said, 'This bibliography's no good. Look – here you put the date of publication before the place – and here the place before the date! That won't do. Take it away. You'll have to do it again. Sort out your bibliography. Get a decent set of footnotes.'

At no time did they consider the content. Probably they never read it. Probably no one ever has. It was a complete waste of time and effort. Still, during the following year I dutifully extracted bits of text and fitted them into the bottoms of pages as footnotes – this involved a fair bit of work with scissors and paste for all four copies – and regularised the bibliography; got it bound again; so at last I got my MA.

However, I discovered something else. I discovered that I loved teaching. I was able to augment my studentship by teaching German to a large class of students. I was quite terrified at first; bought myself a black pencil-slim skirt and a black and white striped blouse, to look professional; worked out exactly what I would teach in the first class; went over it again and again in my mind, imagined possible questions I might be asked, and how to answer them. The great day came. My heart was pounding – it was just like stage fright. No one asked any questions. I went straight through the material I had prepared without stumbling once, right to the end. Then I looked at the clock. Only quarter of an hour had passed. It was a one-hour period. I gulped. I couldn't think of anything else to say except, 'Well, as it's the first lesson, let's knock off early, shall we?' I never made that mistake again. In fact, thereafter the lessons went very well. I had taught some private lessons in English in Zürich, and always enjoyed them. Now I realised that teaching is a great pleasure, akin to performing in a play. Establishing an affectionate rapport with one's students, galvanising their minds, and watching the light of comprehension dawning in their eyes, are real joys. I have been teaching ever since and sometimes marvel that I am paid for indulging in this exhilarating activity.

*****

1956 was the year of my political awakening. This was the year of Suez **and** Hungary. Let me explain.

In July 1956, the Egyptian leader, Nasser, nationalised the Suez Canal. Nasser had been making friendly gestures towards some of the Soviet Bloc countries, and in the lunatic days of the Cold War that meant he could not receive investments from the West. So he nationalised the Canal. Egypt was also very hostile to Israel; had blocked Israel's access to the Gulf of Aqaba, and had sponsored commando raids into Israel. So when the French and the British proposed to regain control of the Canal and depose Nasser, Israel was eager to participate and invaded the Sinai peninsula. Britain and France hypocritically pretended that there had been no collusion with Israel, and a few days later, their forces landed in Egypt and started occupying the Canal zone. Soon the truth came out. There were huge demonstrations against this in London; we felt not only should Egypt own its canal, but we were also furious at Prime Minister Eden's mendacity, embroiling us in an old-style colonial war after secret negotiations with Israel and France. When the Soviet Union threatened to intervene, the constant fear that dominated the world in the Cold War – that any conflict might escalate into all-out nuclear war – made Britain and France withdraw in December. But Israel stayed in Sinai until March 1957, when she was assured of her shipping rights through Aqaba.

Meanwhile – in Hungary – there was an anti-Soviet uprising. It was in February of this same year, 1956, at the 20th Soviet Party Congress, that Khruschev had denounced Stalin's dictatorship (Stalin had died in March 1953). This had encouraged students in Poland and Hungary, and elsewhere in the Soviet bloc, to hold demonstrations and draw up petitions asking for greater freedom. They were greatly encouraged by Radio Free Europe, which broadcast across the Iron Curtain encouraging rebellion and promising Western support. In Hungary, the Army joined forces with the students; Imre Nagy, the Prime Minister, made one concession after the other to popular demands. In a short time, forcibly collectivised land was given back to peasants, local councils were set up; Cardinal Mindszenty returned from exile to great popular acclaim, and the State's atheism was set aside. At first, Khruschev appeared to accept the changes and withdrew Soviet forces from Hungary, but only just across the frontier. When Hungary wanted to withdraw from the Warsaw Pact and possibly join the Western camp in the Cold War, the Red Army tanks were sent back in. Reports of unarmed civilians confronting the armed might of the Soviet bloc was stirring. One wanted to help the little fellow, the David against Goliath. But by December, Nagy was replaced by Kadar, who was more submissive to the USSR; numerous activists had been carried off into the Soviet Union, never to be heard of again, and some 200 000 Hungarian refugees had managed to get to Western Europe before the Iron Curtain clanked down again.

These two parallel developments stirred my passions as few things outside my personal experience had before. I became a newspaper reader. I bought all the newspapers every day, listened to the BBC news, following the events with a pounding heart. I was furious with my government for its imperialist misdeeds in Egypt. Apart from the obvious wickedness of it, it took the wind out of our sails, and meant Britain could not condemn Soviet imperialism in Hungary since we were no better ourselves. I wanted to do something more than join in the demonstrations in Trafalgar Square against Britain's actions in Egypt. When an appeal for support for a joint British Universities' Volunteer Force – BUVF – to fight the Russians in Hungary appeared on a notice board in college, I did not hesitate.

That was how I came to spend my days and most of my nights in a small terraced house in a side-street near Victoria Station, talking endlessly with a motley group of young men about how and where to train (the Lake District was the likeliest), how to get hold of weapons, how to make contact with the Hungarian Freedom Fighters, how to get to Hungary, where, indeed, Hungary was, how to keep our 'plans' secret from the KGB (we should not know what any of the others were doing so that, if caught, we would not be able to betray them), how to get money, how to get more recruits. A few short reports appeared in the *News Chronicle*. My fellow conspirators would slip in through the front door and say, wide-eyed: 'I've got a tail' meaning they thought they had been followed from the bus stop.

One volunteer was a waiter who had been in the army: Jim Cook. He was particularly afraid of the 'slit-eyed' soldiers from the Eastern Soviets, and carried a wicked-looking carving knife in his trouser leg. Tired of the lack of action, he set out for Hungary on his own, pretending to be a tourist. He got to Vienna and from there to the Hungarian border, which he crossed by night, tripping over barbed wire and hurting his feet. He cowered in a ditch all night, watching Red Army trucks moving back and forth. Next day he spent in a camp for Hungarian refugees, sharing their Red Cross food, as he was penniless. In the end, the British Consul in Vienna repatriated him. This heroic venture struck me as fairly futile. The oldest volunteer, and perhaps the most intelligent, a school teacher, Peter Cox, decided that if we were to achieve anything, we had to find out what kind of collaboration was possible with councils of workers and students outside Budapest. Students in Vienna were helping to run refugee camps. They, and a Hungarian academic in Vienna, had contacted us. So in December, he set out for Vienna, and I went with him to translate, as he didn't know German. Nobody knew any Hungarian.

We crossed the Channel to Ostende and started hitch-hiking in a howling gale and torrential rain. Hitch-hiking with Peter Cox turned out to be just as bad as hitch-hiking with Stefan had been, our troubles being exacerbated by his regarding me as a monster of cruelty for not being in love with him. It took us four days to get to Vienna, where we stayed in the youth hostel, and contacted the Hungarian, Istvan, in the university refectory. Yes, he told us, there was an organisation, he himself had just brought a leading rebel's daughter out from Budapest; yes, a radio was being sent in to Budapest University; what they needed most was medical supplies – he gave us a list – if only they could pay for it. Well, my studentship had just been paid into my account in London, so I sent a teleprint message to my bank asking them to wire me £50.

I felt exultant. There really was something useful we could do to justify the BUVF and its endless meetings. We were asked to help in a refugee camp, and after many postponements, Istvan drove us to one of them on Christmas Eve. But there was nothing for us to do there, and I felt quite guilty, sharing the Hungarians' rations and accommodation, and not even able to talk with them. We returned to Vienna and discovered that the radio had not been sent, but Istvan was full of a plan to run a conference in Strasbourg to which BUVF would be invited. It dawned on me that it was all hot air and that we could not in fact do anything at all to help the heroic Hungarian fighters, and Peter Cox too felt that once we got back to Britain, he would leave the organisation and let it collapse.

When we finally got back to the office near Victoria, I was poorer and most of my grant had disappeared. I left the 'debriefing' to Peter and wandered upstairs and into an empty office; and there on a desk lay a stack of books entitled *Protocols of the Elders of Zion*, that notorious forgery which purports to document a secret Jewish plan to take over the whole world. So this building belonged to an anti-Semitic organisation. Why had it given BUVF the use of its downstairs offices? How did we come to have such distasteful bedfellows? Some notion of polarity became apparent to me. To be in support of Hungarians who wished to liberate themselves from Soviet tyranny was to be on the side of the anti-communists; and anti-communists were fascists, and fascists were anti-semitic. Now I was totally disillusioned.

I decided to leave BUVF. I wrote them a letter, begging them not to consider going out to fight, which could only serve to prolong the agony of the country; and that was the end of my connection with them. I did not hear of them again.

All this time David in Bavaria was listening in to the radio messages between sections of the Warsaw Pact forces. These were in Morse code – all he had to do was write down strings of letters which were decoded elsewhere. Still, it was obvious that very alarming events were afoot, and he was not too happy at my being involved.

When he was demobbed, David worked for a time at the Park Lane Hotel, until he got a job as a technical liaison officer at 'Fort Dunlop' – Dunlop's tyre factory – in Birmingham, and we decided to get married. Then on one and the same day, in February 1958, I received letters from Fe and from Peter – who had not spoken to each other for years, remember – containing the same article by JB Priestley cut out of the *New Statesman*, entitled 'Britain and the Nuclear Bombs'. In it, Priestley argued that the monstrous danger posed to the whole planet by the existence of these weapons of colossal destructive power must be averted, that the bombs must be disarmed, and that Britain was ideally suited to lead the world away from the nuclear holocaust. Compared with the USA and the USSR, our nuclear arsenal was insignificant anyway. We could well afford to get rid of them, without affecting the 'balance of terror', and invite others to follow suit, pointing out how much safer we were without them, since then no one would think of a 'pre-emptive strike' to prevent our using them against them. Moreover, we could invite the two Great Powers to use any inspection methods they might want to try out to ensure that we really had dismantled all of them, since the difficulty of 'verification' was always brought up as an argument against nuclear disarmament.

I was completely convinced and so were hundreds of thousands of others. Again, it was a paper on a notice board in the college that alerted me to the plan to march from London to Aldermaston, where the British bombs were being produced. I wrote and told David about it and he was in agreement with me. So we joined the crowd in Trafalgar Square on Good Friday, 1958, and after listening to some speeches set out on the long and gruelling march. We spent the first night on the floor in somebody's house in West London. When we woke up the next morning, it was snowing – the worst Easter weather in living memory. Nobody will want to go on the march in weather like this, we thought, so we had better go. Obviously hundreds of other people had thought the same. As we marched, we were cheered along by bands playing jazz at the road-side; or by singing

Oh when the saints, oh when the saints
Oh when the saints go marching in,

I wanna be of that number
When then saints go marching in

and

Gonna lay down my sword and shield
Down by the riverside, down by the riverside,
Down by the riverside. Ain't gonna study war no more.

and others that grew very familiar. We marched great distances, and to be honest, it was no fun; my feet ached, I got blisters, I longed to stop – as we did, eventually: good people in Slough and Reading fed us and organised sleeping accommodation for us. Once this was in a primary school: one had to bend down to reach the little wash basins, and sitting on one of the tiny children's toilets was like sitting on a crocus. There was some hostility from bystanders along the way, especially in Reading, but in general, people looked at us with astonishment. Even hostile tabloid newspapers grudgingly admired us for turning out in such awful weather – it was cold, and the snow gave way to rain. Our banners, mostly home-made, read:

On the first Aldermaston march

BAN THE BLOODY BOMB!

Use H-Bomb Money To Feed The World's Starving Kids!

READING (and many other towns and villages) SAYS NO!

World in PEACE and not in PIECES!

1.Hiroshima 2.Nagasaki 3. ? ? ? ?

I WANT TO LIVE!

LET BRITAIN LEAD!

There were many others, including simple round ones with the CND symbol. Some showed lurid pictures of the mushroom cloud and children's faces. For hours we marched through open country. From the top of a hump-backed bridge we could see the unruly line of the march stretching in either direction, like a vast, shabby snake with litter stuck to its back, rippling slowly between the hedges; one after the other, the banners rounded a distant bend. There was no one there to see us except a few birds.

Irene Gill

At last, very tired, very footsore, we got to the village of Aldermaston, and walked on, past the huge base, the grim security fence, the queer buildings and structures and pipes, the odd mounds and hummocks inside, the gleams of metal, and the serried ranks of police, till we got to the locked gates – a motley, weary, shabby crowd. We read the warning notices about police dogs and electric wires and felt cowed by the vast, impersonal, deserted, efficient autonomy of it all. Later, in Falcon Field, we listened to speeches, before setting off again for the comforts of civilisation. But as we came past the Atomic Weapons Establishment again, David touched my sleeve and pointed. There, behind all the security fencing, sat a group of rabbits, munching grass and flicking their ears. And we were reassured, to some extent.

That was the first of very many demonstrations. And we wrote letters to politicians, feeling sure that if we only pointed out the simple logic of our case, they would surely be convinced. We wrote to newspapers, we went to meetings, we planned and plotted eye-catching and significant demonstrations in committee meetings; and all the time, the world got steadily worse; France got her Bomb, then China, and Israel, and now India and Pakistan, and Britain, who could have led the world away from the nuclear abyss, keeps up its 'deterrent', its city-killer missiles ever ready on its patrolling nuclear submarines.

255

Once Peter was married, Mu threw herself into her new role as mother-in-law. She would visit Peter and Brenda in Wales, and later in Cambridge, and 'help'. She did not realize that for Brenda, having her cupboards thrown open and the contents pulled out and rearranged by a tut-tutting mother-in-law, Peter's shirts re-washed, his socks darned and his trousers ironed, was not so much helpful as humiliating, and may even have contributed to their ultimate divorce.

While involving herself in family matters, Mu still felt that a career, or at least a useful and meaningful occupation, was what she needed to fight off her feeling of futility and isolation. She applied for various jobs and finally succeeded in getting a residential position at a Borstal Institution for teenage boys at a place called Almondsbury. She felt her long experience with her own teenagers would equip her to help these boys. She was put in charge of a sewing room and spent the days patching and darning and turning sheets 'sides to middle'. Occasionally some of the boys might come and pass the time of day with her, but not often enough to make her feel she was being really helpful to them, as she wished; so she returned to her house in Oxford and her lodgers. She continued to study Russian in evening classes, until she was able to pass the A-level exam, albeit with a disappointingly low grade, and read the great Russian classics in the original. One of her lodgers was a Russian woman, an artist, who had been married to an Englishman: Mrs Kilby. With her she read Lermontov, at first with boundless enthusiasm, especially for the character of the Demon. It seemed that the two women were true soul-mates as they read and discussed the work. In fact they were both in love with the romantic Demon, and jealous of each other. Each accused the other of being incapable of understanding him. They got so excited that they would wake up in the middle of the night and write notes to each other, which they would drop on the floor outside each other's rooms. These grew more and more acrimonious: they would accuse each other of intolerable sentimentality, or of coldness, or simple stupidity; basically each was asserting that the Demon would only find her worthy of his love. In the end they were incapable of speaking to each other at all, and Mrs Kilby moved out. It was a case of romantic rivalry and jealousy between two middle-aged women over a fictional character.

Mu told me more than once that in her mind she was always reliving her childhood; so it was not surprising that when her brother Reinhardt resurfaced after the long silence he had maintained throughout the Third Reich, she went to visit him on the fruit farm in Schleswig Holstein where he was then living and working. She did not write or talk to me about my uncle, but described the low-lying landscape, which had been reclaimed from the sea:

'There are hardly any roads, everything is carried by boat on the canals, every house has a boat or two, just like bikes, tethered to the end of the garden. The canals were full of frogs, which were eaten by storks. Every house had an old wheel on the roof, which the storks accepted with pleasure as the basis for their nests. But everything had been sprayed, and many frogs had been killed as a result, so there are far fewer storks than there used to be. Reinhardt and Annemarie were living quite comfortably, the boys going to a famous old grammar school in Stade. I walked over the soft fruit fields with Reinhardt where the berries had unfortunately just been harvested. However, I found a few forgotten berries, and ate them peacefully. My brother was very upset, as everything had just been sprayed. I had to go to the first aid station, and all sorts of precautionary measures had to be taken – successfully, as you see, since I am still alive.

One evening I walked through the village with Annemarie – it was nice and tidy and as pretty as a picture. I looked at a delightful little house with a garden full of fruit trees and bushes and flowers – but three families lived in it, and several of them had TB. Then we came to a very large empty barn, and I said: "This looks out of place here." – "Oh, this was for Jewish girls, about 300 of them. Then one night there was a lot of noise with dogs and whips, and in the morning none of the girls was there, and none of them were ever seen again." You find places like that all over Germany, and they should be kept as they are, lest we forget.'

*****

In 1958, David and I got married, and lived more or less happily most of the time ever after. David was still a Christian at that time; I was not, but had no strong objection to a bit of Christian mumbo-jumbo if it made him and his parents happy. Wytham Church, in a village just outside Oxford, appealed to me, so one weekend when he came to visit me in Oxford we cycled out to the village and called on the elderly vicar. He appeared to have no experience of marrying two people who did not live in his parish; he would have to consult 'the bishop's surrogate on marriage'. In due course he informed us that the ruling was that I would have to sleep in the village three nights and leave a suitcase for a week. I therefore knocked at the door of a particularly attractive farmhouse in the village and asked if I might

Our wedding at Wytham

sleep there for three nights... The farmer's wife was a bit puzzled but raised no objection – nor to my leaving a suitcase for a week ... So the great day came, David's parents and his sister and a host of uncles and aunts, Mu and Peter, Brenda and little Claire, and Prof. Maas, assembled for the service. One uncle played the organ while his wife worked the bellows: as we turned from the altar to leave the church, her posterior was rising and disappearing behind the parapet of the organ loft. Afterwards there was cake and wine at Beamsend – and then we departed for a honeymoon in Wales.

We lived at first in Birmingham, and while David worked long hours at Dunlop's, I taught in the German Department at the university; thereafter we lived and taught in Hampshire, at Bedales School, where Tom was born in 1960; in 1962, we went to work in Uganda, where Nick was born in 1963. But that's another story.

While we were there, Mu was working in London at Osmond House, a home for elderly Jews. She suffered a great deal of ill health while she was there, and her letters alarmed me. I thought – and she thought – she might have cancer of the stomach. We decided that when we returned to England in 1964 we would fulfil one of her dreams: Beamsend would be our family home, we would live there with her. She would only agree to this if I found work so that she could have a meaningful position, running the house; that was largely why I started teaching German in several Oxford colleges and in the College of Further Education. At first David worked for a language school; then, having mentioned that he was looking for a job to a man who was giving us a lift to a CND demonstration, and who happened to be Bob Stanier, the headmaster of Magdalen College School, he taught German and English there for seven years. Appalled by the hideous war in Vietnam, I started a fund-raising group, Oxford Aid for Children in Vietnam. After a few years, we adopted our third child, Jackie; so there was plenty for Mu to do, and her health was quickly restored. It is not always easy for the generations to live together; she insisted that as a grandmother she had every right to spoil the youngest, Jackie, and ignore any of our attempts to enforce reasonable bedtimes and limit her intake of sweets; and there were occasions when Mu 'took offence where none was intended', and prolonged pleas and explanations were required to get our relations back onto an even keel.

*****

In 1968, at the height of the Cold War, Mu decided to visit the USSR. She wanted to use her hard-won command of the Russian language, and to be for a while in Russia, which, as she often expatiated, was a vast land inhabited by noble, deeply religious peasants, their age-old suffering and oppression as serfs swept aside at last by the communists; the land of brilliant writers like old Tolstoy who, with all his faults, tried to live in accordance with his humane principles; of characters like Dostoyevsky's Staretz Sosima, whose boundless wisdom she would expound; the nation whose singing, in church or by the Red Army choir, stirred one to the depth of one's soul – condemned as sub-humans, like the Jews, by the Nazis, who perpetrated unspeakable cruelties as they pursued their Drang nach Osten (Eastward urge), until at last the 'sub-humans' laid aside their innate love of peace and defeated the 'master race'. To Russia she went, travelling with a small organised group, crossing Germany by train, including areas familiar to her from her childhood. And she wrote a detailed travelogue:

'Early in the morning we were in Germany. It was glorious. My God, how beautiful the country is, and so familiar! No people in the fields, except occasionally a solitary mower with a scythe. We passed through Werder, so close to Ferch. But the oh so familiar view across the lake was blocked by coal trains. But then, quick as a flash, I did get to look right across the lake, and it was as lovely as a fairy tale, incredibly beautiful. I recognised some houses, though there are many new ones, and old ones have vanished. Then Potsdam, with the Star Steamer Bridge, the Garrison Church and many, many things as they used to be. And later the sparse, aromatic pine forests, the sandy paths with the deep ruts made by the cart wheels, bilberry scrub, birch trees – why did I ever leave? I can never love another land as I love this. I could feel dry twigs crackling under my feet, for it was just such a hot summer's day as I remember from the Wandervogel and from the time I spent with the forester at Neubrück.

But there were fifteen passport checks between the West German frontier and the end of Berlin. Only five, actually, but each time there were three louts in uniform who came separately. Each one studied the passports with the same intensity, each one wanted the same signatures. Those East Germans are all armed.

As far as I could see from the train, Berlin is still the same. Some streets have disappeared, but trees and many houses and the canal and the river are still where they were. Even the signs on the stations are still the old ones, only even more dented, and with a lot of bullet holes. In East Berlin the war stares at you. At Friedrichstrasse station two soldiers shouldering their rifles patrolled a bridge across the line. The train waited for ages. It took two hours for this express to cross Berlin. But one was not allowed to get out anywhere – after all, one might have slipped into glorious East Berlin, and entry into paradise is not as easy as that. I saw badly damaged houses, and houses with bullet wounds filled in with plaster; few new buildings.

We left Berlin, and there was Friedrichshagen Station, where we Wandervogel had our "House on the Heath" – from the train I could see the place where we would assemble, where we turned off the road, where we set off on our day-long walks. It was a Sunday, and I saw large numbers of people out in the open, mostly parents and children, all nice and affectionate. This was one of those magical times like when Faust writes to

Margarethe and is still good and innocent. Hardly any cars, no planes, no shouting. Everything bathed in light. Hardly any agricultural machinery. You could see that the furrows in the potato fields had been shovelled by hand, and there were cornflowers, poppies and corn cockles in the wheat fields. And what a joy to see white goats, like our Lotte, tethered at the roadside, and hay making all over the place, and superb lettuce in rows below the railway embankment.

And the villages and the little towns! Poor, often unlovely, they seem to exemplify the Prussian ideals of the nobility of work and of poverty. I was quite apprehensive as we approached what had once been Silesia (Schlesien). What would the Poles have made of the fields and meadows, the fruit of so much labour? But all was well: the fields were splendidly fertile, lush potatoes in dead straight lines, and rye, rye everywhere – as in the past. And have you ever seen a field of ripening rye when the wind wafts over it? It is infinitely more beautiful and graceful than the best wheat field, and barley and oats look almost frivolous by comparison. It is obvious that the Poles love this earth.

At Brest Litovsk at 2 am we had to stand on the platform for an hour while the wheels were changed – and police crawled all over the train, pulled the bunk beds apart, shone their torches into every corner, locked the toilets.

We stopped in Minsk, the capital of Byelo Russia. We were told it was 900 years old. It didn't look it. There are plenty of open spaces, wide, tree-lined streets and big, decent buildings – all built since the war, when 80 per cent of the city was destroyed. It used to have a big Jewish population. I saw few cars, but plenty of buses. I left the conducted tours in the city centre and following my nose headed for any trees I saw, there are plenty in the parks. And plenty of children, very neat and clean and well disciplined, walking in crocodiles – they greeted me politely with a smile and "Babushka". It was so quiet everywhere.

There are still plenty of old streets in Minsk, unpaved and with deep ruts, the wooden houses in need of a lick of paint and the odd nail here and there, but with nice carving in the gables and the window sills, and flowers and fruit trees round them. They are "condemned" and there are big new blocks of flats going up all around. Families were sitting together in their arbours; Babushkas in the grass with the little children. It was quiet – I only heard one radio; and I felt a bit wistful, walking there alone in the evening.

Little old women sweep the streets with huge brooms. There's one now, with her headscarf and a clean apron, sweeping the area in front of the hotel, so busily, so thoroughly, an example to us all. The unpaved side-roads are swept too, the hollows brushed out, dust carefully collected and tipped into a particularly deep rut.

The Pioneers invited us to their camp. It seems every factory has a camp for its workers' children. This one was not far from the town, in open country, but fenced in, understandably - the children are very young, some only three. Their beds stand close together in little wooden huts; between them there are posters showing Lenin, the Hammer and Sickle, famous heroes of the Soviet Union, and a flagpole. There are timed activities for the whole day. The women in charge are very nice and motherly to the children, and quick to notice any who are not joining in properly: these are gently brought back into the group. It would be impossible to be alone. Everything is done in groups. We were given bunches of wild flowers when we arrived. All the children were wearing snow-white shirts; most of the girls had long plaits. They performed traditional dances for us, and patriotic songs, on a platform with a banner over it inscribed: Be ever ready to fight for the Communist Party. Girls in white served us in the refectory, their manners were impeccable. We were given medals and postcards on which they had written: We wish our esteemed guests from England a long life, or: Peace and Unity, etc.

    I noticed several Jewish children in the camp. Minsk had a large Jewish population once. The policy is to accept the surviving Jews fully, provided they cease to regard themselves as a national minority. The Jews call that genocide, and the majority want to go to Israel – and that is regarded as treason – a foolish idea which only makes them more stubborn. Those children in the camp looked serious and restrained, but a bit arrogant, too. One little girl attached herself to me – could it have been "the voice of the blood"? What must her parents have been through? It took the Nazis five days to conquer Minsk, and they stayed for three or four years. There is a building with a lot of pillars and an inner courtyard. That was a Concentration Camp. The pillars were festooned with barbed wire. Beyond, about ten thousand people perished – in the middle of the town.'

::*:*:*

Mu did not really like Moscow – noisy traffic and building sites everywhere. She visited the Kremlin, and saw the queues waiting to see Lenin's grave, and went to museums and art galleries and the little church on Red Square, but the best day was spent with a friend of Peter's, Mrs Grigoreva.

    '...in the forest, while the rest of the group were sweating in museums. One day in the forest is worth more than four in the city to me. The forest is still young – in the war everything was cut or burnt down – but quite dense, with little paths leading to glades with pines and birch trees. There were people lying under the trees in twos and threes, and children playing with the things the forest gave them to play with.

    Mrs G. spoke non-stop, for ten hours, but slowly and patiently – I could understand her easily. We talked about everything under the sun and got on very well. She loves Lermontov's Demon as much as I do. We ate bread and cheese, and coffee from a thermos flask, just the way I like it. She used to live *in Siberia, and her daughter still lives in Irkutsk. Siberia sounds so alluring: clear light, forests, rivers, and people who have never been serfs. Cold? Well, we're not afraid of the cold. The ice on the walls inside the homes an inch thick. But there's no wind. However, during the war seven of her close relatives died either of hunger or of cold. She was working as a nurse and saw young German soldiers – beautiful young men – who were bitterly ashamed of what they had done. Only the leaders are bad, she said. She is completely loyal politically, admires Lenin, who is supposed to have been so human and simple. Stalin, she admitted, was uncultured. She didn't want to talk about Trotsky: he was too vain and selfish, and the success of the Red Army was thanks to the experienced (tsarist) generals, not Trotsky. Still, I could talk about everything with her, including Israel. People here really don't know about Israel, and don't really care.*

✵✵✵✵✵

'In Leningrad, the Friendship League and Intourist met us at the station, with flowers. The hotel was much better than the one in Moscow, and the tempo is quicker: straight after breakfast we were taken to the Hermitage and the Winter Palace with four extensions housing the museum – packed with things, and crowds of people. I went back alone in the afternoon, when it was less crowded; and looked at the collection of Greek vases – and there, like a greeting from long ago, there were Sleep and Death, the two brothers, laying Hector in his grave. Günther showed me that image, and I have never forgotten it. Among all those hundreds of vases, and the dozens of other figures on that particular vase – there they stood, Sleep and Death, my eyes fell on them first of all.

There are no postcards to be had worth buying, which is a pity. I would have liked to get one of a Dutch painting entitled "The Hunter Punished". The hunter and his dogs, having slaughtered numerous animals, suddenly find themselves face to face with the lion, the supreme judge, and are hanged; the animals are free. It appealed to me.

There are solitary old women everywhere – you can feel their loneliness. No doubt their loved ones are all dead. But all signs of the war have been cleared away. In the 900-day-long siege, a million civilians died of the cold and the hunger. It's no wonder the Russians are demanding such high reparations and keeping the German prisoners of war to clear up the rubble. But no one ever mentions the help they got from the West – they did it all alone, alone they saved Europe. All the tour guides say things like: "The Germans burned all the books in this library" – "Many paintings were taken to Germany" – "This is where the German cannons stood that bombarded Leningrad" – "Hitler had had invitations to a ball to celebrate the conquest of Leningrad and of Moscow printed" – and so on: and yet there are swarms of well-fed Germans here, speaking very loudly. The Germans deliberately

262

gutted the great Summer Palace of the tsars at Tsarskoye Selo (now renamed Pushkin) outside Leningrad and destroyed the park; it has been beautifully restored, but few of the stolen works of art have been found – and here too you hear German spoken loudly and see posters in German: "Willkommen in der Soviet Union". In "Friendship House", a former palace, the Anglo-Russian friendship league entertained us, young people keen to practise their English. One was a Jewish girl called Eva who knew nothing about Israel except what she had read in "Pravda" and was keen to learn more. There was also a professor from the polytechnic; after we had watched a film about the war years he said, sadly: "And now the Jews are inflicting the same suffering on the Arabs." There was a general feeling about that the Arabs needed to be protected against the big bad Israelis. I read about meetings passing resolutions condemning Israel, and sending parcels of food and baby clothes to the Arabs, (well that's better than sending weapons) – people here were swallowing all the nonsense about all-powerful Israel murdering and wanting to exterminate the vulnerable Arabs.'

*****

The return journey was by boat through the Baltic, stopping at Helsinki and Stockholm. In Copenhagen they tied up next to an American cruiser with many 'bombs' on board.

'It was the Fourth of July and there was a band, and flags, and the captain was standing by the gangway – but I saw no visitors for him to welcome on board. Instead, about fourteen trains had been painted with slogans against the Vietnam War.'

She spent some of the time in Denmark wandering around in the woods, feeling very much at home – the gnats were just like the ones in Ferch – and with an old friend, Ilse Bock, in Copenhagen. In the park at Jägerspris she suddenly remembered Günther, and wrote:

Halb ausgelöscht war sein Gesicht (His face was half forgotten)
Doch seiner Worte Kraft noch nicht (But not the force of his words)
'...and after all not a day passes without my thinking of him, somehow or other. Somehow – because try as I will, I cannot recall his face, though I sometimes see it in one of the children, recently in Tom. But memories come and go like clouds, and don't even leave me feeling wistful. A bit puzzled, perhaps – but I don't want them to return. I do feel a bit envious when I see an elderly couple, both rather unlovely and worn, being friendly together. I have got used to being alone, have had plenty of time to get used to it, after all.'

*****

Israel was one area where we all disagreed with my mother. She gloried in the 'Six-Day War', in 1968, when Israel had launched a pre-emptive strike against Egypt, smashed her air force on the ground, occupied the Sinai peninsula, defeated the Jordanian army, occupied East Jerusalem and the West Bank, driven the Syrian army almost as far as Damascus, and occupied the Golan Heights – she gloried in this triumph of the Israeli David against the Arab Goliath; it was like her pride, as a child, in the German army holding out alone against so many enemies in the First World War; it was part and parcel with her passionate empathy with whatever was small and weak, and also, of course, with her loyalty to all the Jewish victims of Nazism.

'And Israel,' (she wrote in her diary), 'I can hardly say the name without tears. All the sensible, generous, far-sighted proposals made by the Jews are turned down, there is to be a war of annihilation. They don't talk about that in the UN, nor about the daily murders. Israel will not be able to stay GOOD.'

But the next note in her diary is

'Again I wake up with a start and realise that I've been in Ferch again. Happens so often. It's always the meadow path with the three willows at the beginning, the glorious round meadow, the sun-warmed hill with the wild pinks and the cats' feet. And looking through to the lake. I could paint it all if I could paint. I used to wake up with such a burning pain, starting to cry in my sleep. It doesn't hurt so much now. But I think that means I am near the end of my journey. But I'm always alone, I never dream of another person – or rather, there is someone walking beside me, I look up, and he has no face – who is it? I'm always dreaming about Death, my friend.'

She never did go back to Ferch, though quite a few people tried to arrange a visit for her: she would always find some reason to refuse at the last moment, such as the East German authorities demanded that she should stay in an official guest house, they would not allow her to sleep in the open. Perhaps in her heart of hearts she feared that the Ferch of her dreams and of her reminiscences was too precious to be exposed to reality – a bit like Fe not wanting to go to modern Greece. Perhaps she had unspoken doubts about Israel, too: but finally, in 1969, she did set out for that object of her love. Not without qualms – or rather, in view of her life-long death wish, not without hope. In her notebook, she wrote:

'If anything should happen to me, Gabi is to distribute my estate. 50 per cent of the house and about 50 per cent of the furniture belong to me, and I rely on Gabi to be fair. I would love the house to be kept as a holiday home for the others, but I must leave such decisions to the brothers and sisters.'

Some of her impressions of Israel echo those of her mother, Olga, more than 30 years earlier, who stressed the contrast between the well-tended Jewish farms with the Arab ones, but expressed her doubts about the 'orthodox Jews who are now in charge'. Oma made no mention of the conflicts between Jews and Arabs, which were uppermost in Mu's mind (and still seem to me to be by far the most important factor in the Middle East). Here's what she wrote:

'Our departure was two hours late. Of course my first thought was sabotage, but no: Ben Gurion was on the same plane, so they wanted to avoid a hijacking. We didn't reach Lod till midnight – a most unpleasant reception: coarse officials kept us waiting for two hours. It was hot and close, but there was air conditioning in the hotel.

The road to Haifa went through a lot of desert, but there were some fine plantations. But it all left me cold – if you can say that when the weather was so hot. Haifa looks impressive, big airy buildings climbing up the steep slopes of Mount Carmel, but I hated it: such turmoil, so many damaged buildings, as in Tel Aviv, but building sites everywhere – no time for repairs. Some parts are rather like I imagine a Polish "stetl" must have been: booths and street traders everywhere selling extremely unhygienic food. The booths are so small that there is only just room for one person in it. Dreadful. Of course there are also some very smart shops – but not a sign of socialist planning. Very disappointing.

I visited Aunt Elsbeth, who has a balcony overlooking the sea – but also the oil refinery: an alarming sight, especially at night – like an evil cyclops. But Elsbeth was so kind, so relaxed, despite a recent death in the family, it was lovely to be with her.

Then I visited Ehrlichs, who live in a village. They are independent farmers now, as at the Winkelhof 40 years ago, though they are not looking after orphans any more. Their land is leased from the state, which also provides settlers like them with a house like a bunker, 50 hens, one cow, two and a half hectares of irrigated land, more that is not irrigated to be used for corn, which the tractor station ploughs, sows, harvests and sells: the farmer has nothing to do with it. All the poultry are kept in batteries. It is a terrible thing to see. Like a concentration camp. And the wretched creatures under corrugated iron: when the hot wind blows in from the desert these almost red hot roofs have to be cooled with water. 150 hens died of heat on one kibbutz. How people can treat animals like that for profit is beyond me. Ehrlichs thinks it can't be helped, so they have no livestock: they grow roses, which are exported to Europe, which seems absurd. The butter on their table is American. The valley looks very pleasing, green and well cared for. It was a malaria swamp when they came in 1937 and the Arabs had left and gone into the mountains. But the malaria has been wiped out and the Arabs complain that their good land has been taken from them. The mountains look magnificent. Now, in September, everything is deathly white, and the forests are grey with dust – the trees, mostly pines, have grown in the 30 years since they were planted, but of course it isn't a "forest". International Jewry paid for the land which was now being farmed so admirably; but the money was paid to the Arab title holder, and not to the wretched peasant or squatter.

We drove from Ehrlichs' village in a battered but admirable jeep across fields where melons had been harvested. After about ten minutes there was a little wood on the right: that was where the spring was from which they had at first carried their water home on their shoulders. A little later a few trees on the left: that was where the Arab women got their water, carrying it on their heads. The Israelis gave them a piped water supply when they laid on their own. In 1948 the Arabs accidentally blew up their own pipeline – of course they had meant to blow up the Jews'. "They had to wait 20 years before we made them a new one," said Ehrlich. Now it's hard to imagine Israel without water: there are showers and sprinklers everywhere. But in those early days, in 1948, when the state of Israel was declared, five Arab armies attacked Israel, and there were numerous minor attacks on the early kibbutzim and settlements. The Jews formed terrorist gangs which were as bad as any other terrorists, and the Israelis are very ashamed of them now: but they say there was no alternative then. There was an exodus of Arab Palestinians, the founding fathers of today's terror gangs. The Arab nations keep the Palestinians in camps instead of integrating them into their societies, knowing that they represent an ever-ready weapon to attack Israel. The Palestinian refugees in Jordan were expelled, and now the camps in Lebanon have been the scene of horrific massacres. I was shown a place where there had been an Arab village: it was razed to the ground in the first days of fighting. It was an eerie experience. There was just one mulberry tree, and the foundations of the mosque. There was bitter fighting, evil deeds were committed, and no Israeli denies this but now, the Israelis feel, the time has come for reconciliation. The Arabs refuse.

The Arab villages look prosperous, but passing through them made me anxious: never a greeting, never a smile. Crowds of children trained to beg. Very rarely does one see a man working. Mostly they sit and talk. The children play in the street, are very badly dressed, but nothing suggests poverty, rather: neglect. One only sees women in the distance. Isolated houses look almost like caves. There are always numerous olive trees by them; they give no shade and are always a dusty green. Israelis don't pick olives – the labour costs are too high! Instead they lease the fruit on the trees to Arabs.

Despite the unbearable tensions, life goes on quite normally. There are losses every day, terrible threats from all sides, and when you look at a map and see how small Israel is, and how big the hostile Arab countries, you feel it can hardly survive for a single day. But people here are used to it. Their attitude seems to be one of "don't care". No matter what Israel does, world opinion is negative; so why waste time waiting for approval? They get on doing what needs to be done. Opinions are divided as to what it is that needs to be done. Most are in favour of keeping the Occupied Territories because it is impossible to negotiate. Hence the new settlements. Those new settlers live the hard lives of pioneers. But they are quite confident. Others, for instance the communists, are against the new settlements and in favour of unconditional surrender of the Territories. I think the communists are living in cloud cuckoo land. They still think Russia can do no wrong – despite everything we now know.

What is bad is Israel's Western orientation. There are memorials to Churchill, Truman, Balfour etc all over the place – there would be better uses for the money! I think the Suez Crisis of '56 was a disaster for Israel. Merrily aligning herself with the capitalists' war of pillage and robbery was a big mistake – but no one here agrees with me.'

She came home from Israel considerably chastened by what she had seen and learned, and for a short time it was possible to have a reasonable conversation about it with her. But not for long. Soon we could never express so much as a doubt about any of Israel's actions without unleashing a torrent of counter-argument; if we remained silent, so much the worse: it meant we didn't care, didn't understand the permanent crisis with which the Jews had to deal. She was fired by her awareness of the Holocaust, and her irrational sense of guilt for having survived – having lived a charmed life, as she often said, when so many had suffered and died, she had to give her loyalty to Israel. In June 1970 she wrote:

'Israel, my Israel! Slandered by the whole world, and so alone. Any ceasefire is better than war. But the Arabs will use any breathing space to build up their forces. Then the time will have passed and the blood-hounds will be at the door.'

Chapter 25

Mu's Last Years

Mu often reminded herself that her old age was not the worst part of her life. She had her house, and took the English saying 'my home is my castle' to heart – not by pulling up a drawbridge, but by inviting people to live in it.

She dreamed of recreating the hospitable atmosphere of the Heights of Erwin in Freiburg. Peter's children spent most of their holidays at Beamsend, especially after their parents' divorce. Lorchen was busy and happy at such times; and she visited the growing families often.

Mu with grandchild

There was no communication now between her and Fe, but I kept in touch with him and visited him and Stella occasionally with David. Fe achieved one of his ambitions when he was promoted to professor at manchester, rather than just senior lecturer, and when he was elected a fellow of the British Academy. He produced learned tomes on the playwright Euripides and on the goddess Persephone, and articles. When he retired, he and Stella moved to Cambridge and he devoted himself to producing a three-volume course in Greek, using only authentic texts by classical authors to illustrate points of grammar. This was drudgery, but he did it willingly, as part of his lifelong service to the Greeks, and he was helped by the University of Tübingen, who accommodated him for long periods of time while he was working on it. It was on one of our visits there that he handed me the plastic shopping bag containing all my letters to him over the years, and drafts or copies of many of his replies, which I have quoted from.

Fe in old age

*****

In 1972, David got a job in teacher training, which involved our moving to High Wycombe, and later to Maidenhead; but we still visited Mu frequently (though never often enough, in her view) when we would take her out for a walk, often in Wytham Woods – these walks got slower and slower as she grew older, and stopped from time to time to comment at length on the news, or to reminisce. As each grandchild was born, she opened a post office savings account for them, and paid in a little money as often as she could. She knitted squares from scraps of wool and crocheted them together into patchwork bedspreads, intending to make one for each. She was deeply interested in each of the children, their personalities and progress, and worried about them, especially as the years went by and they entered the turmoil of adolescence and early adulthood. Several lived with her for extended periods – Kurt's Gabriel, Peter's Claire and Liz, Maleen's Nicolette – and often their friends stayed too. Maleen and Bob, driven out of their beloved Beirut, where Bob was the director of the American Community School, by the terrible events following Israel's invasion in 1982, lived with her at Beamsend throughout her last years.

There was no shortage of distressing news for her to comment on – Solzhenitsyn's revelations about Stalin's dictatorship, the horrors of the 'Cultural Revolution' in China; communism itself, that cherished philosophy of 'From each according to his ability, to each according to his need' was hard to support as Cambodia came under Pol Pot's Khmer Rouge mass-murderers, who claimed to be communists. But she maintained her emotional love of Israel, which led to severe disagreements with Bob and Maleen. She supported the Peace Movement actively, taking part in demonstrations at Greenham Common, Upper Heyford, Molesworth and others.

Her thoughts reverted constantly to her own life, the injustices done her, her failure to achieve anything: she had to face the fact that despite her intelligence and empathy and erudition, the only work she had done was housework, at home, or for other people, or in hospitals and care homes. (It is probably an unconscious attempt to justify all her years of cleaning etc. that makes me devote a good deal of time to housework, pouncing on dusty skirting boards or grubby corners with a sort grim satisfaction.) Mu's memories of Ferch grew ever more nostalgic. It became a paradise of peace and harmony, of closeness to nature, of childhood friends and loving relatives: even her parents were at peace with each other there, before the First World War. And even during that war, Ferch was sunlit in front of the black clouds.

It was in Ferch that her death wish had begun, and it never left her. Almost every page of her late writings includes an expression of her longing to die. When she was 72 it seemed that her wish would at last be granted. The pains in her abdomen turned out to be cancer of the womb, and she confidently expected to die soon. She rejected the suggestion that she should have an operation. She wrote, in English, expecting her English-speaking grandchildren to read it after her imminent death:

'1. *One has to accept the fact that we all have to die, and I am ready to go at a moment's notice. I have had my life, bad and good, with the best years now in my old age. I'd rather die when I am on top of things than when I am down, crawling, and reduced to a whimpering, stinking clot of flesh. I demand from those who love me the freedom to decide when I want to go. I shall not do anything in a hurry, feeling, on the whole, quite strong and healthy, with some bad periods in between, but not too bad. As long as I am alive, I shall be cheerful, helpful and undemanding. I do not want my grandchildren to remember me as decaying and an object of pity, intermingled with abhorrence.*

2. The Welfare State is one of the few worthwhile achievements of modern times; however, it goes to pieces if people exploit the health service, unemployment benefits etc. I do not want to speak about the despicable greediness of the medical profession, but about the patients who crawl to the doctor for any little woe and take up their time and enrich the chemical industry. We grow older and older and demand more and more without giving much in return. I do not want to be one of them. An operation needs doctors, nurses and a place in hospital, for quite a considerable time. And then? Shall I undergo all this and demand all this in order to prolong my life for two, three years, and then die for a second time?'

Seven months later, she wrote a cheerful farewell letter:

28.9.77

'Dearest children and grandchildren, you must never forget how much I love every one of you, even if we meet very rarely here on earth, and soon not at all. But I firmly believe that love can never die, that love changes the texture of life. I am very proud of this scientific remark. For now I will tell you something, which the clever eyes of Tom, Alex, probably Nick, in any case Peter and Kurt, will think is nonsense and balderdash. But I want to tell you how I experienced the love of God, the all-pervading, in spite of all the horrors which I have seen and of which I have heard.

The normal way of proving the power of God is to show that he can upset the laws of nature. The sun for instance stood still in the valley of Jericho in order to finish a battle – that is, in my eyes, a blasphemy, though it is in the bible. The power of God is, the miracles of God are: that the laws of nature do not change. The sun warms us, or burns us, and the moon softens our hearts or makes us frightened. What has been heated up expands, and what has been cooled down or frozen, contracts. There is only one example, as far as I know, where God has deliberately changed the law of nature, which he himself has created: ice takes up more room than water. Imagine what would happen if the merciless law of nature had been applied to ice and water. What would happen to the algae and fishes and snails or whatever else lives in the ponds and rivers if the heavy ice would sink to the bottom? The creation would have been a murderer. In the bible it says constantly: and God looked at the creation, and saw that it was good. So out of compassion

God upset the rhythm of nature.

Tom and Alex have explained to me that H_2O (the formula for water) is some sort of triangle and that the molecules have been assembled in some sort of order which makes ice lighter than water. But why has this been arranged like that, and who has done it?'

However, when the pain became too intense to bear, she let herself be persuaded to go to hospital for the operation. She recovered remarkably quickly, and had to admit that she was grateful. She had fifteen more years to live.

'November '78

"Recalled to life" ... Do you want to live? I don't know.

I really thought that my cancer would be my escape route, and I was all set to go. But things did not work out like that ... My well-laid plan has come to nothing, and I am still alive, and, on the whole, enjoying it. For I am really quite restored and can walk and even read (I mean, concentrate) without much trouble. The children seem to be glad that I am still here, and without Maleen's and Alex's wonderful nursing I would never have got onto my legs again.

I now have the opportunity to enjoy the remaining years and make other people glad that they insisted on my operation, or to become a nuisance and misery. I have decided on the first way, and up to now I have succeeded; it was made easy for me because after a miserable summer with much rain and cold the September and practically all October have been so warm and radiantly bright. Even today I was sitting in the garden, reading. Well, I never doubted that the world is wonderful and beautiful. And happily, Claire came to stay here.

Thus the year runs out. I try to be cheerful. But sometimes beside me I see black shadows, and only my conscience keeps me from falling into the soft embrace of the shadows. I must go on, I know, and there is so much I can be grateful for. And the golden Autumn is like balm.

The other day I got the definite NO to my attempt to go and stay in Ferch for one or two weeks. I would have had to live in Potsdam in the Crown Princess's palace, which is now the official hotel for foreigners. I do not want to do this, as the daily journey would be too exhausting and the whole thing too expensive. I am quite content, for when I am dead I can be in Ferch every day and perhaps live in one of the old oaks or in the sycamore in the little alder wood. Meanwhile, the pictures of Ferch are crowding in on me, and often I am walking the old paths and seeing everything so clearly.'

*****

In the 1980s, as our three children made themselves independent, David and I took early retirement from our teaching posts and bought a house in

Oxford, intending to sub-let it while we spent some years as English language teachers abroad. We spent one year in Portugal and that Christmas we had Mu come and stay with us. She was in a strange state of mind, seeming to be quite disorientated, convinced that the sun was setting in the east. The next year we spent in Japan, where our first grandson was born – our son Tom had married Kazuko. Then we came back to Oxford and set up our own micro-school, still teaching English as a foreign language. I would visit my mother almost every day. As the years passed I would sometimes find her curled up on her bed, and she would say, "I'm as weak as a kitten" – but then assure me that this was just an off day and she would soon be back to normal. In fact she suffered very little ill health, none of the arthritis that plagued her mother and her sister for years: a touch of asthma, occasional colds, insomnia was all she complained of.

Christmas with a great-grandchild

Soon there were more great-grandchildren to bask in her love. When she was alone, she would open her typewriter and write, instead of talking: detailed descriptions of the grandchildren, and their partners and children; letters to her scattered friends and relatives; when she heard that someone had died she would write down everything she could remember about them; she also wrote comments on the news, and large fragments of an autobiography and of family history, sometimes in her rather special English for her grandchildren. Much of this has been reproduced in these pages. She allowed herself to type some wry comments on her houseguests. For instance, here is what she wrote about her beloved granddaughter Liz and her friends:

In the garden with another great-grandchild

'Her most outstanding characteristic is her social conscience, and she doesn't look down on people, no matter how screwed up they are. The creatures she brings into my house are often a bit much for me. The mere fact that someone is an alcoholic, dirty and ragged, does not automatically make him a pleasant person to have in my home. There it is,

I'm a petty bourgeois. The other day I found a note by the telephone: "Oma, I've found someone who needed a bath, he's asleep in my bed at present". I managed to get this honoured guest to leave without too much trouble. A few days later another fair youth with long locks came for a bath, which is of course always to be applauded. Then another one with shining eyes and long greasy hanks of hair came to spend the night here. Unfortunately he was a bed wetter. He spent a long time in front of the mirror, arranging his hanks as daintily as possible; he claimed he had been the Director of the Art Academy in Leicester (which does not exist) and had given it up in order to seek self-fulfilment. So. You can find masses of these creatures in the Peace Camps, which are admirable places in themselves, but which attract a lot of dross due to their great hospitality.'

At other times she would apostrophise her grandchildren:

'Can I ever hope to tell you convincingly how wonderful it was to live in Germany? How wonderful that this was my country? No, I cannot. For even while I swim in those beautiful memories, the horror of the Nazi years is upon me. And the First World War. But it was a wonderful country, well worth living for, while unfortunately so many young and idealistic people thought, well worth dying for. In some respects this is easier, for it does not last so long. A long life, like mine, is like a long road over a heath, and to the right and to the left lie the lifeless cadavers of lost hopes and dead friends. How radiant were the eyes of the boys who went to the front, in order to defend the homeland, die Heimat, not knowing how cruelly they had been deceived, like the young men in all the other countries who were driven against each other with murder weapons in their hands; how dimmed were the eyes of the women and girls who saw them go away; how lonely were the woods and the paths we had walked together, and never again…'

She lived very frugally. She seldom bought clothes, and when she did she prided herself on only getting them second-hand from Oxfam gift-shops. Her food consisted mainly of porridge with tomato puree stirred into it, or apple sauce, except when Maleen was allowed to cook for her. But she never refused a gift of whisky or cherry brandy or wine, and would sit in her garden sipping and talking with a visitor or reading and dreaming. I found her there one sunny day, and she said, 'Here I sit and contemplate murder.' Who did she want to murder? A bramble. It had forced its way through the wall from next door at the back of the garden. 'Just think what a struggle it had,' she said. 'Push here! Squeeze here! And – ah! At last! I'm through! Now I can stretch, and throw out leaves and thorns, roots and flowers – and what do I do? I sit and work out the best way to kill it.' And the ever-ready tears began to flow. 'But I cannot allow it in! It will take root, it will spread over the whole garden! And isn't that exactly what people always said about the Jews? And the others, all over the world, who try and try to find somewhere to live!' As I rose to comfort her, I caught sight of the cap of a whisky bottle tucked into the plants by her side. I knew what the caps of whisky bottles looked like. There were numerous ones in the garden on sticks supporting plants – to protect one's eyes as one bent down to pull up weeds. Nothing was ever wasted.

She would have her bath and go to bed early, and fall asleep listening to the radio. She would often wake up after a very short time, from a startling or distressing dream, and try to calm herself down by reading, or walking around the house, or out into the garden, especially if there was a moon to adore, before going back to bed for another snatch of sleep. However, she was fit; for years she had gone for long country walks with Mr Loveridge's group of ramblers, and for a time regularly once a week with her friend Gau Maas, Professor Maas' daughter. She read her favourite German books over and over again, especially the big anthology of poetry, *Der Echtermeier*, as well as Russian literature, in Russian, and historical and political books from the city library. She listened to news bulletins on the radio and cut out interesting reports from the newspaper to stick into her diary. Despite her highly unorthodox views on Christianity (she loved Jesus but detested the dogma) she attended the German-language Lutheran services in St Mary's Church, out of loyalty to the pastor and appreciation of the generosity of St Mary's, which had given the German community in Oxford houseroom throughout the war; and she was a familiar figure at the meetings of her local CND branch and at demonstrations. On 8 February, 1985, when she was 81, she wrote:–

'Yesterday I was at Molesworth, where the Americans want to put more of their Cruise missiles. It was really very bad. The landscape there is not at all lovely, quite flat, and the farming all "agro-industry". It rained all day, everything was sodden, and then we got sleet and a bitterly cold wind. But the worst part was seeing the wilful destruction of the land – like at Greenham Common – the huge fences and the awful structures inside. In fact, the policemen stood four deep everywhere, we could not get through anywhere, there were helicopters overhead. The Peace Campers had even built themselves a little chapel, but that didn't help – the police stood in the window niches. They must have felt very silly. But what won't a person do for money. It makes me more tolerant towards all the unemployed, who prefer to be out of work rather than being obliged to perform dishonourable actions.

Mu at Greenham Common

Robert gave me a fabulous present, and

sent me and Maleen to Freiburg. Of course, there is nothing more beautiful than the Black Forest and Freiburg. We had a wonderful week together, it is most pleasant to travel with Maleen ... We both enjoyed the beautiful town. I also had one day quite alone in the Sternwald, Kybfelsen, etc. It was a cool, wet day, and the mists rose out of all the valleys and swirled around me. I was quite alone, there was no other sound than the dripping wet from the trees and the murmur of the rivulets. Maleen went to see Schwester Goswina, her old nursery teacher ... a very delightful person, but very old and apparently suffering with cancer. She will go joyfully! I had actually intended to spend another week in Marburg and other places; but I lost my nerve on the central railway station in Frankfurt. I remember so well the time when these people were wolves and tigers, and I know they can be like that again, drunk as they are with success, too much food and too much money. I fled, and took the next plane home. Home is my house, thank God for it. England will never be my home, my roots are in Germany, but cut completely.

I am not happy, however, with our Tory government. "Selling the family silver" is bad enough, but Thatcher's constant sabre-rattling disturbs me much more. It's as if she was looking for war. She tells Brezhnev, who has announced a token reduction of forces on the German frontier, that one false move by Russia would lead to much heavier punishment by NATO than she got from the Nazis – it's too bad to be believed. What is happening to the world? What happened to us pales in comparison with what is happening in South America, Cambodia, South Africa, China ... and Israel! The orthodox Gush Enumin are nearly in the majority now – and how can Israel survive if she does as much wrong as the others?'

*****

She was greatly stimulated by her hatred of Margaret Thatcher, Conservative Prime Minister from 1979 until 1990. She called her 'Goldilocks' or 'Boadicea', and would utter these names with sneering contempt, as she had always for her pet aversions, like Chiang Kai-Shek and 'shareholders'. She detested Thatcher's affected manner almost as much as her monetarist policies, her militarism, which led to the Falklands War, and her hob-nobbing with Reagan, the 'cowboy', and her support of his 'star wars' and nuclear policies. But Mu's central obsession was still with Israel. For her, the PLO and its leader Arafat were terrorists against whom Israel had to defend herself. However, she was critical of much of Israel's behaviour. It was hard to brush aside the fact that Prime Minister Begin had also been a terrorist, and she could not condone the illegal settlements on the West Bank, or the invasion of Lebanon. But she would always return to the fact that Israel's very existence was threatened by the hostile Arab countries, and the emotions she always experienced when aware of a weak being in mortal danger would well up and obliterate any criticism of Israel.

Like her mother when she became old, Mu felt guilty for being unhappy at times, realising that her daughter, Maleen, was taking excellent care of her, as Marianne had of Oma, and that it was ungrateful to expect more – more time, more interest, more conversations, more affection:

'Have I any right to be so terribly depressed? I feel I am a non-person, and believe I have so much knowledge and ability which has never seen the light of day.'

But then at the end she found some fulfilment. First because her grand-daughter Ann and her husband asked her – asked her – to write our family history for them: they were genuinely interested. Of course she set about the task with enthusiasm and typed eleven letters, or chapters, in English, varying in length – 60 pages in all, covering the familiar topics in random order: her brother's life – Prussian history – her parents, aunts, grandparents – Judaism – Greek history and drama – the rise of the Nazis – her parents' divorce, her own marriage, the Zuntz family – with plenty of detours to take in her own very original thoughts and opinions. Her deep emotional identification with whatever was small, vulnerable, helpless – Chinese women in the past with bound feet – African slaves lying chained on their backs in rows on ships crossing the Atlantic, and maltreated on the plantations – beggars – street children – battery hens – sows imprisoned in narrow pens, forced to give birth to one litter after the other – even the saplings that thrust up through the asphalt pavements on the Woodstock Road, only to be trodden on – all this emotion was subsumed into her partisanship for Israel and Judaism, though she could not entirely silence her irony. She wrote:

'Judaism has given a lot to the world. First, most important, the idea of the invisible god. Next, the Mosaic laws. They are the foundation of any civilised life, and as far as I know, the first ones. For instance, thou shalt not kill: indeed, we agree, but are ready to break that law at the drop of a hat. The Old Testament is full of wars and the extermination of tribes, brazenly breaking the law, and with dire consequences. Has there ever been a time when man did not kill man? But does this mean it is, after all, right?

Next, thou shalt keep the Sabbath holy – perhaps the most humane law ever, for it did not concern only the master of the house and his family, but the slaves, and the animals. But alas! What have people made of this wonderful idea? The Sabbath, if kept in the orthodox way, is a cruel burden. Okay, thou shalt not work: but neither can you do anything like reading a good, non-religious book, or exert yourself, so you can only walk a certain number of steps, carefully counted out by the rabbi, or you cannot attend the Sabbath service. If more steps are reported, you are severely reprimanded.

You cannot turn on the electricity – but a clever device makes the electricity turn itself on, or a Christian neighbour is paid to come and do things for you, draw the curtains, and so on, leaving you more time for reflection.

Next, respect your neighbour's property, including his wife and servants. And honour your father and mother, showing that even thousands of years ago children found it hard to live peacefully with their parents.

Jews are not particularly creative. There are brilliant Jewish violinists, but few composers; they understand people, and make good psychologists and lawyers and teachers and doctors. All this is quite honourable: so why have Jews been hated, persecuted, despised, humiliated, murdered? I do not know. I have a few suggestions, but they don't add up to a proper answer. First: they had no country of their own, like the gypsies, and depended on the goodwill and hospitality of diverse host countries. Now they have got their own country; it is not very peaceful, they have all the faults that other nations have – aggression, conceit, intolerance, and so on – but they are more stigmatised – could it be that one expects more morality from those who call themselves "the chosen people"?

Jews used to be rejected because "they" had murdered Christ. So they became more and more apart; wore their old costumes, used a mixture of languages called Yiddish, celebrated Saturday, not Sunday; the women had to cut off their hair and wear wigs so as not to appear too sexy for their men-folk (this nonsense has started again in Israel). The men were on top, women had to serve them. Men should not dirty their hands, but sit in the synagogue and study the Talmud. They have this morning prayer: I thank you, God, for not creating me a woman.

They felt no affection or obligation to their host countries, being only concerned to take advantage of their circumstances as best they could. This opened the door to all sorts of cheating, and dealing in money, which they could take with them if they had to leave. Which came first: the Jews' fear of expulsion, or the Christians' fear of exploitation by the Jews?

Intermarriage was virtually impossible throughout the Middle Ages. A Jew who had anything like that to do with a non-Jew was declared dead; a Christian who had a liaison with a Jew was similarly outcast. Being of mixed blood some thought we would be infertile, like mules These ideas evaporated to a large extent with the Enlightenment in the eighteenth century. My mother was one of many who believed fervently in assimilation, a powerful factor in her decision to marry the son of a Saxon peasant, my father. I believed in assimilation, too. The result was that when the Nazis came we had nowhere to go. To the Nazis we were "Non-Aryans". The orthodox Jews accused us of betraying our Jewish ancestors.

My mother grew up in Danzig (Gdansk), where Germans, Jews and Poles lived together if not in great love, still quite decently. Jews answered the general call-up and joined the hussars along with everyone else. But once a Jewish hussar was insulted on the parade ground; he came home in tears and told his family about it. His father decided to put things right. Every day at noon the hussars, led by their general, rode across the market place, which was always a great attraction. The father stepped forward from the crowd of onlookers when the general came, took hold of his horse's reins and said politely: "Would his Excellency please get off the horse?" The general was so surprised that he did so, whereupon the old man gave him two well-tailored smacks in the face: "This for the treatment of my son." Of course there was a court case, and the result was that the Jew got an apology and the general had to leave the army. You see, in those days Germany was still ein Rechtsstaat – a state where the rule of law was supreme.

Not under the Nazis. There are many books about the Jewish experiences. We escaped the worst, but 22 of my relatives and friends perished in the camps.

I have lived in this country far longer than I lived in Germany, but I am still a foreigner. Nobody has hurt me, but nobody wants the foreigner. I am very privileged in having this house, which I have made a HOME for quite a lot of people, not only my family. But when I go out into the street, I feel the cold wind of the alien life.'

Later still, three women, Annette, Margaret and Cordula, whom she had met on a demonstration at Greenham Common, asked her to read German literature with them. This was her greatest pleasure: to read her favourite poems and explain them, to recite long poems from memory – ones she had recited to her mother while they picked raspberries in Ferch; to study Goethe's *Faust* with these women who loved and admired her. She was teaching.

It was as if then, right at the end of her long life, some of the early traumas, her failures at school and after, her inferiority complex – were all lifted off her and her true, gifted self was revealed.

She died on 25 February 1993, aged 88. The evening before, Maleen watched her go along the corridor from the bathroom – she didn't walk, she ran, she danced. It was as if she knew that her life-long longing for death was about to be fulfilled. Next morning, she did not wake up. Her breathing was very slow, very loud. The doctor came and gave her an injection. She died surrounded by daughters and a grand daughter, and is buried

Mu's grave at Wytham

in Wytham. And now, according to one of her beliefs, she is absorbed into trees and hills and streams. Perhaps she has entered one of the trees in Ferch.

Fe had died less than a year before her. His grave is in Cambridge.

✳✳✳✳✳

This story – Oma, Mu, and Me – covers more than a century. It is tempting to trace the influences in great and trivial respects. For instance, why can I never sleep without opening the window? Surely it goes back to Oma's conviction that it was fresh air that cured little Marianne of TB, and her life-long insistence on its vital importance was passed on to me through Mu, who would sooner have died of cold than risk shutting a bedroom window. Oma's 'Puritanism' and Mu's Wandervogel memories have surely contributed to my scorn of 'fashion' and make-up and fuss, and like them I feel the need for long country walks from time to time. My head is always full of the songs Mu used to sing, tuneful folk songs, military songs from the First World War and the Hitler period, some hits – Schlager – from her

Fe's grave in Cambridge

youth, and the Bach chorales and Schubert Lieder and Mendelssohn duets that Oma sang – and her mother, Rose, too. And Mu's and Oma's lives have made me deeply suspicious of religious, nationalistic, and political fervour. Like Oma, I am rational; like Mu, I get emotional about the weak and helpless, be they nations, races, people, animals or plants, and I feel responsible for them.

Oma seems to have been blessed with an extraordinary degree of self-confidence, possibly as a result of the freedom and independence of her childhood, free to roam with Harras, her dog-protector. It was her self-esteem, I think, which made her for so long unable to accept that she was not going to marry Schubert, the man she loved. Her decision to study medicine was really a determined and rational effort finally to come to terms with it. She got into the habit of setting herself targets, and achieving them. She even seems to be a little bit pleased with herself for admitting that it was a mistake to marry Hugo; but she didn't feel responsible for the untimely birth of Mu, or for the deep distress she caused by letting Mu know, from an early age, that her coming was unwelcome; she expressed no compunctions over her unfairness, so obviously favouring her first daughter over her second, nor for the brutal way she tried to deal with Mu's stammering and her nail-biting. But Mu's reaction was to extend her undoubted self-pity to a passion of pity for all victimised beings.

The influence of political developments on our lives is overwhelming. Oma's self-confidence reflects Germany's self-assertive optimism in the prosperity of the Gründerjahre following the Franco-Prussian War, which so infuriated France and Britain. The emancipation of the Jews at that time led to their disproportionate achievements in all areas of German life, business, politics, academia, art, music – and to many discarding ancient Jewish traditions, becoming fervently patriotic Germans, and marrying non-Jews, as she and indeed my other Jewish grandparent, Leo Zuntz, did. That did not prevent the Nazis and their precursors from resenting them and identifying them as Jews, not Germans.

Oma's non-Jewish husband, my grandfather Hugo, whom I never met, briefly dazzled by Oma's brilliance, his emancipated Jewish wife, was a son of the soil, and in his development he chimes in with Germany's admiration turning to jealousy. The First World War, and Germany's defeat, rekindled his anti-Semitism and led to his growing coarseness and brutality, just as it did in Germany at large. Reinhardt, denying his mother, his half-Jewish ancestry, preferring to be seen as a bastard if it meant he could keep his farm, reflects the 'Blu-Bo' – the 'Blut-und-Boden' – 'Blood and Soil' – dogma of the Nazis.

Oma's serene self-confidence stood her in good stead when the Nazis came to power, and enabled her to create a good life for herself in Persia in her seventies; but it probably contributed to Mu's total lack of self-respect. I think she felt guilty for her existence, and this accounts for her life-long death-wish. Yet Oma was a loyal mother to her and repeatedly cared and provided for her, and for us, her children, during those turbulent early years of her marriage; and her letters throughout the years were a lifeline to Mu. However, Mu plunged into her ill-advised marriage at an early age, and for years she accepted Fe's frequent and prolonged absences and his arrogant behaviour as if it was in some way a 'just punishment', though justifiable anger did arise at times. Caring for her children and grandchildren and for wartime dependents went some way towards justifying her existence to herself. The Second World War gave her a sense of purpose, legitimate objects for her concern, as well as the family, I, the youngest, in particular, and various 'good causes', and Israel.

As for me: I believed, for many years, that there was a special relationship between me and Oma, and I have plenty of beautiful letters from her; yet in her memoirs there is scarcely so much as a mention of me. Being so much younger than my siblings meant I felt insignificant in the family, but very close to Mu. I always felt that it was my duty to reassure her, to justify her existence, to respect her, to spend time with her, to communicate with her; but nothing was ever adequate to her needs, so I was chronically guilty. I loved her dearly, and ached for her, and enjoyed her company, the never-ending stream of songs, poems, stories, reminiscences, jokes, historical and political expositions with which she entertained me; I admired her. But I was also aware of her faults and failings, and secretly resented the demands I felt obliged to respond to, all the time. Sometimes I blamed her for the loss of my father. History had made me an outsider, a foreigner, a refugee, an enemy alien, and then my father's disappearance took away what little self-confidence I might have possessed. The year in Switzerland gave me a taste of being an 'insider'. But it also threw me off course, causing me to give up my plan to become a doctor and to go in for the theatre, which did nothing for my self-esteem. A partial reconciliation with my father was partly responsible for my finally going to university and becoming a teacher; and a happy marriage has very slowly driven away my self-doubt. My family history and current events have made me angry with those placed in authority above us and the lunacy of their policies. I have been brought up to feel responsible as a citizen in a democracy: had the Good Germans resisted the Nazis, instead of averting their eyes from their distasteful ravings, the Second World War and the Holocaust would have been averted. So now, as a British citizen, I must join forces with those who are resisting the disastrous military and nuclear policies of our successive governments. This does not prevent me enjoying my life and my very comfortable circumstances; I am more fortunate than Mu or Oma – largely because I did not make a catastrophic mistake in marriage as they did; for most of the time, private, daily life outweighs all other factors.